Microsoft® Windows® XP

Home Edition, Third Edition

Contents

Easy Microsoft Windows XP Home Edition, Third Edition

U.S. International Standard Book Number: 0-7897-3337-4
Non-U.S. International Standard Book Number: 0-7897-3338-2

Library of Congress Catalog Card Number: 2004111745

Printed in the United States of America

First Printing: October 2004

06 05 4 3 2

Trademarks

All terms mentioned in this book that are known to be trademarks or service marks have been appropriately capitalized. Que cannot attest to the accuracy of this information. Use of a term in this book should not be regarded as affecting the validity of any trademark or service mark.

Warning and Disclaimer

Every effort has been made to make this book as complete and as accurate as possible, but no warranty or fitness is implied. The information provided is on an "as is" basis. The authors and the publisher shall have neither liability nor responsibility to any person or entity with respect to any loss or damages arising from the information contained in this book.

About the Author

Shelley O'Hara is the author of more than 100 books, including the best-selling Easy Microsoft Windows 98 and other top-selling titles. She recently published her first novel, The Marriage Trifecta, and has a B.A.in English from the University of South Carolina and a M.A. in English from the University of Maryland. She lives in Indianapolis with her husband (Sean), son (Michael), English Bulldog (Jelly Roll), and Doberman (Xie).

Dedication

To Michael Raymond O'Hara —Shelley O'Hara

For John Nol Sr. and his beautiful family. —Kate Shoup Welsh

Acknowledgments

Thanks to Kate Shoup Welsh for her part in the revision of this book. Thanks also to Greg Wiegand for setting up the revision, Sharry Gregory for handling all the project management details, Maureen McDaniel for her development and copy editing, Kyle Bryant for his review.

—Shelley O'Hara

Associate Publisher
Greg Wiegand

Acquisition Editor
Stephanie J. McComb

Development Editor
Maureen A. McDaniel

Technical Editor
Mark D. Hall
Kyle Bryant

Managing Editor
Charlotte Clapp

Project Editor
Lisa Wilson

Copy Editor
Maureen McDaniel

Indexer
Chris Barrick

Interior Designer
Anne Jones

Cover Designer
Anne Jones

Page Layout
Brad Chinn
Eric S. Miller

We Want to Hear from You!

As the reader of this book, *you* are our most important critic and commentator. We value your opinion and want to know what we're doing right, what we could do better, what areas you'd like to see us publish in, and any other words of wisdom you're willing to pass our way.

As an associate publisher I welcome your comments. You can email or write me directly to let me know what you did or didn't like about this book—as well as what we can do to make our books better.

Please note that I cannot help you with technical problems related to the topic of this book. We do have a User Services group, however, where I will forward specific technical questions related to the book.

When you write, please be sure to include this book's title and author as well as your name, email address, and phone number. I will carefully review your comments and share them with the author and editors who worked on the book.

Email: `feedback@quepublishing.com`

Mail: Greg Wiegand
Associate Publisher
Que Publishing
800 East 96th Street
Indianapolis, IN 46240 USA

For more information about this book or another Que title, visit our Web site at `www.quepublishing.com`. Type the ISBN (excluding hyphens) or the title of a book in the Search field to find the page you're looking for.

Bulk Sales

Que offers excellent discounts on this book when ordered in quantity for bulk purchases or special sales. For more information, please contact:

U.S. Corporate and Government Sales
1-800-382-3419
corpsales@pearsontechgroup.com

For sales outside of the U.S., please contact:

International Sales
international@pearsoned.com

 Each step is fully illustrated to show you how it looks onscreen.

It's as Easy as 1-2-3

Each part of this book is made up of a series of short, instructional lessons, designed to help you understand basic information that you need to get the most out of your computer hardware and software.

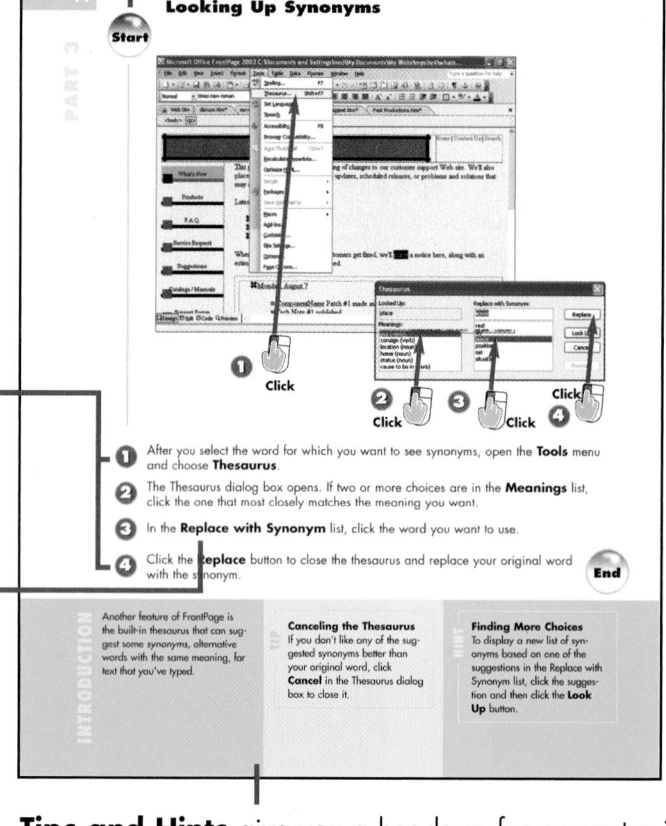

44
PART 3
Looking Up Synonyms
Start
Click
Click
Click
Click
After you select the word for which you want to see synonyms, open the Tools menu and choose Thesaurus.
The Thesaurus dialog box opens. If two or more choices are in the Meanings list, click the one that most closely matches the meaning you want.
In the Replace with Synonym list, click the word you want to use.
Click the Replace button to close the thesaurus and replace your original word with the synonym.
End
INTRODUCTION
Another feature of FrontPage is the built-in thesaurus that can suggest some synonyms, alternative words with the same meaning, for text that you've typed.
TIP
Canceling the Thesaurus
If you don't like any of the suggested synonyms better than your original word, click Cancel in the Thesaurus dialog box to close it.
HINT
Finding More Choices
To display a new list of synonyms based on one of the suggestions in the Replace with Synonym list, click the suggestion and then click the Look Up button.

2 Each task includes a series of quick, easy steps designed to guide you through the procedure.

3 Items that you select or click in menus, dialog boxes, tabs, and windows are shown in **bold**. Information you type is in a `special font`.

Tips and Hints give you a heads-up for any extra information you may need while working through the task.

How to Drag:
Point to the starting place or object. Hold down the mouse button (right or left per instructions), move the mouse to the new location, then release the button.

See next page:
If you see this symbol, it means the task you're working on continues on the next page.

End Task:
Task is complete.

Selection:
Highlights the area onscreen discussed in the step or task.

Click:
Click the left mouse button once.

Right-Click:
Click the right mouse button once.

Click & Type:
Click once where indicated and begin typing to enter your text or data.

Double-Click:
Click the left mouse button twice in rapid succession.

Pointer Arrow:
Highlights an item on the screen you need to point to or focus on in the step or task.

Introduction to Easy Microsoft Windows XP

Becoming proficient with an operating system, such as Windows XP, can seem like a daunting task. There's so much to learn: How do you create and edit documents? How can you customize the desktop? How do you connect to the Internet? Sometimes these questions can seem overwhelming.

That's why *Easy Microsoft Windows XP* provides concise, visual, step-by-step instructions for handling all the tasks you'll need to accomplish. You'll learn the basics of getting started in Windows XP. In addition, you can find out how to start and use applications, how to organize your documents, how to print, and how to personalize how your computer looks and works. This book also covers the key task of using your computer to hook up to the Internet. Once connected, you can then send and receive e-mail and browse the many, many sites on the Internet. All of the skills you need to use your computer and Windows XP are covered and in an easy format.

You can read this book cover to cover or use it as a reference when you encounter a problem or a feature you don't know how to use. Either way, *Easy Microsoft Windows XP* lets you see it done and then do it yourself.

PART 1

Getting Started

You don't need to do anything to start Windows XP other than turn on your PC. Windows starts automatically when you turn on your computer, and you see a screen called the desktop. The desktop is your starting point. Here you find the key tools for working with your computer. From your Windows desktop, you can open and switch between applications, search for specific folders, print documents, and perform other tasks. This section covers the basics of working with the desktop.

Tasks

Task 1: Understanding the Desktop

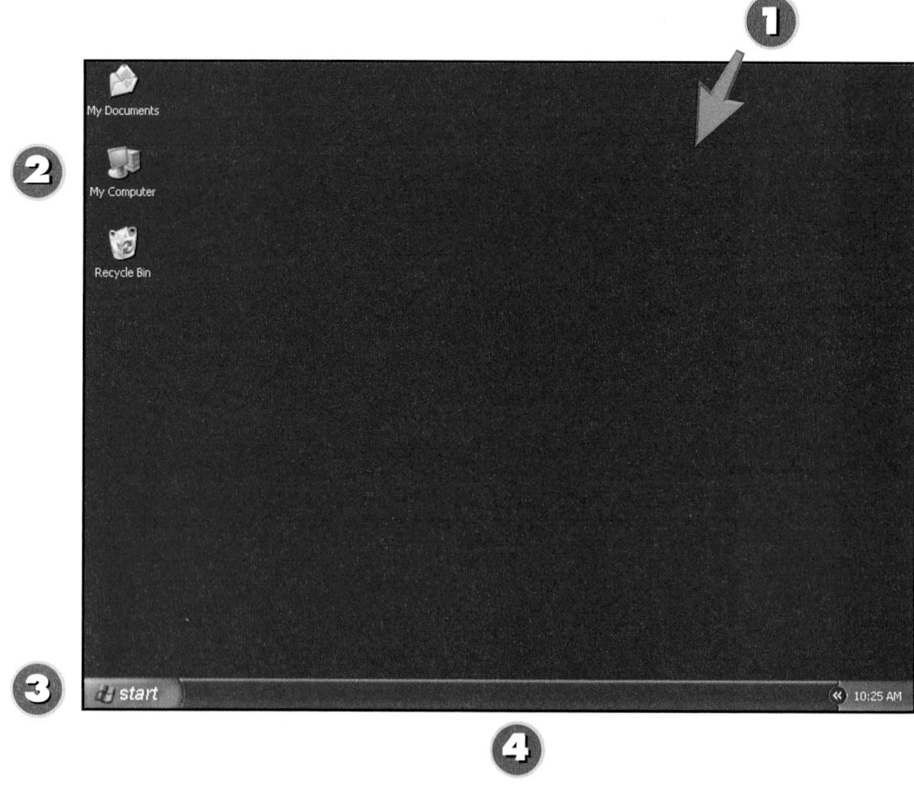

1. The desktop background is the area you see where icons are placed.
2. Desktop icons provide access to commonly used programs, folders, and files. Some icons are displayed by default. You can add other icons.
3. The Start button is where you access programs and open folders.
4. The taskbar displays buttons for open windows and programs. The status bar part of the taskbar displays the date and status icons. For example, if you are printing, you see a printer icon in this area.

INTRODUCTION

The desktop is your starting place, what you see when you first start your computer and Windows XP. This opening screen provides access to all the programs and files on your computer. This task introduces the main parts of your desktop.

TIP

Change the Desktop Background

You can change the appearance of this background. See Part 10, "Personalizing Windows," for more help on changing the appearance of the desktop.

TIP

Add Desktop Icons

By default, the Windows XP displays the Recycle Bin. You can also display the My Documents folder and the My Computer icon, as shown here. For help on adding these particular icons to the desktop, see Part 10.

Task 2: Understanding the Start Menu

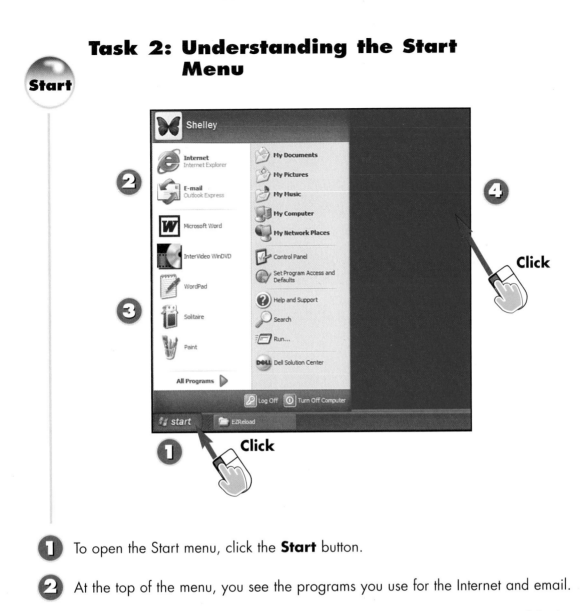

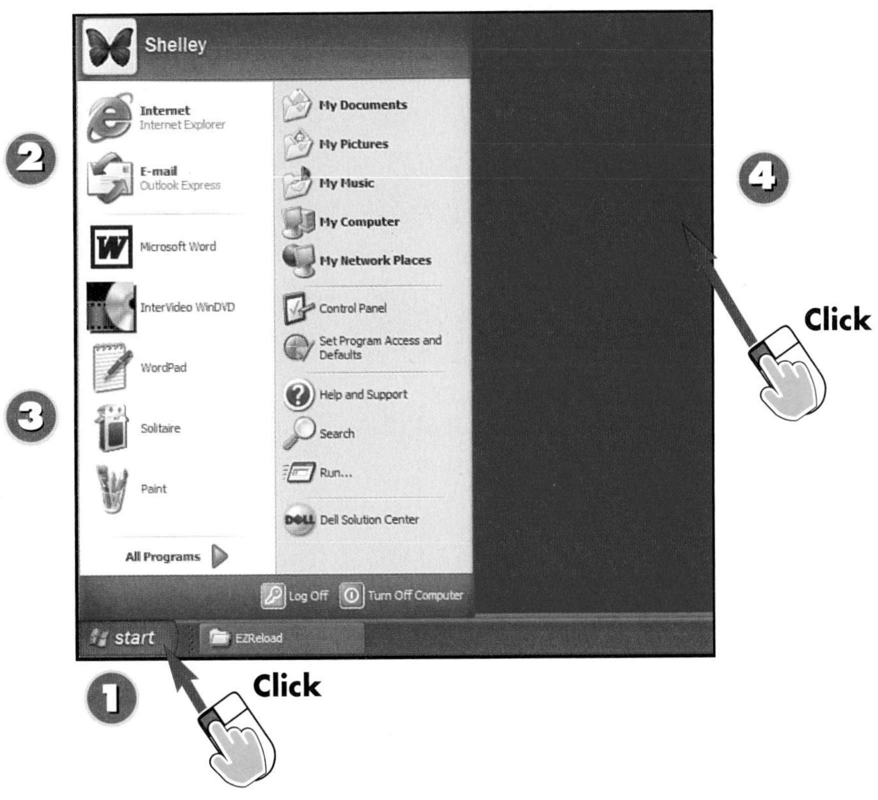

1. To open the Start menu, click the **Start** button.
2. At the top of the menu, you see the programs you use for the Internet and email.
3. The Start menu lists the programs you last used here. You can click any of the listed programs to start that program. To display additional programs, click the **All Programs** button.
4. Press **Esc** or click outside the Start menu to close it.

INTRODUCTION

The Start menu is where you can access common programs and folders. The Start menu in Windows XP has a new look, so if you are upgrading for a previous version, take a look at how the Start menu is organized. If you are new to Windows XP, you can get a good sense of how to use the Start menu from this task.

TIP

Your Menu Is Different

What you see in your Start menu will be different than what appears here. You see the programs you last used and your selected Internet and e-mail programs.

TIP

Start a Program

For help on starting a program, see Part 2, "Working with Programs," which covers the various ways you can start a program, including from the Start menu.

Task 3: Opening and Closing a Window

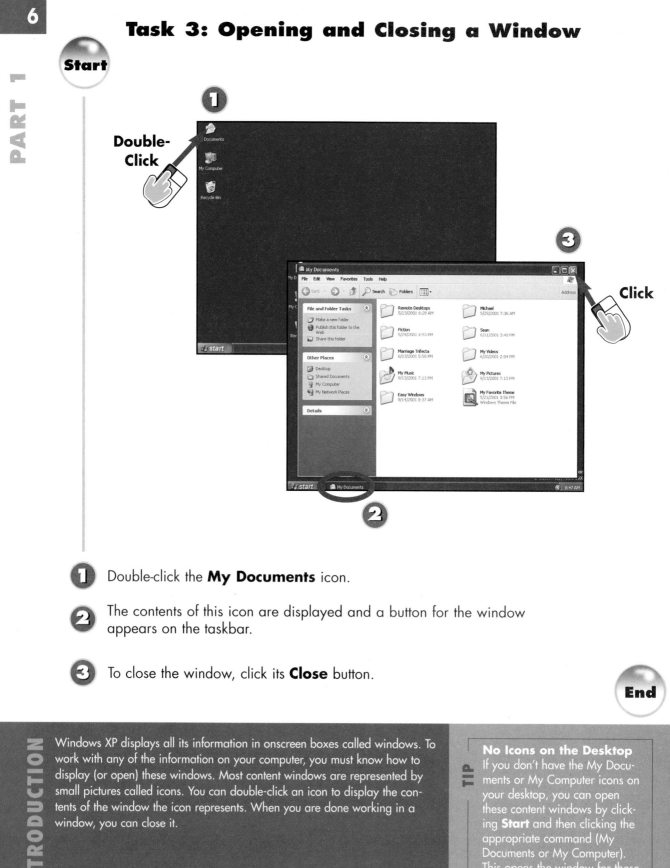

Double-Click

Click

1. Double-click the **My Documents** icon.

2. The contents of this icon are displayed and a button for the window appears on the taskbar.

3. To close the window, click its **Close** button.

INTRODUCTION

Windows XP displays all its information in onscreen boxes called windows. To work with any of the information on your computer, you must know how to display (or open) these windows. Most content windows are represented by small pictures called icons. You can double-click an icon to display the contents of the window the icon represents. When you are done working in a window, you can close it.

TIP

No Icons on the Desktop
If you don't have the My Documents or My Computer icons on your desktop, you can open these content windows by clicking **Start** and then clicking the appropriate command (My Documents or My Computer). This opens the window for these icons.

Task 4: Minimizing a Window

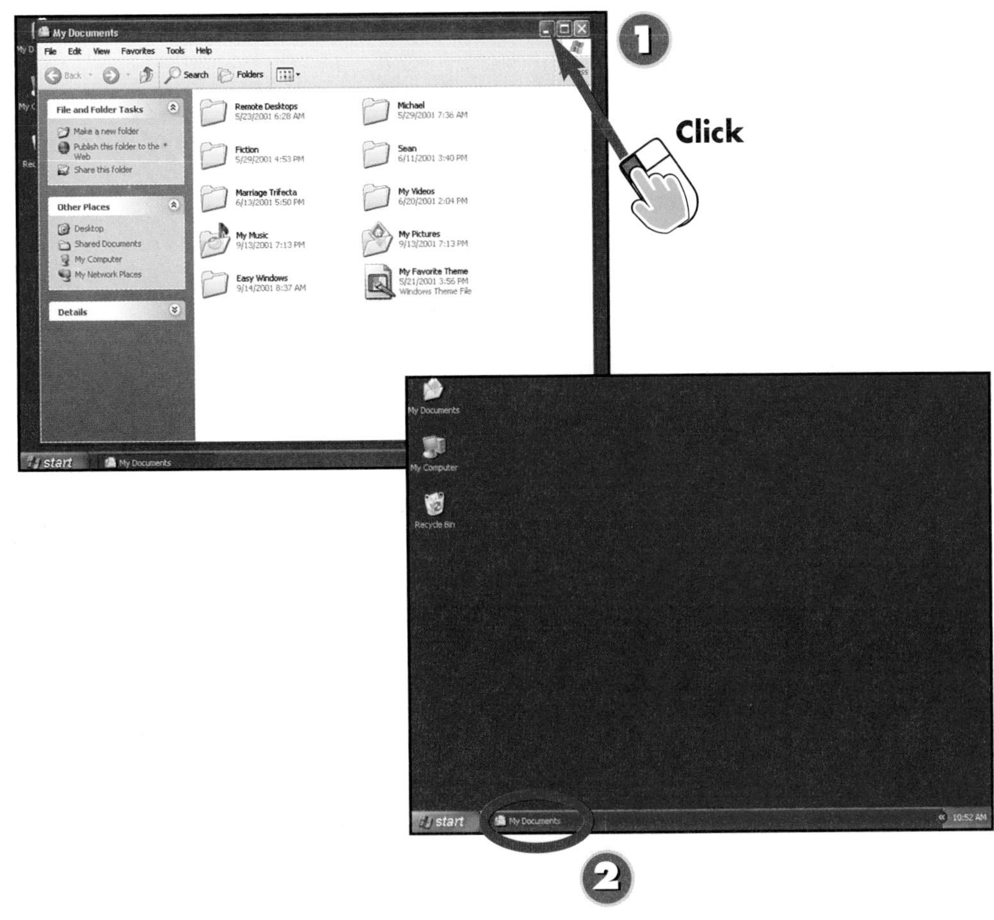

1. Click the **Minimize** button in the window you want to minimize.
2. The window disappears from the desktop, but a button for this window remains on the taskbar.

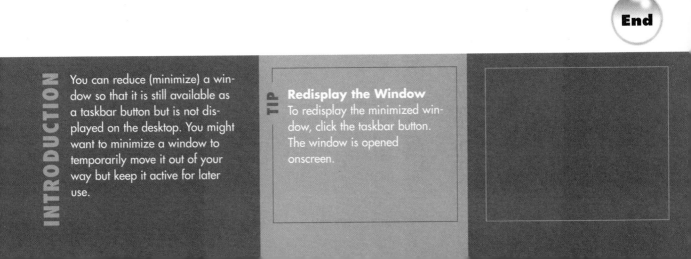

INTRODUCTION

You can reduce (minimize) a window so that it is still available as a taskbar button but is not displayed on the desktop. You might want to minimize a window to temporarily move it out of your way but keep it active for later use.

TIP

Redisplay the Window
To redisplay the minimized window, click the taskbar button. The window is opened onscreen.

Task 5: Maximizing a Window

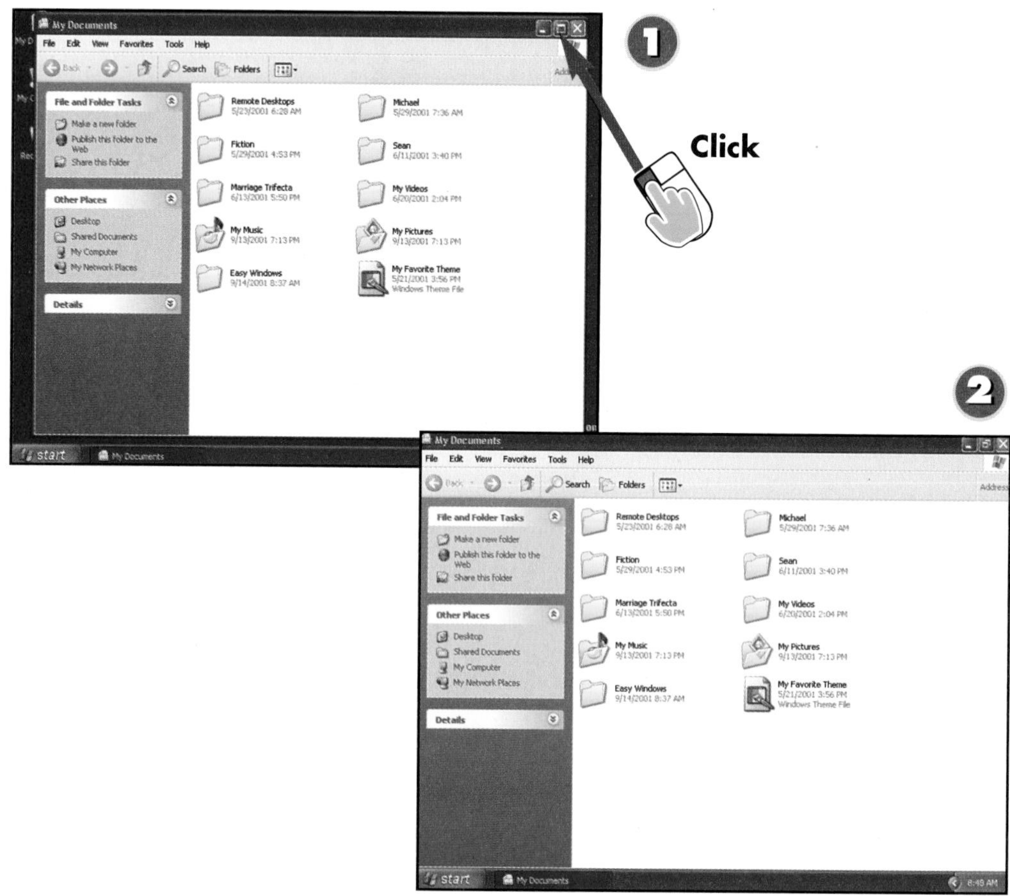

1. Click the **Maximize** button.
2. The window enlarges to fill the screen and the Maximize button changes to the Restore button.

You can enlarge (maximize) a window so that it fills the entire screen. Doing so gives you as much room as possible to work in that window.

TIP

Restore the Window
You can restore the window to its original size. To do so, click the **Restore** button.

TIP

Moving and Resizing Windows
Note that when a window is maximized it does not have borders so you cannot move or resize it, as covered in the next tasks. To resize or move a window, you must restore it so that it has borders.

Task 6: Moving a Window

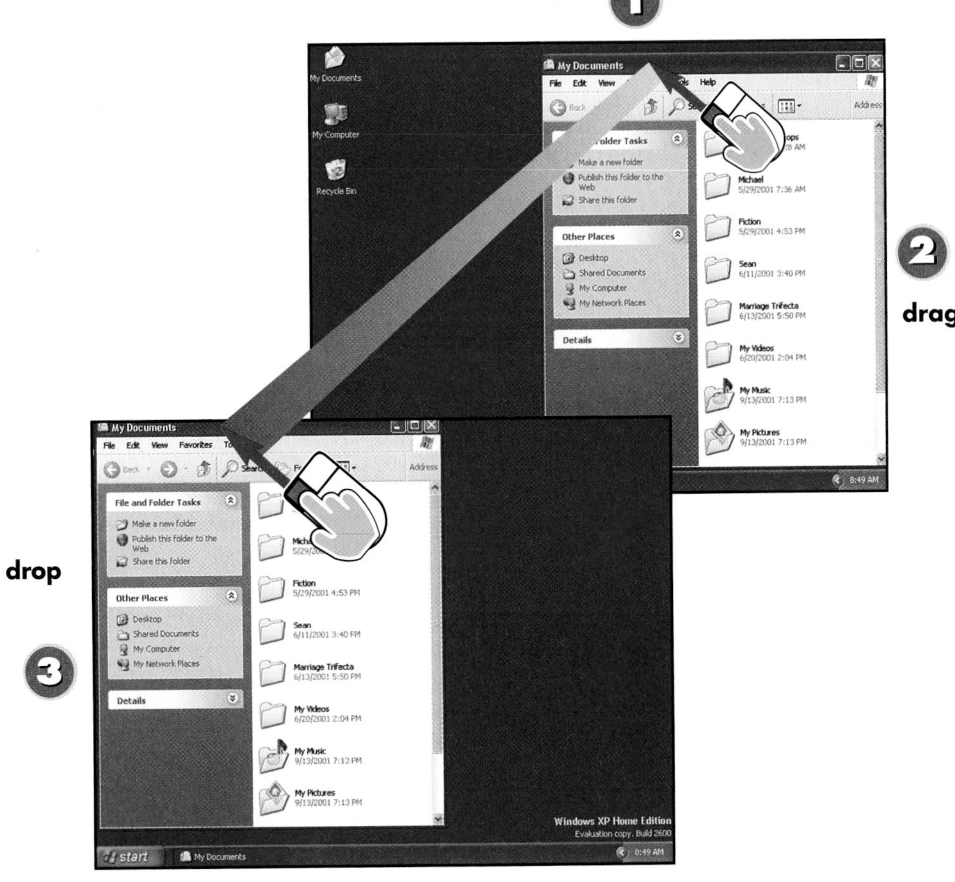

1. To move an open window, point to its title bar. Click and hold down the mouse button.
2. Drag the window to a new position.
3. Release the mouse button. The window and its contents appear in the new location.

INTRODUCTION

As you open more applications, folders, shortcuts, and so on, you'll need more room to display these windows on the desktop. You can easily move them around so you can see more open windows at one time.

TIP

The Title Bar

Be sure to point to the top row of the window, the title bar. If you point to any other area, you might resize the window instead of move it.

Task 7: Resizing a Window

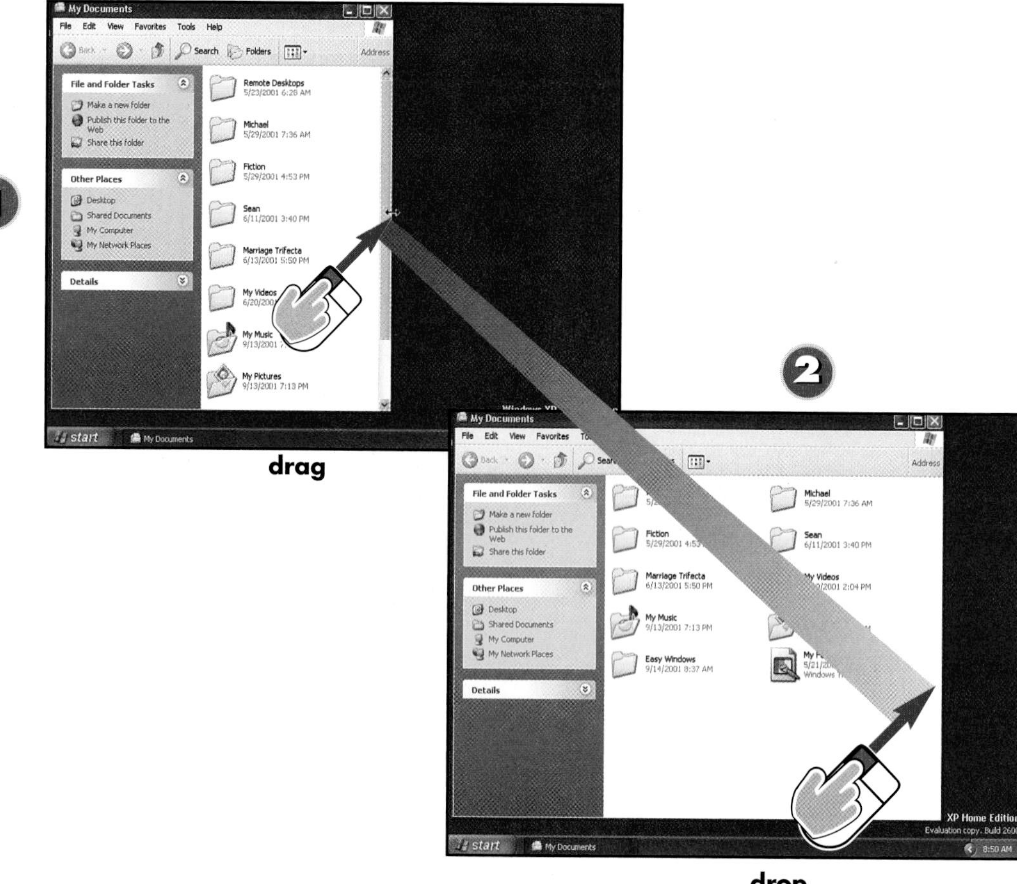

1. Point to any window border. You should see a double-headed arrow pointing out the directions in which you can size the window.

2. Drag the border to resize the window, and then release the mouse button. The window is now resized.

INTRODUCTION

If you want to see more of the window or less of the window, you can resize the window.

TIP

Resize from Corner

You can drag a corner of the window to proportionally resize both dimensions (height and width) at the same time.

TIP

Scroll Through a Window

If a window is too small to show all its contents, *scrollbars* appear along the edges of the window. Use these bars to scroll through the window and view the other window contents. Click the arrows to scroll in that direction or drag the box to scroll quickly through the contents.

Task 8: Arranging Windows on the Desktop

Start

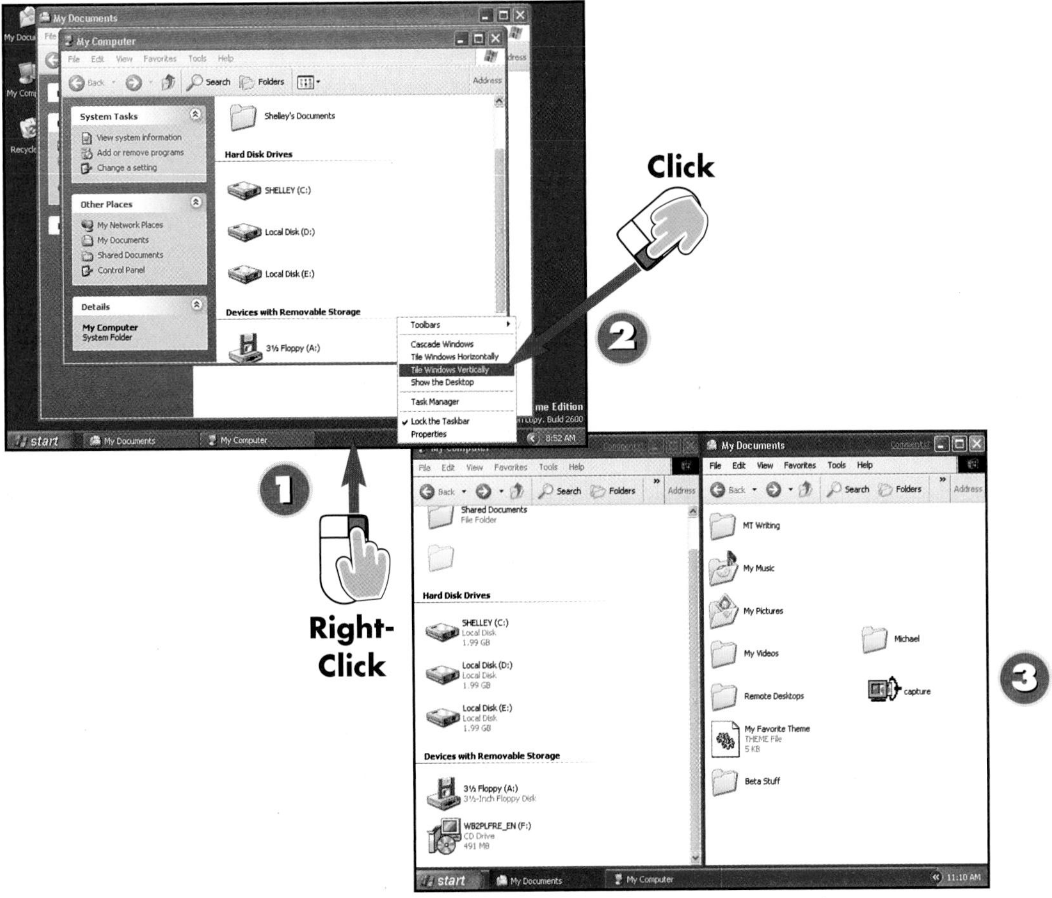

1. With multiple windows on the desktop, right-click a blank area of the taskbar.

2. Click the arrangement you want.

3. Windows arranges the windows; here they are tiled vertically.

INTRODUCTION

As you work, you will often have several windows open on the desktop at one time. The windows probably overlap each other, which can make it difficult to find what you want. To make your work easier and more efficient, Windows enables you to arrange the windows on the desktop in several different ways.

TIP

Right-Click a Blank Part
When choosing a window arrangement, be sure to right-click a blank area of the taskbar, not a button.

Undo
Undo the arrangement by right-clicking and choosing **Undo**.

TIP

Select a Window
To work in any of the open windows, click the desired window to make it active. The active window moves to the front of the stack, and its title bar changes to a brighter color.

Task 9: Using Menus

Start

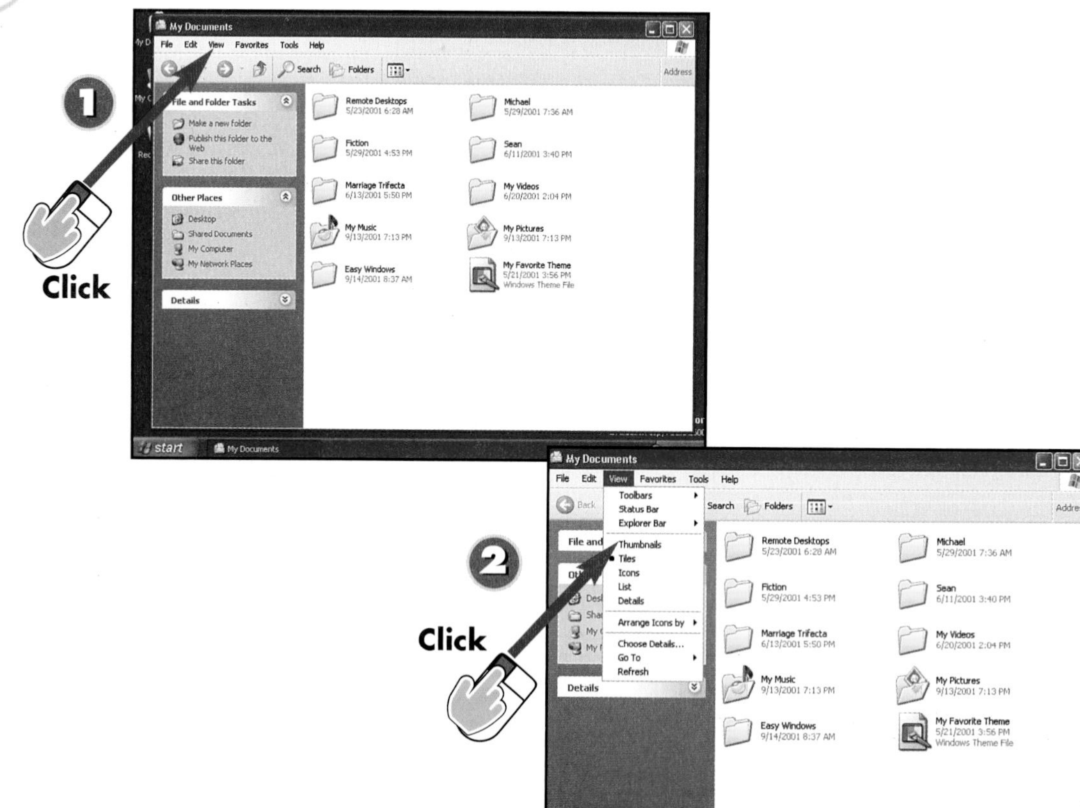

1. In the window or program, click the menu name (in this case, the menu name is **View**).

2. Click the command you want.

INTRODUCTION

Although you can perform many tasks by clicking the mouse on different onscreen objects, you must choose commands to perform the majority of Windows tasks. Commands are organized in menus. Most windows contain menu bars that list the available menus; each menu then contains a group of related commands.

TIP

See an Arrow or Ellipsis?
Selecting a command that is followed by an arrow will display a *submenu* (a menu within a menu). Select the command you want from the submenu by clicking it. Clicking a command that is followed by an ellipsis will display a dialog box.

TIP

Close a Menu
To close a menu without making a selection, you can press the **Esc** key on your keyboard or click outside the menu.

Task 10: Using Shortcut Menus

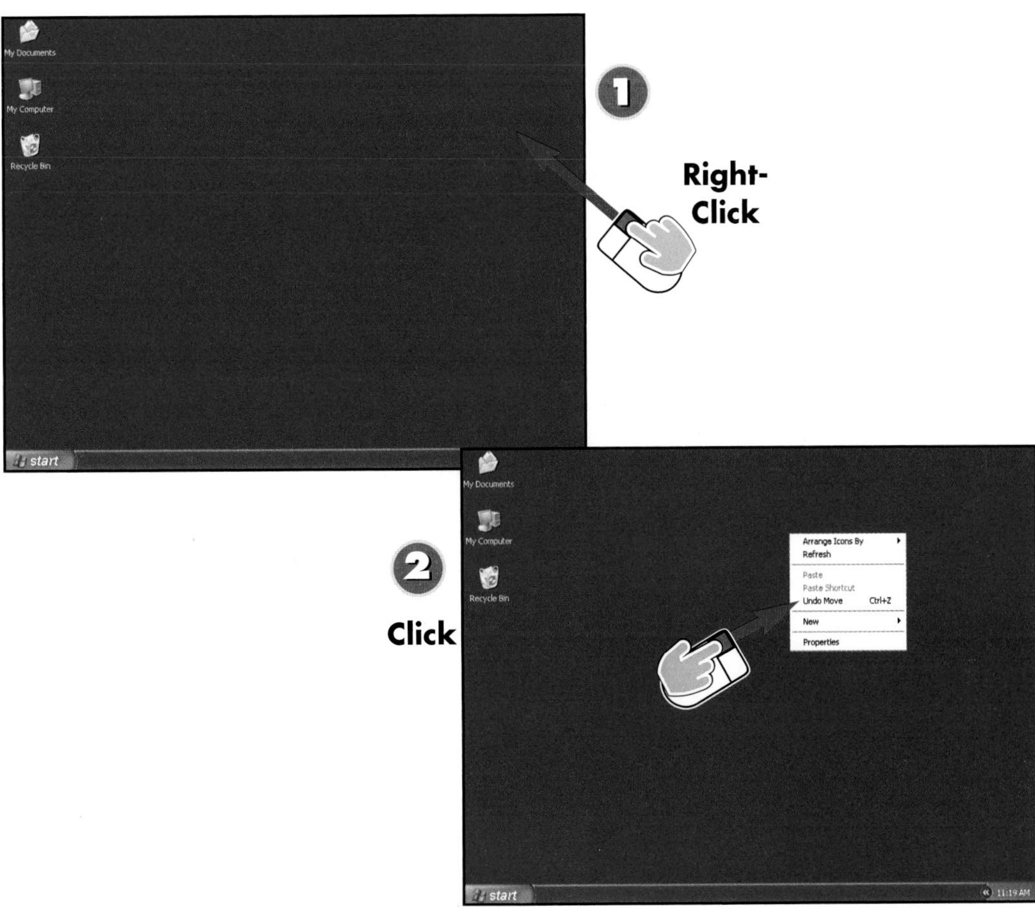

1. Right-click the item for which you want to display a shortcut menu. For example, right-click any blank part of the desktop.

2. Click the command you want in the shortcut menu.

INTRODUCTION

Shortcut menus, also called *quick menus* and *pop-up menus*, provide common commands related to the selected item. You can, for example, quickly copy and paste, create a new folder, move a file, or rearrange icons using a shortcut menu. You can also display properties about the selected item, as shown in this task.

TIP

Menus Vary
Different shortcut menus appear depending on what you're pointing to when you right-click the mouse.

Task 11: Using a Dialog Box

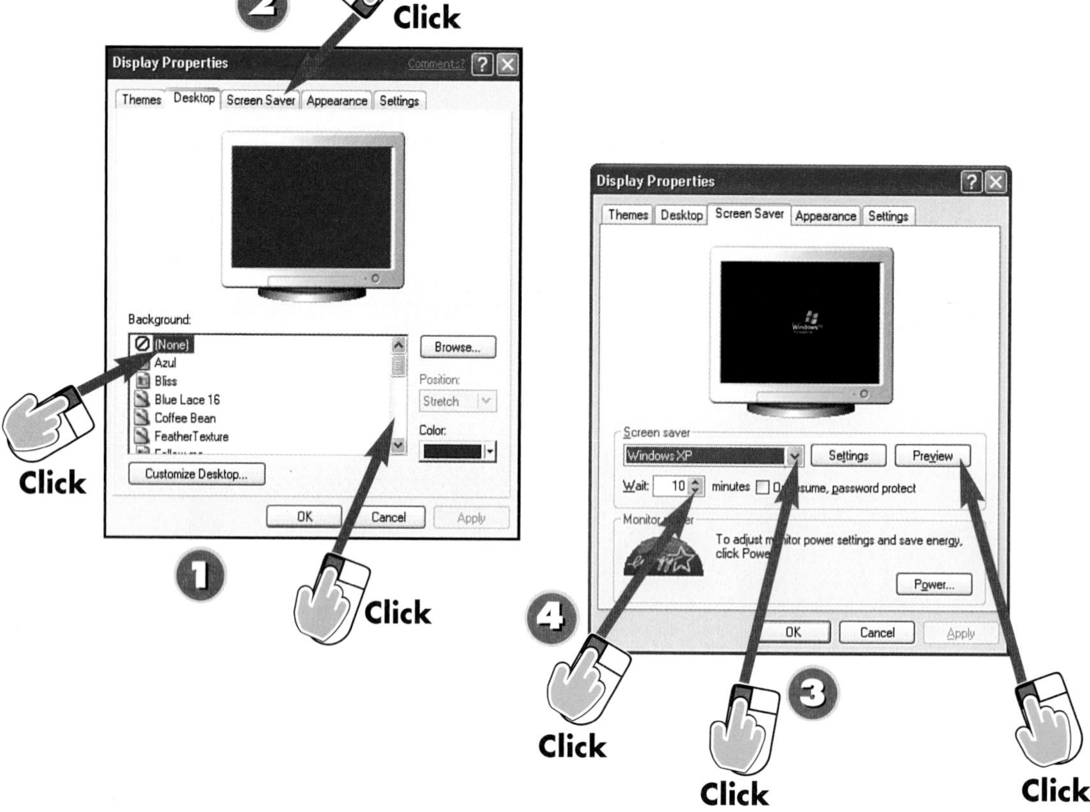

1. To use a list box, scroll through the list and click the item you want to select.

2. To view a tab, click it.

3. To use a drop-down list box, click the arrow, and then select the desired item from the list.

4. To use a spin box, click the arrows to increment or decrement the value, or type a value in the text box. To use a command button other than OK or Cancel, click the button.

INTRODUCTION

When you choose certain commands, a dialog box prompts you for additional information about how to carry out the command. Dialog boxes are used throughout Windows; luckily, all dialog boxes have common elements, and all are treated in a similar way. This task uses various dialog boxes from Windows to illustrate the common elements you can expect to find and how to make selections using the different elements.

TIP

Make a Selection

When a dialog box is open, you cannot perform any other action until you accept any changes by clicking the **OK** button. To close the dialog box without making a selection, click the **Cancel** button.

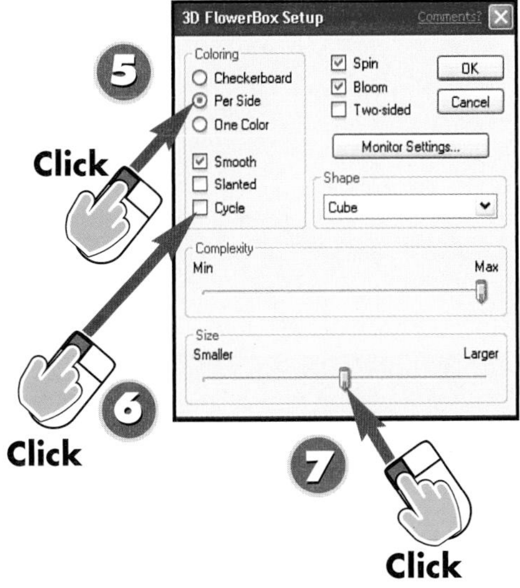

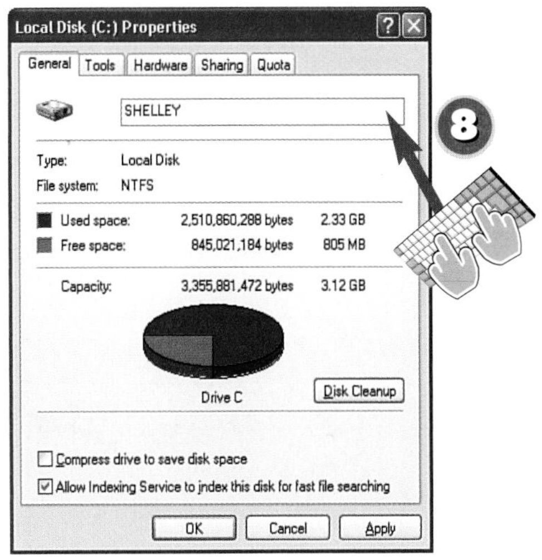

5. Click an option button to activate it.
6. Click a check box to select it (or deselect it if it is already selected).
7. Drag a lever to increase or decrease the setting.
8. Type an entry in a text box.

TIP

Option Buttons and Check Boxes

You can choose only one option button within a group of option buttons; choosing a second option deselects the first. However, you can select multiple check boxes within a group of check boxes.

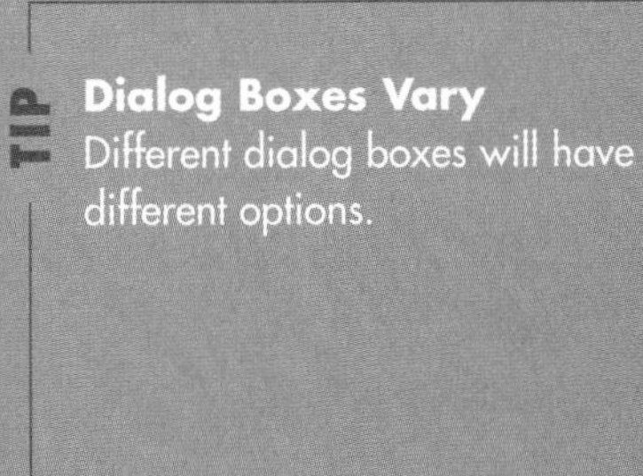

TIP

Dialog Boxes Vary

Different dialog boxes will have different options.

Task 12: Getting Help

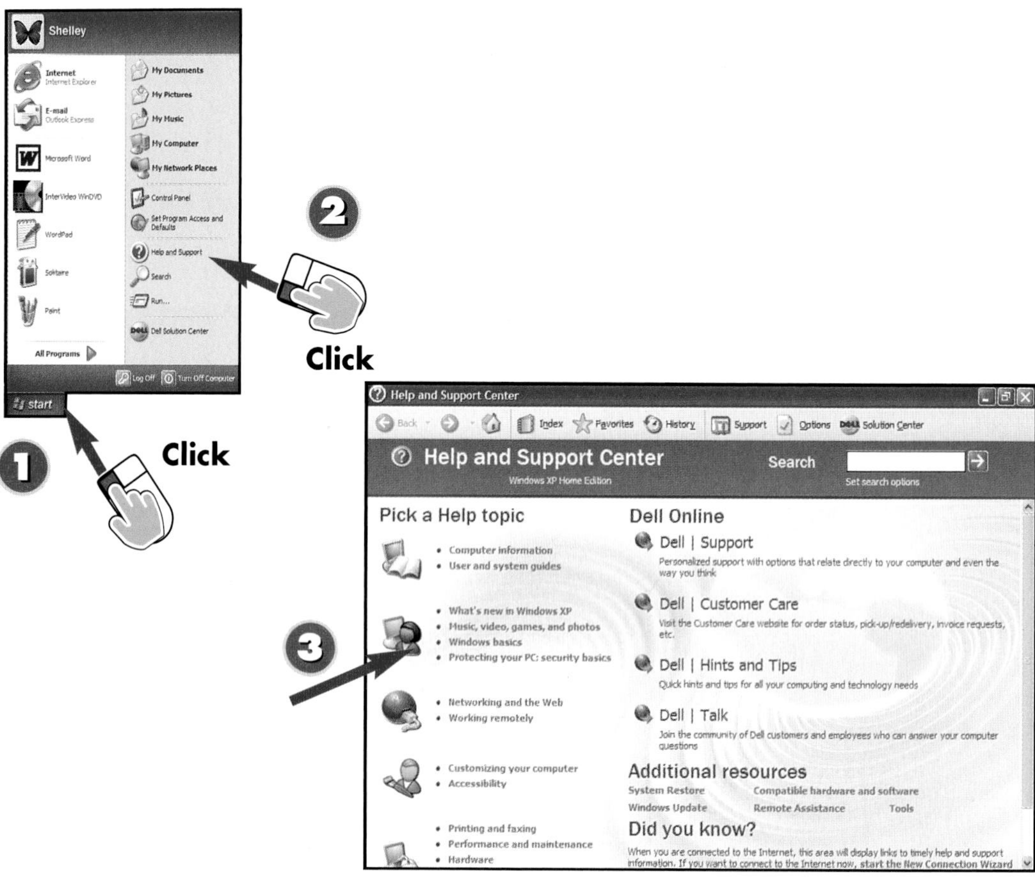

1. Click **Start**.
2. Click **Help and Support**.
3. Click the topic you want help on.

INTRODUCTION

You can use the Windows **Help** command to get help on common topics. You can select from a list of topics, as covered here.

TIP

Search for Help

As an alternative to browsing the contents, you can search for help. Type the topic in the Search box and then click the **Search** button. The matching topics are listed in the Search Results pane on the left. Click a match in this pane to display the help topic in the pane on the right.

Go Back

You can click the **Back** button to go back to the previous help page.

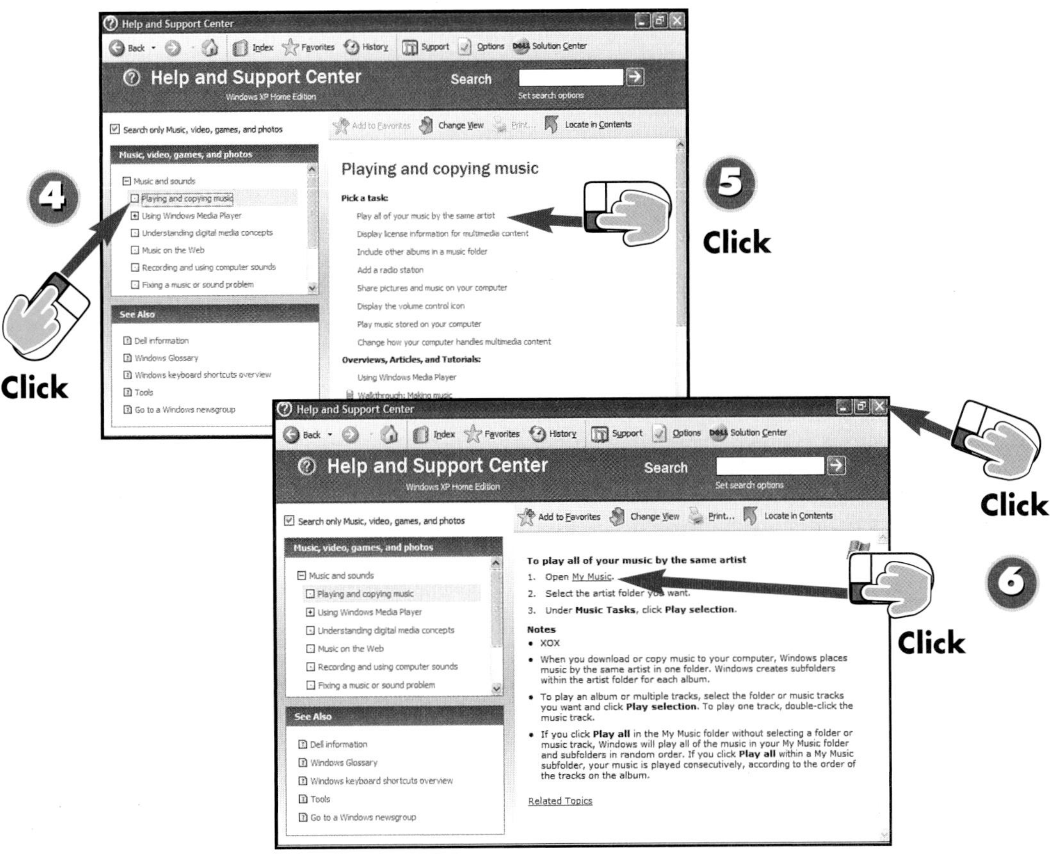

4 In the list of available topics, click the topic you want.

5 The right pane displays a list of subtopics within this topic. Click the topic you want help with.

6 The help information appears in the pane on the right. When you have reviewed this information, click the **Close** button to close the Help window.

TIP

Use the Index
For help, you can look up words in the Index. Click the **Index** button in the Help window toolbar. The Index appears in the left pane. Type the keyword in the text box; the index scrolls to matching entries. Click any of these entries to display the relevant help topic in the right pane of the help window.

Print Topic
To print the current help topic, click the **Print** button.

TIP

Related Topics
To view related help topics, click this link in the help window, if available. You can also click any underlined text to view additional help on that help topic step or to display a definition of the item.

Task 13: Getting Context-Sensitive Help

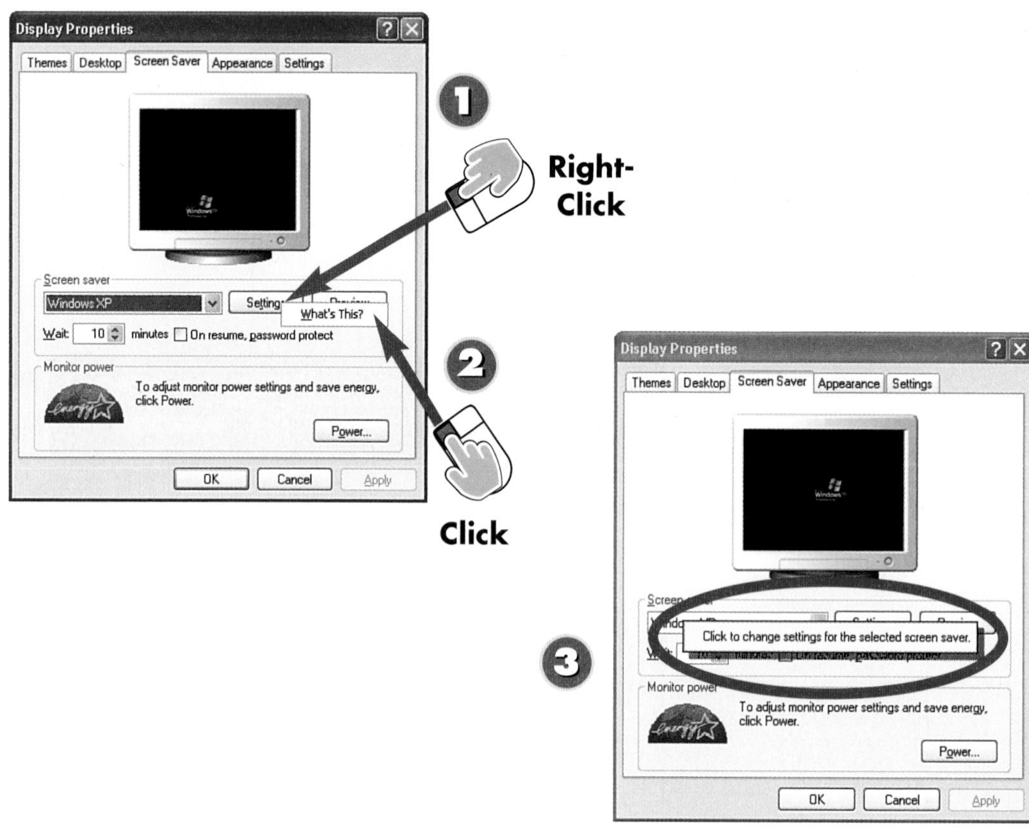

1. In a dialog box, right-click the option with which you want help.
2. Select **What's This**.
3. After you review the explanation, click outside the pop-up tip to hide the explanation.

Often when you open a dialog box, you might not know what each feature does. To help you understand all of your options, you can display context-sensitive help on any of the options. You see a pop-up explanation of the feature.

TIP

Use Help Button

If the window includes a Help button, you can click this button and then click any of the options in the dialog box to get help.

Task 14: Restarting and Shutting Down the Computer

Start

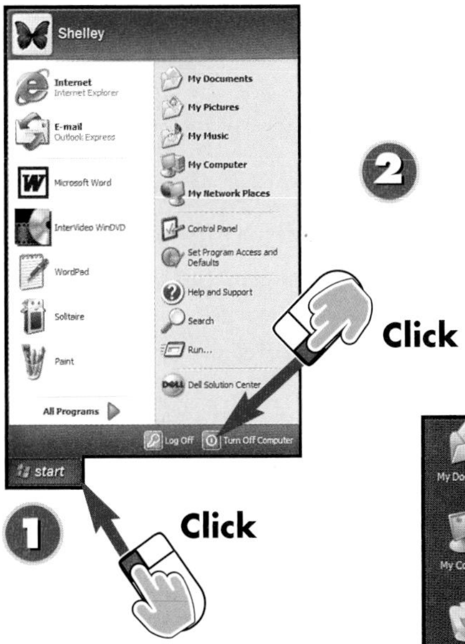

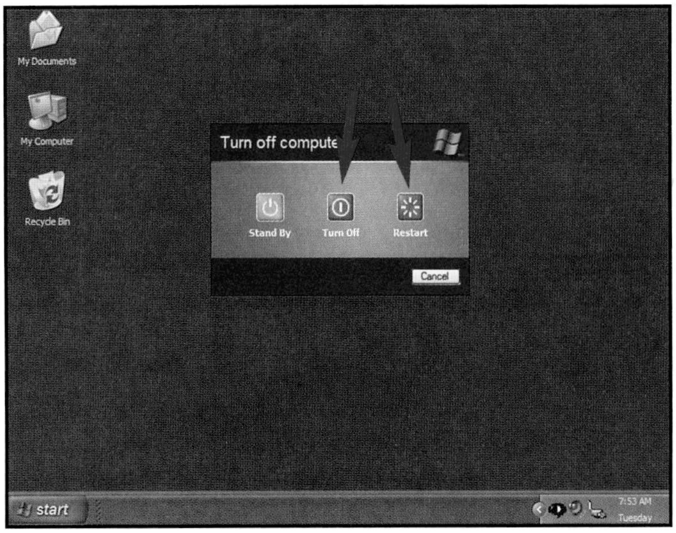

1 Click Start.

2 Click the **Turn Off Computer** button.

3 Select **Restart** to restart the computer, or select **Turn Off** to turn off the computer. If you selected to restart, the computer is restarted. If you selected to turn off, the computer is shut down.

INTRODUCTION

Sometimes you will need to restart your computer. You might do this if the computer gets stuck or if you make changes and need to restart to put the changes into effect. When you are done working on your computer, you should turn it off.

TIP

Save Documents and Close Programs
Before you shut down or restart, save any documents that you are working on and also close any open programs. You can find out more about these topics in the next part, Part 2.

TIP

Hibernate
To hibernate the computer to conserve power, select the **Stand By** button. This is most commonly used for laptops.

PART 2

Working with Programs

One advantage to using Windows XP is the enormous number of available Windows programs. You can use many word-processing, database, spreadsheet, drawing, and other programs in Windows. This variety of programs provides all the tools you need to perform your everyday tasks.

Windows programs are easy to open and use, and enable you to create documents. In addition to learning how to open and exit programs, you also learn some skills for working with documents you create with those programs. Two important tasks are saving your work and opening your saved work, both covered here.

Tasks

Task 1: Starting a Program from the Start Menu

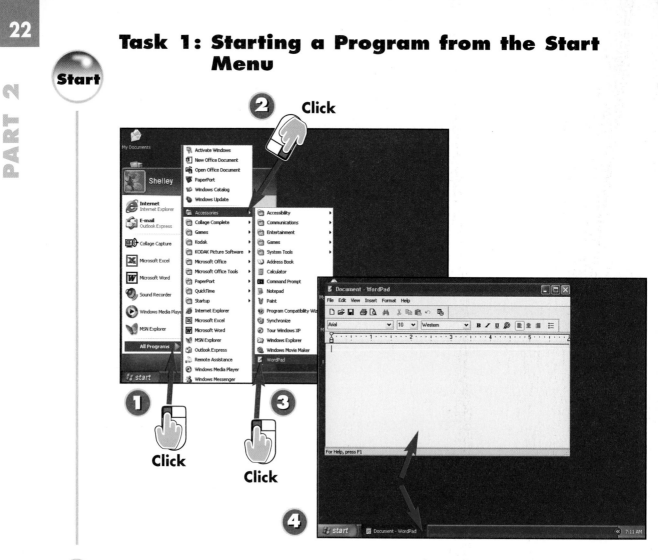

1. Click **Start** and then click **All Programs**.
2. Select the program group that contains the program you want to start (in this case, **Accessories**).
3. Click the program you want to start (**WordPad** is selected here).
4. The program opens in its own window, and a taskbar button for the program appears in the taskbar.

INTRODUCTION

Most of the time you spend using your computer will be spent working in some type of a program—a word processing program to type letters, a spreadsheet program to create budgets, and so on. You can start a program in any number of ways, including from the Start menu. When you install a new Windows program, that program's installation procedure will set up a program folder and program icon on the Start menu.

TIP

Shortcut

Windows XP keeps track of th last several programs you hav opened and lists them on the opening Start menu. If the pro gram is listed here, click it to start the program.

Task 2: Exiting a Program

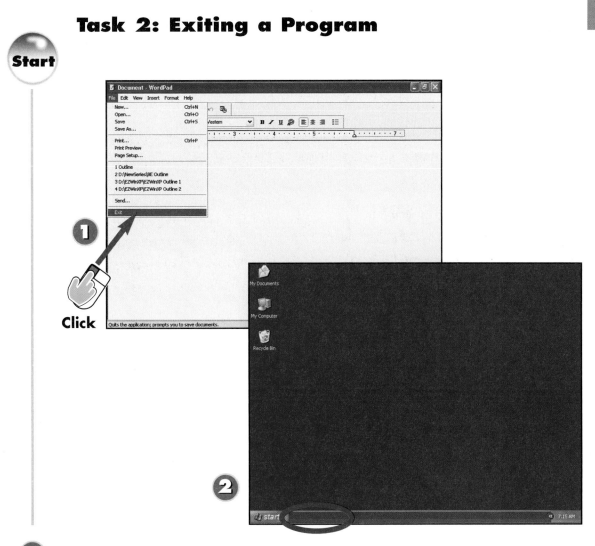

1 Click **File**, and then click the **Exit** command.

2 The program closes. Notice that the taskbar button for the program (here WordPad) has disappeared.

INTRODUCTION

When you finish working in a program, close it to free system memory. Too many open programs can tax your system's memory and slow the computer's processes, such as saving, printing, switching between programs, and so on.

TIP

More Ways to Close
You can also press **Alt+F4** or click the **Close** button in the program's title bar to close a program.

TIP

Saving Your Work
If you have not saved a file and close that file's program, a message box appears asking if you want to save the file. If you do, click **Yes**; if not, click **No**. If you want to return to the document, click **Cancel**.

Task 3: Starting a Program from a Shortcut Icon

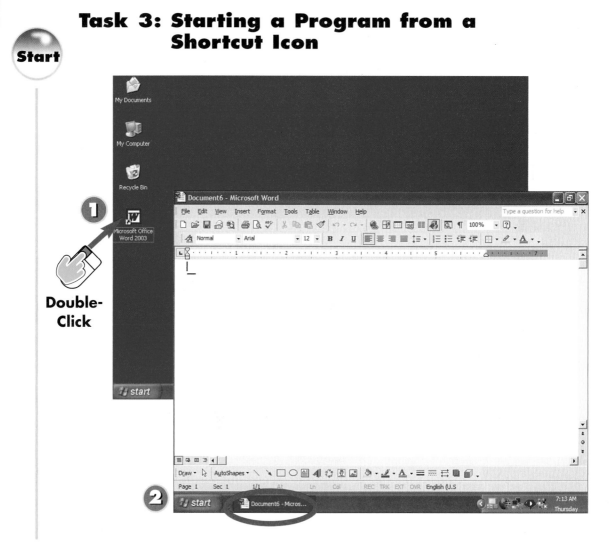

1 Double-click the shortcut icon on the desktop (shown here is the shortcut icon for Word for Windows).

2 The program starts and displays in its own window. A taskbar button appears for the program.

INTRODUCTION

In addition to the Start menu, you can also start programs from shortcut icons. Some programs automatically create shortcut icons, placing them on the desktop. You can also add shortcut icons to programs yourself. This task covers how to start a program from a shortcut icon.

TIP

Create Shortcut Icons

You can create shortcut icons to any of your installed programs. To do so, see Part 11, "Setting Up Programs."

Task 4: Switching Between Programs

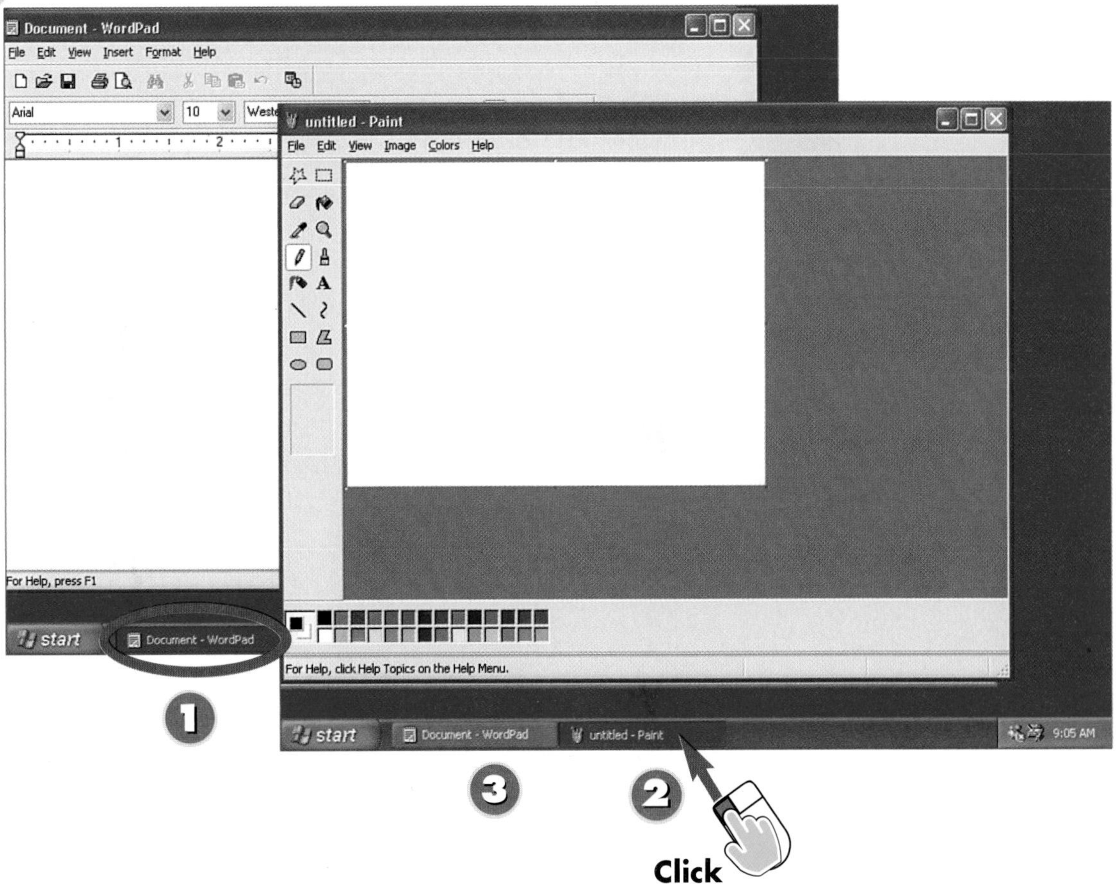

1. After you've started two programs, look at the taskbar. You should see a button for each program.
2. Click the button for the program you want to switch to (in this case, **Paint**).
3. That program becomes the active program.

INTRODUCTION

You may often work with more than one type of program at the same time. Windows XP enables you to quickly switch from one program to another. For example, you might want to compare price figures from an Excel worksheet with a price list you've set up in Word. You might want to copy text from a WordPad document to a Paint picture. Switching between programs enables you not only to compare data, but also to share data among programs.

TIP

Close a Program

To close a program, use the **File, Exit** command or click the **Close** button for the program window.

Task 5: Saving and Closing a Document

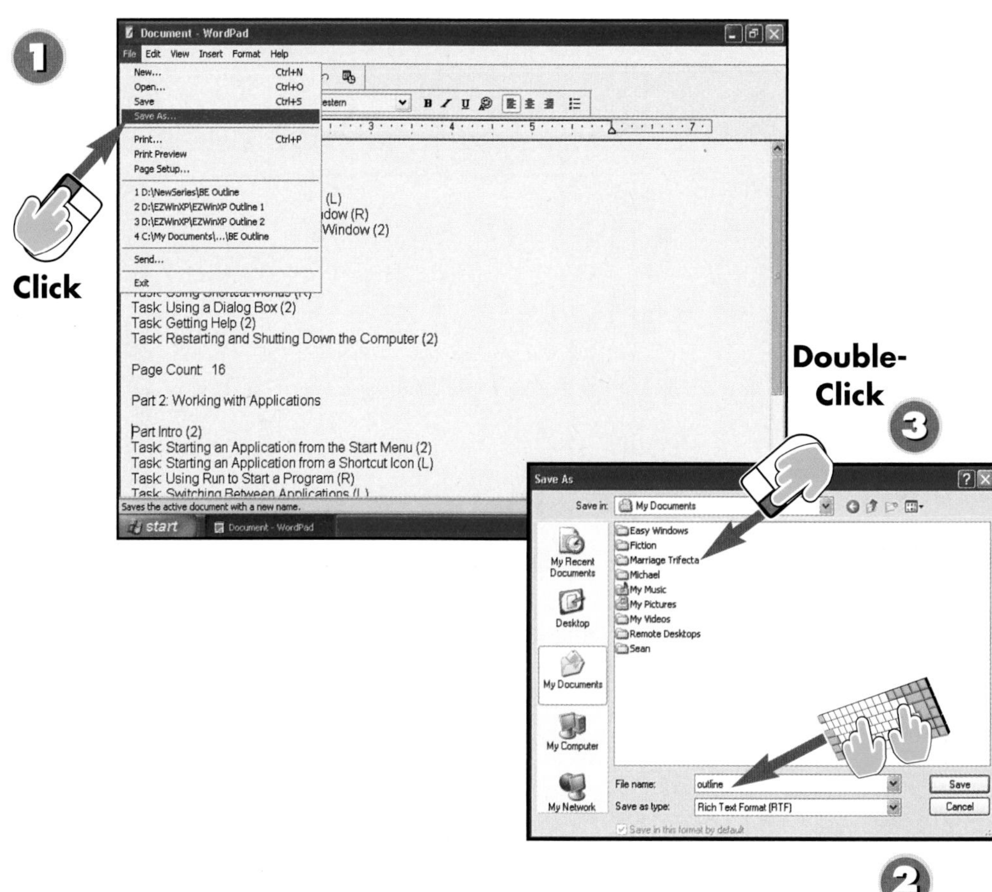

1. Click **File**, **Save As** in the program.
2. Type a new name, replacing the default name.
3. To save the document in another folder, double-click that folder.

INTRODUCTION

You save documents and files so that you can open them later to print, edit, copy, and so on. The first time you save a file, you must assign that file a name and folder (or location). You save documents pretty much the same way in all Windows programs; this task shows you how to save a document in WordPad.

TIP

Save Again
After you've saved and named a file, you can simply click **File** and select **Save** to resave that file to the same location with the same name. Any changes you have made since the last save are reflected in the file.

TIP

Open Another Folder
If the folder is not listed, you can open the folder. To do so, select it from the Save in drop-down list or use the Up One Level button to move up through the folder structure until the folder is displayed.

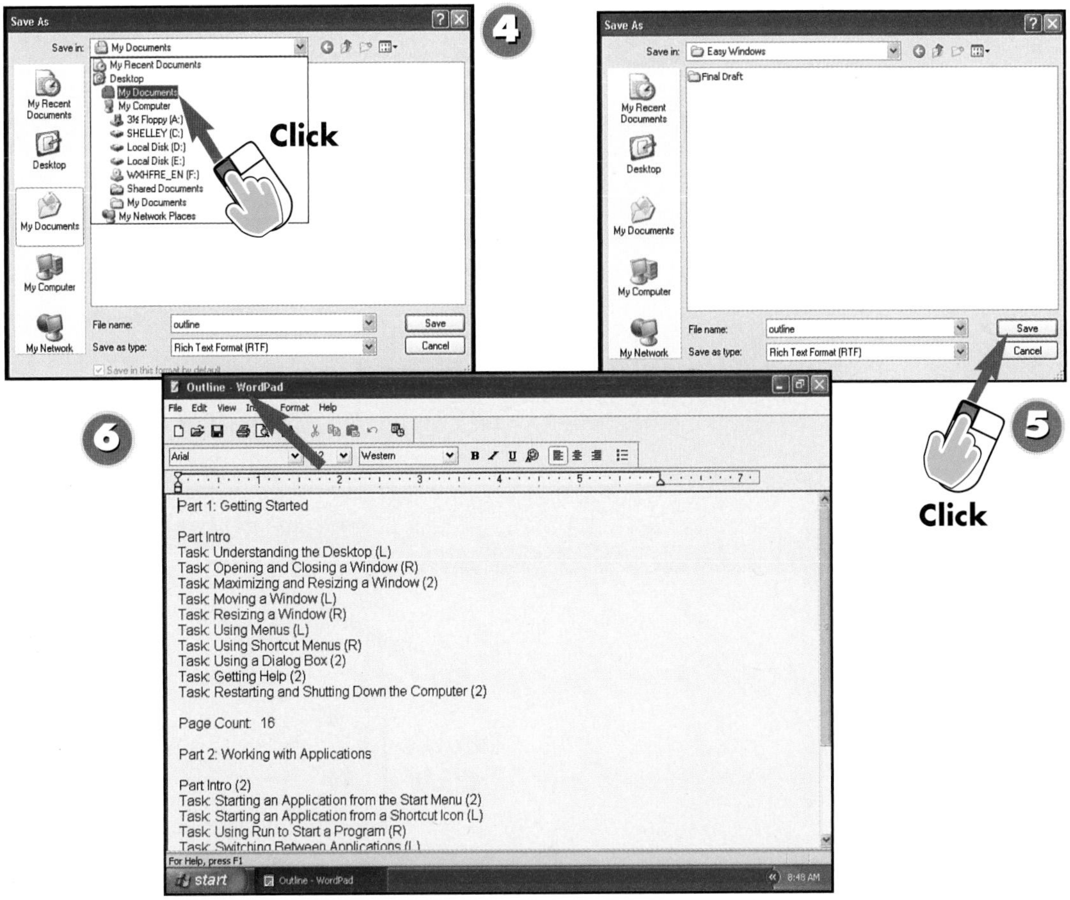

4 To save the document in another drive or folder, display the Save in drop-down list and select the drive or folder you want.

5 Click the **Save** button.

6 The program saves the file. The document name is listed in the title bar.

TIP

Create a New Folder
You can create a new folder from within the Save As dialog box. To do so, click the New Folder button, type the new folder name, and press Enter.

TIP

Close the Document
Most programs, with the exception of WordPad and Paint, include a Close command and a Close button for the document window. To close the document, select **File**, **Close** or click the Close button for the document window. In WordPad and Paint, you must open another document, create a new document, or exit the program to close the document.

Task 6: Opening a Document

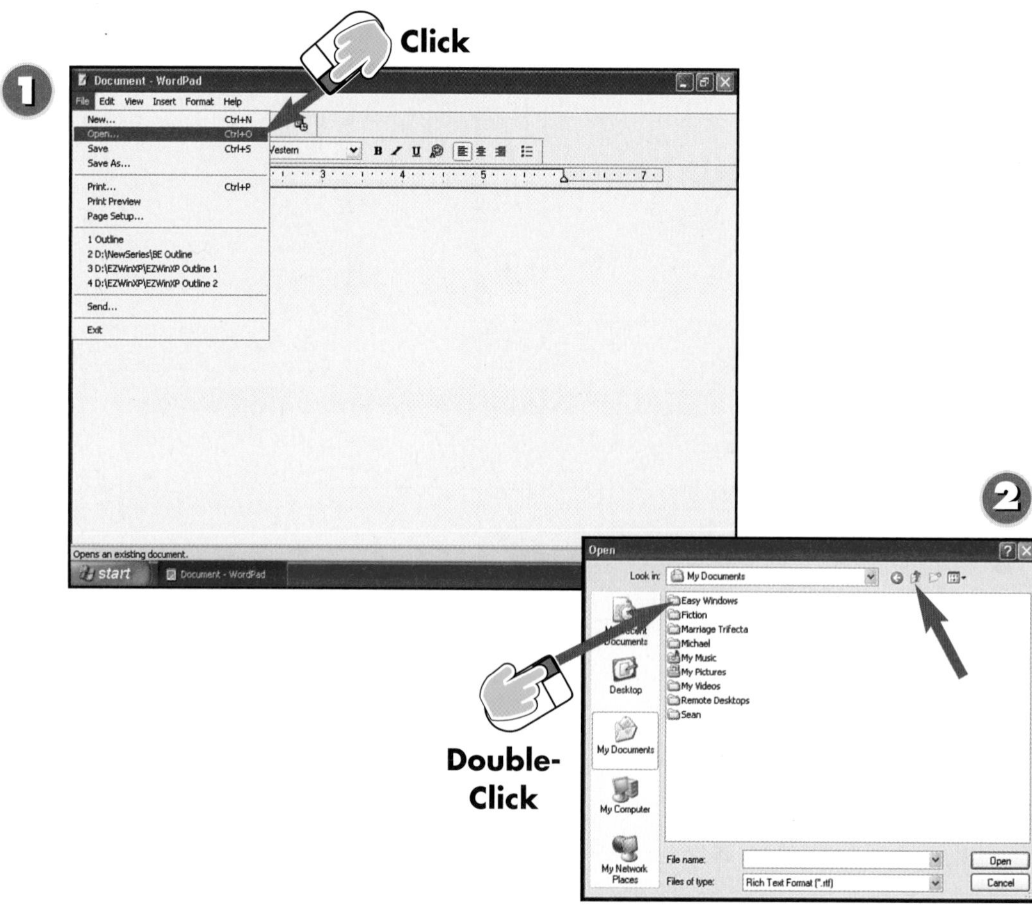

1. Click **File**, and then click the **Open** command.
2. Double-click the folder that contains the file. You can click the **Up One Level** button to move up through the folders and display other folders to open.

INTRODUCTION

When you save a document, the program saves the document information as a file with the name you entered and in the location you specified. The purpose of saving a document is to make it available for later use. You can open any of the documents you have saved. You can then make changes or print the document.

TIP

Can't Find a File?
If you can't find the file you want to work with, it could be because you did not save it where you thought you did. Try looking in a different drive or folder. If you still can't find it, try searching for the file (see Part 4, "Working with Files").

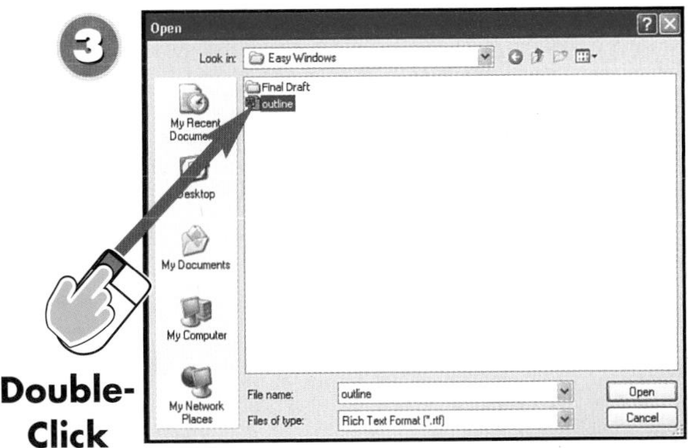

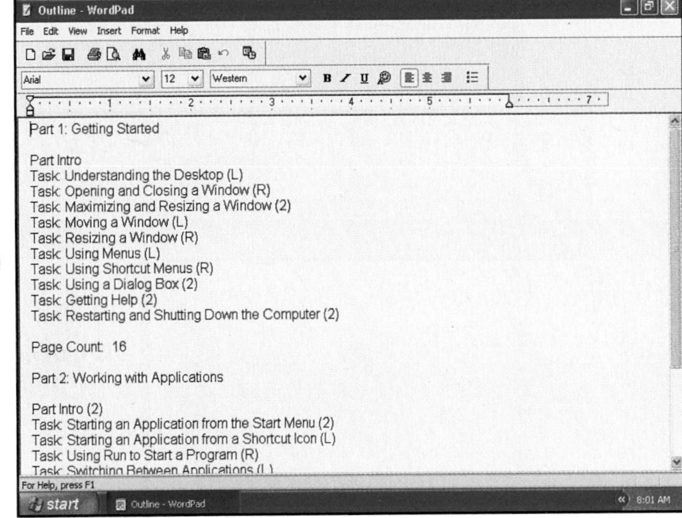

3. When you find the file you want to open, double-click it.

4. The file is opened and displayed in the program window. Here you see a WordPad document opened.

TIP

Shortcut

As a shortcut, click **File**. Notice that the last files opened are listed near the bottom of the menu. You can open any of these files by clicking them in the **File** menu.

TIP

Change to Another Drive

If the file is on another drive, display the Look in drop-down list and select the drive where you placed the file.

TIP

Use Recent Documents Command

You can also add the Recent Documents command to the Start menu. Then you can click **Start**, **Recent Documents**. From this list, you can select the document you want to open.

Task 7: Switching Between Open Documents

Start

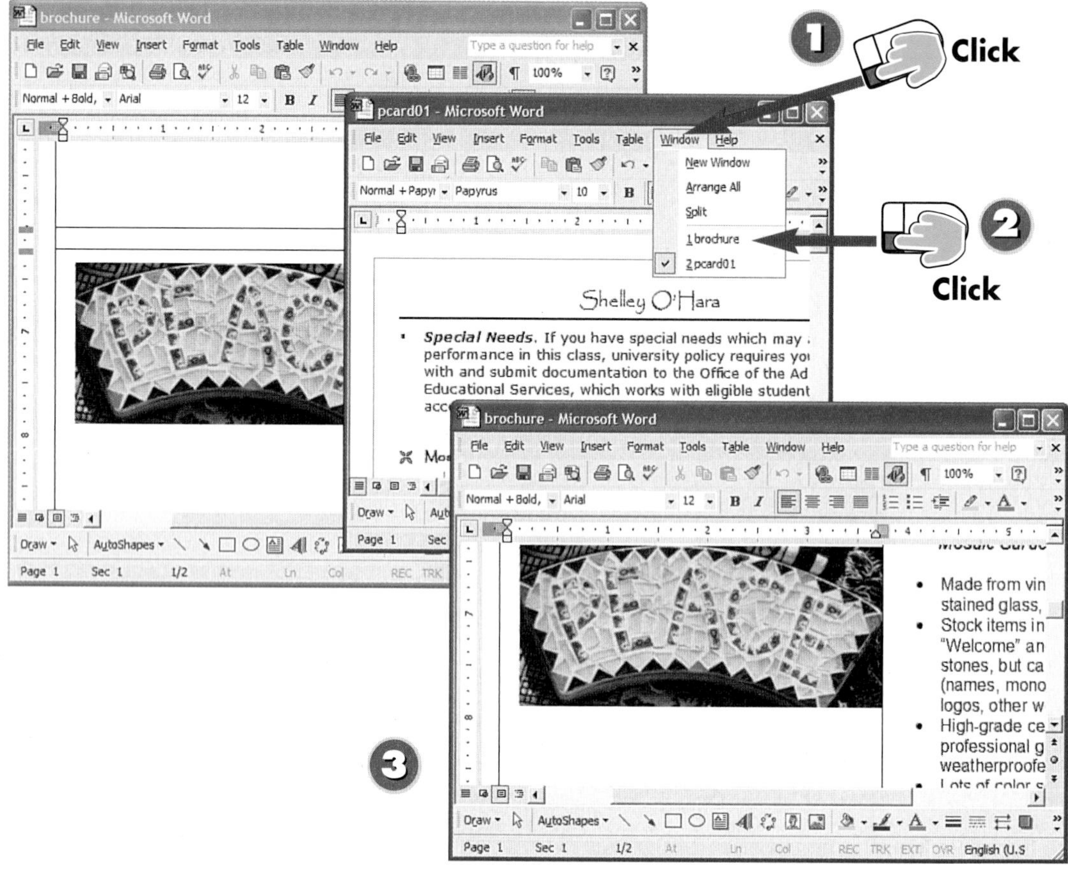

1. Click **Window**.
2. Notice that the current document has a check mark next to its name. Click the document that you want to switch to.
3. The document you just clicked in the **Window** menu becomes the active document.

INTRODUCTION

In most programs, you can work with several documents at once. The number of documents you can have open depends on your system memory and the program. Simply click File and select the Open command to open the files you want to work with. Then you can easily switch between any of the open documents.

TIP

Switching Documents Versus Programs

Don't confuse switching between documents with switching between programs. For more information, refer to Task 4, "Switching Between Programs."

TIP

No Window Menu?

If the program does not have a **Window** menu, you probably cannot work in multiple documents. For example, in WordPad, you cannot have more than one document open at a time.

Task 8: Creating a New Document

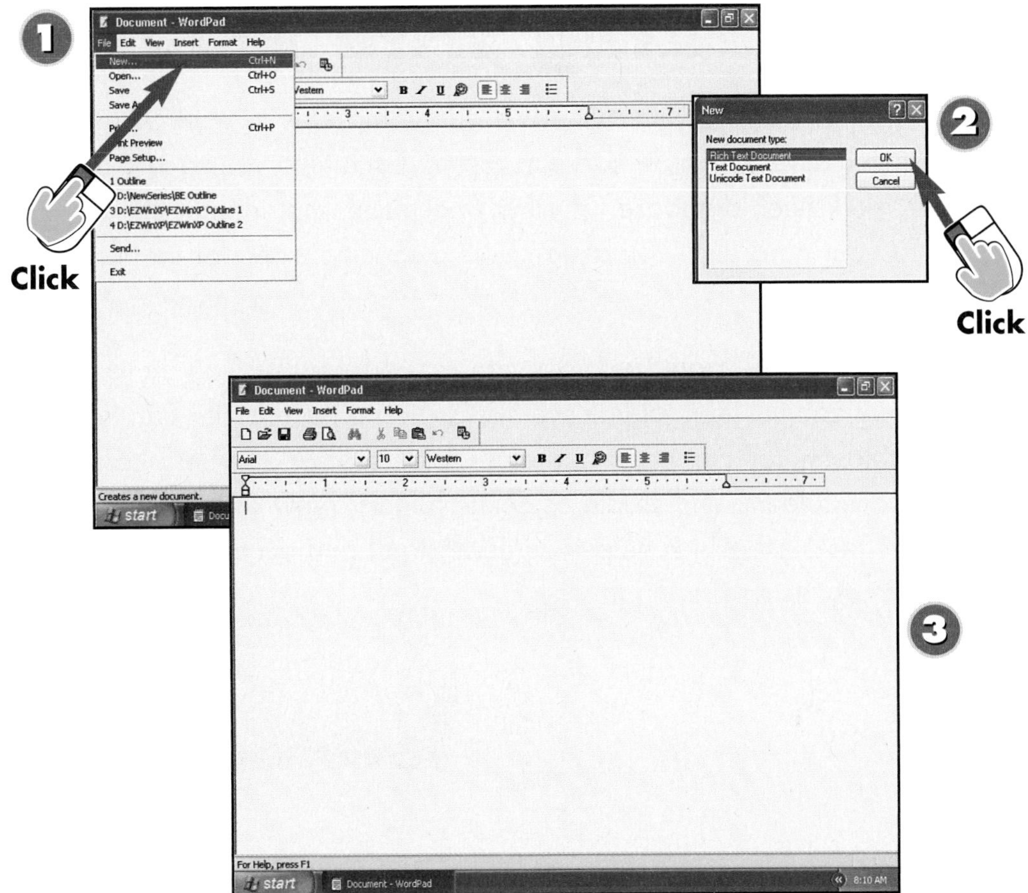

1. In the program, click **File**, **New**.
2. If you see a **New** dialog box, click the type of document you want to create and then click the **OK** button.
3. A new document is displayed.

INTRODUCTION

When you want a new "sheet" of paper, you can create a new document. Many programs prompt you to select a template on which to base the new document. A *template* is a predesigned document. You can select the template, if prompted, and create the new document.

TIP

Shortcut
As a shortcut, you can click the **New** button to create a new document based on the default template.

TIP

Exceptions
For complex programs such as PowerPoint and Access, you might be prompted to make some selections before the new document is created. Use your program documentation for help for creating new documents with these programs.

PART 3

Working with Folders

One part of working with Windows is learning how to work with the documents you save and store on your system. Each time you save a document (a letter, worksheet, database, or other document), that information is saved as a file on your hard disk. You assign both a specific place for the file and a name.

To keep your files organized, you can set up folders. If your hard drive is like a big filing cabinet then folders are like drawers. Each folder can hold files or other folders. You can open and close folders, view a folder's contents, copy and move folders, and create or delete folders. New with Windows XP is the Folders Tasks list, which helps you understand and access the common folder commands, as covered in this part.

Tasks

Task 1: Opening My Computer

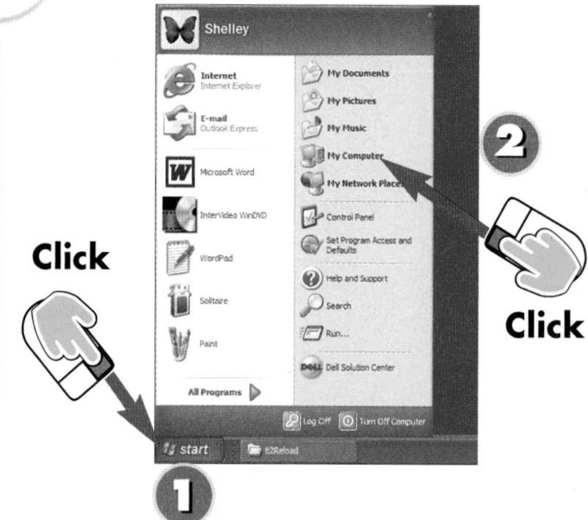

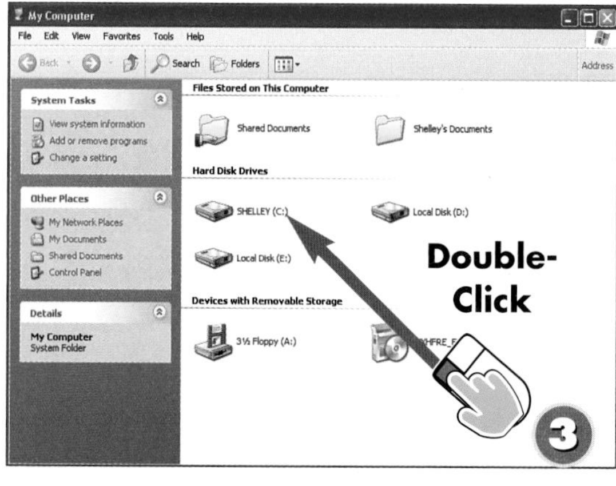

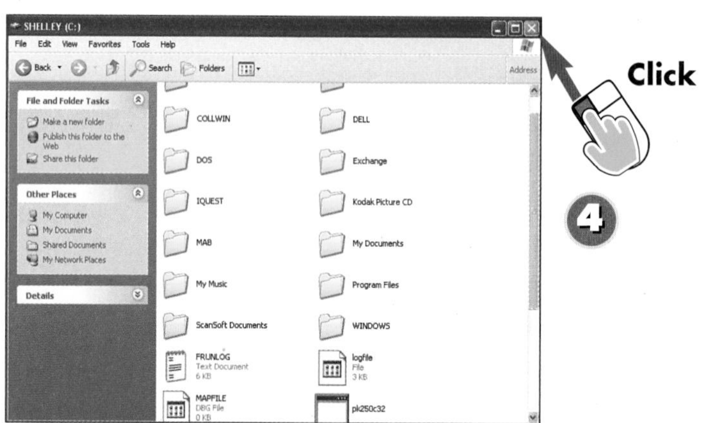

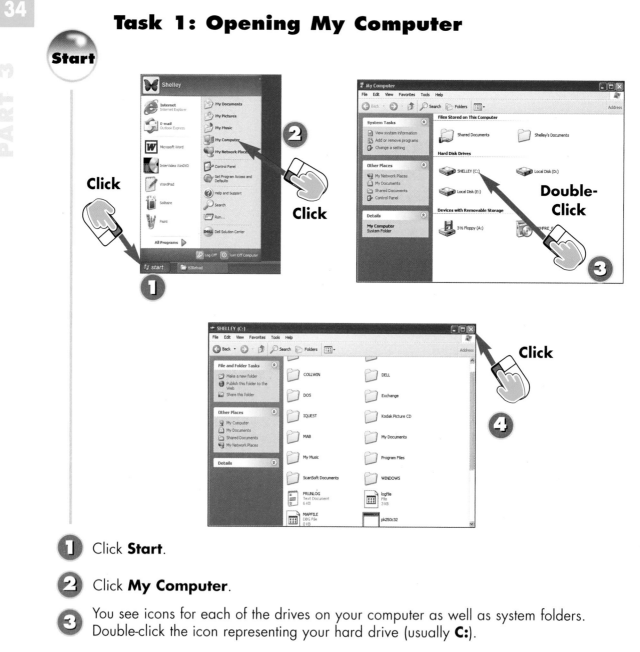

1. Click **Start**.
2. Click **My Computer**.
3. You see icons for each of the drives on your computer as well as system folders. Double-click the icon representing your hard drive (usually **C:**).
4. Each folder icon represents a folder on your hard drive. Each page icon represents a document (file). Click the **Close** button to close the window.

INTRODUCTION

My Computer is an icon that represents all of the drives on your system. To open folders and display files, you often start by opening My Computer. Once you open this window, you can then open any of your drives to see the folders and files contained on that drive.

TIP

Use Shortcut Icon
If you have added the shortcut icon for My Computer to your desktop, you can double-click this icon to open My Computer, as covered in Part 10, "Personalizing Windows."

TIP

Tasks Pane
Windows XP displays a Tasks list with common tasks as well as Other Places and a Details area. When you click an icon, you can see information about the icon in the Details area.

Task 2: Opening the My Documents Folder

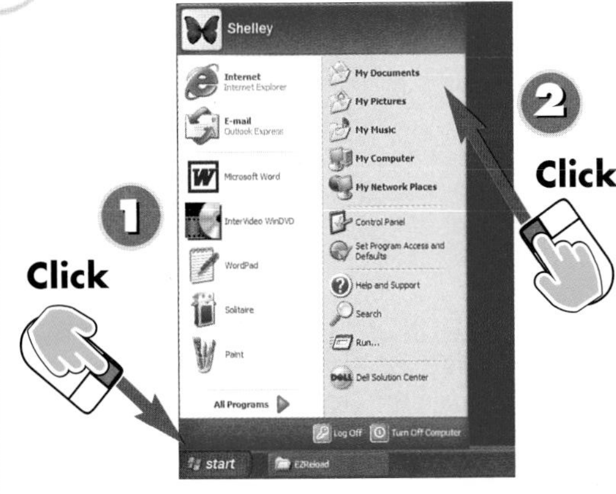

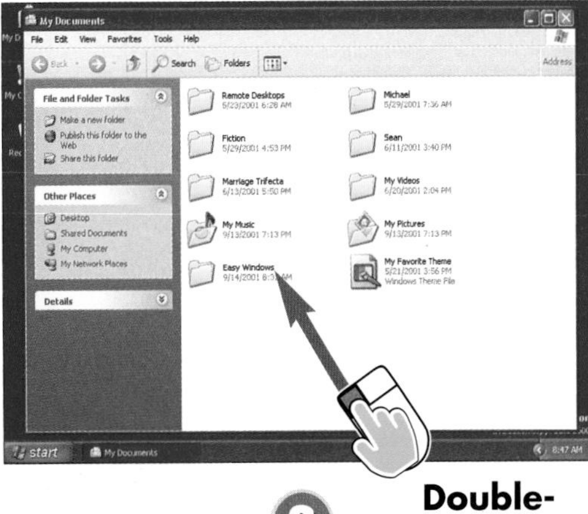

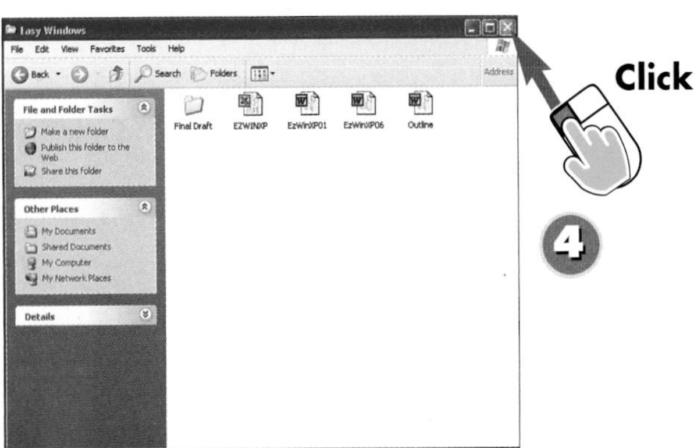

1. Click **Start**.
2. Click **My Documents**.
3. If you have added any folders to this folder, you see them listed. Double-click any folder to display its contents.
4. You see the contents of this folder. Folder icons indicate folders and page icons indicate documents. Click the **Close** button to close the window.

INTRODUCTION

To help you keep your documents organized, Windows sets up a special folder called My Documents. You can view the contents using the **My Documents** command. When you organize your own documents, it's a good idea to use the My Documents folder, creating subfolders within this folder to store your work.

TIP

Add Folders
You can add folders to the My Documents folder. To do so, see Task 11, "Creating a New Folder."

TIP

Shortcut
If you have added the My Documents icon to your desktop, you can double-click this icon to open this folder. See Part 10 for information on customizing the desktop.

Task 3: Opening the My Pictures Folder

Click

Click

Click

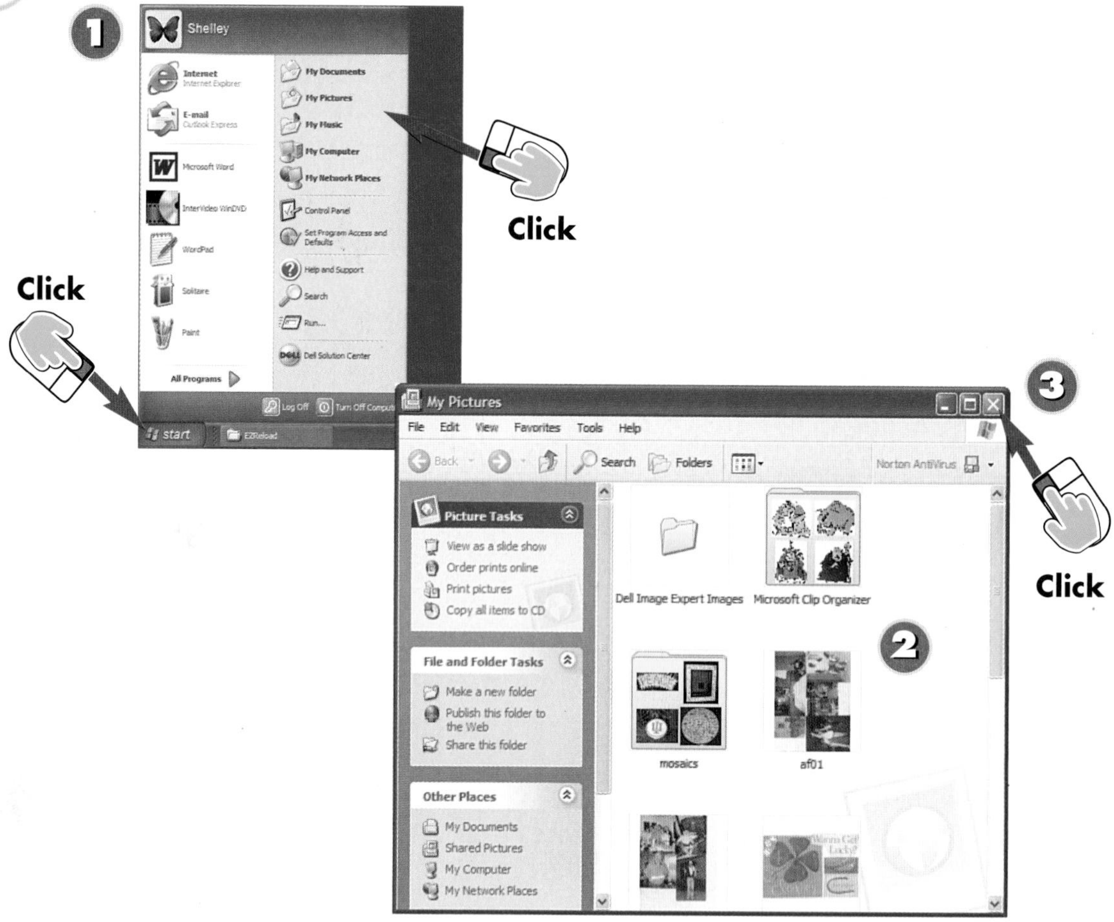

1 Click **Start** and then click **My Pictures**.

2 You see the contents of this folder. If Windows can display the image file type, you see the picture in thumbnail form. If not, you see an icon.

3 Click the **Close** button to close the window.

INTRODUCTION

Windows also sets up special folders within the My Documents folder. One folder is the My Pictures folder, which you can use to store graphic images. These might be pictures taken with a digital camera, images created with a scanner, or images you have created with a drawing or paint program. Windows XP includes a Picture Tasks list with commands for handling pictures.

TIP

Thumbnail View

You should see the contents in Thumbnail view, which shows miniature pictures of each graphic file. You can change to another view (or switch to Thumbnail if you don't see this view) using the **Views** command or button.

Task 4: Opening the My Music Folder

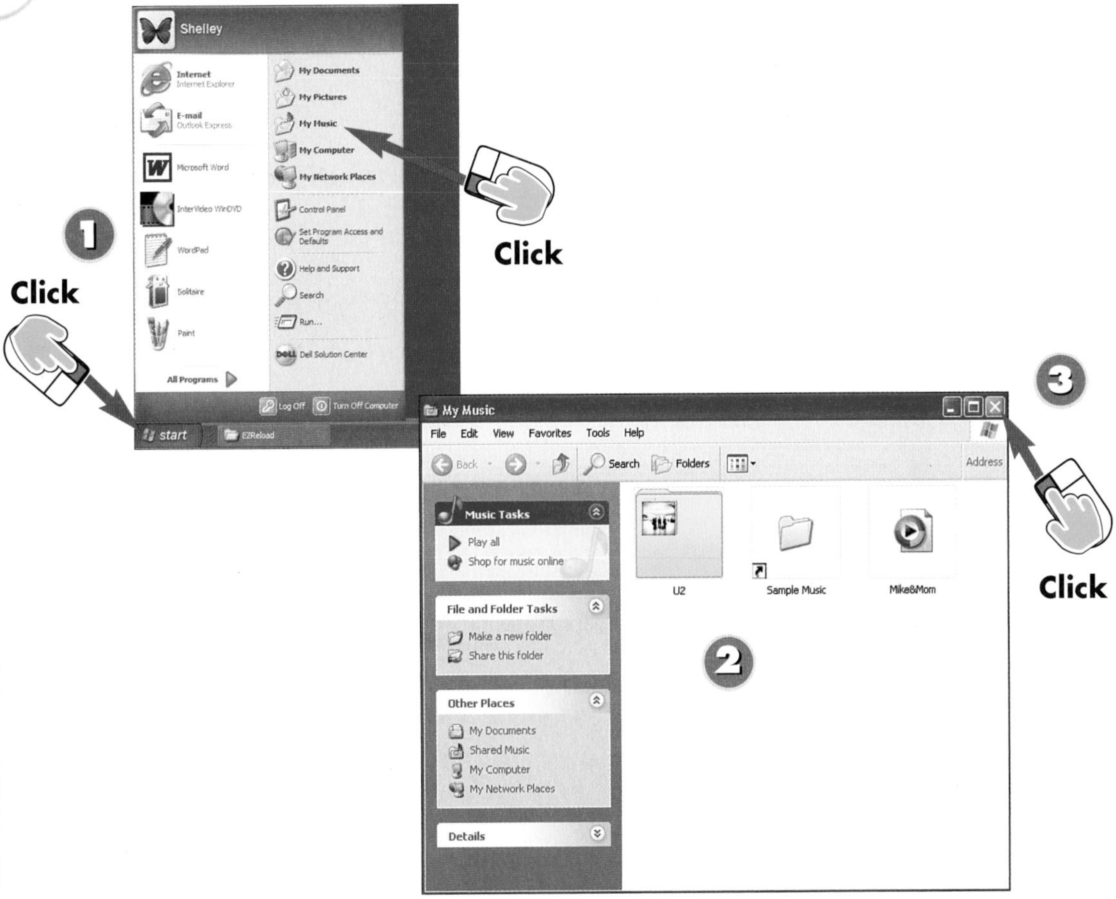

1 Click **Start** and then click **My Music**.

2 You see the contents of this folder including any music files you have stored here.

3 Click the **Close** button to close the window.

INTRODUCTION

Within the My Documents folder, you see special folders set up by Windows to store particular types of content. For instance, you can use the My Music Folder to store music files. You not only see the contents when you open this folder, but new with Windows XP, you see a Music Tasks list with commands for working with music files.

TIP

My Videos

Windows XP also includes a My Videos folder within the My Documents folder. You can use this folder to store video files. To open My Videos, open **My Computer** and then double-click the icon for the **My Videos** folder.

Task 5: Selecting a Folder

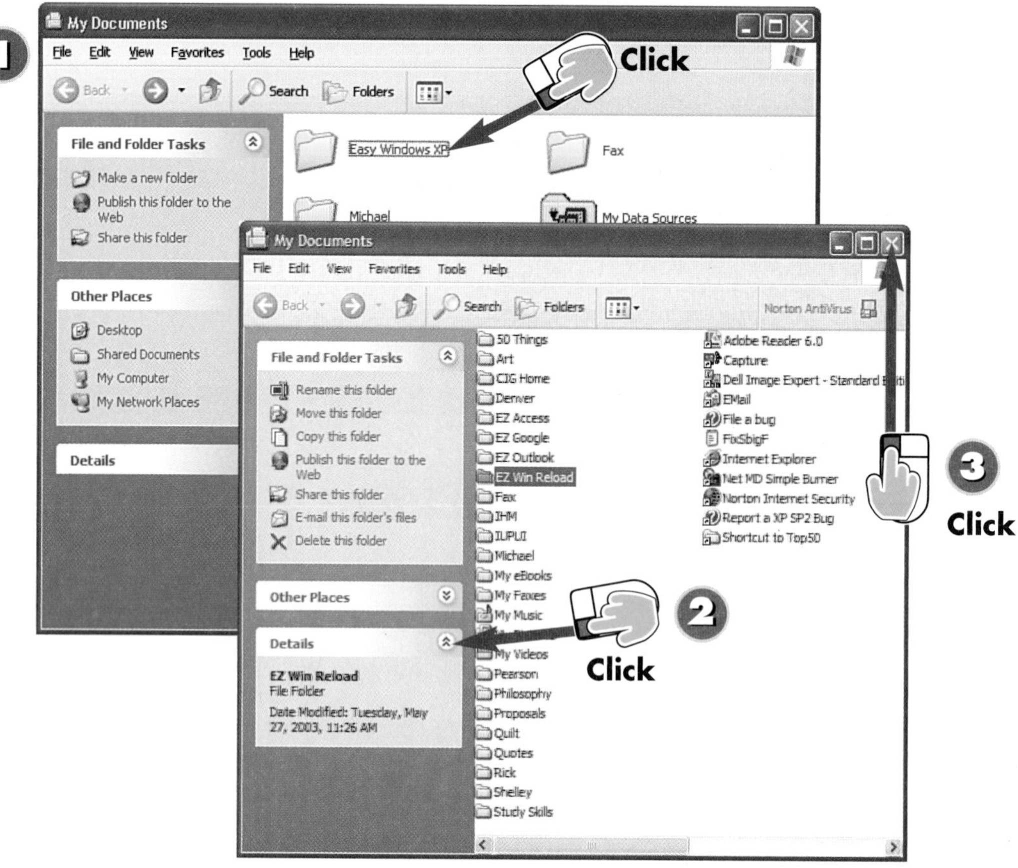

1. Click the folder you want to select.

2. In the File and Folder Tasks list, you see folder-related tasks. Click [expand button] to display Details about the folder. The details are displayed.

3. Click the **Close** button to close the folder window.

INTRODUCTION

When you are working with folders, you start by selecting a folder. You can then rename, delete, copy, or move the folder. When you select a folder, you see commands for all the folder-related tasks. You can also view detailed information about the selected folder.

TIP

Hide and Display Panes
You can hide or display any of the areas in the Explorer Bar of a window. Click the Expand button [expand button] to display the area. Click the Hide button [hide button] to collapse and hide the area.

Task 6: Navigating Folders

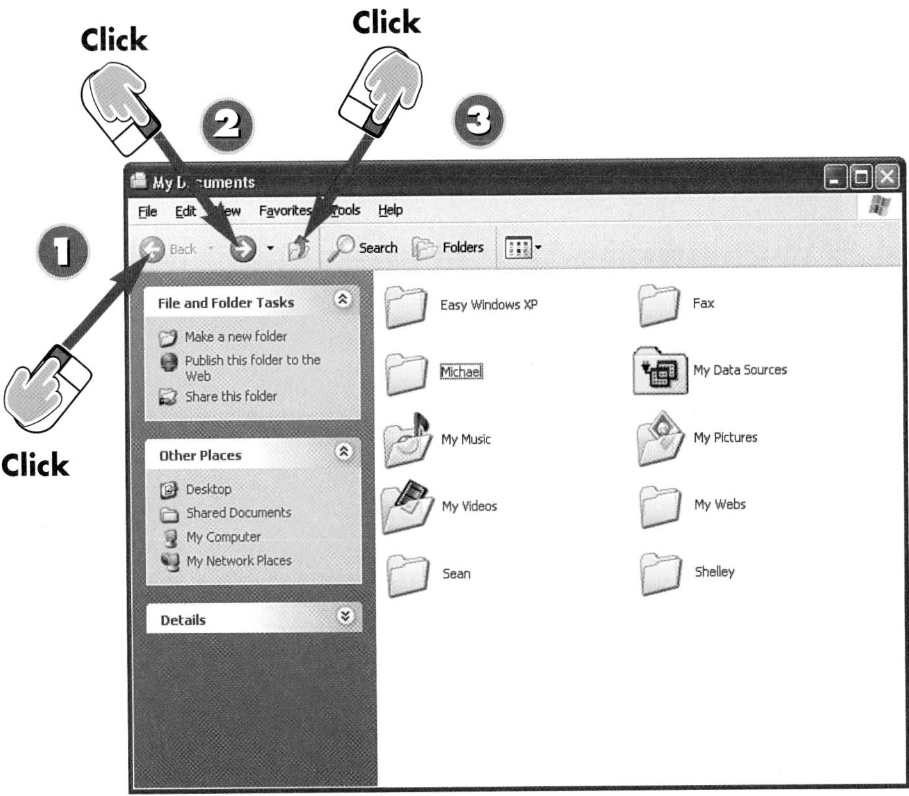

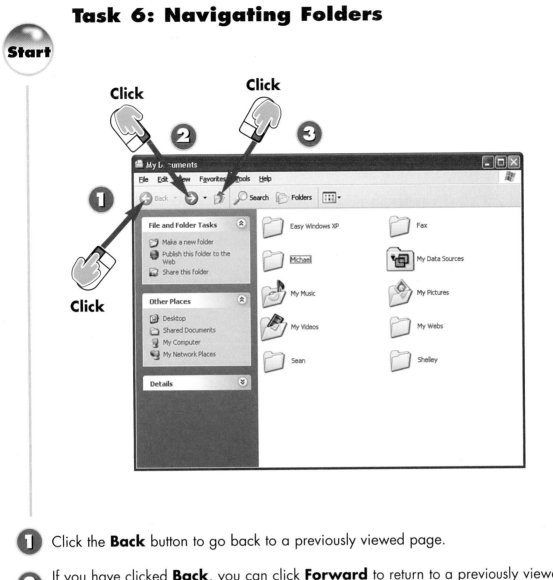

1. Click the **Back** button to go back to a previously viewed page.
2. If you have clicked **Back**, you can click **Forward** to return to a previously viewed page.
3. Click the **Up** button to display the next level up in the folder structure.

INTRODUCTION

Each folder window includes a toolbar that you can use to navigate from folder to folder. You can go back and forth among previously viewed content windows. You can also move up one level in the folder structure to the containing folder. For instance, you might move up to the desktop level and then open drives and folders to move to another branch of the folder structure.

TIP

Search and Folders Button

You can find information on searching for a file in Part 4, "Working with Files." For help on displaying a Folders List with the Folders button, see Task 12, "Displaying the Folders List," in this part.

Task 7: Changing the Window View

Click

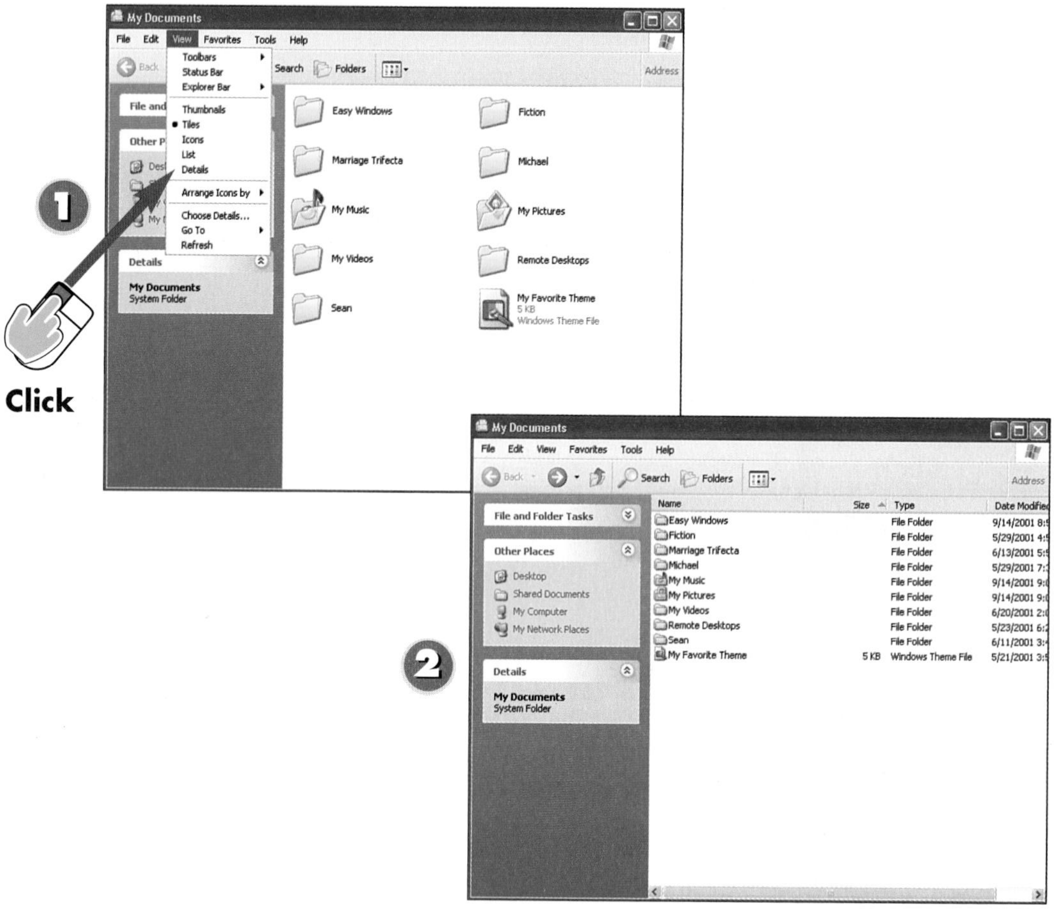

1. In the window you want to change, click the **View** menu, and then select the view you want.

2. The window displays the contents in that view (in this case, the Details view).

INTRODUCTION

You can view the contents of a window in a variety of ways. If you want to see more of a window's contents at one time, you can change the view to List. Click **View**, **Details** to view information about the contents of a window (size, name, type, modification date). You can also select **Thumbnails**, useful for pictures, or **Tiles** which shows an icon along with file information. Changing the way a window displays its contents can make it easier to find what you need.

TIP

Use the Views Button

You can also click the down arrow next to the Views button and select another view.

Task 8: Sorting the Contents of a Window

Click

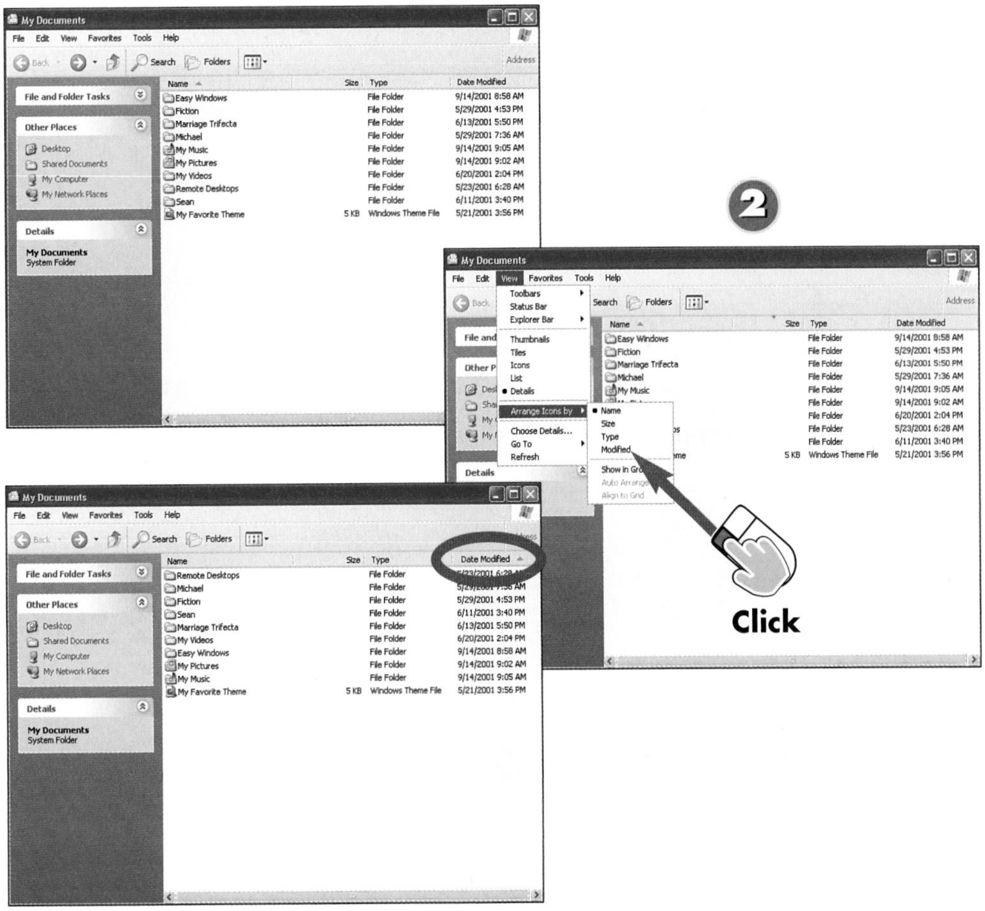

1. Open the window you want to sort. In this case, the window is displayed in Detail view so that you can see the results of sorting.

2. Click **View**, **Arrange Icons By** and choose the sort order you want (in this case, **Modified**).

3. Windows sorts the files in the selected order. For example, this view shows the files sorted by modification date. Note the sort column is indicated with shading and an icon in the heading.

INTRODUCTION

You sort the contents of a window so that you can more easily find the folders and files you want. Windows enables you to arrange the contents of a window by name, type, date, and size. All views show the sort, but the change is most apparent in Details view.

TIP

Sort in Details View
You can also click the column header in the Details view to sort by that column. Click once to sort in ascending order; click the column heading again to sort in descending order.

TIP

My Computer Sorts
If you are working in the My Computer window, you have different options for arranging the icons. You can arrange by name, type, total size, free space, or comment.

Task 9: Choosing Content Details

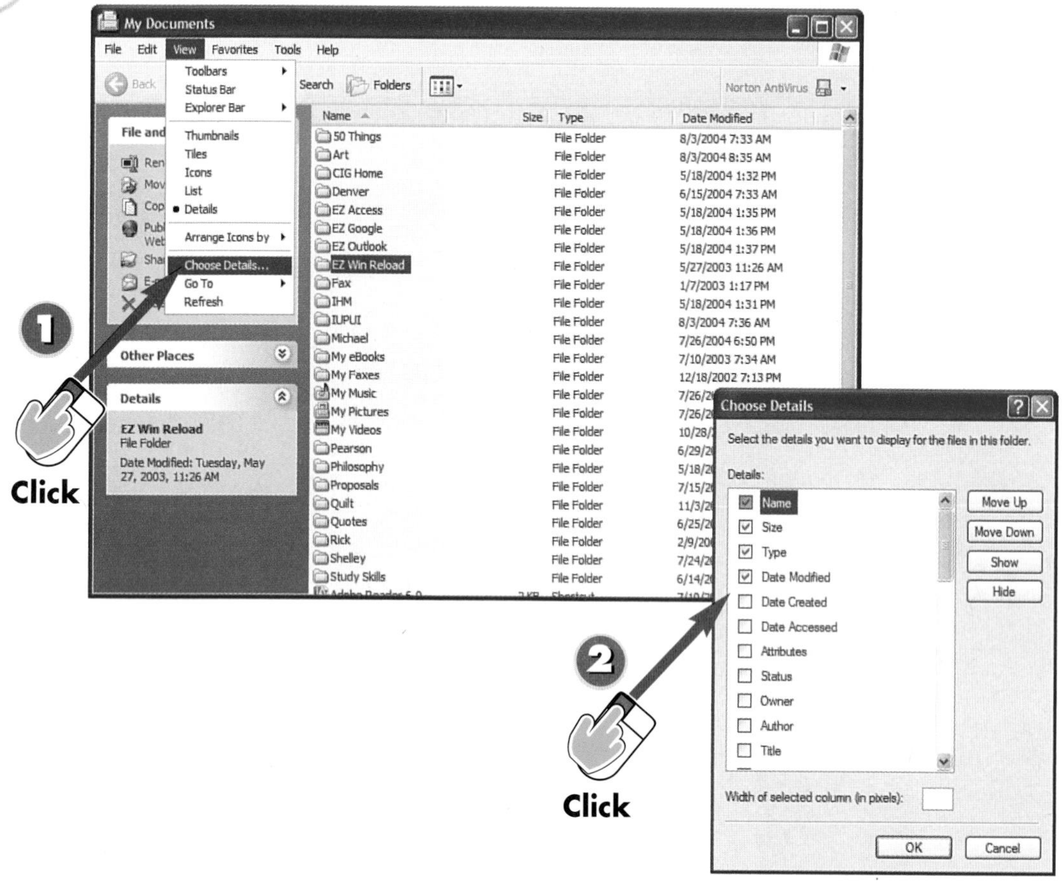

1. Click **View**, **Choose Details**.

2. In the Choose Details dialog box, check any details you want to include. To hide any details, uncheck the check box.

INTRODUCTION

When you view the contents of a window in Details view, you see the Name, Size, Type, and Date Modified. You have other options which you can include in the Details view, including Date Created, Author, Date Accessed, and so on. These other details may be useful in finding a file you need.

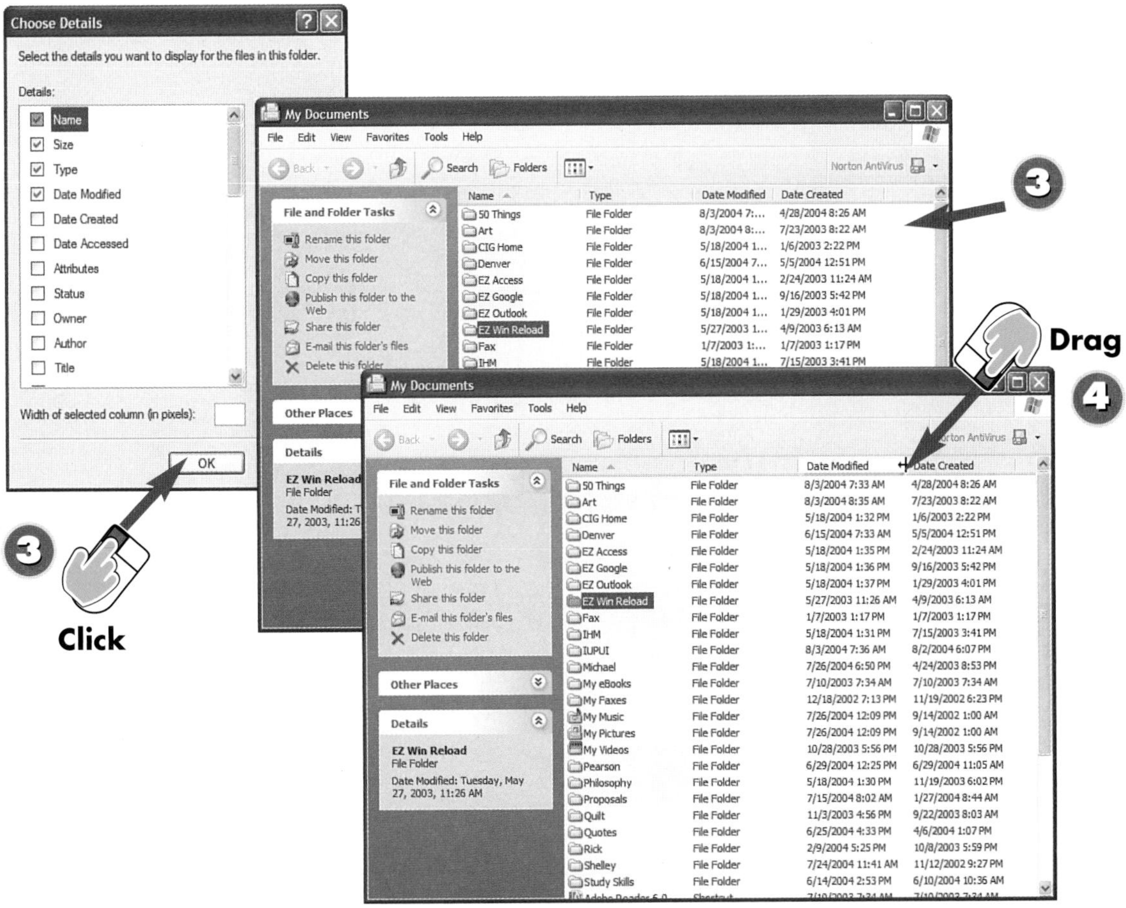

3. Click **OK**. You see the results of your selections. (Here the Size column is not displayed, and the Date Modified and Created columns are displayed.)

4. If you want to resize any of the columns, put the cursor at the edge of the column heading and drag. Do this so you can see the complete contents of the column.

TIP

Only in Details View

If you make these changes in any other view, you won't notice any change. This feature works only in Details view.

Task 10: Grouping Icons

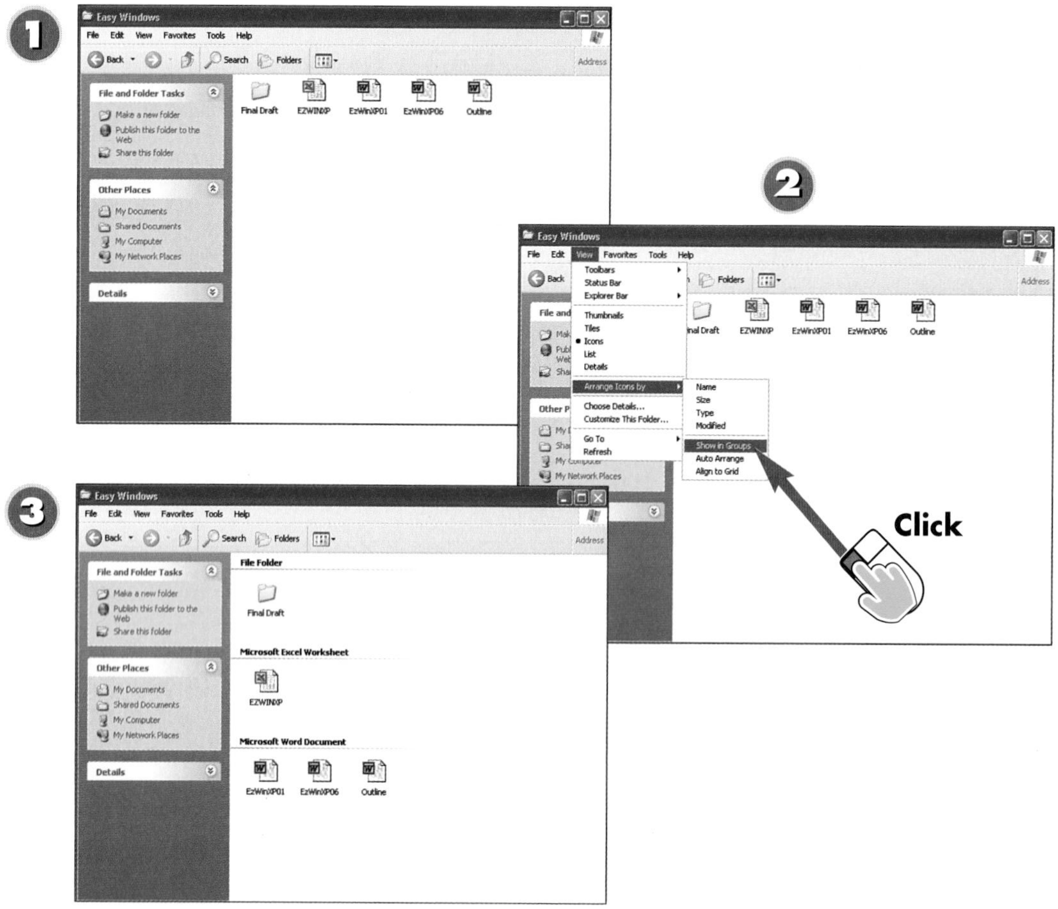

1 Sort the contents by how you want them grouped. For instance, to group by type, sort by type.

2 Click **View**, **Arrange Icons by**, **Show in Groups**.

3 Windows groups the icons by the sort order (here by type).

INTRODUCTION

Another way to view a window's content is to group icons. The grouping depends on how the items are sorted. If you sort by name, the contents of a window are grouped alphabetically. If you sort by type, the contents are grouped by type. Therefore, sort first and then group. You can group in any view.

TIP

Undo the Groups
To undo the groups, select **View**, **Arrange Icons by**, **Show in Groups** again to remove the checkmark.

Task 11: Creating a New Folder

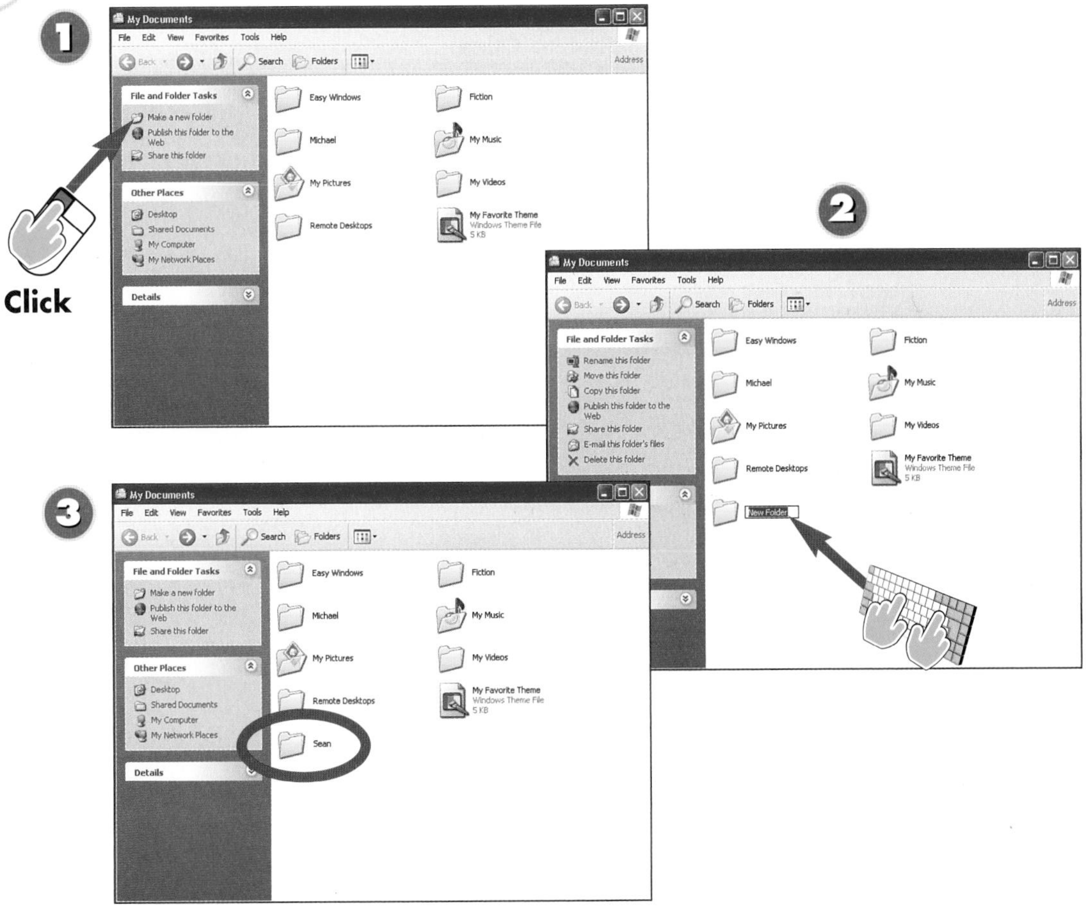

1. Open **My Documents** and click **Make a new folder**.
2. The new folder appears in the window, and the name is highlighted. Type a new name and press **Enter**.
3. The folder is added.

INTRODUCTION

Finding and opening documents is easier if you group related files into folders. For example, you might want to create a folder for all your word processing documents. Creating a folder enables you to keep your documents separated from the program's files so that you can easily find your document files.

TIP

Delete a Folder

If you change your mind about the new folder, you can always delete it. To delete the folder, select it, and then press the **Delete** key on your keyboard. Click the **Yes** button to confirm the deletion.

TIP

Folder Name

The folder name can contain as many as 255 characters and can include spaces. You cannot include these characters:

| ? / : " * < > \

Task 12: Displaying the Folders List

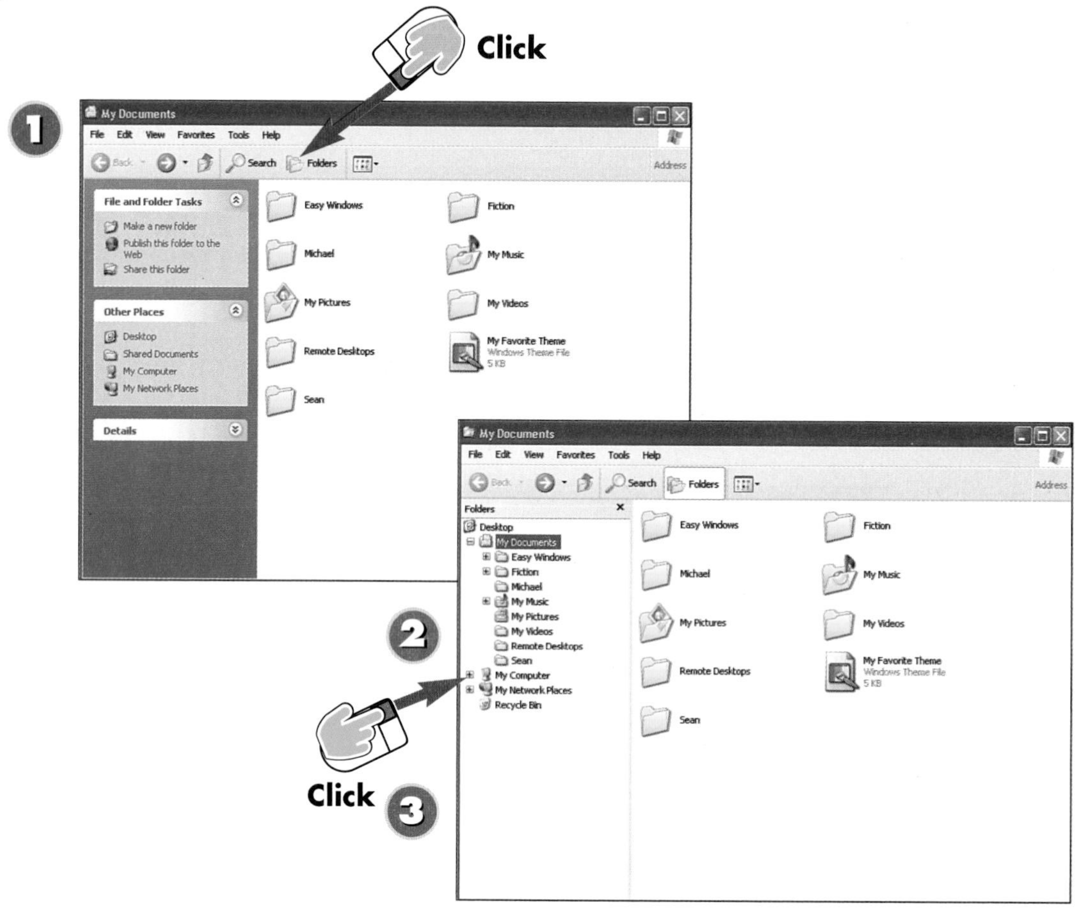

1. Click the **Folders** button.
2. You see the Folders List. The top level is the Desktop; beneath that you see the icons on the desktop.
3. You can expand or collapse any of the folders and drives in the list by clicking the plus sign next to the drive or folder.

INTRODUCTION

To see a hierarchical listing of all the folders on your system, display the Folders List. You might prefer this view when working with folders and files because you can see the contents of the selected folder as well as all the other drives and folders on your computer.

TIP

Hide Content

When you click a plus sign to expand the folder or drive, the icon changes to a minus sign. You can click the minus sign to hide the contents of that item. For instance, you might hide content if the Folders List becomes too long.

TIP

Select Folders

You can select folders in the Folders List by clicking the folder you want. The right pane then shows the contents of the selected folder.

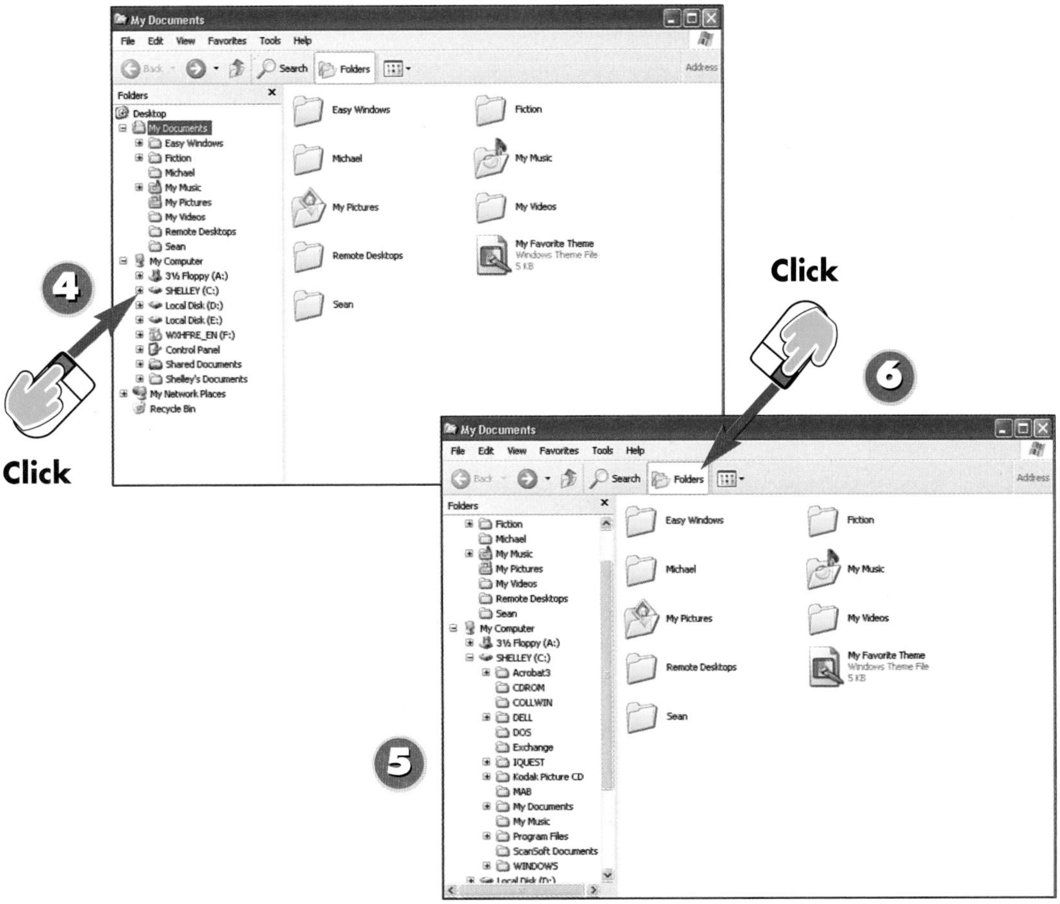

Click

Click

4 You see the drives and folders on My Computer. You can continue to expand the listing. For example, click the plus sign next to your hard drive.

5 You see the contents of that drive. You can continue to expand the listing to display other nested folders.

6 To close the Folders List, click the **Folders** button again.

TIP

Display Other Bars
You can display other bars within a folder window. To do so, click **View**, **Toolbars**, and then **Explorer Bar**. Select the Explorer Bar you want to display.

TIP

Windows Explorer
You can use Windows Explorer in much the same way you use the My Computer window: to copy and move folders, to create and rename folders, to view details, and so on. Basically, Windows Explorer is a file window with the Folders List displayed. Click **Start**, **All Programs**, **Accessories**, and then **Windows Explorer** to use this feature.

Task 13: Copying Folders

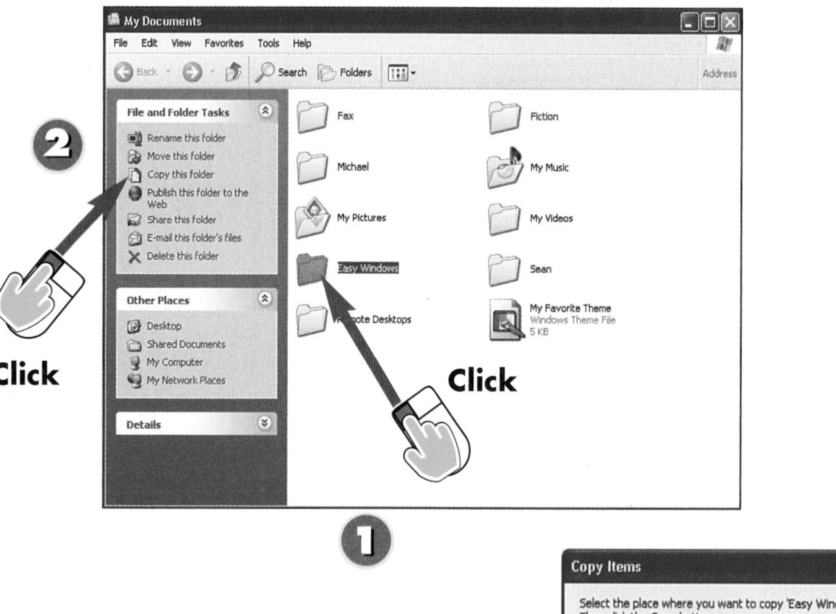

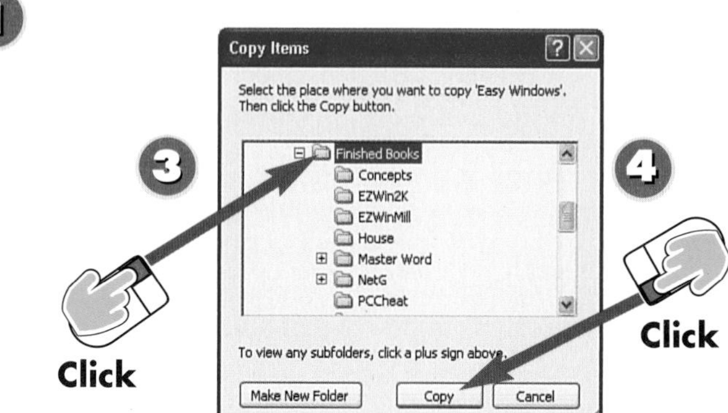

1. Click the folder you want to copy.
2. Click the **Copy this folder** button.
3. Select that folder where you want to place the copy.
4. Click **Copy**. Windows copies the new folder and its contents to this location.

INTRODUCTION

You can copy a folder and its contents to a new location. For example, you can copy a folder to a floppy disk to use as a backup or to use the folder contents on another computer. In addition, you can copy a folder and its contents to another location on the hard drive if, for example, you want to revise the original files for a different use.

TIP

Use Commands
You can also use the **Edit**, **Copy** command to copy a folder. Move to the drive or folder window where you want to paste the folder, and select **Edit**, **Paste**.

TIP

Drag a Copy
As another shortcut, you can display the Folders List (see Task 12, "Displaying the Folders List") and then hold down the **Ctrl** key and drag the folder from the content window to the folder or drive in the Folders List.

Task 14: Moving Folders

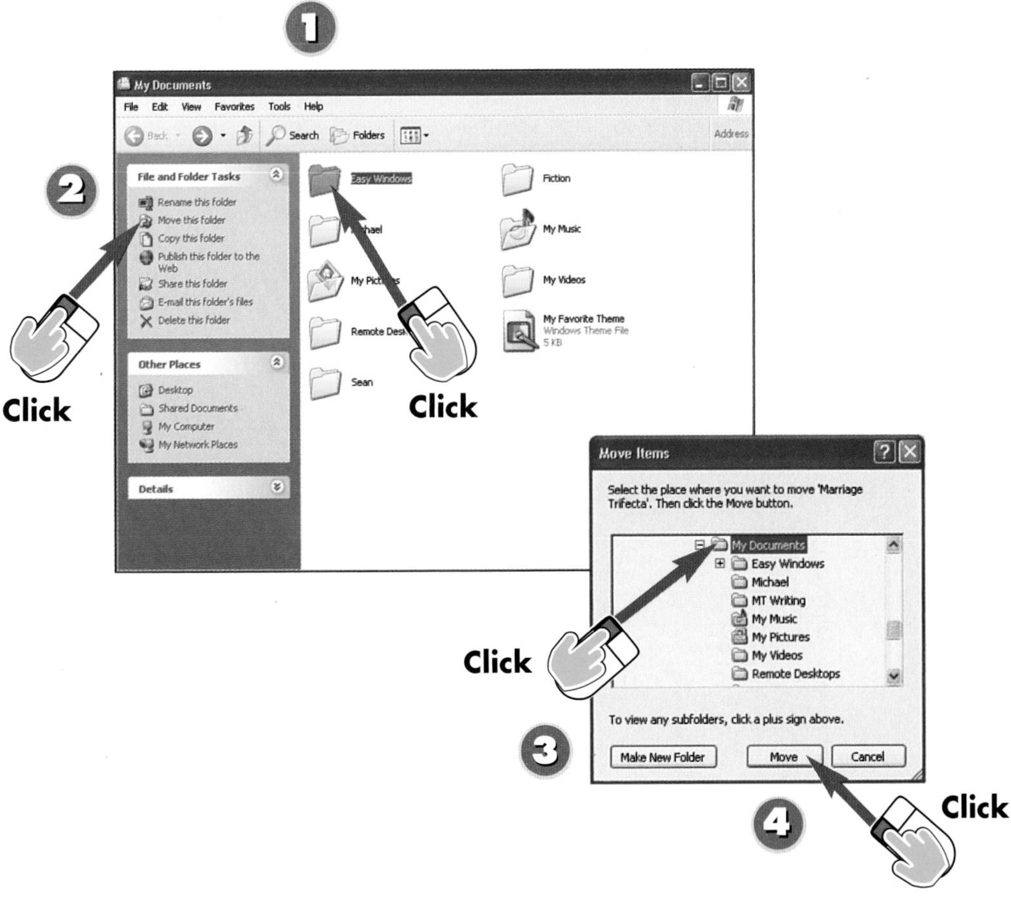

1. Click the folder you want to move.
2. Click the **Move this folder** link.
3. Expand the folder listing until you see the drive and folder you want. Select the folder.
4. Click **Move**. Windows moves the folder and its contents to this location.

INTRODUCTION

You can move a folder and its contents to another folder or to a disk so that you can reorganize your folder structure. For example, you might want to move a document folder to My Documents to place all of your folders within the one main My Documents folder.

TIP

Drag and Drop
You can also display the Folders List and drag a folder from the content pane (the one on the right) to the drive or folder in the Folder List on the left.

TIP

Undo Move
You can select the **Undo** command from the Edit menu to undo the move if you change your mind.

Task 15: Renaming Folders

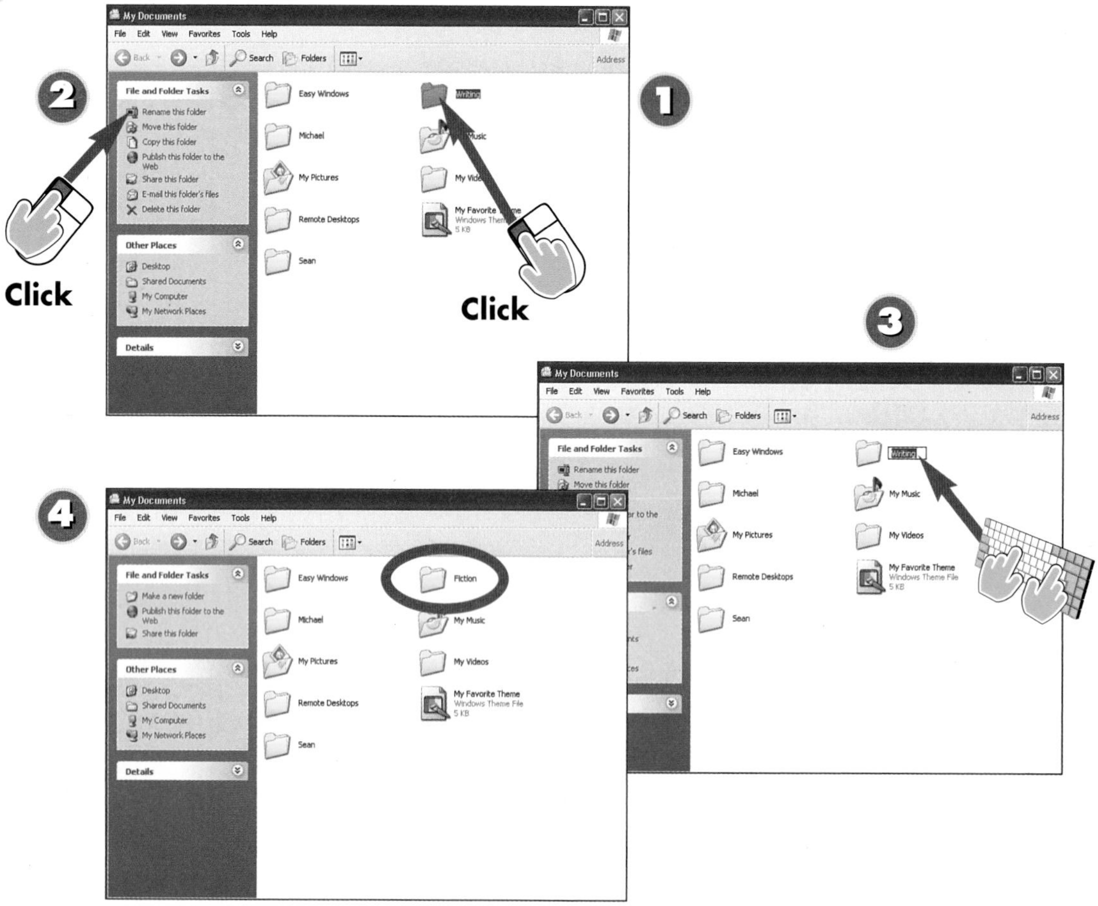

1. Select the folder you want to rename.
2. Click the **Rename this folder** link.
3. The current name is selected. Type the new name and press **Enter**.
4. The folder is renamed.

INTRODUCTION

If you did not type a descriptive name for a folder, you can rename the folder to a more fitting name. Using descriptive names helps you identify at a glance the contents of a particular folder.

TIP

Folder Names
Folder names can contain as many as 255 characters, including spaces. You also can include letters, numbers, and other symbols except the following:
| ? / : " * < > \

TIP

Single-Click Renaming
Click the folder once to select it, and then single-click within the name to edit the name.

Task 16: Deleting Folders

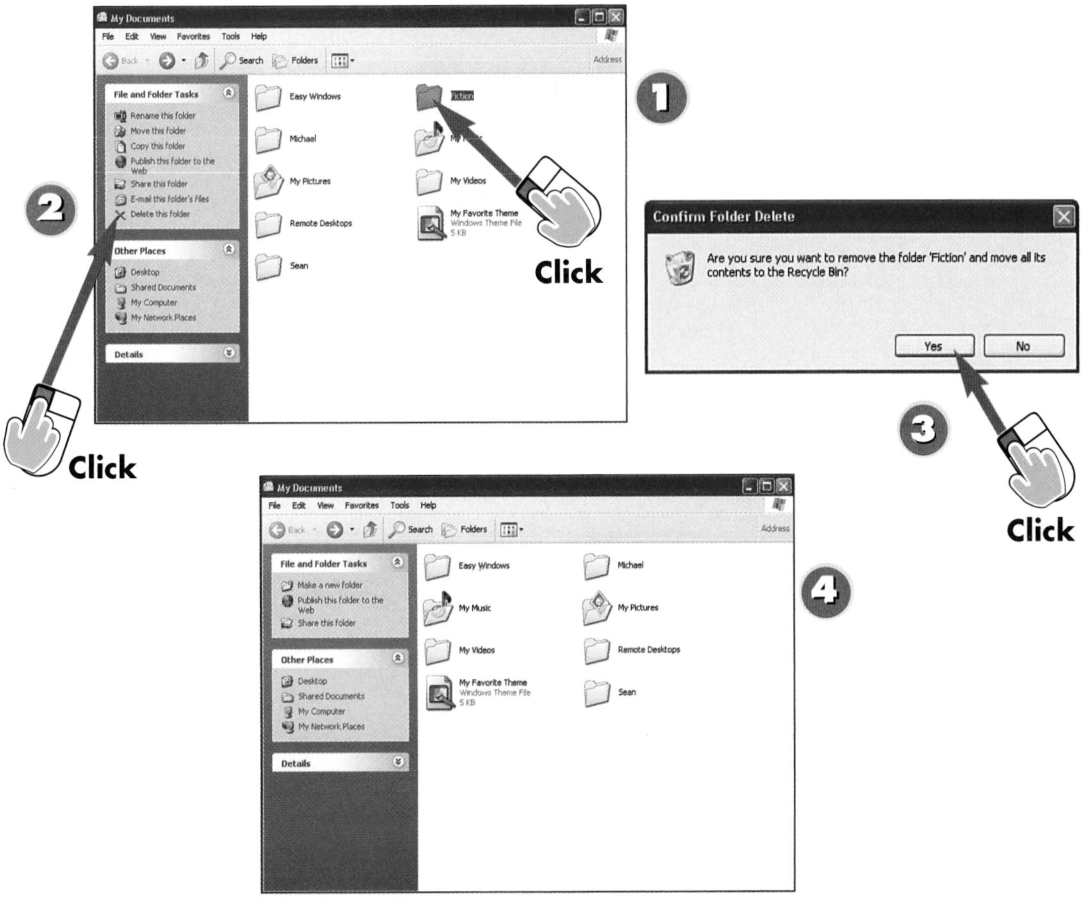

1. Select the folder you want to delete.
2. Click the **Delete this folder** link.
3. Click the **Yes** button to confirm the deletion.
4. The folder and all its contents are deleted.

INTRODUCTION

You can delete folders when you no longer need them. When you delete a folder, you also delete its contents. Windows XP places deleted folders in the Recycle Bin. You can restore deleted items from the Recycle Bin if you realize you have placed items there by accident.

TIP

Cancel Deletion
If you change your mind, click **No** in the Confirm Folder Delete dialog box. Or undo the deletion by selecting the **Edit**, **Undo** command. As another option, restore the folder from the Recycle Bin. See Part 4 for information on opening and restoring items from the Recycle Bin.

WARNING!
When you delete a folder from a floppy drive, that item is not placed in the Recycle Bin; it is immediately deleted from your system.

Task 17: Changing the Folder Options

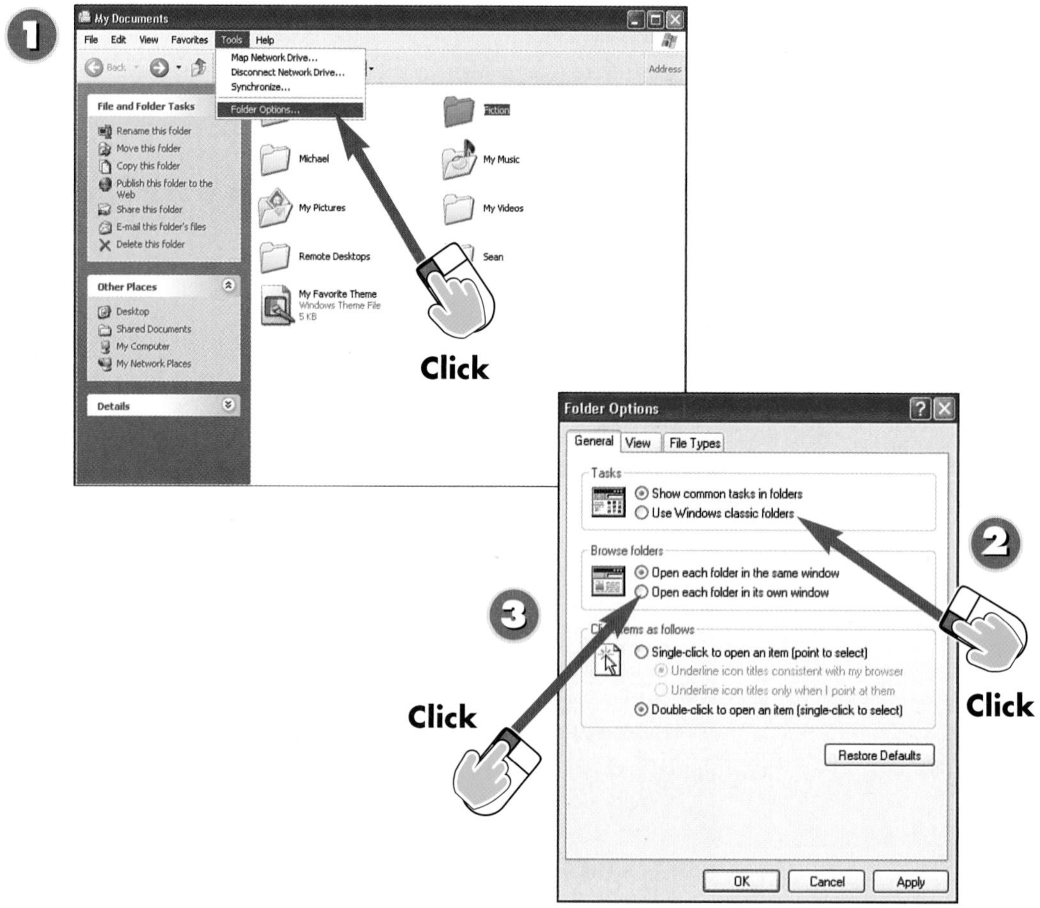

1. Click **Tools** and select the **Folder Options** command.
2. To use Windows classic folders (like previous versions of Windows), click **Use Windows classic folders**.
3. To open a folder in separate windows, click **Open each folder in its own window**.

INTRODUCTION

By default, Windows opens each new folder or drive in the same window, replacing the contents of the current window with the one you open. To open a folder or drive, you double-click. You can change these and other folder options. For instance, you can choose to single-click an icon to open it, similar to clicking links on a Web page.

TIP

Go Back to Original Settings

To go back to the original settings, select **Tools**, **Folder Options**, and then click the **Restore Defaults** button. Then click **OK**.

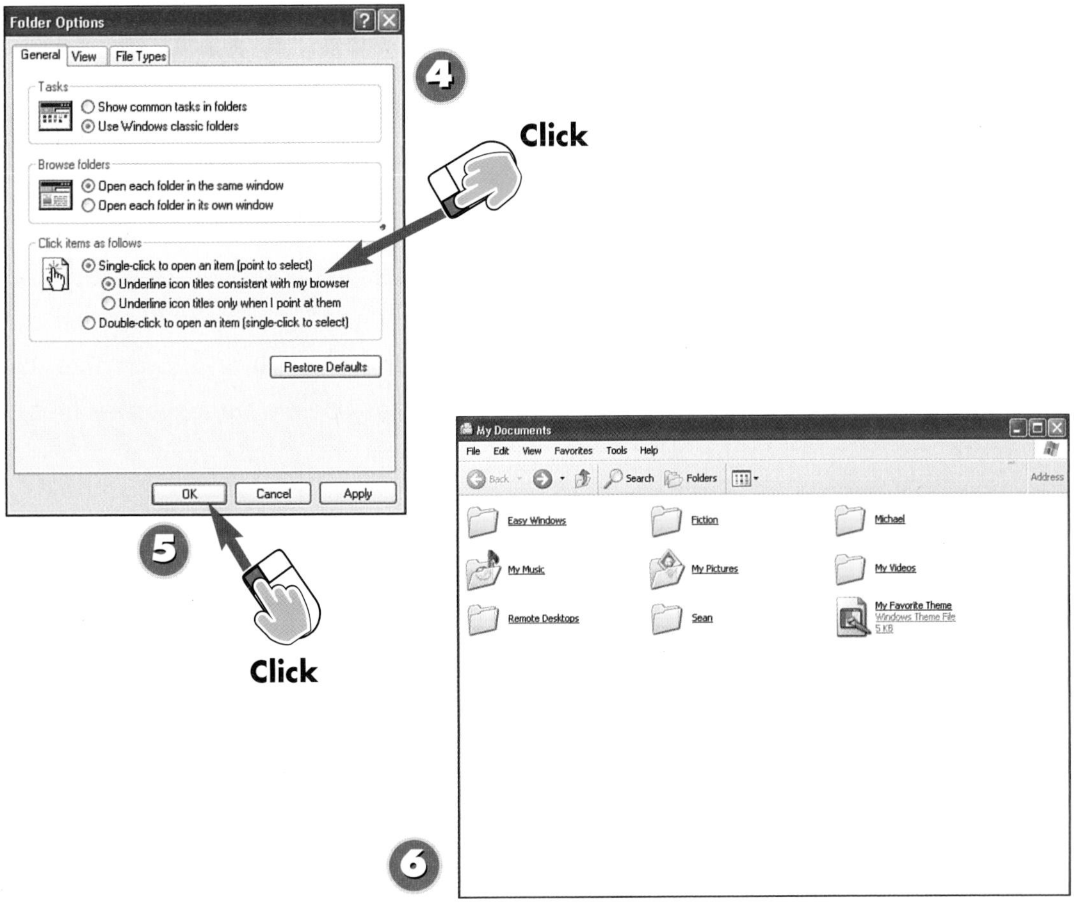

4 To single-click rather than double-click to open an item, select **Single-click to open an item**.

5 Click the **OK** button.

6 The folder is displayed with the options you selected. Here you see Windows classic folders with single-clicking.

TIP

Single-Click

If you select **Single-click to open an item**, the contents of the window are displayed as links. Single-click any item to display its contents.

TIP

Other Tabs

You can use the other tabs in this dialog box to set more complex view options (View tab) and to view the list of recognized file types and their associated programs (File Types). See Part 4 for more information on file types.

PART 4

Working with Files

As mentioned in the last part, each time you save a document, that information is saved as a file on your hard disk. When you save that document, you assign both a specific place for the file (a folder) and a name.

The more you work on your computer, the more files you add. After a while, your computer will become cluttered, and you'll need a way to keep these files organized. Windows provides features that can help you find, organize, and manage your files. You can copy files, move files, delete unnecessary files, and more, as covered in this part.

Tasks

Task 1: Selecting Files

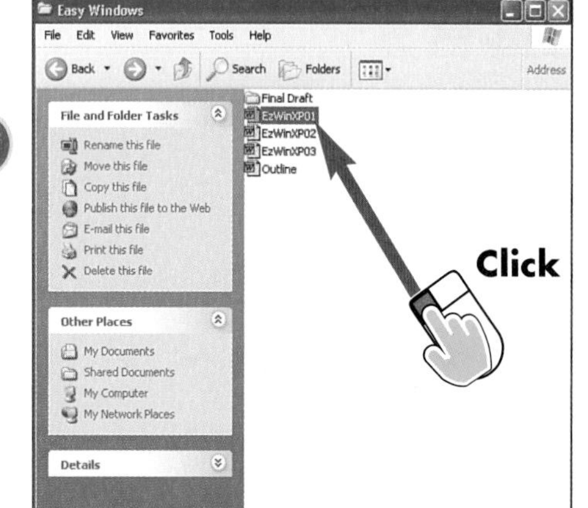

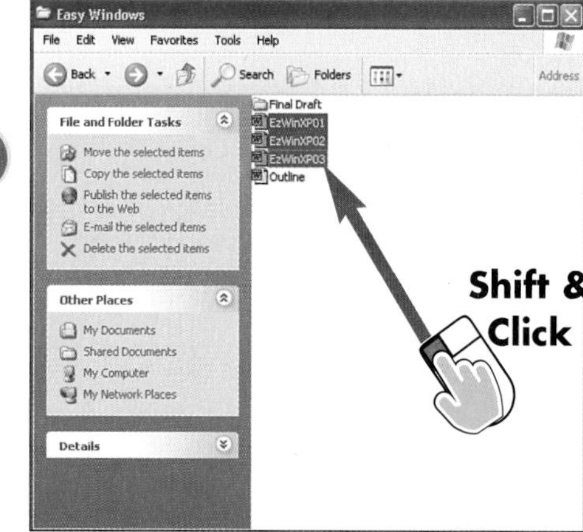

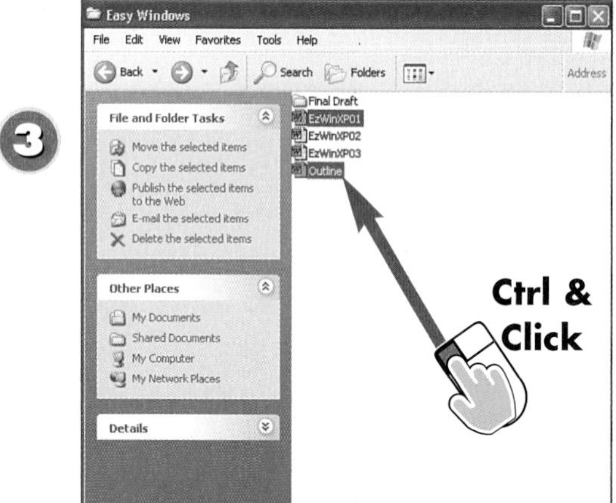

1. To select a single file, click it. The file is selected.
2. To select several files next to each other, click the first file of the group that you want to select, and then hold down the **Shift** key and click the last file. The first and last files and all files in between are selected.
3. To select several files that are not next to each other, hold down the **Ctrl** key and click each file you want to select.

INTRODUCTION

When you want to work on files (copy, move, print, delete, and so on), you start by selecting the files you want. You can select a single file or several files.

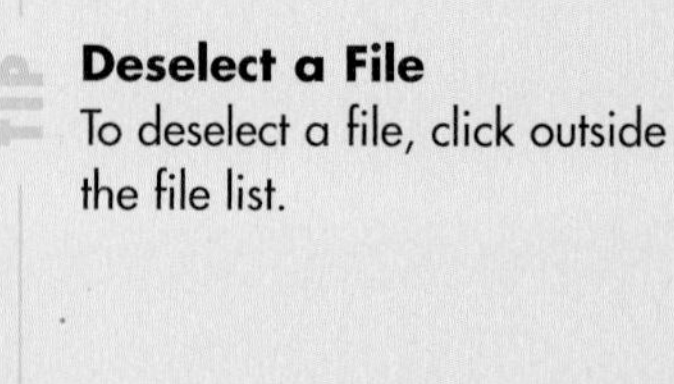

TIP

Deselect a File

To deselect a file, click outside the file list.

TIP

Select All Files

To select all files, open the **Edit** menu, and then click the **Select All** command. Or press **Ctrl+A**.

Task 2: Viewing File Details

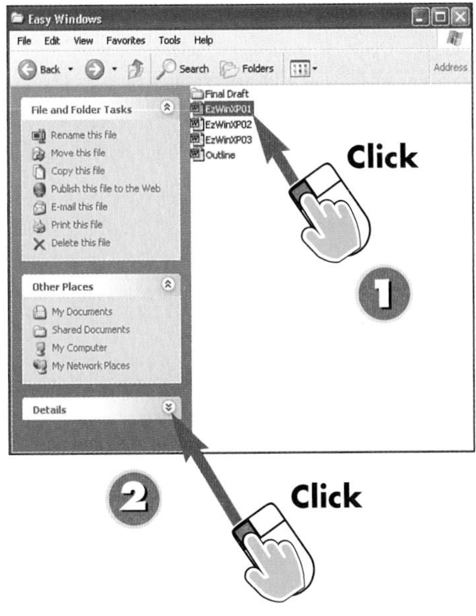

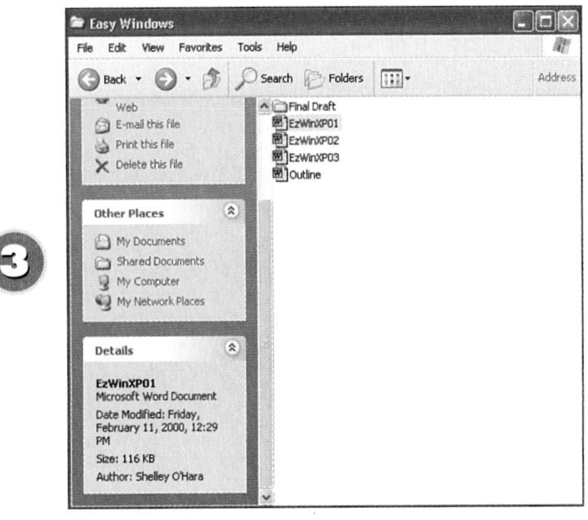

1. Select the file.
2. If necessary, click the **Expand** button for the Details area.
3. You see file information on the selected file. You may need to scroll through the Explorer Bar to view all of the information.

INTRODUCTION

When you are working with files, you may not be able to tell from the file name what the file contains. In that case, you can view basic file information by expanding the Details area of the folder window.

TIP

Change Views

Another way to get an idea of the content of a file is to change how the window content is displayed. You can display a list (shown here), icons, tiles, or a detailed list. See Part 3, "Working with Folders," for more information.

TIP

Several Files Selected

When you select more than one file, you see information about the total number of files selected, the total file size of the selected files, and a list of the selected files in the Details area.

Task 3: Viewing File Properties

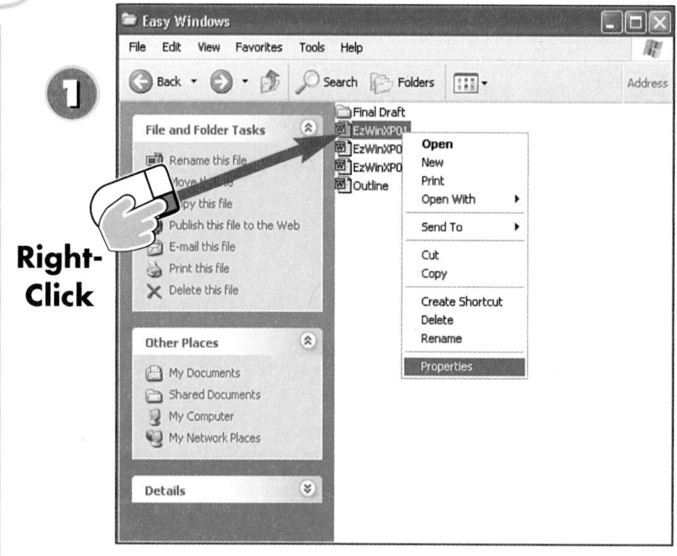

Right-Click

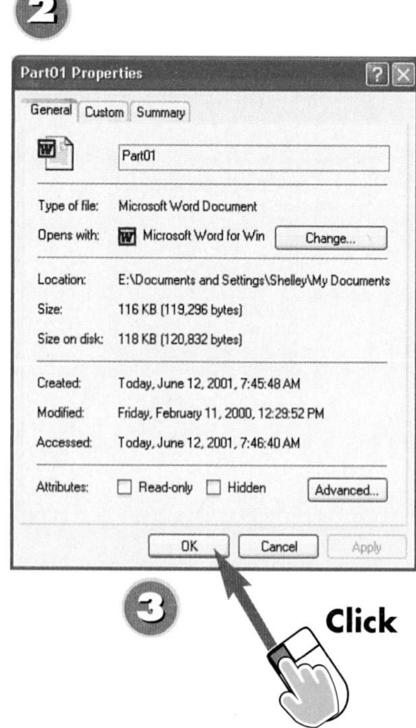

Click

1. Right-click the file and select Properties from the shortcut menu.
2. You see the Properties dialog box for the file, which lists the type of file, the program used to open that file, the location where the file is stored, and other important file information.
3. When you are done viewing the file properties, click the **OK** button.

End

INTRODUCTION

If you want detailed information beyond the file name, size, author, and modification dates, you can display the file properties. You might display file properties if you cannot remember what a file contains or if you want to compare this file with another file, for example, a backup of the same file.

TIP

Other Tabs

Depending on the type of file, other information tabs may be available. Microsoft Office documents, for instance, have a Summary tab that displays key information about the document. Click the tab to view the information.

TIP

Make Changes

You can make changes to the file properties. Check **Read-only** to allow users to open the file, but not change anything in the file. To change the associated program, see Task 12, "Setting File Associations" later in this part.

Task 4: Renaming a File

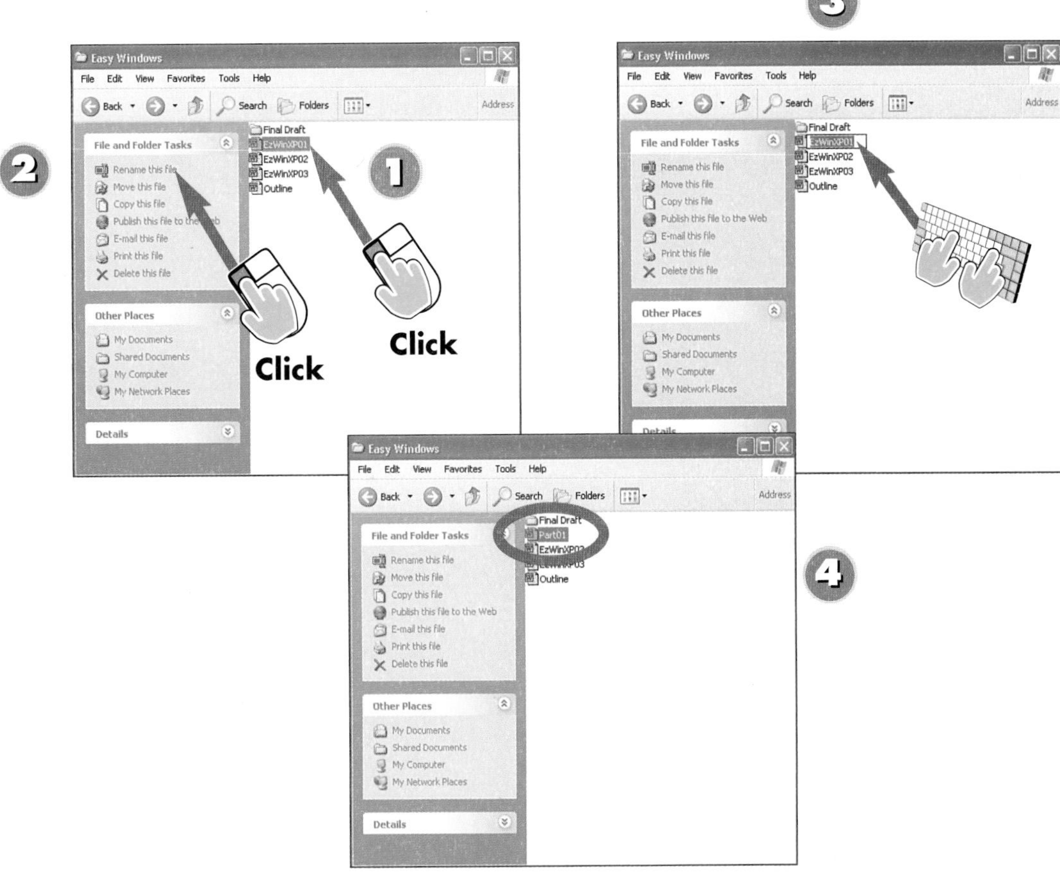

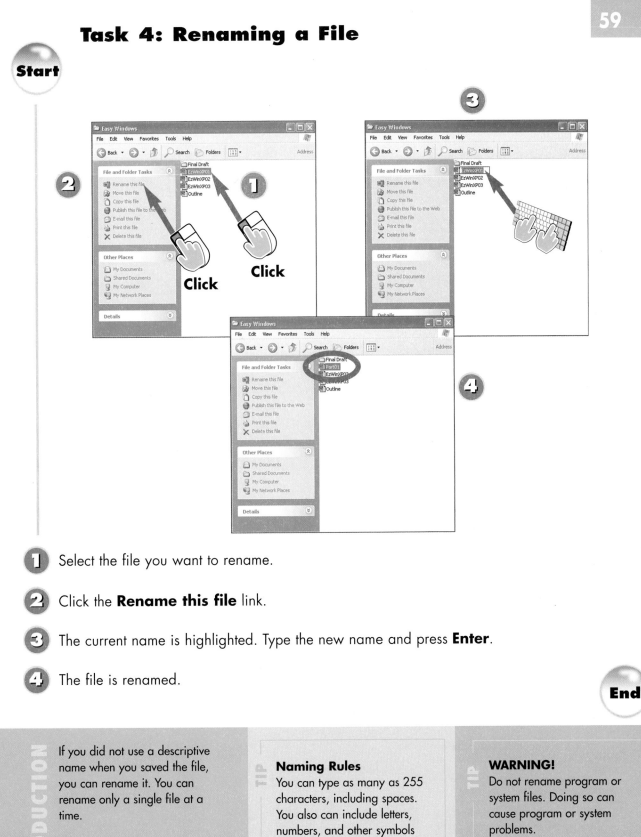

1. Select the file you want to rename.
2. Click the **Rename this file** link.
3. The current name is highlighted. Type the new name and press **Enter**.
4. The file is renamed.

INTRODUCTION

If you did not use a descriptive name when you saved the file, you can rename it. You can rename only a single file at a time.

TIP

Naming Rules

You can type as many as 255 characters, including spaces. You also can include letters, numbers, and other symbols except the following:

| ? / : " * < > \

TIP

WARNING!

Do not rename program or system files. Doing so can cause program or system problems.

Task 5: Moving a File

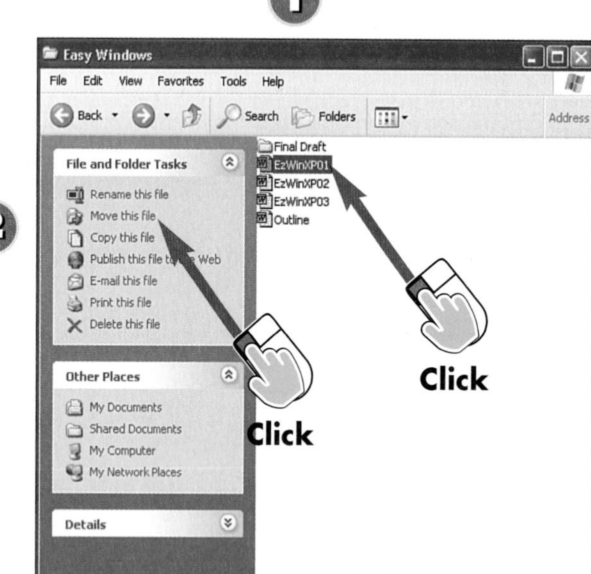

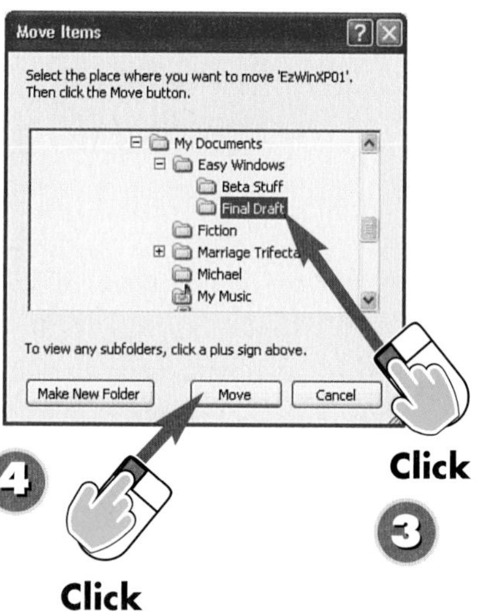

1. Select the file(s) you want to move.
2. Click the **Move this file** link.
3. Display and then click the folder where you want to place the file. You can expand the folder listing by clicking the plus sign next to the icon, drive, or folder.
4. Click the **Move** button.

INTRODUCTION

You might need to move files from one folder or drive to another (for example, to reorganize folders by putting similar files together in the same folder). You can also move a file that you accidentally saved in the wrong folder.

TIP

Undo Move
If you make a mistake, you can undo the move by selecting the **Undo** command from the **Edit** menu.

5

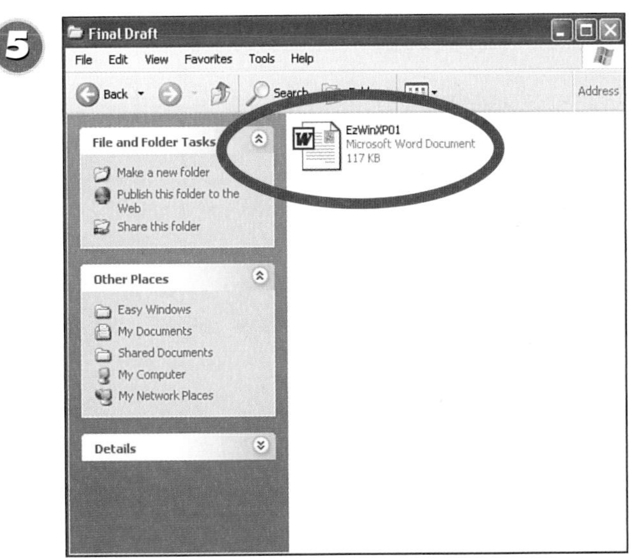

5 Windows moves the files to the new location. You can open that folder, as shown here, to confirm the move.

TIP

Drag to Move

You can also drag a file to a different folder. Display the Folders List by clicking the **Folders** button. Then in the right pane select the file(s) you want to move. If you are moving from one folder to another, simply drag the files from that window to the drive or folder in the folders list on the left. If you are moving from one drive to another, hold down the **Shift** key and drag.

Task 6: Printing a File from a File Window

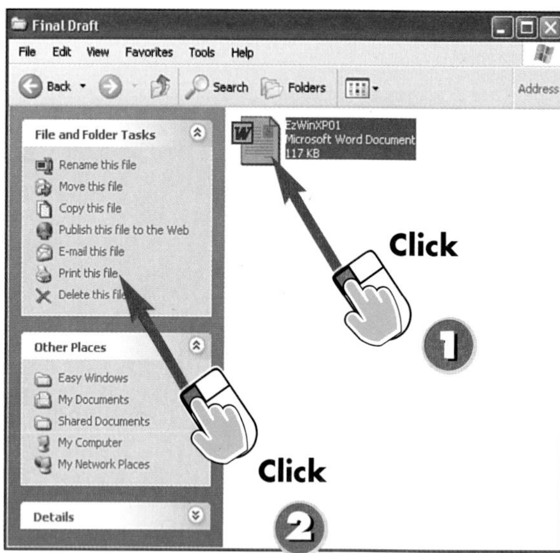

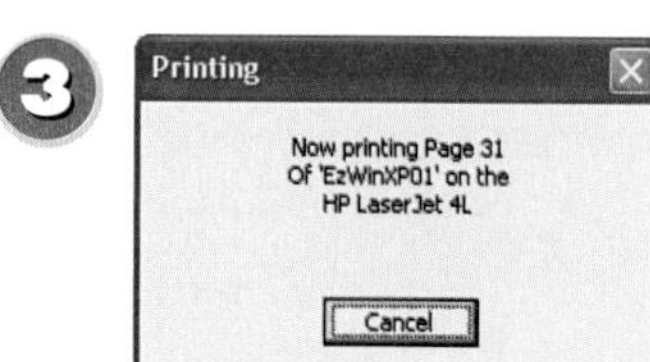

1. Select the file(s) you want to print.
2. Click the **Print this file** link.
3. Windows opens the associated program and prints the file(s). You see a status message as the file(s) are printed.

INTRODUCTION

If do not want to open a document and then print from the program, you can print from a folder window. Printing from a folder window is helpful when you want to print several files; you can select all of the files and print them with one command.

TIP

Printer Setup
Windows XP uses the default printer you have selected. For more information on setting up printers and printing, see Part 5, "Working with Printers, Scanners, and Digital Cameras."

TIP

Email a File
You can email a file by selecting it, clicking **E-mail this file**, and then completing the mail window (entering the address and any text to accompany the file attachment). See Part 7, "Sending Faxes and E-mail" for more information.

Task 7: Copying a File

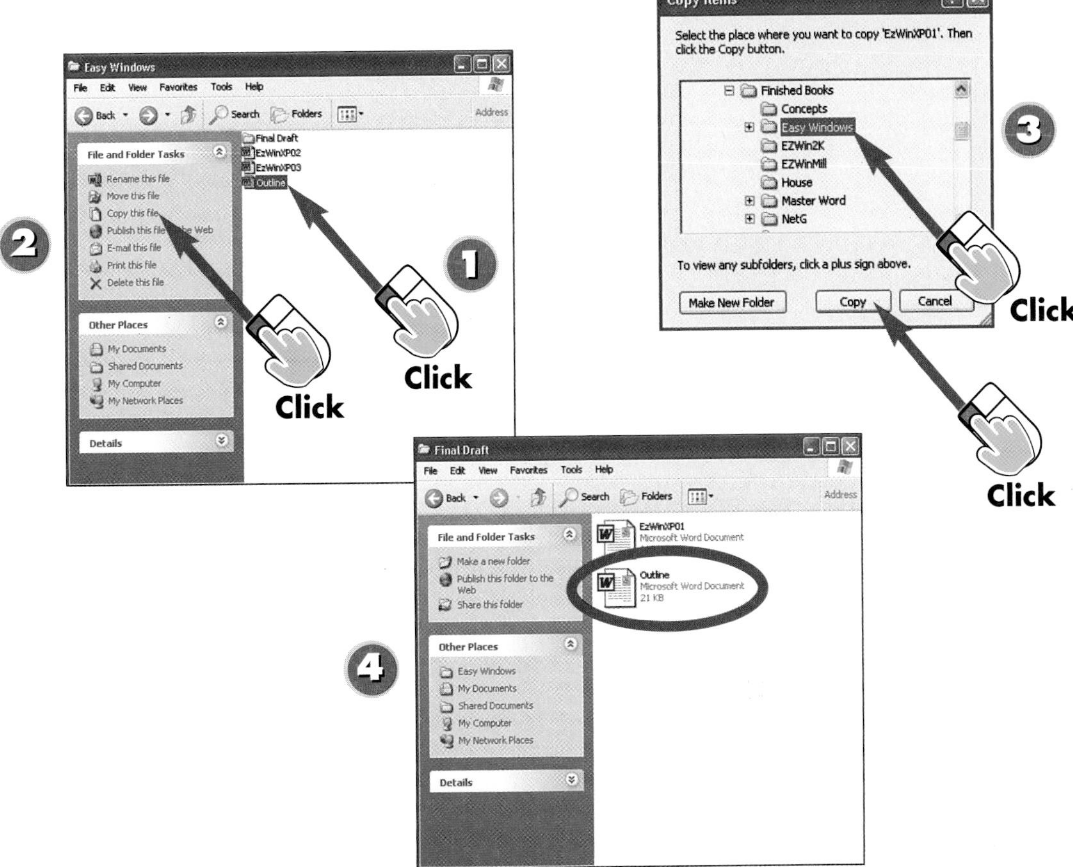

1. Select the file(s) you want to copy.
2. Click the **Copy this file** link.
3. Select the folder in which you want to place the file. Click the **Copy** button.
4. Windows copies the files to the new location. You can also open that folder.

INTRODUCTION

Windows makes it easy to copy files from one folder to another and from one disk to another. You might copy files to create a backup copy or to revise one copy while keeping the original file intact.

TIP

Drag-and-Drop Copying
To use drag-and-drop to copy files, display the Folders List by clicking the **Folders** button. Then in the pane on the right, display and select the files. Hold the **Ctrl** key and drag the file to its destination in the folder list on the left.

TIP

Expand Folder List
You can expand the folder listing by clicking the plus sign next to the icon, drive, or folder.

Task 8: Copying a File to Another Disk

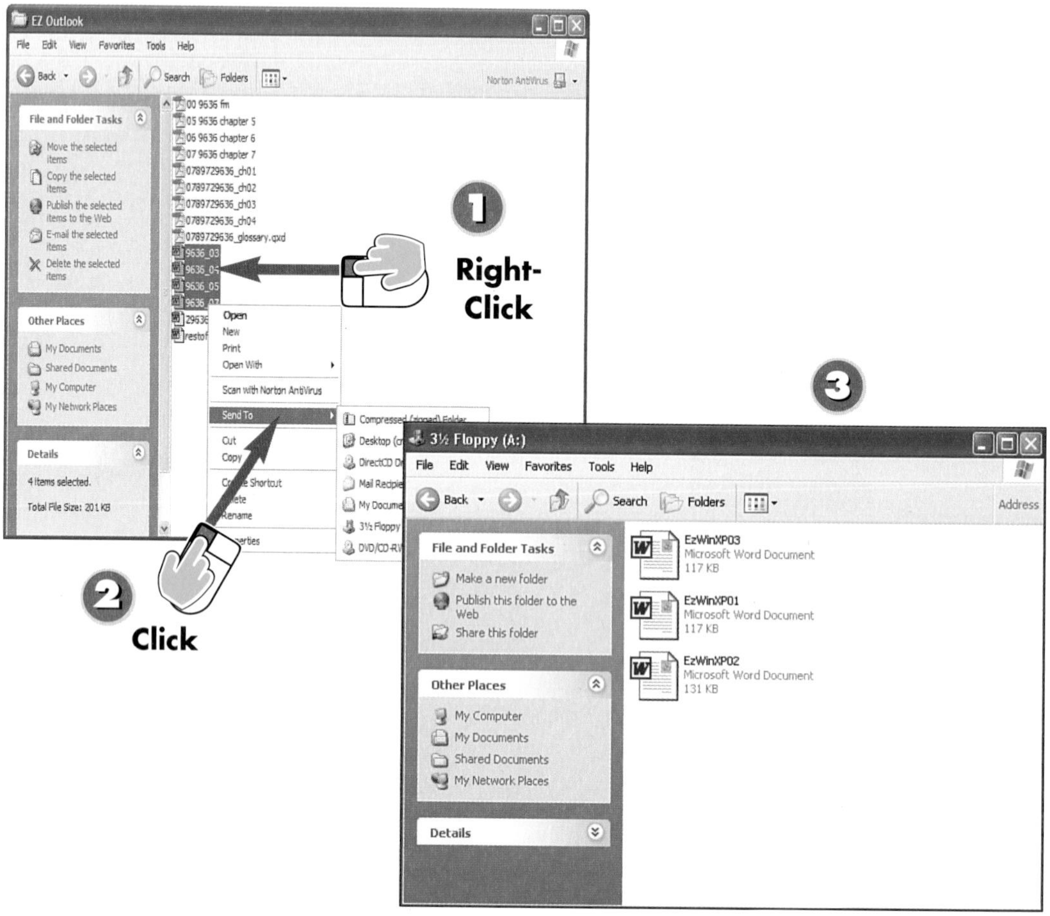

1. After you've inserted a disk into the drive, select the files you want to copy to the disk. Right-click the selected files.
2. Select the **Send To** command from the shortcut menu, and choose the appropriate drive.
3. The files are copied to that disk. You can open that disk from My Computer to verify that they are copied. As shown here, files are copied to a floppy disk.

End

INTRODUCTION

You might want to copy a file to a floppy disk to take the file with you or to make a backup copy. If you have a CD drive, you can also copy folders and files to a CD disk. Windows provides a shortcut (the Send To command) for copying a file to another disk.

TIP

Disk Full?
If the disk is full, you see an error message. Insert another blank disk and click the **Retry** button. The files are copied to the next disk.

TIP

Check File Size
If you want to check the size of the selected files to make sure they'll fit on the disk, expand the Details view. This shows you the total file size of all selected files.

Task 9: Deleting a File

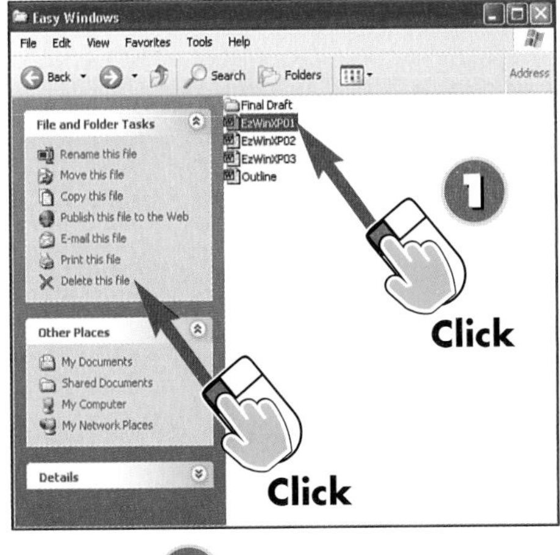

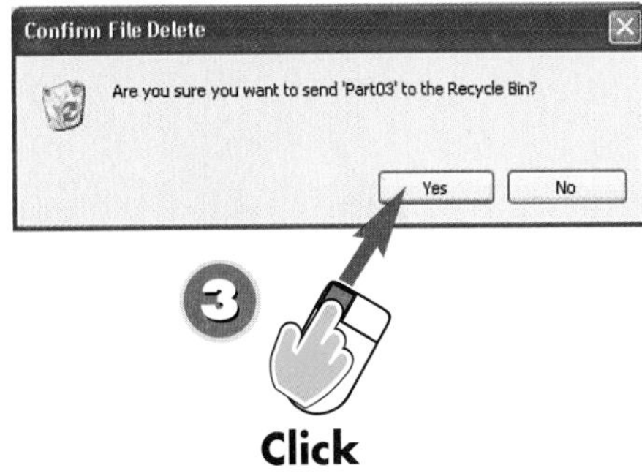

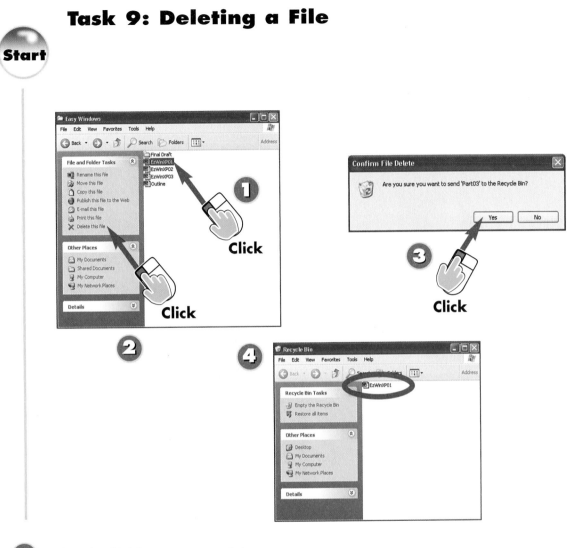

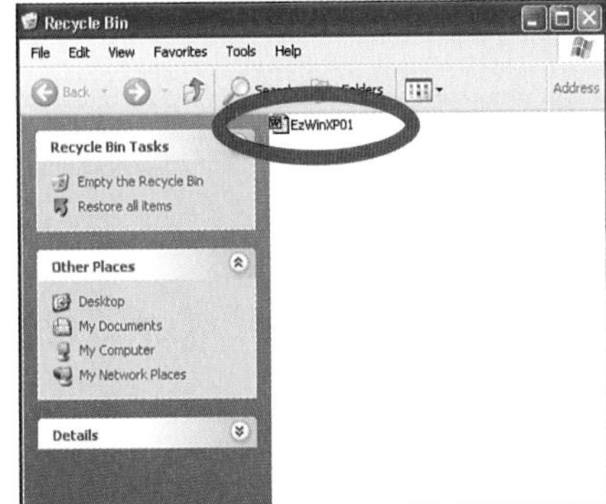

1. Select the file(s) you want to delete.
2. Click the **Delete this file** button.
3. Click **Yes** to confirm the deletion.
4. Windows removes the file(s), placing it in the Recycle Bin.

INTRODUCTION

Eventually, your computer will become full of files, and you'll have a hard time organizing and storing them all. You can delete any files you no longer need. You can also make room by copying files you want to keep, but don't need to work with again, to a disk. Then you can delete the files from your hard drive.

TIP

Undo the Deletion
You can undo a deletion by selecting the **Undo** command from the **Edit** menu. Alternatively, you can retrieve the deleted item from the Recycle Bin, as covered in the next task.

TIP

Delete Shortcuts
Other alternatives for deleting files include right-clicking the file and choosing Delete from the shortcut menu, or selecting the file and pressing the **Delete** key on your keyboard.

Task 10: Undeleting a File

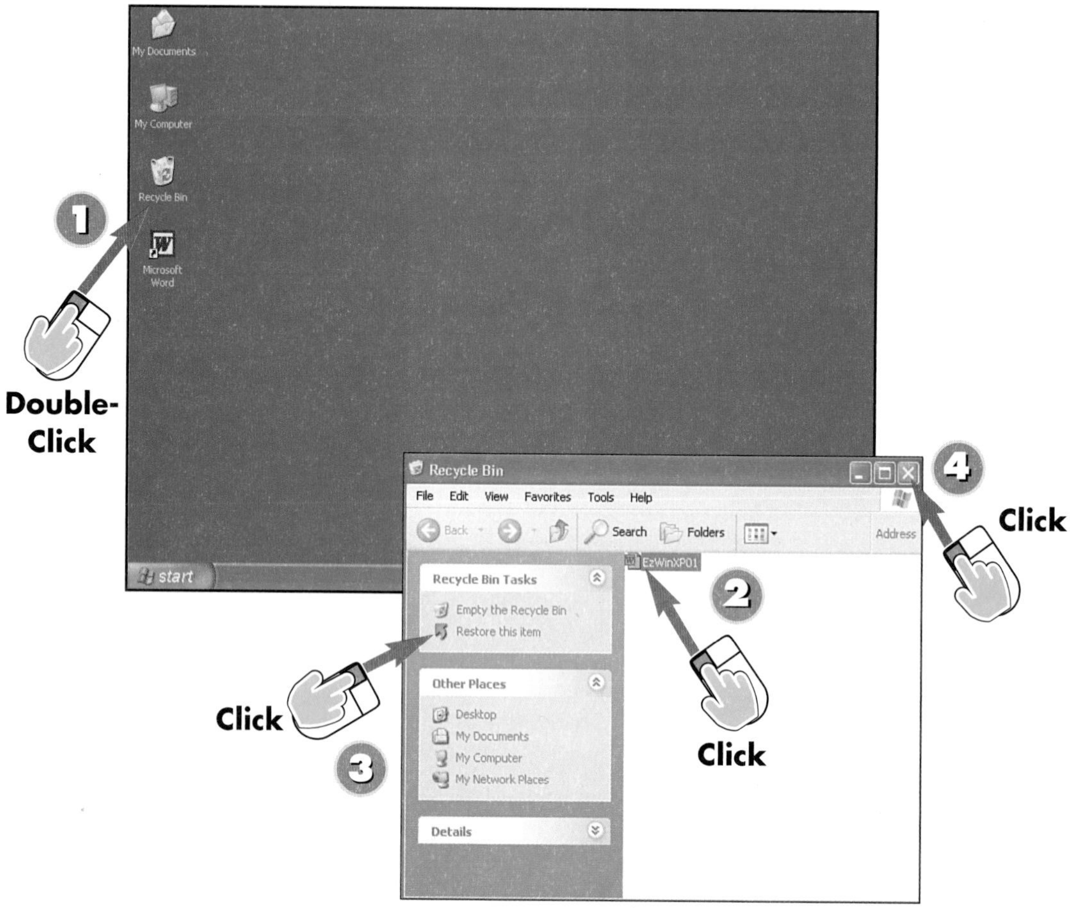

1. Double-click the **Recycle Bin** icon on your desktop.
2. In the Recycle Bin window that appears, you see all the files, programs, and folders you have deleted. Select the file(s) or folder(s) you want to undelete.
3. Click the **Restore this item** link. The file(s) or folder(s) are moved from the Recycle Bin to their original locations.
4. Click the **Close** button to close the Recycle Bin.

End

INTRODUCTION

Sometimes you will delete a file or folder by mistake. If you make a mistake, you can retrieve the file or folder from the Recycle Bin (as long as the Recycle Bin has not been emptied) and return it to its original location.

TIP

Clean Out the Recycle Bin

If you want to permanently delete the files in the Recycle Bin, you can empty it. Double-click the **Recycle Bin** icon and make sure that it doesn't contain anything you need to save. Then click the **Empty the Recycle Bin** link. Windows displays the Confirm Multiple File Delete dialog box; click **Yes** to empty the Recycle Bin.

Task 11: Opening a File from a File Window

Start

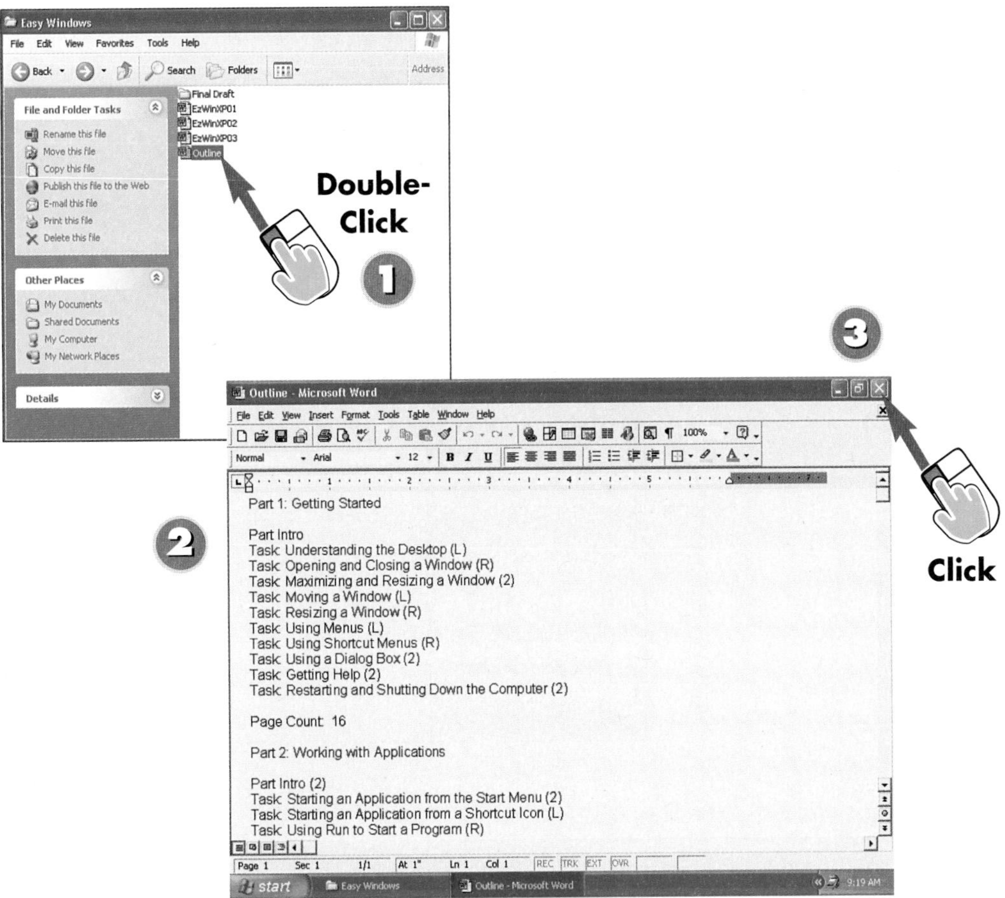

1. Double-click the file you want to open.
2. The associated program is started, and the file is displayed.
3. When you are done viewing the file, click the **Close** button to close the document and program.

INTRODUCTION

As you are organizing your files, you may need to open a file to view its contents. You may also browse through folder windows to find a particular file and then open it, rather than open it from within the program. When you open a file, the associated program is started, and the file is opened.

TIP

Use My Recent Documents Command

You can also click **Start**, **My Recent Documents** and then select the document to open. If this command is not displayed, see Part 10, "Personalizing Windows."

Task 12: Setting File Associations

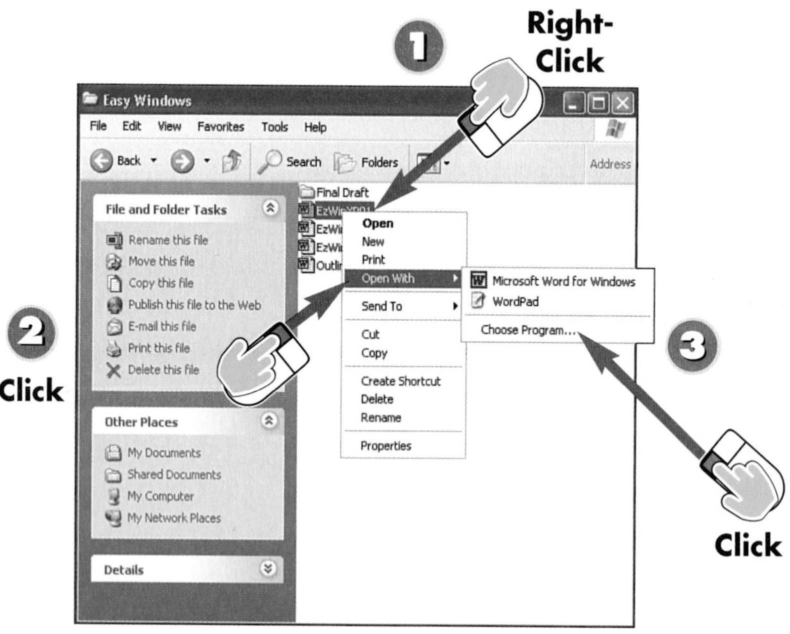

1. Right-click the file icon for which you want to check or change the associated program.
2. Select **Open With** from the shortcut menu. The current program is listed. If it is correct, you can skip the remaining steps.
3. To change the program, click **Choose Program**.

INTRODUCTION

When you double-click a file icon, Windows opens the program associated with that file type. If no program is associated, you are prompted to select the program. You can set and check program associations so that you don't have to continually tell Windows which program to use.

TIP

Program Not Listed?
If the program isn't listed, click the link at the bottom of the dialog box. You see the Open With dialog box. You can open any program folder on your computer and select a particular program file to use to open the selected file type. Click **OK**.

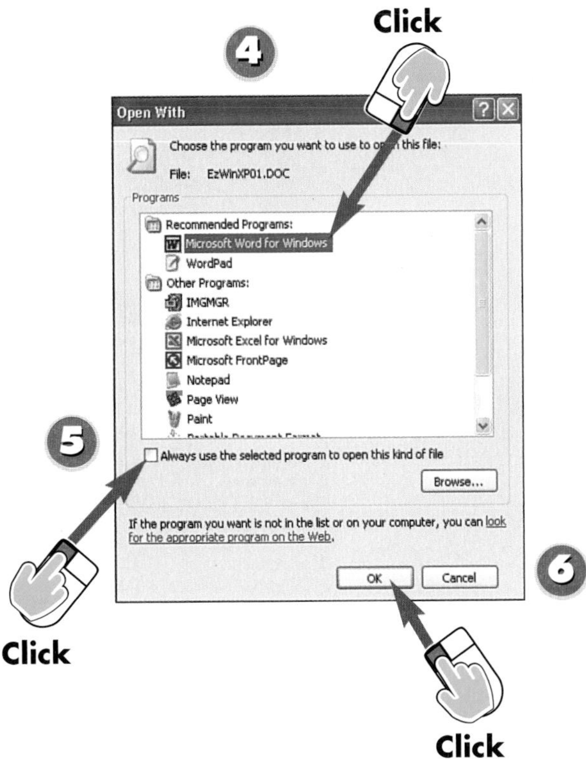

4 The Open With dialog box appears. Select from any of the listed programs.

5 To always use the program you selected to open the file, check **Always use the selected program to open this kind of file**.

6 Click **OK**.

TIP

View All File Types
To view, verify, and change the list of associated programs for all file types, click **Tools**, **Folder Options**. Click the **File Types** tab. In the Registered file types list, select the file type to check or change. Use the **Change** button to select a different program. Use the **New** button to set new file associations.

Task 13: Searching for Documents

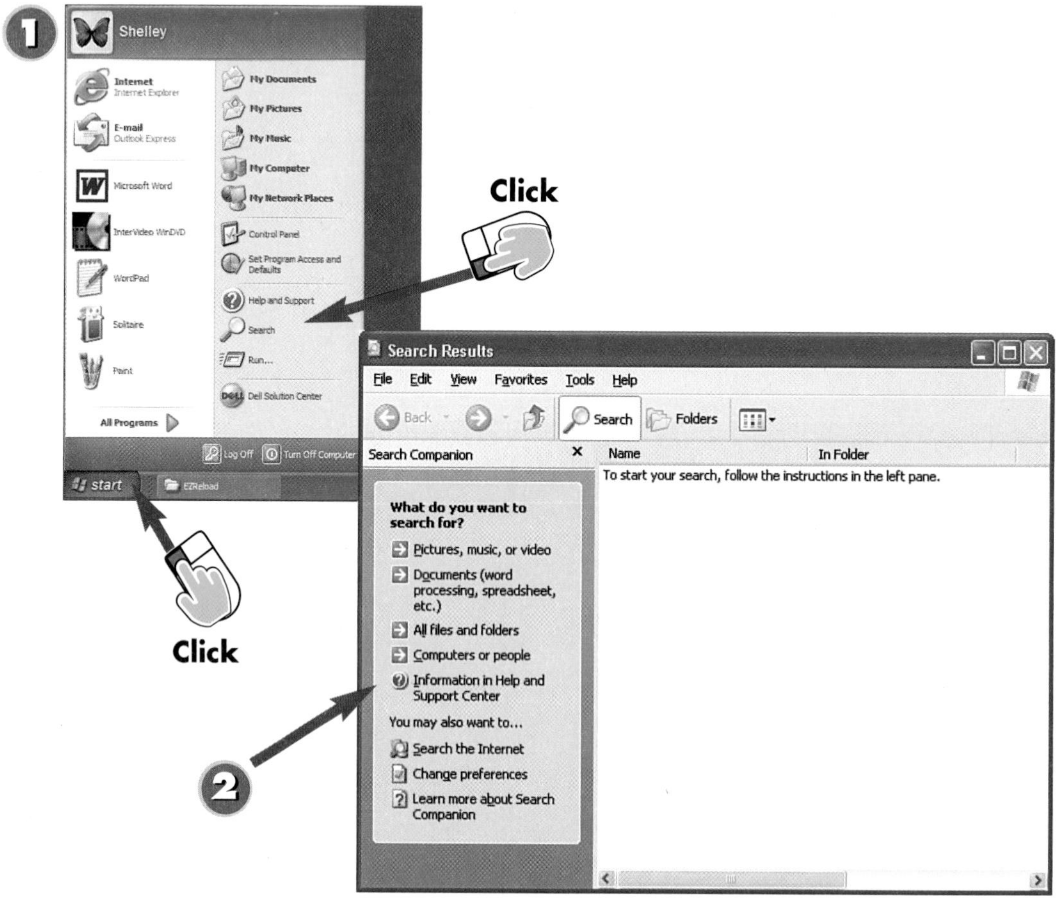

1 Click **Start** and then **Search**.

2 Select what type of item you want to search for. You can select a particular type of file or search all files.

INTRODUCTION

It is easy to misplace a file. If you have saved a document, but cannot locate it by browsing through your folders, search for it. You can search for several different file types. From the search results, you can then open, print, copy, or move the file.

TIP

Search from Folder Window

You can also search from within a folder window. To display the Search Bar, click the **Search** button. Then perform the search.

TIP

Stop the Search

If the search is taking too long and your results have already been found, you can stop the search. To do so, click the Stop button.

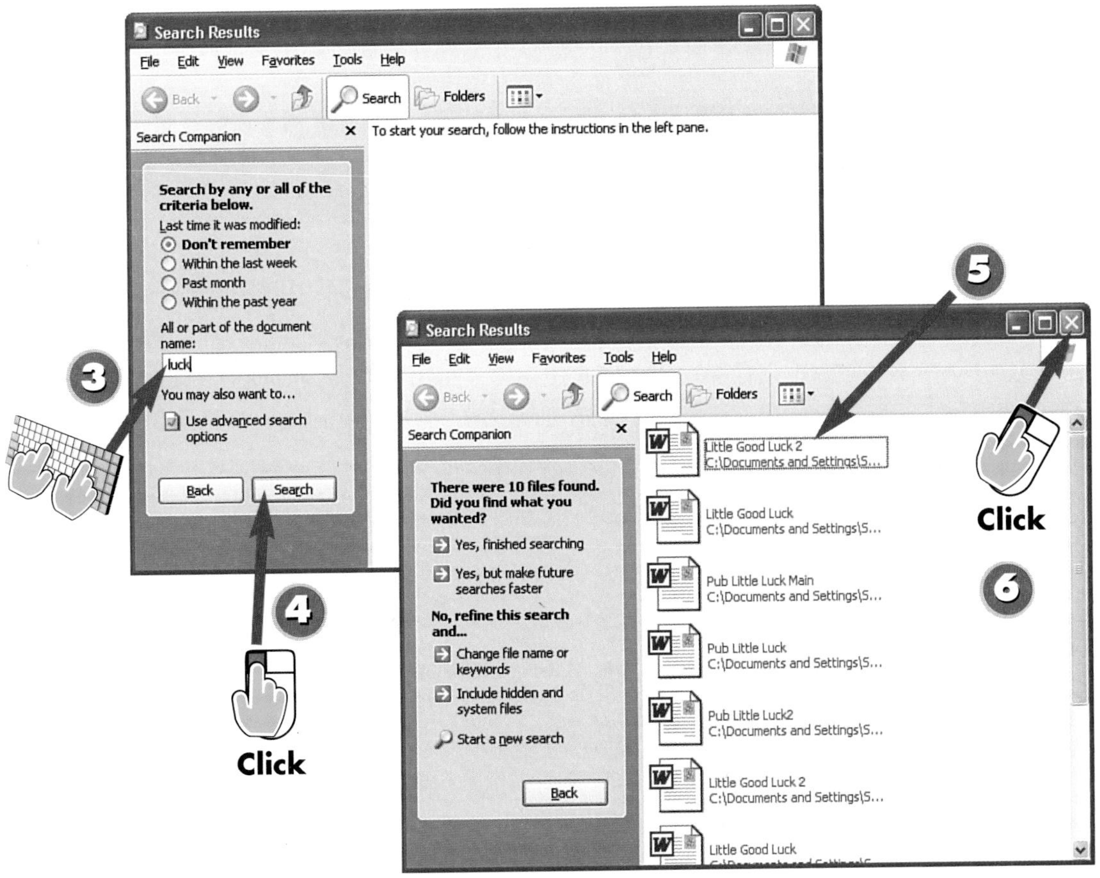

3. You see the options for this file type (here, documents). Type all or part of the name.

4. Click the **Search** button.

5. Windows searches the selected folder or drives and displays a list of found files. You can double-click any of the listed files or folders to go to that file or folder.

6. To close the search window, click its **Close** button.

End

> **TIP**
> **No Search Results?**
> If the search did not find a match, you can try searching using a different word. Or you can try searching all file types. Use the options in the Search bar.

> **TIP**
> **Use Other Search Options**
> You can also use the other search options, such as last time the file was modified. These options vary depending on what type of item you are searching for.

PART 5

Working with Printers, Scanners, and Digital Cameras

All Windows programs use the same setup for your printer, which saves time and ensures that you can print from any Windows program without resetting for each program. When you first install Windows, it sets up your printer. If needed, you can set up more than one printer in Windows and choose the printer you want to use at any given time. In addition, you can easily manage printing for all your programs from Windows.

Related to printing are scanners, which you can use to scan illustrations and documents. While the specifics of using your particular scanner will be different, you can learn how to set up your scanner in this part.

Finally, digital cameras have become popular add-ons to the home computer. If you have a digital camera, you can find out in this part how to set up that camera and manage the picture files.

Tasks

Task 1: Adding a Printer

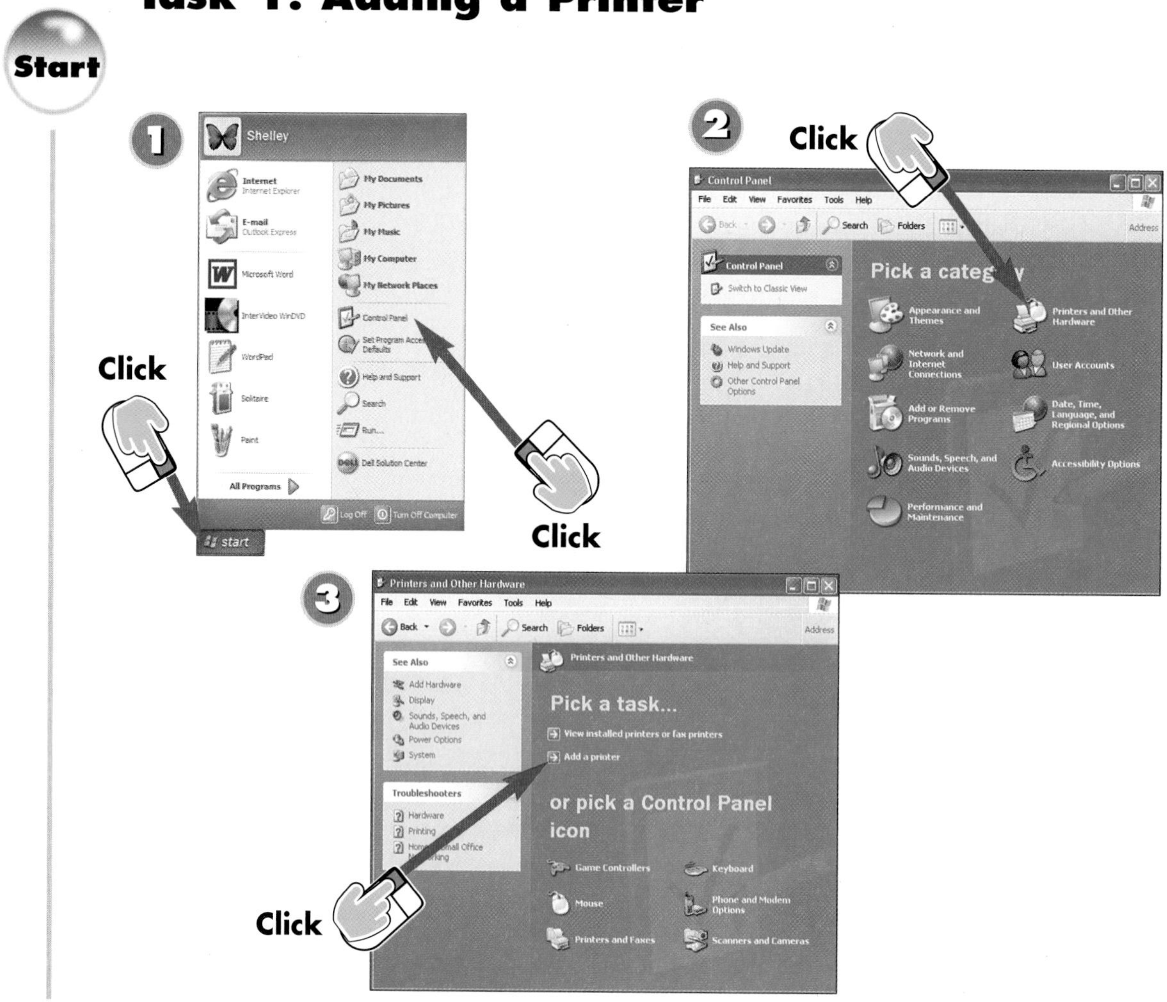

Click Start and then click **Control Panel**.

Click **Printers and Other Hardware**.

Click the **Add a printer** link to start the Add Printer Wizard.

INTRODUCTION

You can add a new printer to your Windows setup using a step-by-step guide called a wizard. In many cases, Windows can automatically set up your printer once you attach it. If this doesn't work for some reason, you can use the wizard to set up the printer if you get a new printer or change printers.

TIP

Install Network Printer

If you are installing a network printer, you select different options for the type of printer and printer sharing. For help on installing a network printer, see Part 13, "Home Networking Basics."

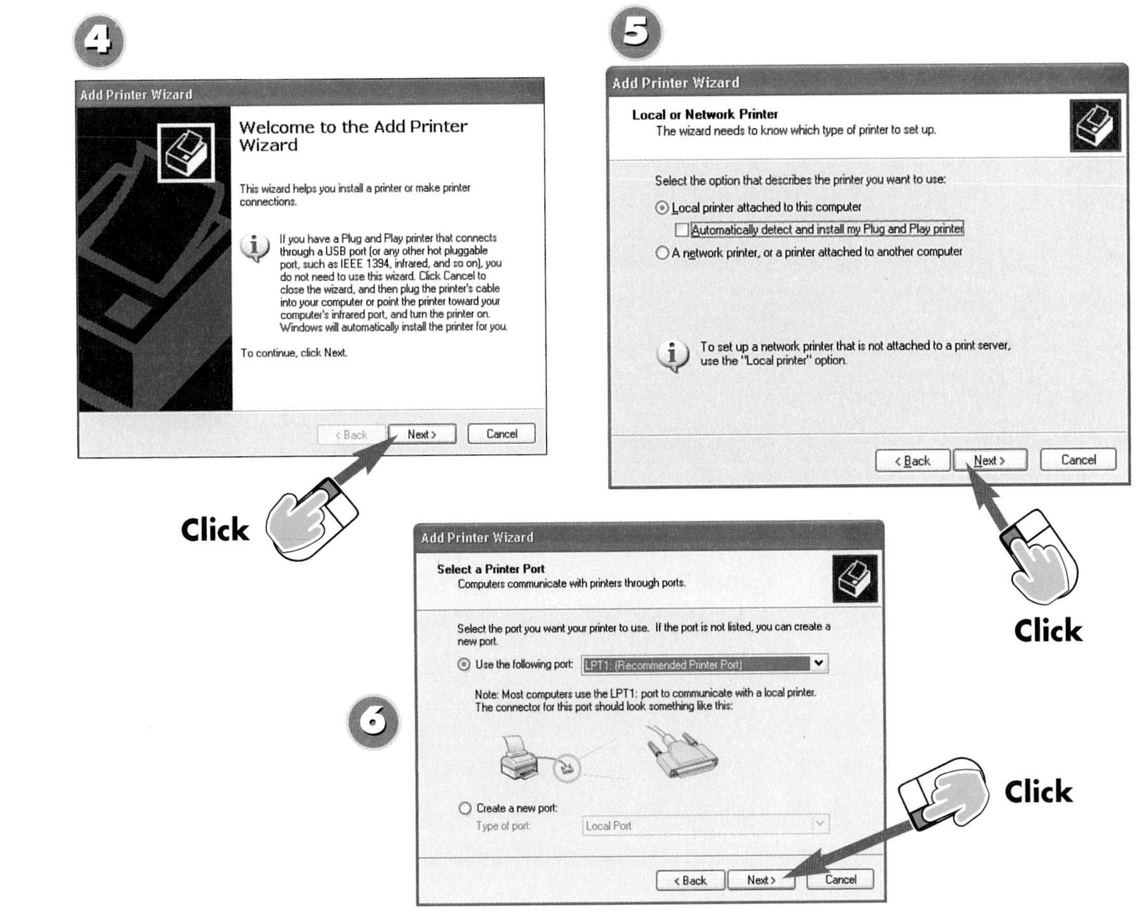

4. Click **Next** to move from the welcome screen to the first step.

5. For the first step, select **Local printer** and then click **Next**.

6. Select the port to which the printer is attached and click **Next**.

TIP

Automatic Detection
If you select automatic detection, Windows looks for the new printer and installs it if possible. If that doesn't work, uncheck this option and follow these steps to manually install the printer.

TIP

Use Printer Disk
If you have the printer disk with the printer driver file (the file that tells Windows the details of that particular printer), click **Have Disk**, insert the disk, and then select the drive to search for the file.

Adding a Printer (Continued)

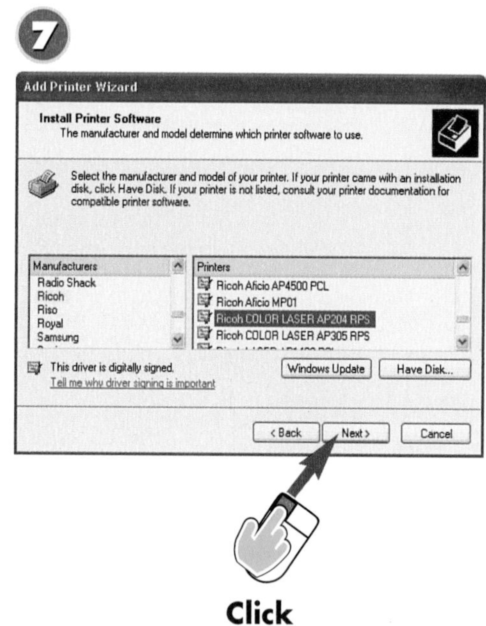

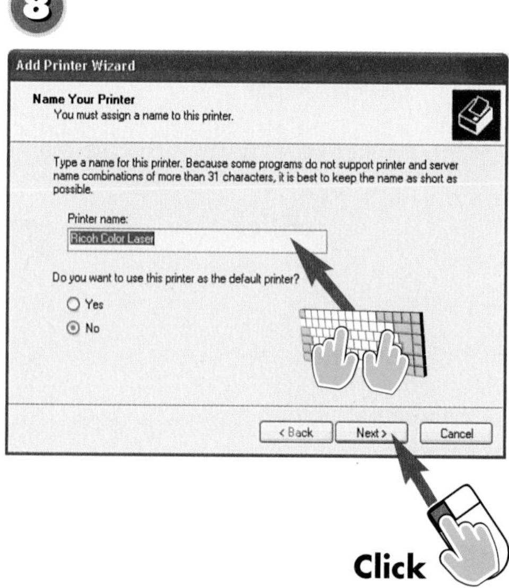

7. Select your printer manufacturer in the list on the left. Then select your particular printer from the list on the right. Click **Next**.
8. Type a name to identify the printer and click **Next**.

Delete a Printer
If you replace a printer, you can delete the icon for the other printer so that you are not confused. To delete (and uninstall a printer), right-click the icon (see the next task "Displaying Installed Printers" for help on displaying printer icons). Select Delete and then click Yes to confirm the deletion.

Go Back a Step
Click the **Back** button in a wizard dialog box to return to the previous dialog box and review or modify your selections.

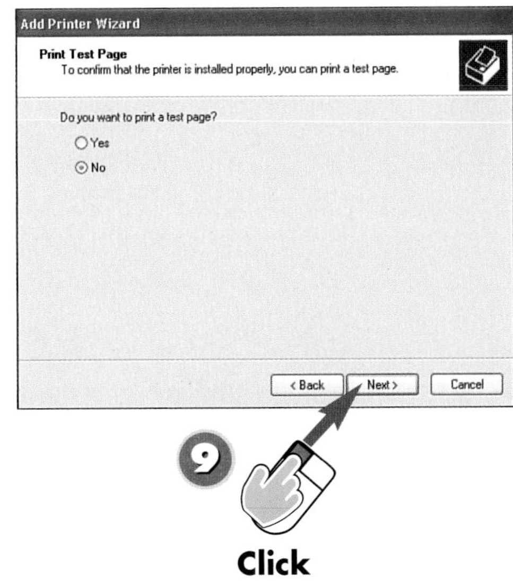

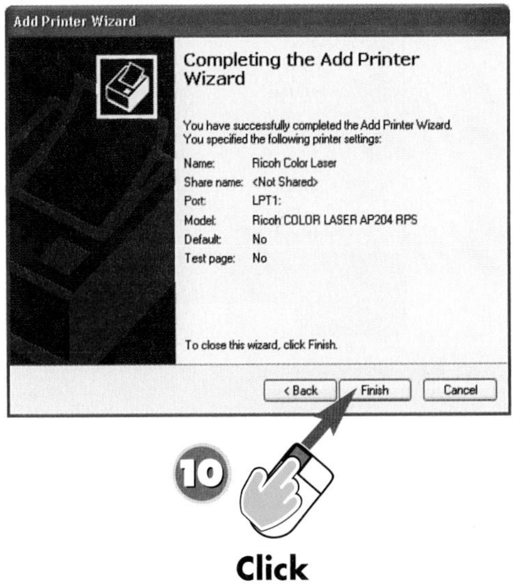

9. Select **Yes** or **No** for the test page question and then click **Next**.

10. The final step of the wizard lists all of your selections. Click **Finish** to finish the printer setup. The printer is set up and added to Windows XP.

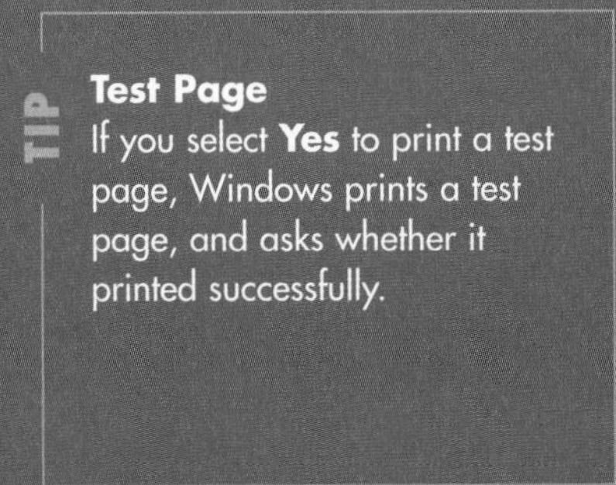

TIP

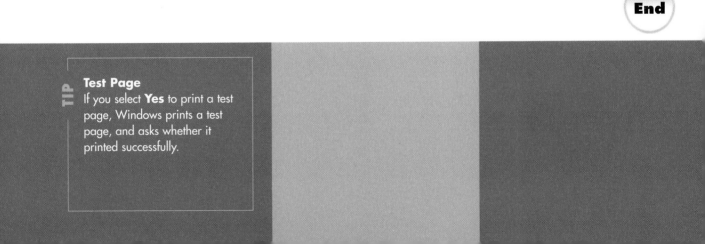

Test Page
If you select **Yes** to print a test page, Windows prints a test page, and asks whether it printed successfully.

Task 2: Displaying Installed Printers

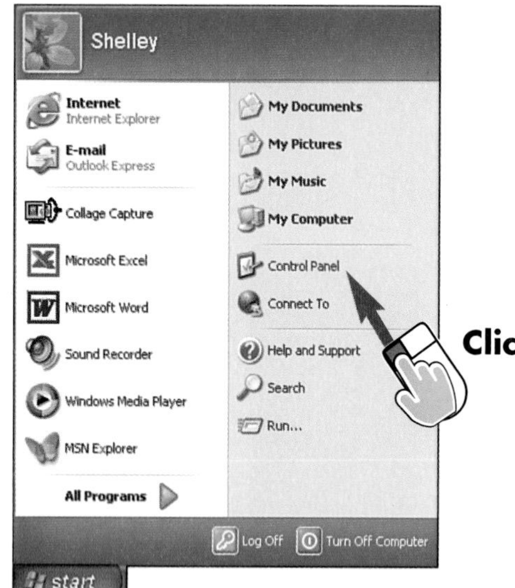

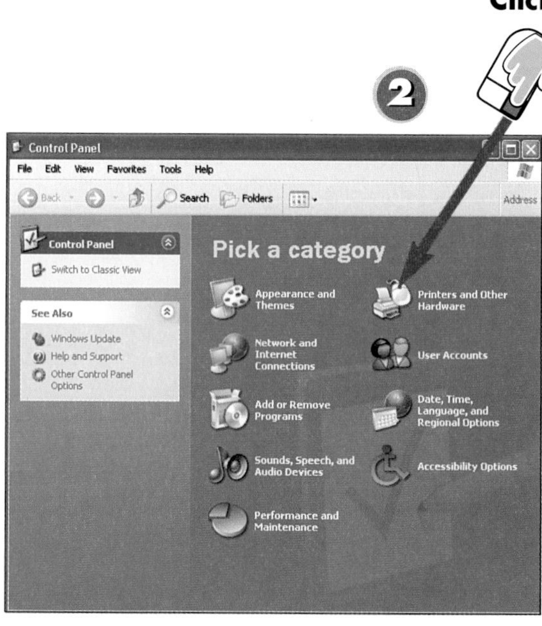

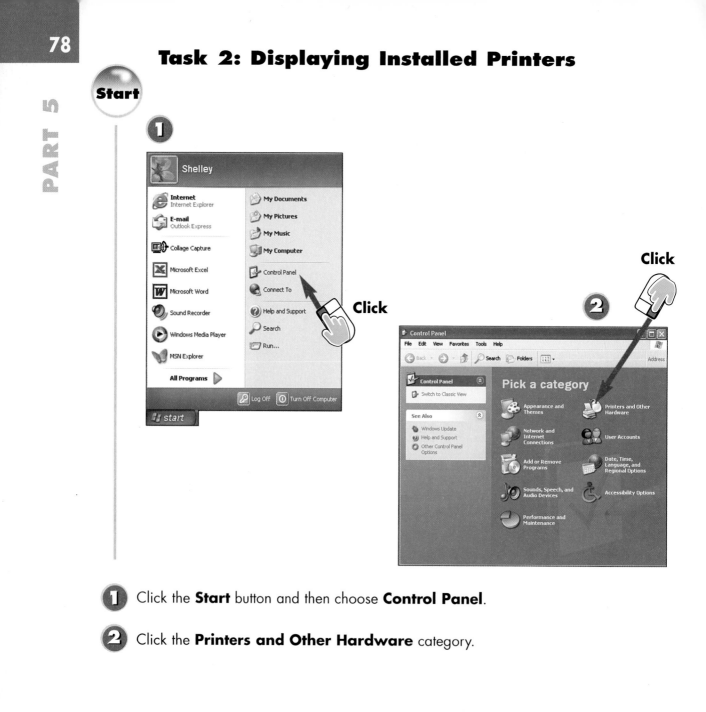

1. Click the **Start** button and then choose **Control Panel**.

2. Click the **Printers and Other Hardware** category.

INTRODUCTION

If you want to modify a printer's settings or delete an installed printer, you start by opening the Printers & Faxes Control Panel. You can then view and change the preferences and properties for any of the printers. You can also access the print queue to pause, restart, or cancel a print job.

TIP

Default Printer
The default printer is indicated with a checkmark. To select another printer as the default, right-click the icon for that printer and select **Set as Default Printer**.

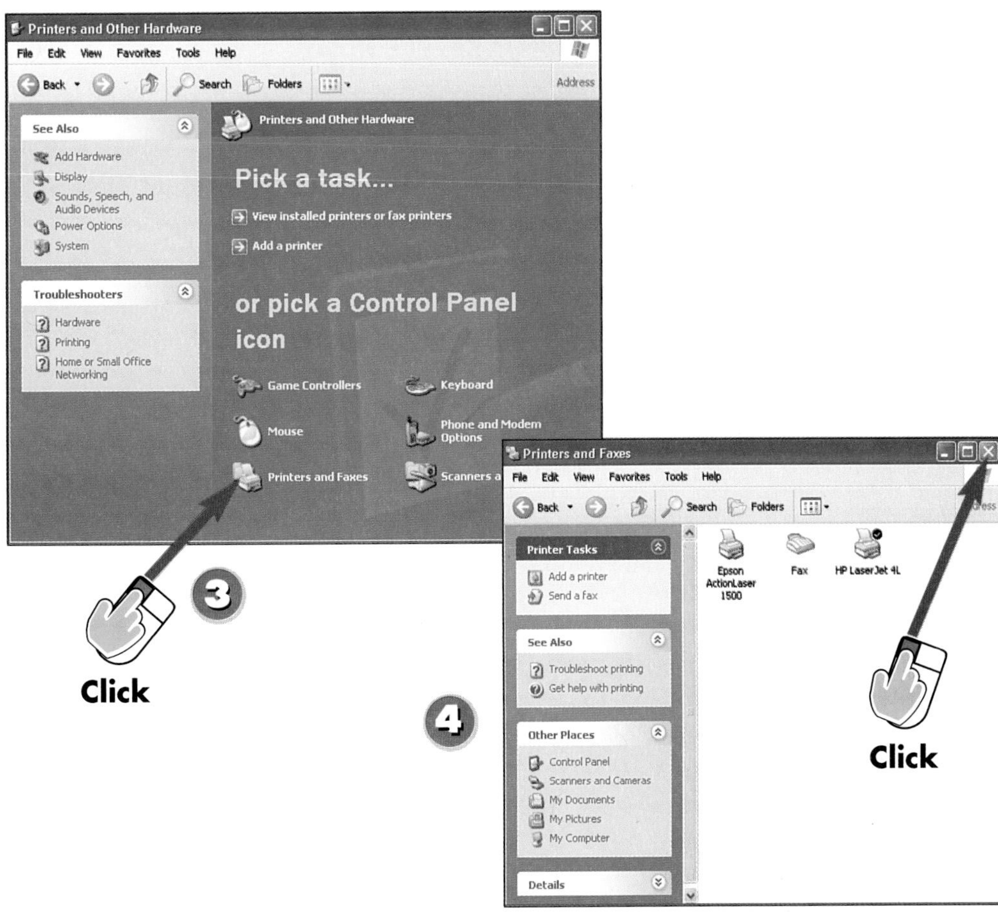

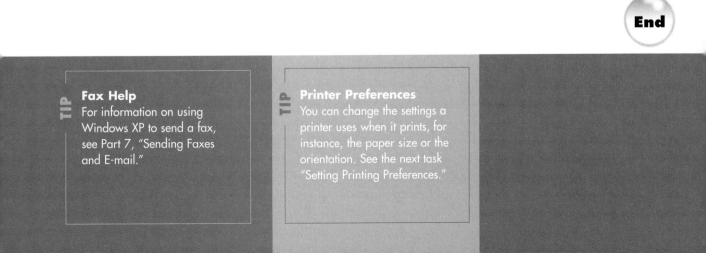

3. Click the **Printers and Faxes** Control Panel icon.

4. You see a list of all the installed printers and faxes. To close this window, click its **Close** button.

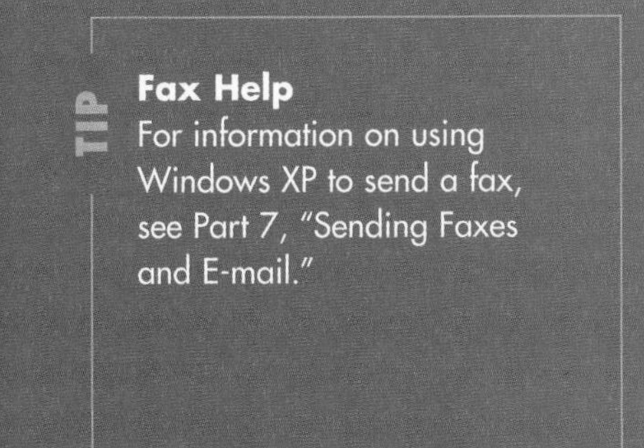

TIP

Fax Help

For information on using Windows XP to send a fax, see Part 7, "Sending Faxes and E-mail."

TIP

Printer Preferences

You can change the settings a printer uses when it prints, for instance, the paper size or the orientation. See the next task "Setting Printing Preferences."

Task 3: Setting Printing Preferences

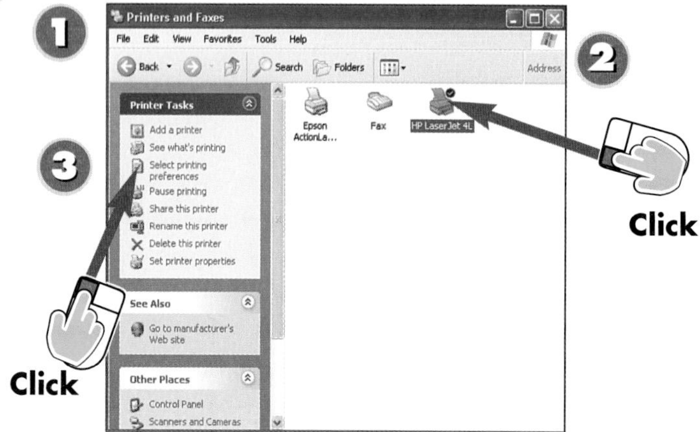

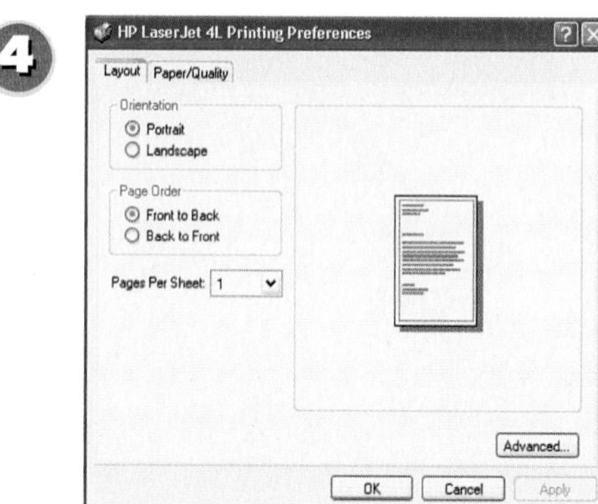

1. Display your installed printers. See Task 2, "Displaying Installed Printers," for help with this step.
2. Select the printer you want to modify.
3. Click **Select printing preferences**.
4. Select a default orientation and default page order.

INTRODUCTION

Printing preferences are settings such as the order pages are printed (beginning to end of document, or end to beginning), landscape (portrait or landscape), and paper source. If you always print a certain way, you can change these settings.

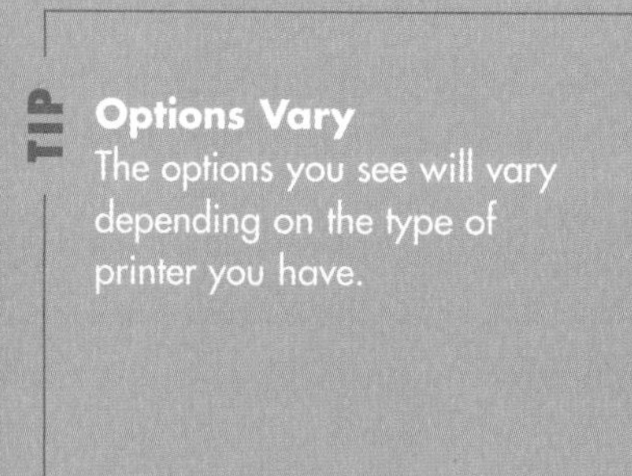

TIP

Options Vary
The options you see will vary depending on the type of printer you have.

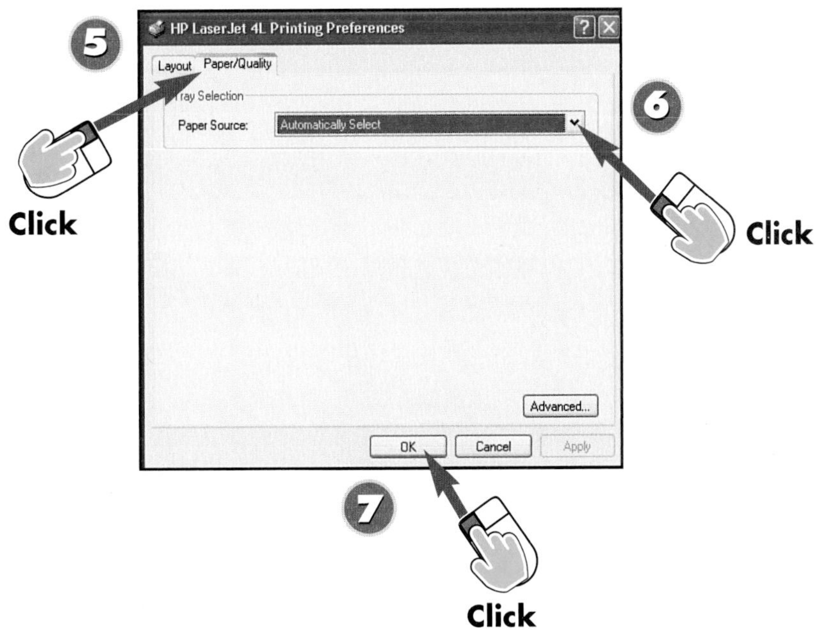

5 Click the **Paper/Quality** tab.

6 Display the Paper Source drop-down list and select a default paper source.

7 Click **OK**.

TIP

Advanced Options

To change options for paper size, graphic quality, copy count, and others, click the **Advanced** tab. Make any changes and click **OK**.

TIP

When to Change Preferences

Changing the printer's preferences changes them for all documents you print on this printer. If you want to change settings for just one document, change the setting in that document instead.

Task 4: Viewing Printer Properties

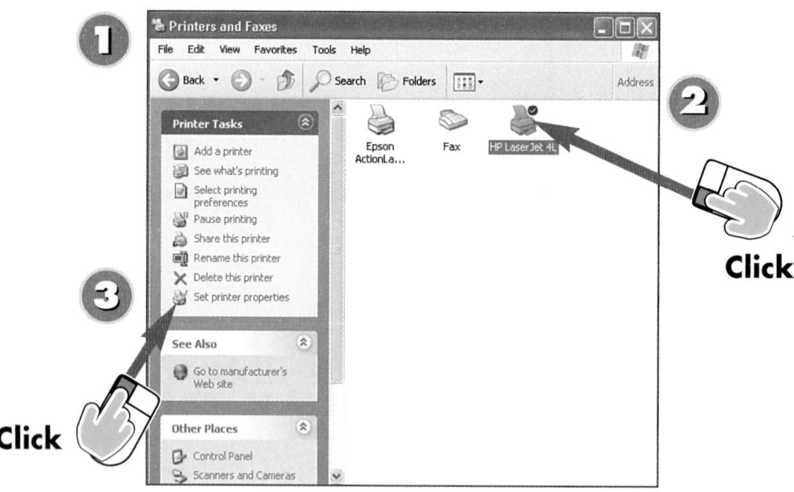

1. Display your installed printers. Refer to Task 2, "Displaying Installed Printers," for help with this step.
2. Select the printer you want to modify.
3. Click **Set printer properties**.

INTRODUCTION

In addition to printing preferences, you can also view and change printer properties. These are more technical details of how your printer works—for instance, when the printer is available, the port to which the printer is attached, whether printer sharing is enabled, and other options.

TIP

What Is Spooling?

Spooling is the action of copying a document temporarily to the hard disk when printing. The document is then fed to the printer from the spooler. Spooling lets you get back to work within the program faster.

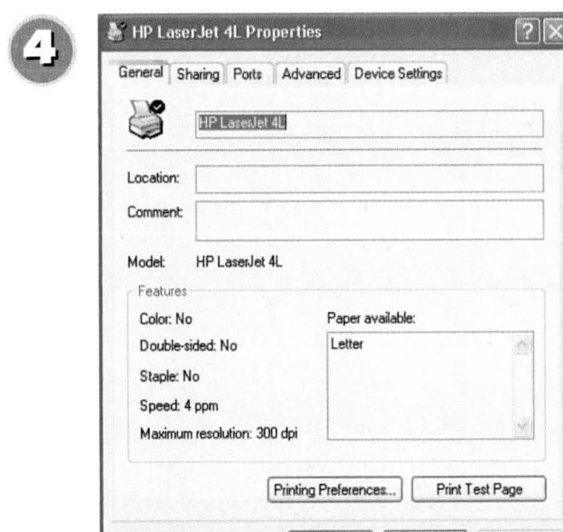

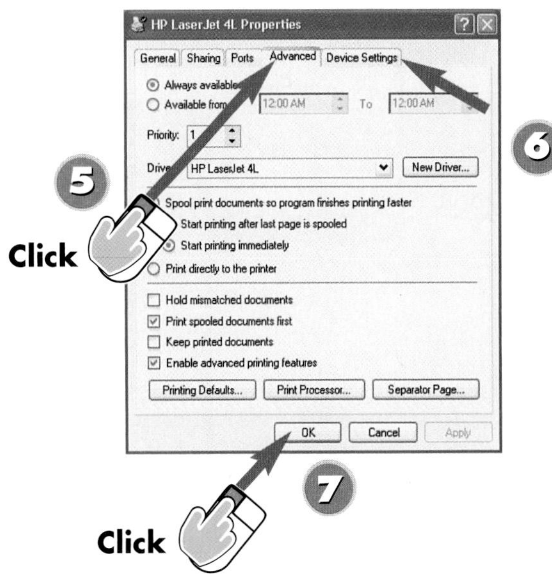

4. The General tab contains useful information about the features of your printer.
5. Click the **Advanced** tab to set when the printer is available as well as spooling options.
6. View and make changes to any of the other tabs.
7. Click **OK** when you are done.

End

TIP

Other Tabs

Use the **Sharing** tab to enable printer sharing, usually a network feature. Use the Ports tab to change the port to which the printer is connected. For printer memory and font options, click the **Device Settings** tab.

Task 5: Previewing a Document

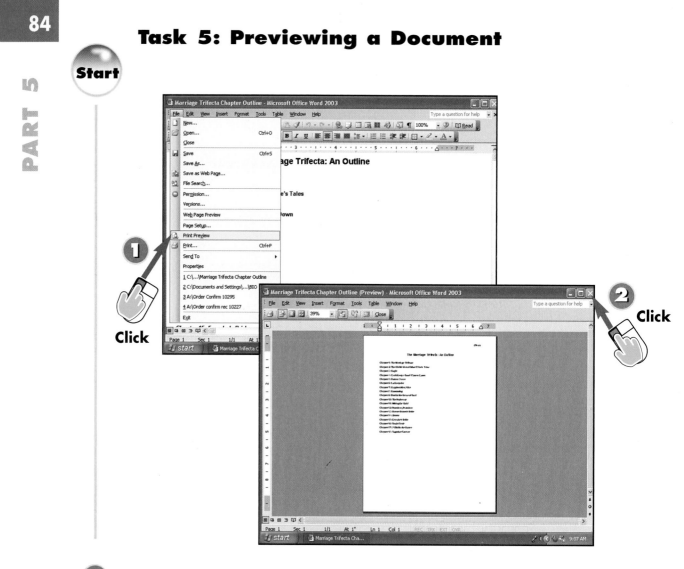

1. Click File and select the **Print Preview** command.

2. You see a preview of the current document. After you finish viewing the preview, click the **Close** button.

INTRODUCTION

Once your printer is set up, you can print your documents. Most programs enable you to preview a document to check the margins, heads, graphics placement, and so on before you print. Previewing can save time and paper because you can make any needed adjustments before you print.

TIP

Toolbar

The Print Preview window usually includes a toolbar for working with the document. Using buttons in this toolbar, you can magnify the view, print, change the margins, and more.

TIP

No Preview?

Most programs have a preview option, but if you don't see this command listed in your program, it is not available. You will have to print the document to see how it looks.

Task 6: Printing a Document

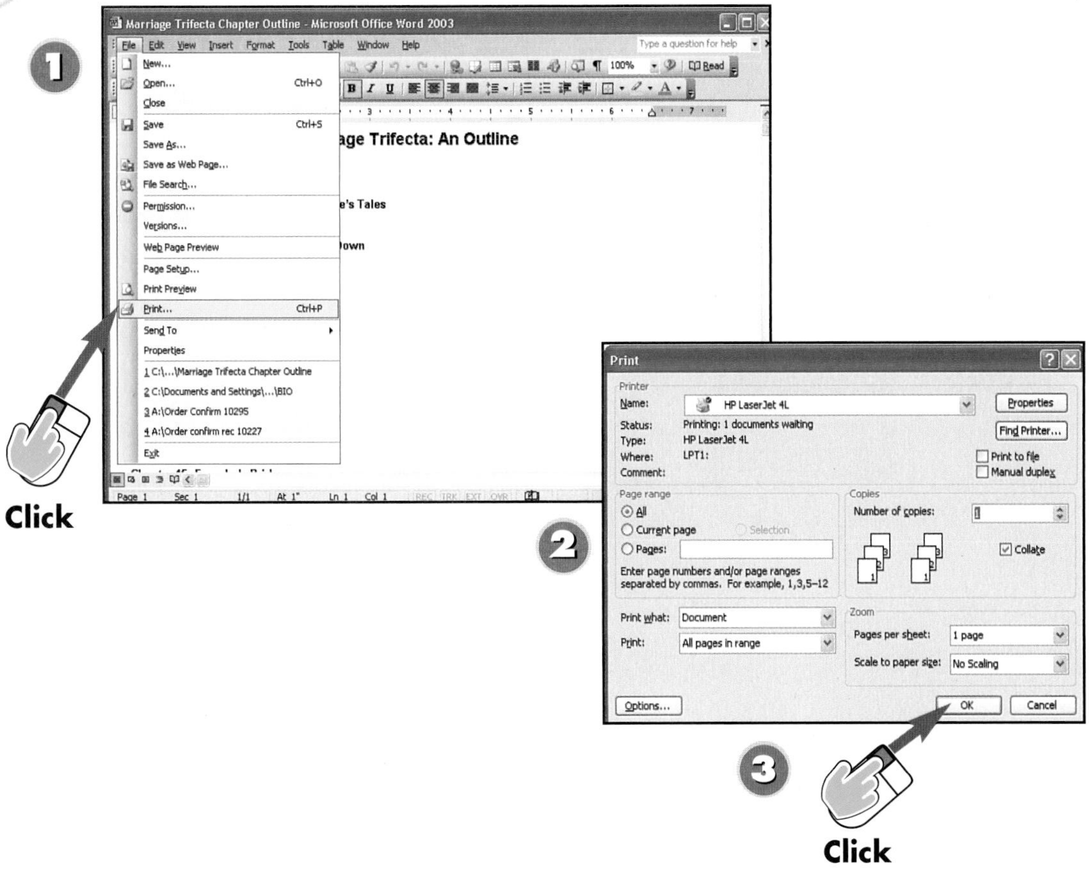

1. Click **File** and then click the **Print** command.
2. Make any changes to the print options.
3. Click the **OK** button. The document is printed.

INTRODUCTION

Printing your documents gives you a paper copy you can proofread, use in reports, give to co-workers, and so on. The options for printing vary from program to program, but the basic steps are the same.

TIP

Shortcut

As a shortcut, look for a **Print** button in the program's toolbar. Alternatively, you can use a keyboard shortcut (usually **Ctrl+P**) to print.

TIP

Use Another Printer

If you want to use a printer other than the default, choose the printer you want to use from the Name drop-down list in the Print dialog box.

Task 7: Viewing the Print Queue

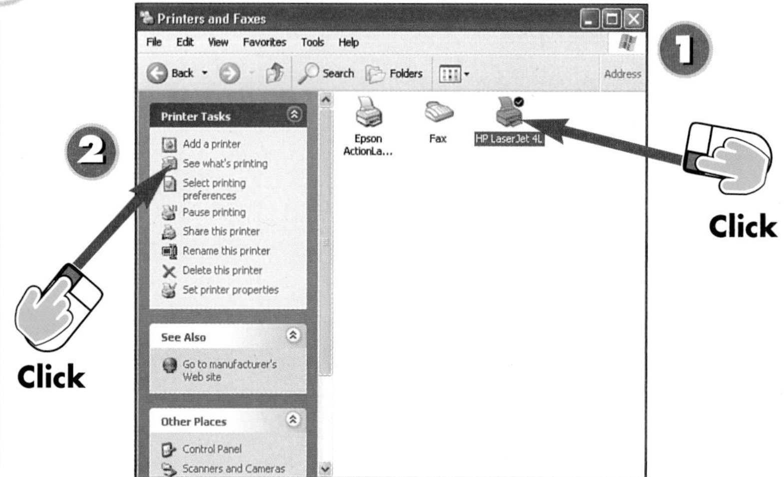

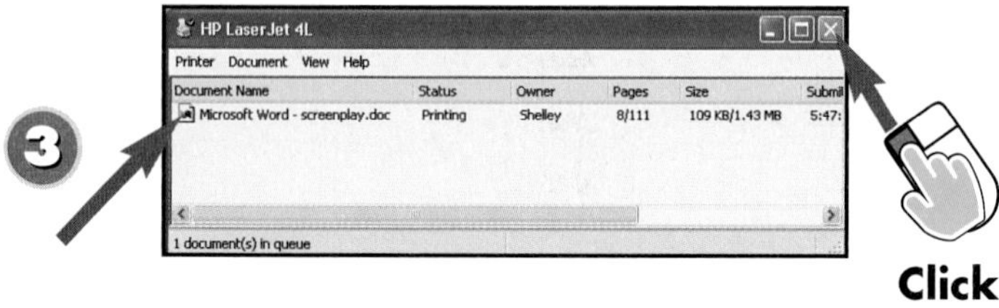

1. Select the printer you want to view. See Task 2, "Displaying Installed Printers," for help with this step.
2. Click **See what's printing**.
3. The printer window displays a list of the documents in the queue as well as information about the documents being printed. Click the **Close** button to close the queue.

End

INTRODUCTION

The print queue lists the documents that have been sent to a printer, and it shows how far along the printing is. Using the print queue, you can pause, restart, or cancel print jobs. This task shows how to view the print queue.

TIP

Double-Click the Icon

You can display the print queue by double-clicking the **Printer** icon in the status bar of the taskbar (on the left side). The Printer icon appears whenever you are printing a document.

TIP

Empty?

If the print queue window is empty, either the print job never made it to the queue or it was already processed by the printer.

Task 8: Canceling a Print Job

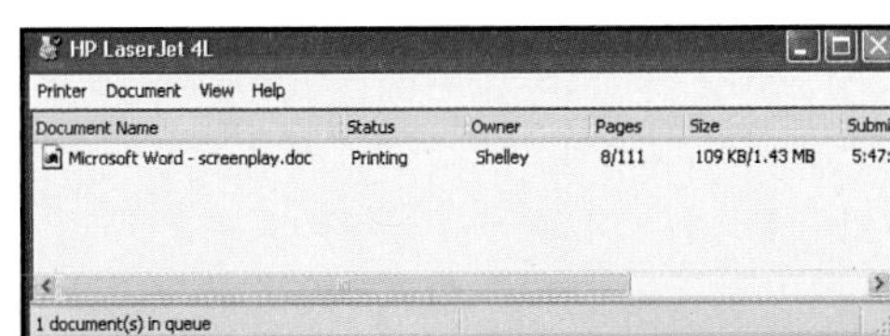

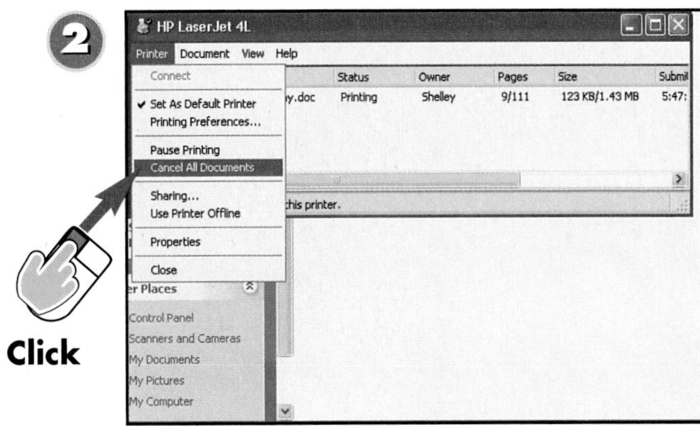

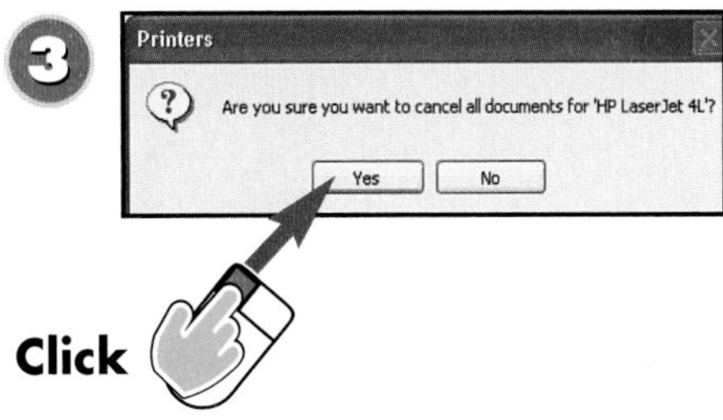

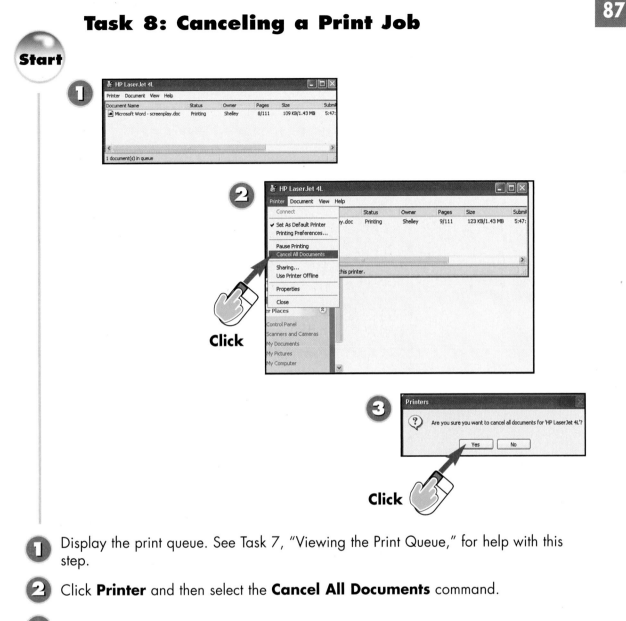

1. Display the print queue. See Task 7, "Viewing the Print Queue," for help with this step.
2. Click **Printer** and then select the **Cancel All Documents** command.
3. Click **Yes** to confirm the cancellation.

INTRODUCTION

If you discover an error in the job you are printing, or if you decide that you need to add something to it, you can cancel printing. Canceling printing prevents you from wasting time and paper.

TIP

Nothing Listed?
You must be quick to pause or stop a short print job. If nothing appears in the print queue, it probably means that the entire print job has already been sent to the printer.

TIP

Pause the Printer
To pause all print jobs, click **Pause Printing**. To restart the printer after you have paused it, click **Printer** and then click the **Pause Printing** command again.

Task 9: Viewing Fonts

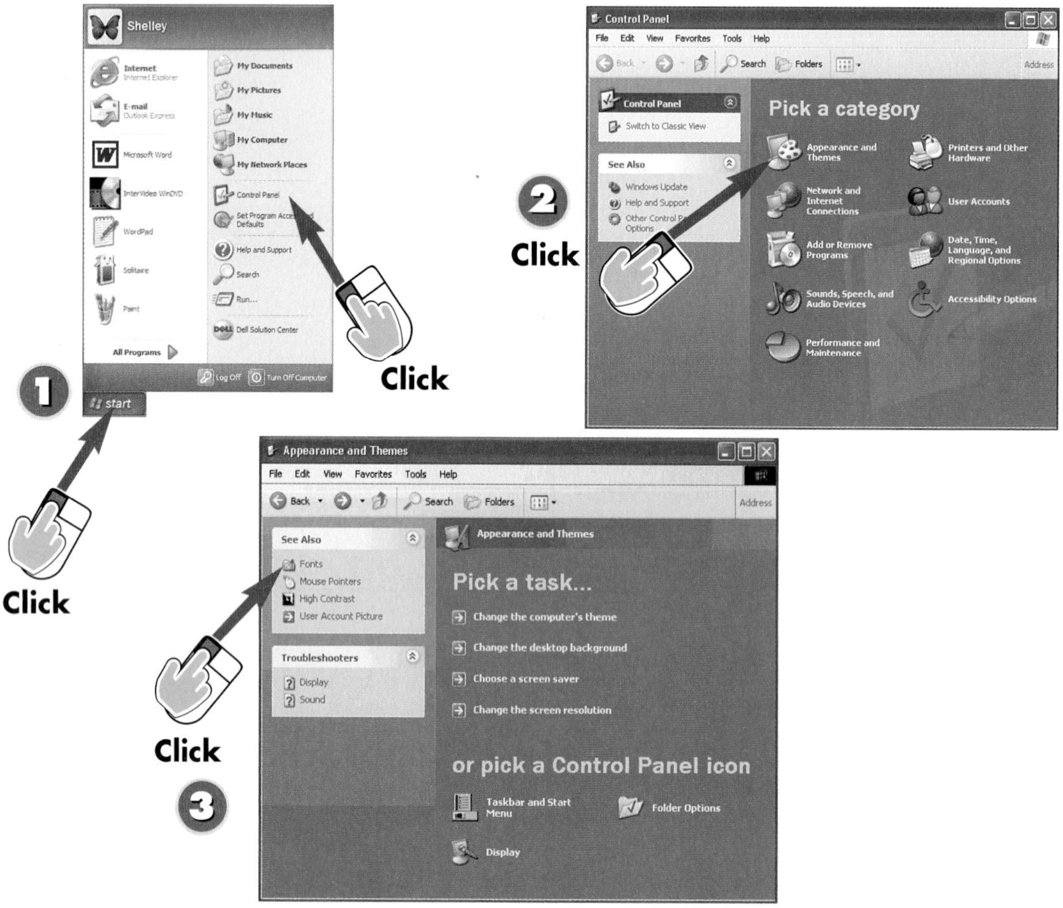

1. Click **Start** and then select **Control Panel**.
2. Click **Appearance and Themes**.
3. In the See Also area, click **Fonts**.

INTRODUCTION

Windows can use two types of fonts: the fonts built in to your printer and the fonts installed on your system. The installed fonts are files that tell Windows how to print in that font. The fonts you can select to use in a document depend on the fonts installed on your system. You can view a list of fonts and see an example of any of the available fonts.

TIP

View List

You can view the fonts by list rather than by icon. To do so, click **View** and then **List**. You can also view similar fonts by selecting **View**, **List Fonts by Similarity**.

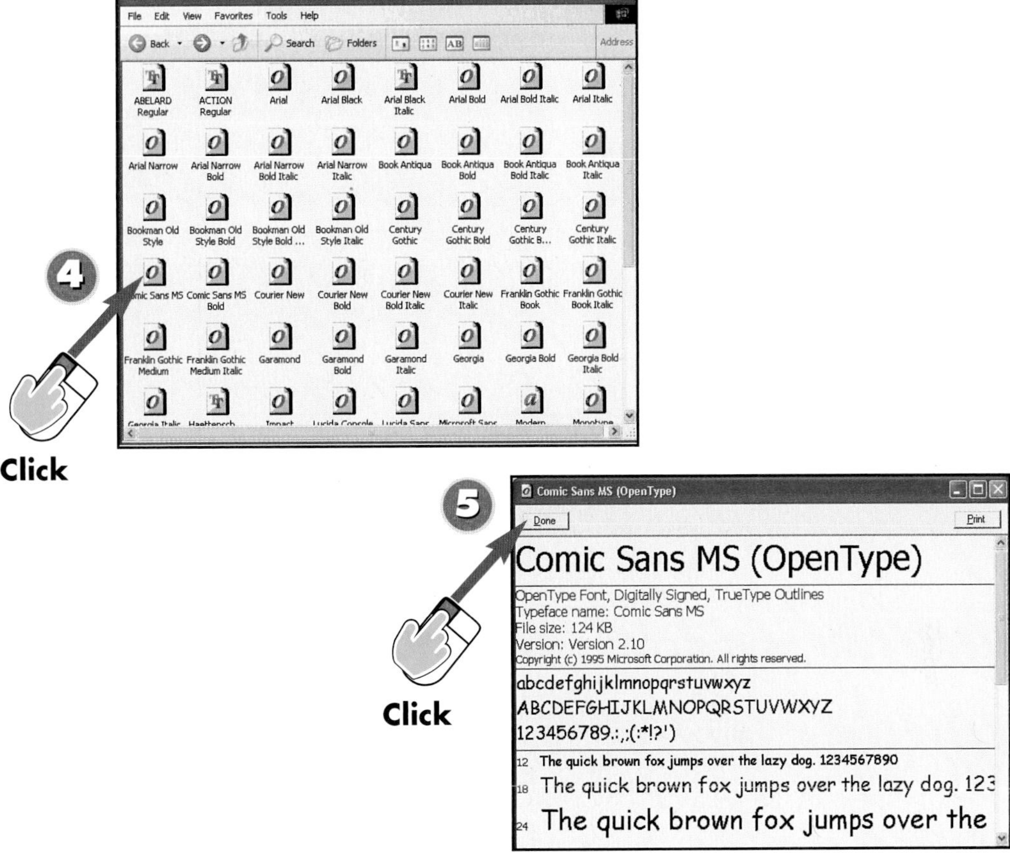

4. You see the Fonts folder with icons for all of the installed fonts. To view a font, double-click the icon.

5. You see a sample of the font in various sizes. Click the **Done** button to close the font window.

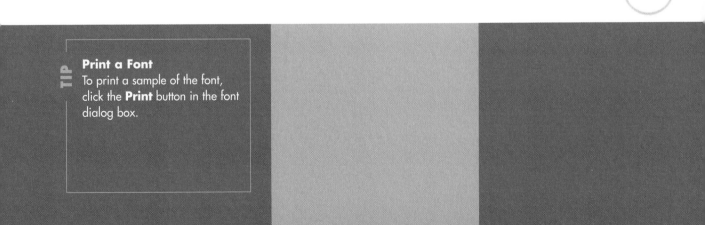

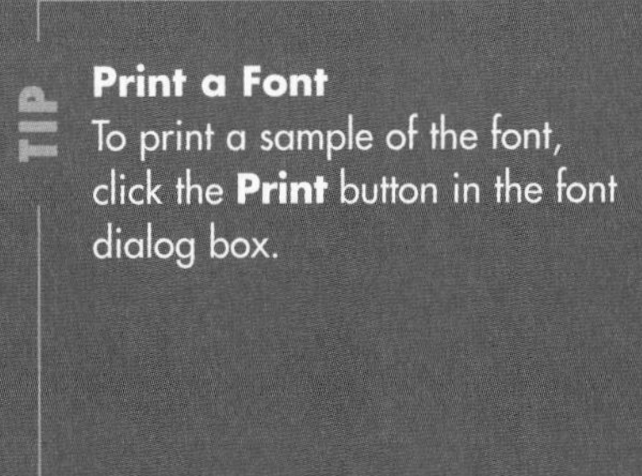

TIP

Print a Font

To print a sample of the font, click the **Print** button in the font dialog box.

Task 10: Adding Fonts

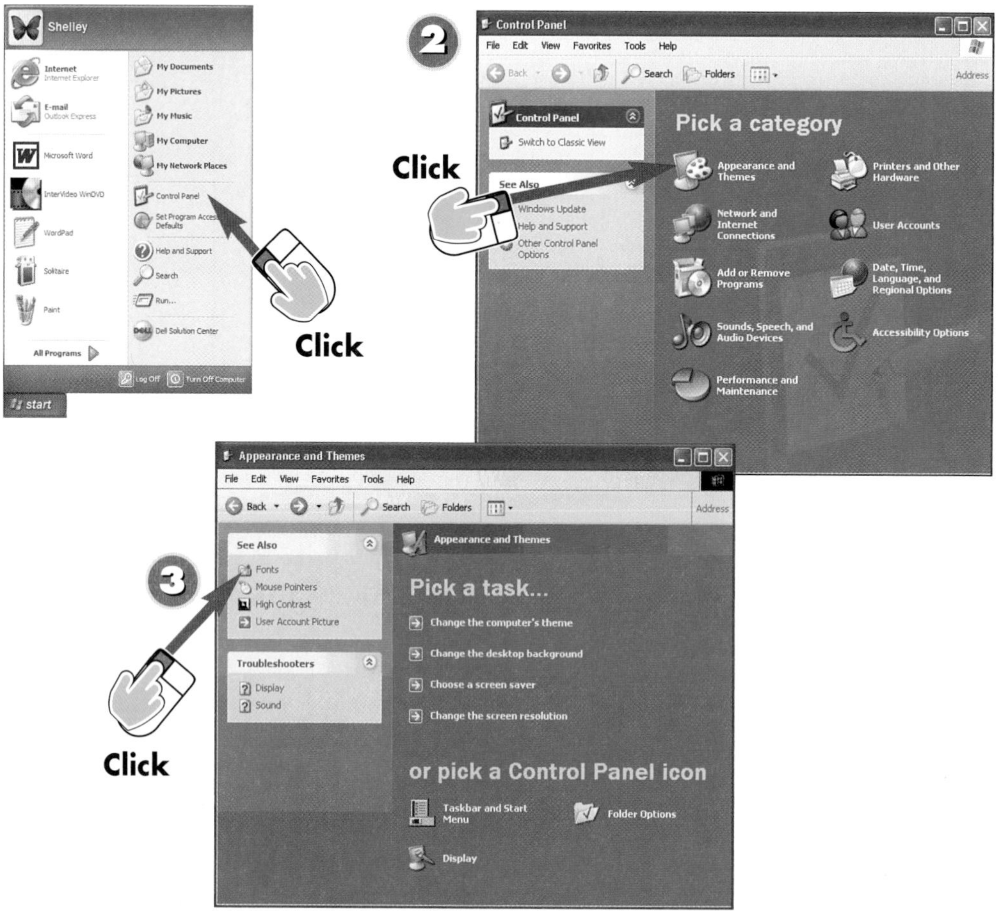

1. Click **Start** and then select **Control Panel**.
2. Click **Appearance and Themes**.
3. In the See Also area, click **Fonts**.

INTRODUCTION

You can purchase additional fonts to add to your system. When you do so, you need to install them in Windows so that you can use them with any Windows programs.

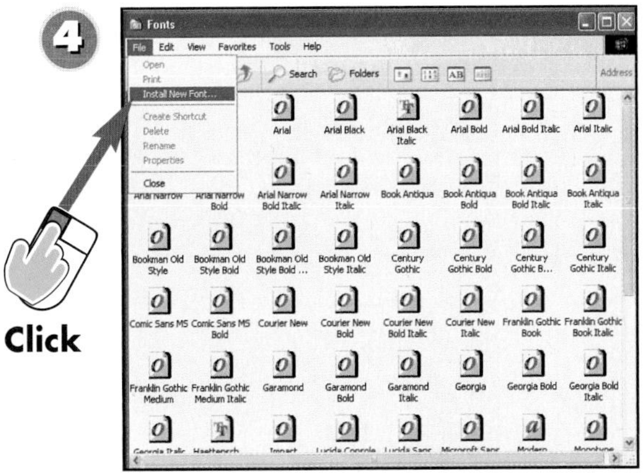

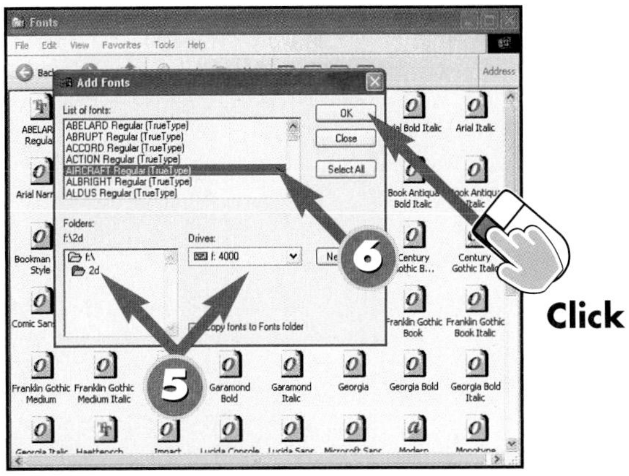

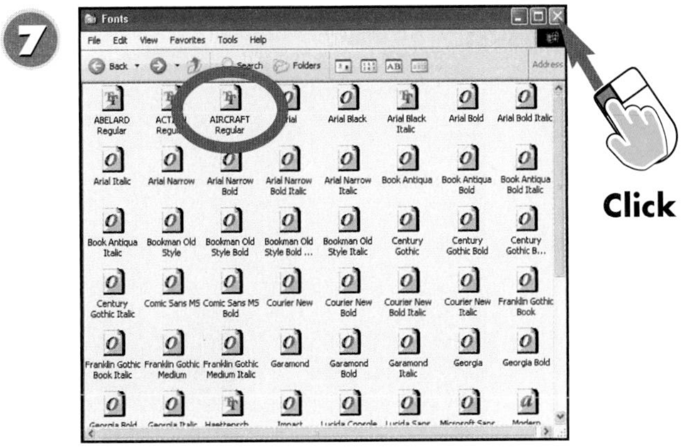

4. You see the Fonts folder with icons for all of the installed fonts. Click **File** and then **Install New Font**.

5. Select the drive and folder that contains your font files.

6. Select the font(s) you want to install and click **OK**.

7. The font(s) are installed. Click the **Close** button to close the font window.

TIP

No Fonts Listed?
If no fonts are listed, it's because no font files are in the selected folder. Be sure to select the drive and folder where the files are stored.

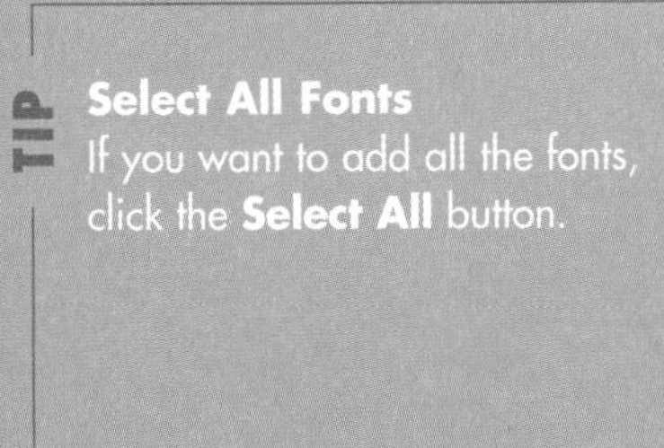

TIP

Select All Fonts
If you want to add all the fonts, click the **Select All** button.

Task 11: Setting Up a Scanner

Start

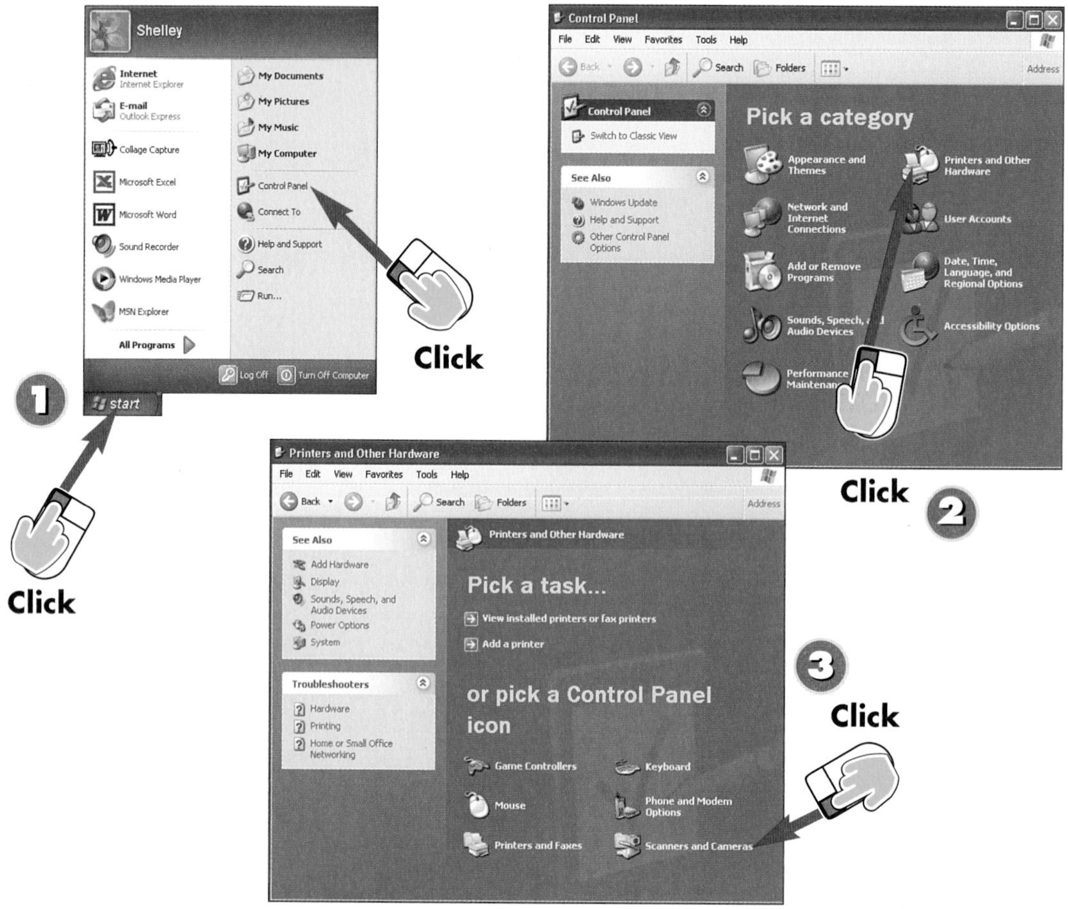

1. Click **Start** and then click **Control Panel**.

2. Click **Printers and Other Hardware**.

3. Click the **Scanners and Cameras** Control Panel icon.

INTRODUCTION

If you have a scanner, you can set it up and then use it to scan documents and illustrations. When you connect a scanner, Windows XP should query the scanner and then prompt you to install the proper driver (the scanner file that tells Windows about the scanner and how it works). If this automatic set up does not occur, you can use the Add Device wizard to set up the scanner.

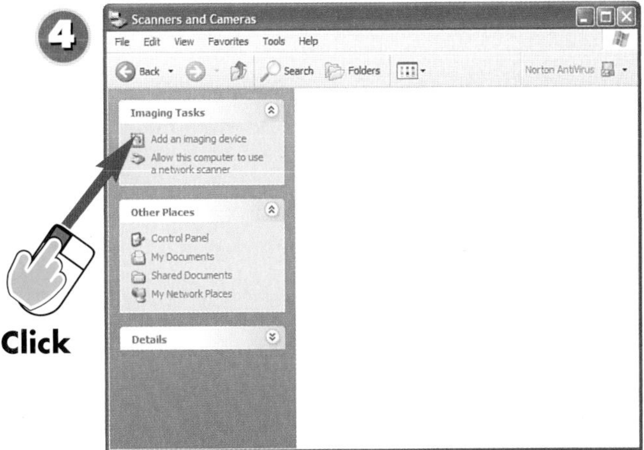

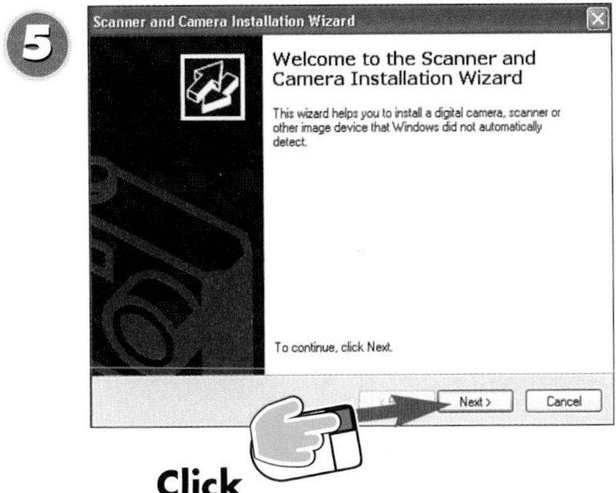

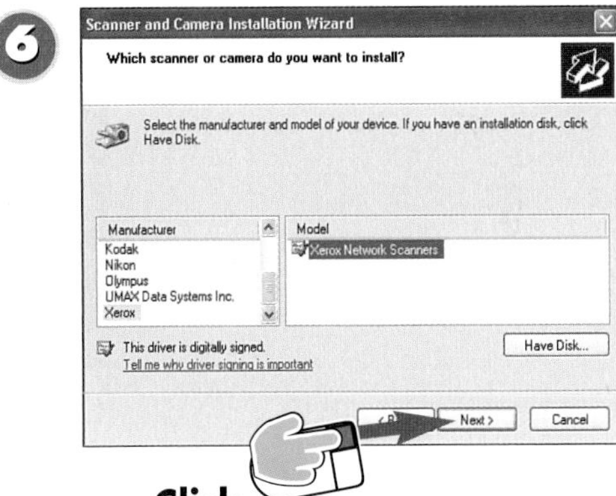

4. Click the **Add an imaging device** link to start the Scanner and Camera Installation Wizard.

5. Click **Next** to move from the welcome screen to the first step.

6. Select your scanner manufacturer in the list on the left. Then select your particular scanner from the list on the right. Click **Next**.

See next page

TIP

Automatic Installation

You will know if Windows XP automatically located your scanner because a status bar message will appear listing the new hardware (scanner). You can then click **OK** to have Windows install the driver for the hardware.

TIP

Use Disk

Windows XP does not list many scanners for manual setup. If the scanner was not automatically installed when connected, you most likely have to use your scanner disk. When prompted to select a manufacturer and model, click **Have Disk**. Select the drive that contains the disk and click **OK**. Windows XP should install the driver from this disk.

Setting Up a Scanner (Continued)

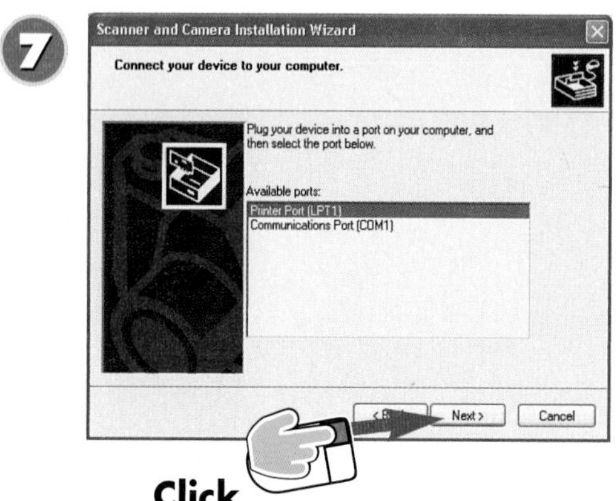

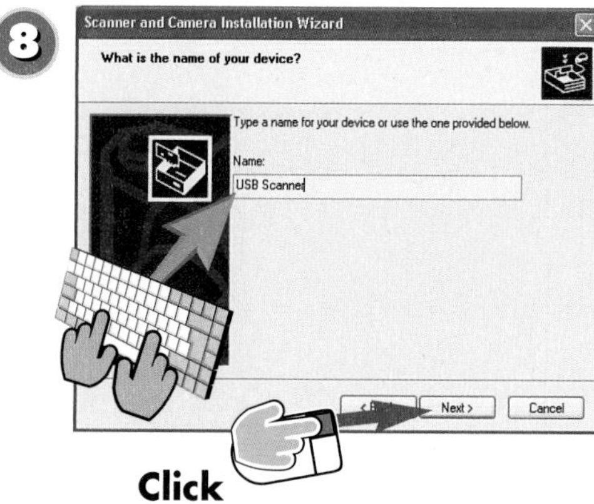

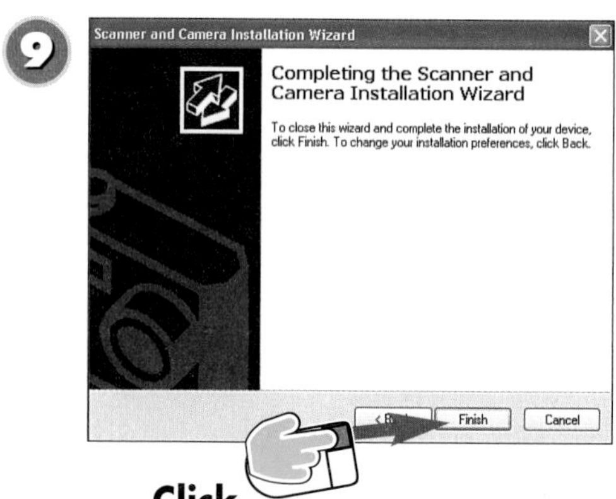

7. Select the port to which the scanner is connected and click **Next**.
8. Type a name for the scanner and click **Next**.
9. Click **Finish** to install the new scanner and its appropriate device driver.

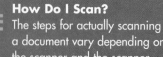

How Do I Scan?
The steps for actually scanning a document vary depending on the scanner and the scanner software, so you need to consult your scanner documentation for help on scanning.

Task 12: Setting Up a Digital Camera

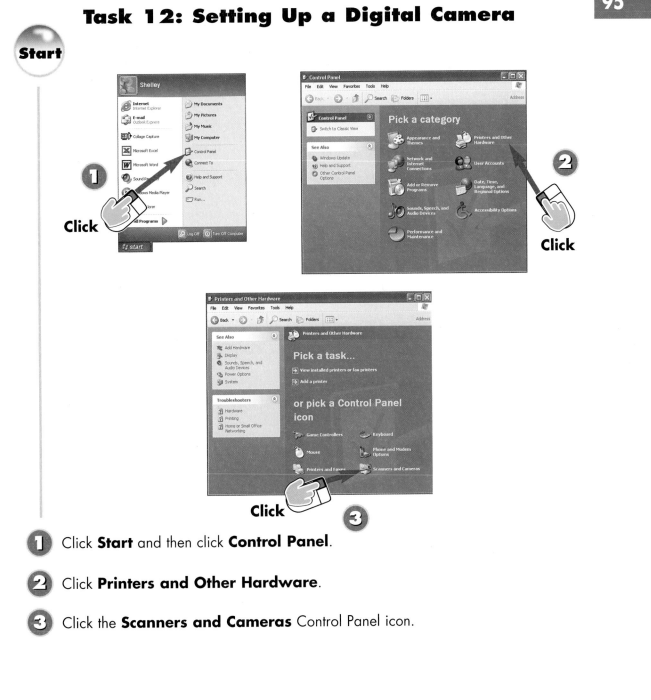

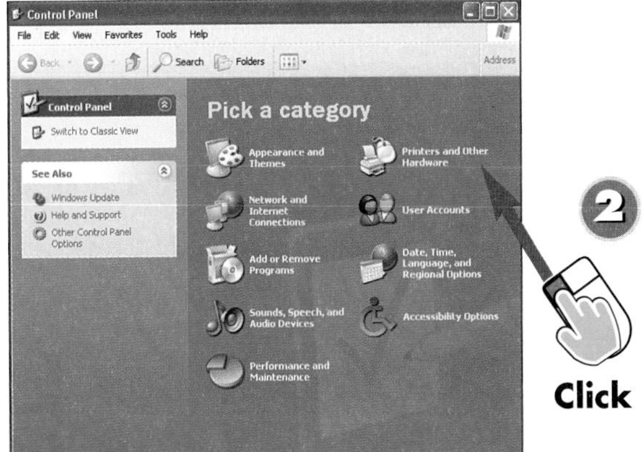

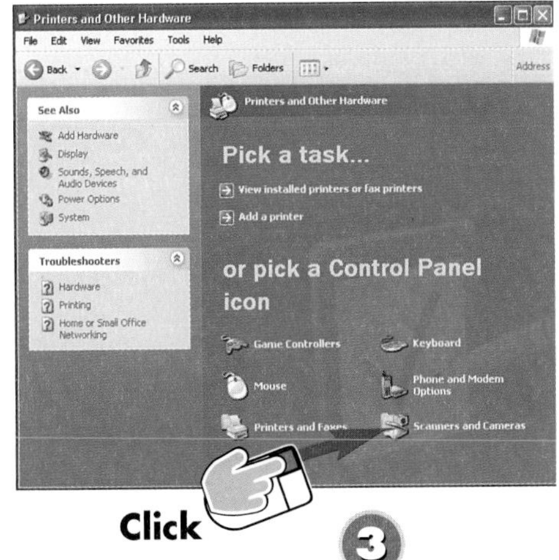

1. Click **Start** and then click **Control Panel**.
2. Click **Printers and Other Hardware**.
3. Click the **Scanners and Cameras** Control Panel icon.

INTRODUCTION

Another hardware component you may add to your system is a digital camera. You can snap pictures using this camera and then copy them from the camera's memory or media card to your computer. From your computer, you can then print, e-mail, and store the pictures. To start, you first set up your particular camera.

Setting Up a Digital Camera (Continued)

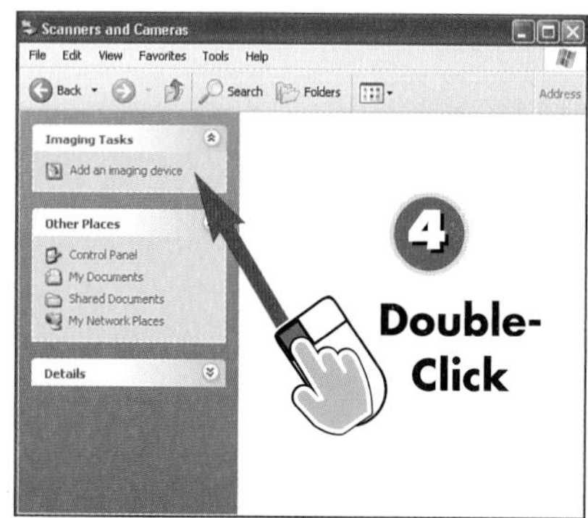

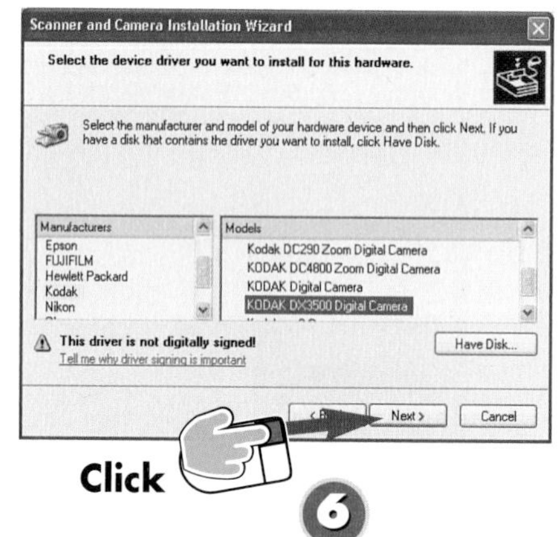

4. Double-click the **Add an imaging device** link to start the Scanner and Camera Installation Wizard.

5. Click **Next** to move from the welcome screen to the first step.

6. Select your camera manufacturer in the list on the left. Then select your particular camera from the list on the right. Click **Next**.

See next page

TIP

Automatic Installation
Before you use the wizard, try automatic installation. Connect the camera to your computer. Windows should recognize the new hardware and prompt you to install the appropriate driver. Click **OK** to install the recommended driver.

TIP

Take Pictures
The features of your camera as well as how to use that camera vary from camera to camera. Check your camera documentation to learn how to take pictures and transfer them to your PC.

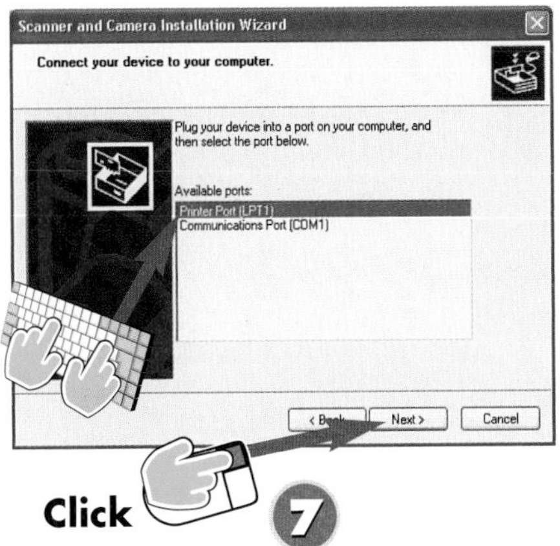

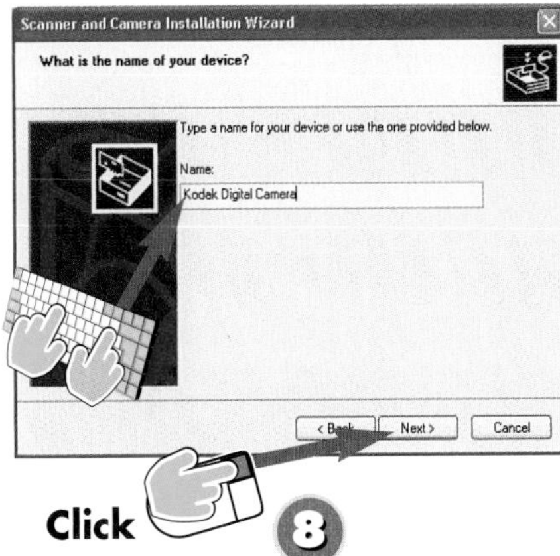

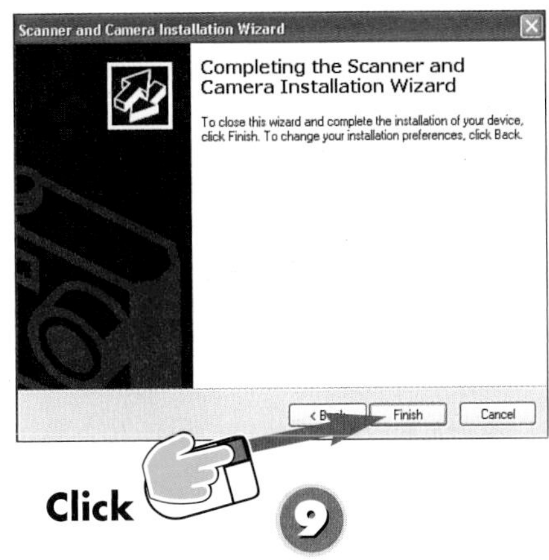

7. Select the port to which the camera is connected and click **Next**.

8. Type a name for the device and click **Next**.

9. Then click **Finish** to install the new camera and its appropriate device driver.

My Pictures Folder
Consider storing your pictures in the My Pictures folder which includes a handy Pictures Tasks list with picture-related tasks.

Task 13: Printing Photographs

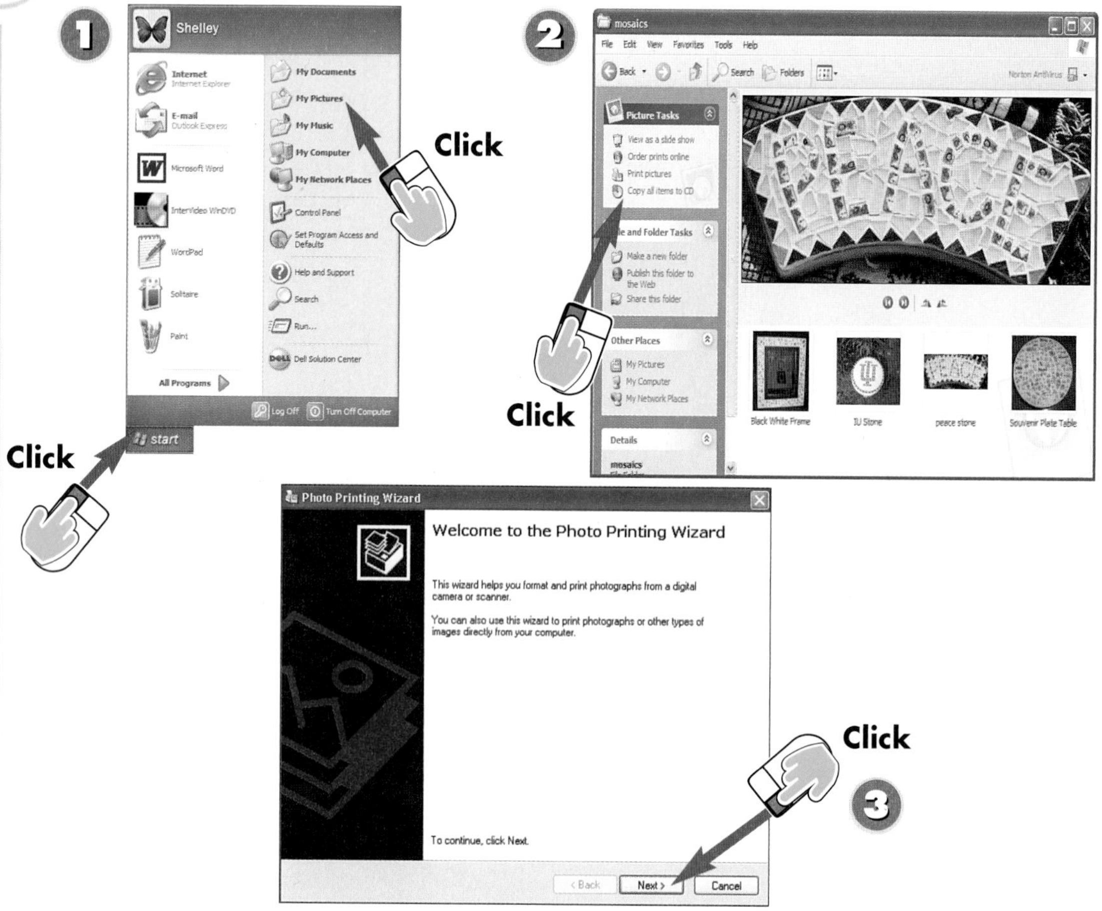

1. Click **Start** and then click **My Pictures** to open the My Pictures folder.

2. Click **Print pictures**.

3. You see the opening screen of the Photo Printing Wizard. Click **Next**.

INTRODUCTION

If a folder contains picture files, you can use the Picture Tasks list to print pictures. If you have a "regular" printer, the quality won't be great, but will be OK for some purposes. You can purchase special photo paper for the printouts. You can also purchase and use a special photograph printer.

TIP

Photo Printers

You can expect to pay from $200 to $800 or more for a special photo printer. Visit computer retail stores and check the actual printouts from various printers to choose one with an acceptable print quality.

TIP

Open Other Folders

If your pictures are stored in another folder, open that folder for step 1.

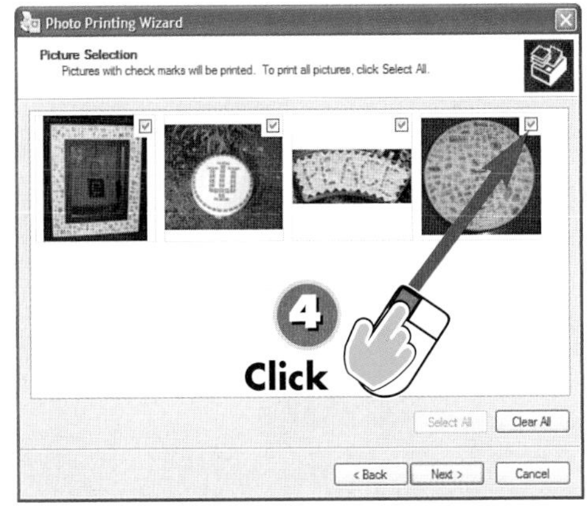

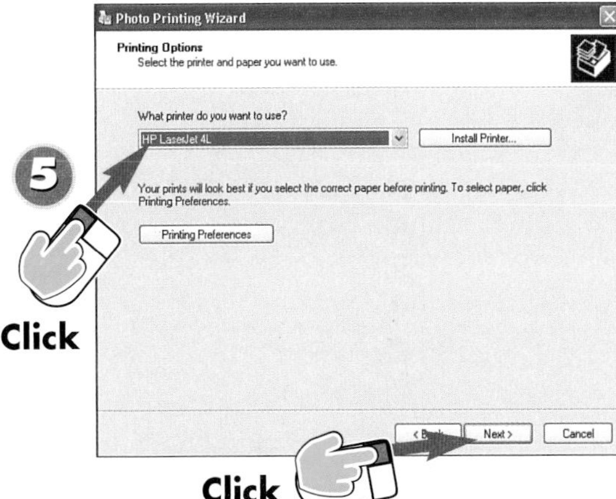

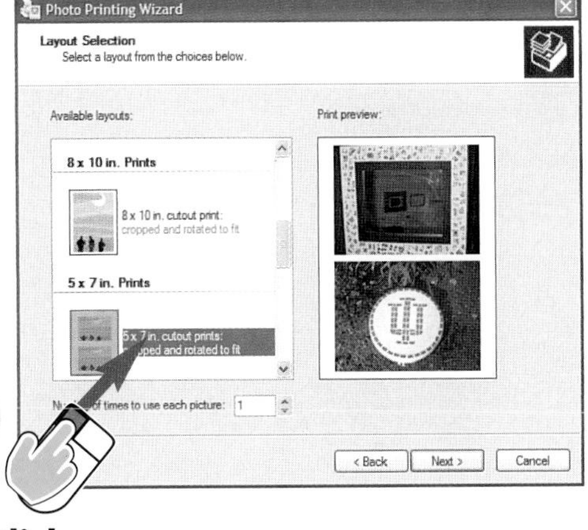

4 Select which pictures you want to print. Then click **Next**.

5 Select the printer and click **Next**.

6 Select a picture layout and click **Next**. The photos are printed.

7 Click **Finish**.

End

TIP

Email Pictures

To email pictures, click the e-mail picture link. Windows prompts you to optimize the image (which speeds sending and opening the picture). Make your selections, complete the e-mail address and message, and click **Send**.

TIP

Working with Picture Files

You can rename, delete, move, or copy picture files just like any file. See Part 4, "Working with Files," for more help on managing files.

TIP

Transfer Pictures

You can transfer pictures from the camera to your computer using the software that came with the camera or with Windows XP's.

Task 14: Ordering Photo Prints from the Internet

Start

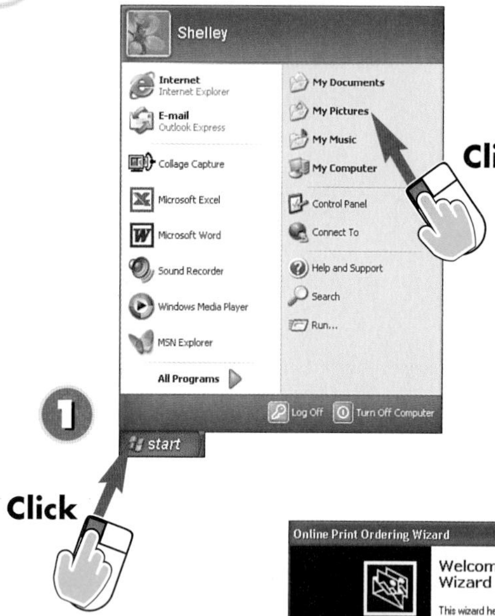

1. Click **Start** and then click **My Pictures** to open the My Pictures folder.

2. Click **Order prints online**.

3. You see the opening screen of the Online Print Ordering Wizard. Click **Next**.

INTRODUCTION

You can also select to order photo shop quality prints from the Internet. Windows XP includes a wizard that leads you step-by-step through the process of ordering prints.

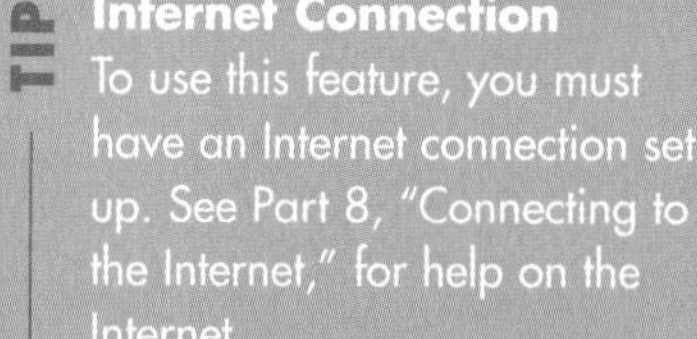

TIP

Internet Connection

To use this feature, you must have an Internet connection set up. See Part 8, "Connecting to the Internet," for help on the Internet.

TIP

Open Other Folders

If your pictures are stored in another folder, open that folder for step 1.

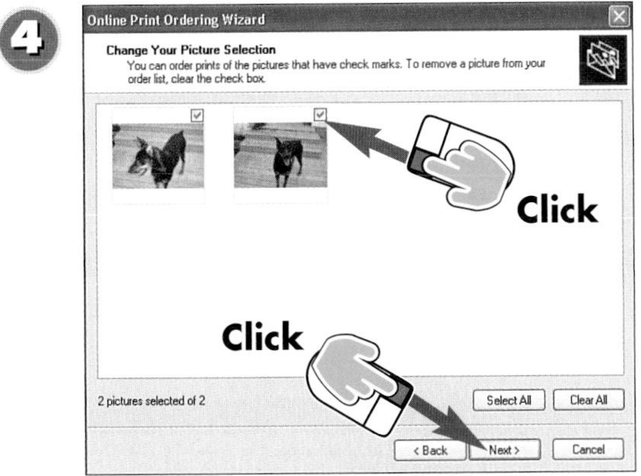

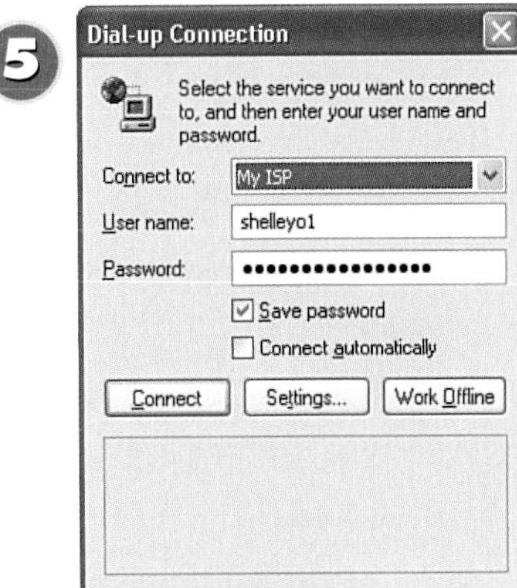

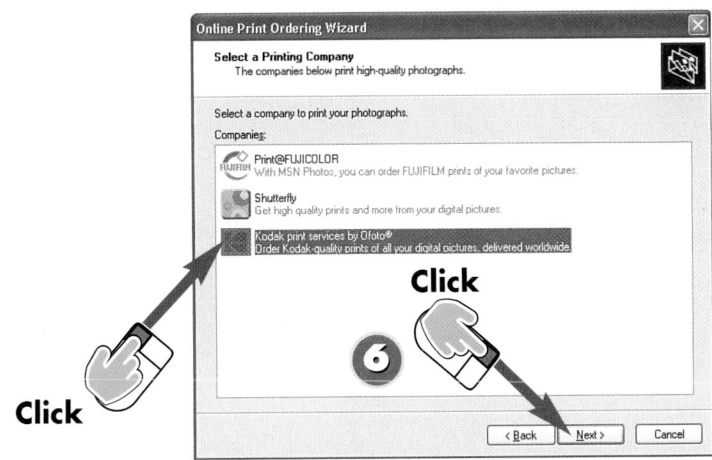

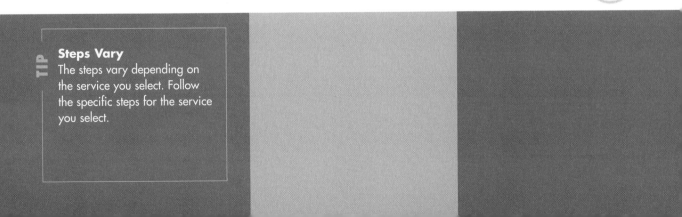

4. Select the pictures you want to order and click **Next**.

5. You are prompted to connect to the Internet. Follow the appropriate steps to log on.

6. Select a printing company and click **Next**.

See next page

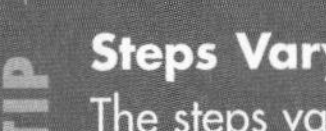

TIP

Steps Vary
The steps vary depending on the service you select. Follow the specific steps for the service you select.

Ordering Photo Prints from the Internet (Continued)

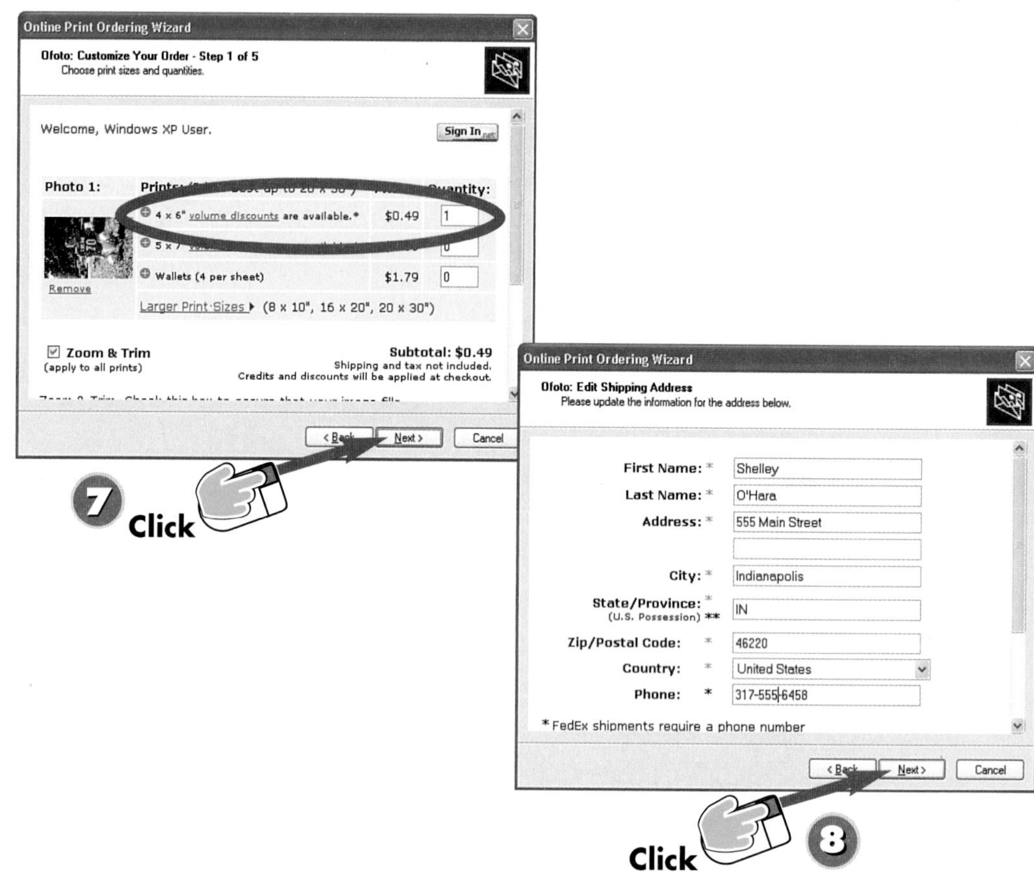

7. Select the size and quantity for each print. Click **Next**.
8. Complete any additional information, clicking **Next**. For instance, you usually are prompted to enter the shipping address.

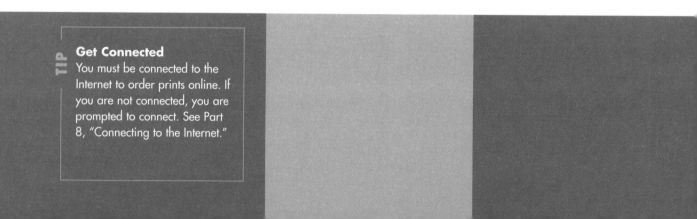

TIP

Get Connected

You must be connected to the Internet to order prints online. If you are not connected, you are prompted to connect. See Part 8, "Connecting to the Internet."

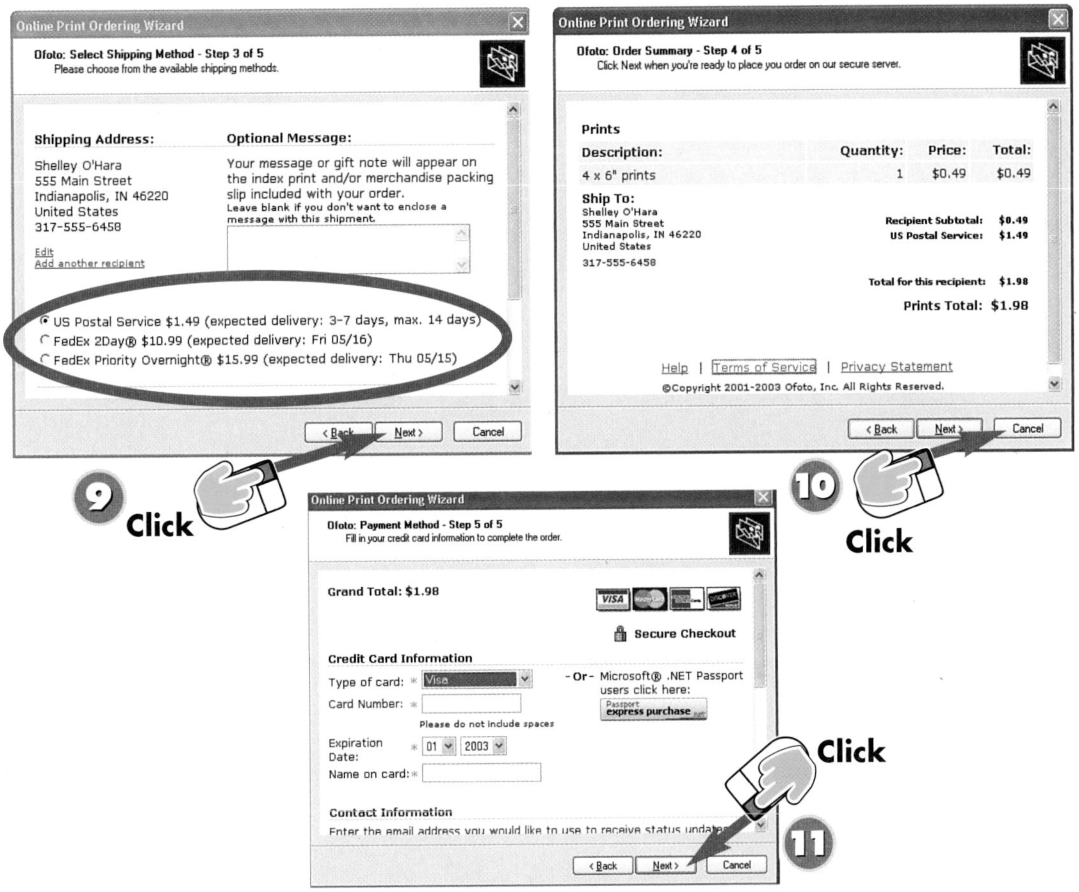

9 Click

10 Click

11 Click

9 Complete any additional steps as prompted. For instance, select a shipping method.

10 You may see an order summary to check before placing the order.

11 Complete billing information by clicking **Next**. Files are copied and sent to printing company.

Cost
Before you order the prints, you see the pricing information for printing. You must also pay shipping and handling. You see the grand total and can cancel at any time by clicking **Cancel**.

Task 15: Copy Pictures to CD

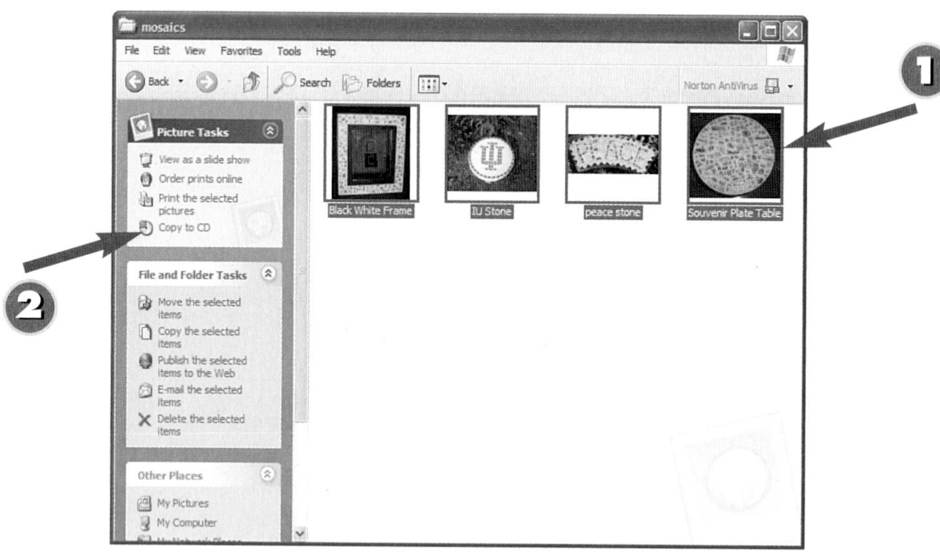

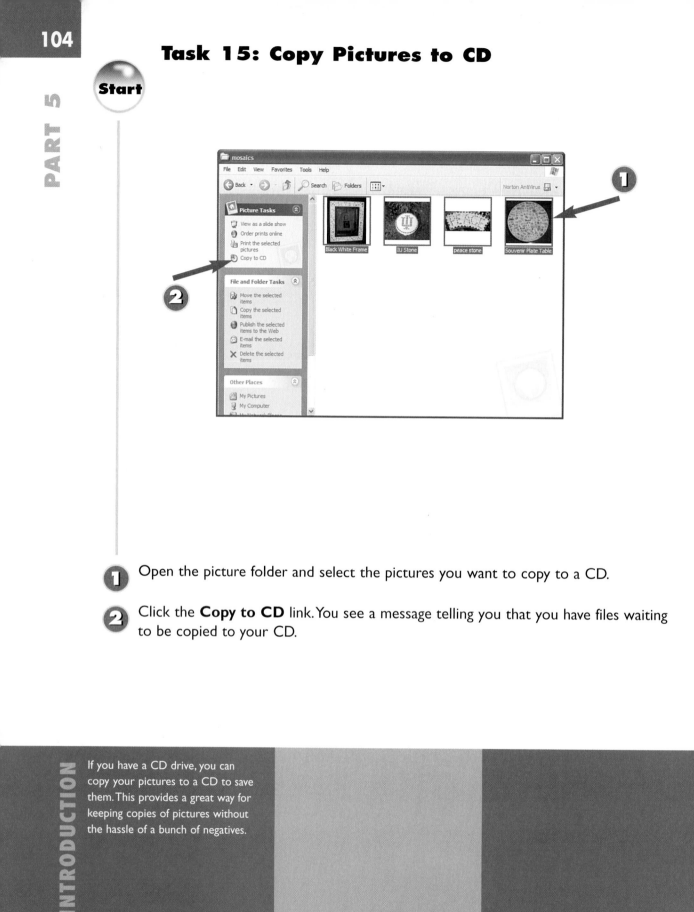

1. Open the picture folder and select the pictures you want to copy to a CD.
2. Click the **Copy to CD** link. You see a message telling you that you have files waiting to be copied to your CD.

INTRODUCTION

If you have a CD drive, you can copy your pictures to a CD to save them. This provides a great way for keeping copies of pictures without the hassle of a bunch of negatives.

Click

Double-click

Click

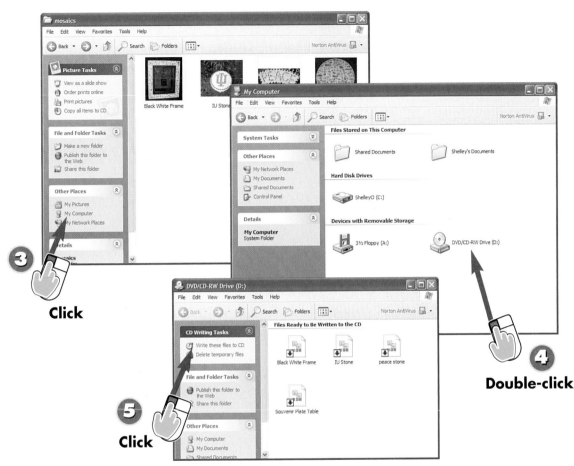

3 Click **My Computer** in the Other Places area in the taskbar.

4 Double-click the CD drive.

5 You see the files that are ready to be written. Click **Write these files to CD**. The files are copied to your CD drive.

TIP

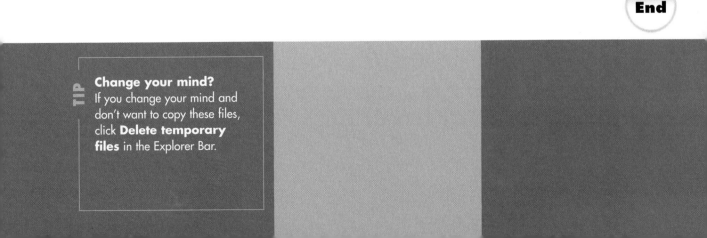

Change your mind?
If you change your mind and don't want to copy these files, click **Delete temporary files** in the Explorer Bar.

PART 6

Entertainment

Computers are not all work and no fun. Windows XP includes entertainment programs for playing CDs, viewing multimedia files, and recording and playing back sounds. You'll also find a new program for creating and editing movies.

Tasks

Task 1: Playing Games

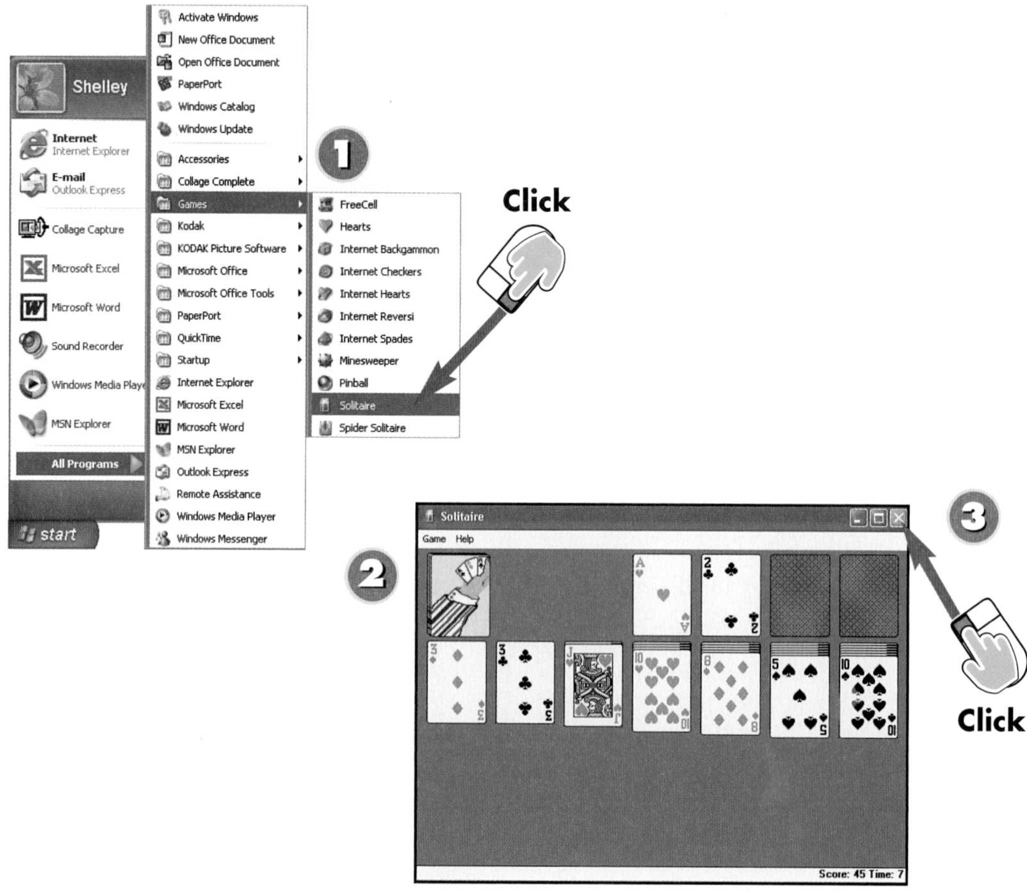

1. Click **Start**, **All Programs**, **Games**, and then click the name of the game you want to open (in this case, **Solitaire**).
2. Play the game.
3. When you are finished, click the **Close** button to exit.

INTRODUCTION

Windows provides several games that you can play to break up your work-day with a little entertainment. Use any of the games to fill a lunch hour or coffee break and to ease the tensions of the day. Playing games is also a good way to help you get the hang of using the mouse. For example, playing Solitaire can help you practice such mouse skills as clicking, dragging, and so on.

TIP

Get Help

If you aren't sure how to play a game, get instructions using the online help. Open the **Help** menu and select the **Help** command.

Task 2: Changing the Volume

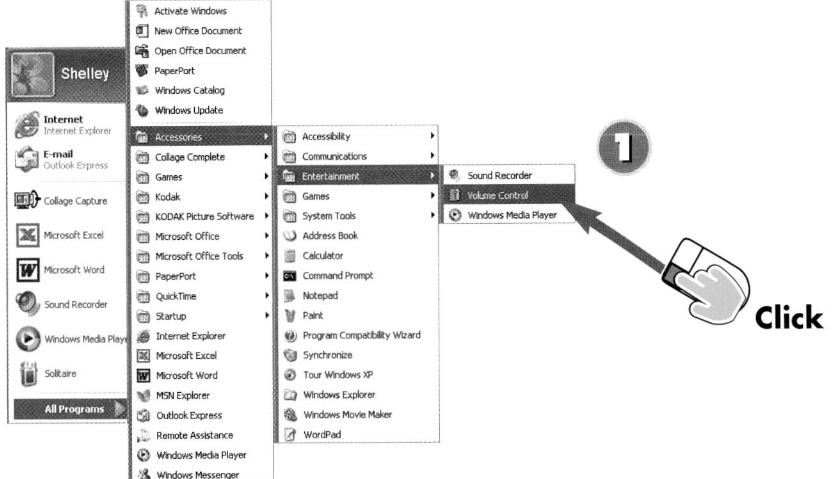

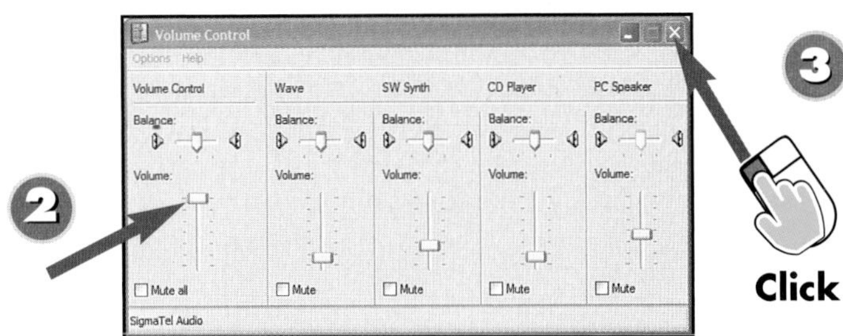

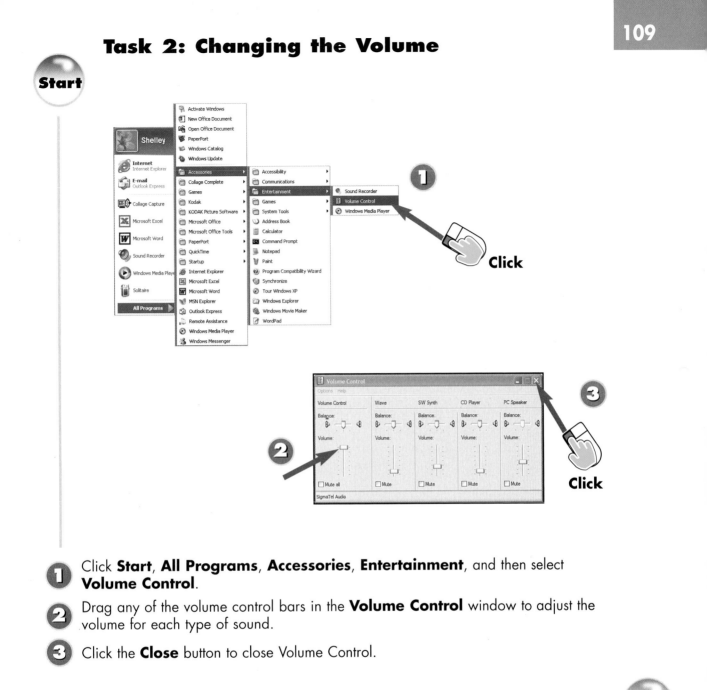

1. Click **Start**, **All Programs**, **Accessories**, **Entertainment**, and then select **Volume Control**.
2. Drag any of the volume control bars in the **Volume Control** window to adjust the volume for each type of sound.
3. Click the **Close** button to close Volume Control.

INTRODUCTION

If the sound on your PC is too loud or too quiet, you can adjust the volume. To do so, use Volume Control. This feature enables you to set the volume for several types of audio input and output devices.

TIP

Speaker Volume
You might also have a volume control on your speakers or on your keyboard. You can also use these to adjust the sound.

TIP

Double-Click Icon
To display the Volume Control panel, you can also double-click the **Speaker** icon in the taskbar.

Task 3: Playing a Sound with Sound Recorder

Start

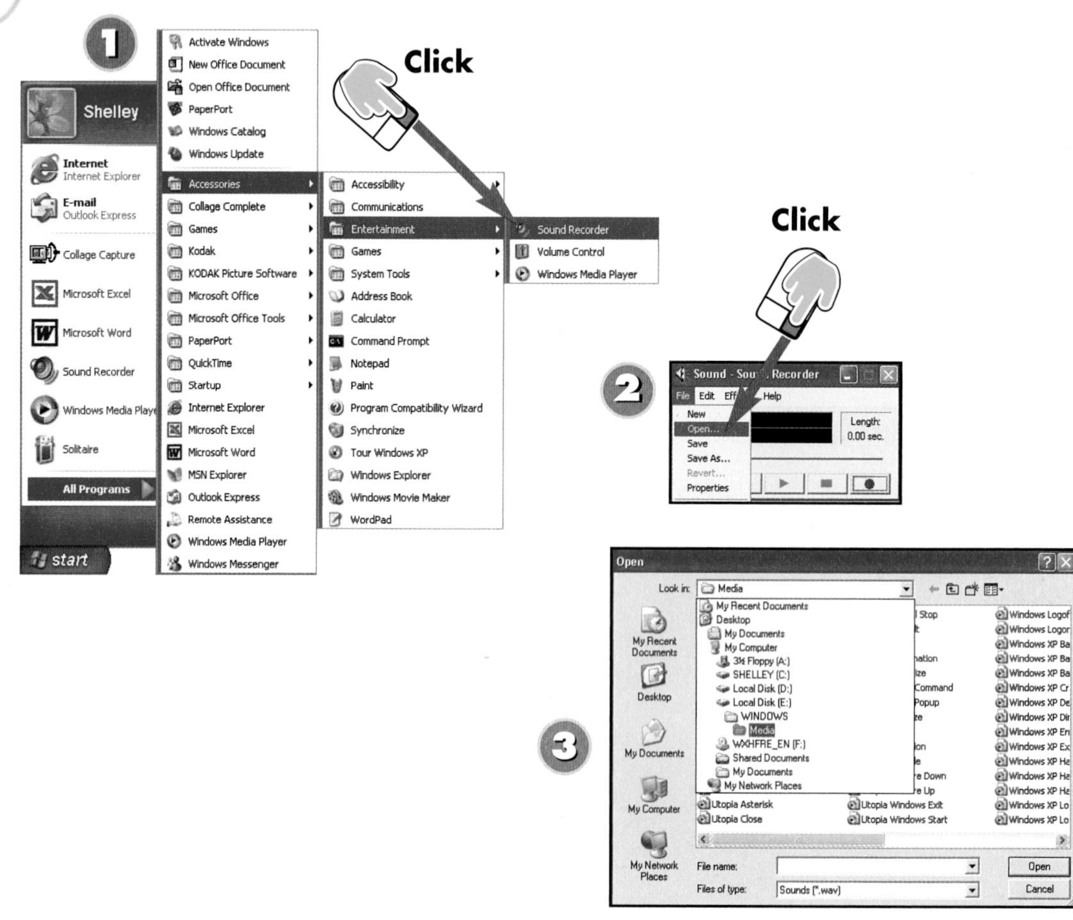

1. Click **Start**, **All Programs**, **Accessories**, **Entertainment**, and then select **Sound Recorder**.
2. The Sound Recorder window appears. Click the **File** menu, and then choose **Open**.
3. From the Look in drop-down list, select a folder that contains sound files. (To sample one of the Windows sounds, select the **Windows\Media** folder.)

INTRODUCTION

You can use the Sound Recorder to play back and record sounds. You can record your own sounds and insert the sound files into your documents for clarification or interest. You can play back any of the sound files on your computer. To use Sound Recorder, you need a sound card and speakers, which are standard on nearly all newer computers.

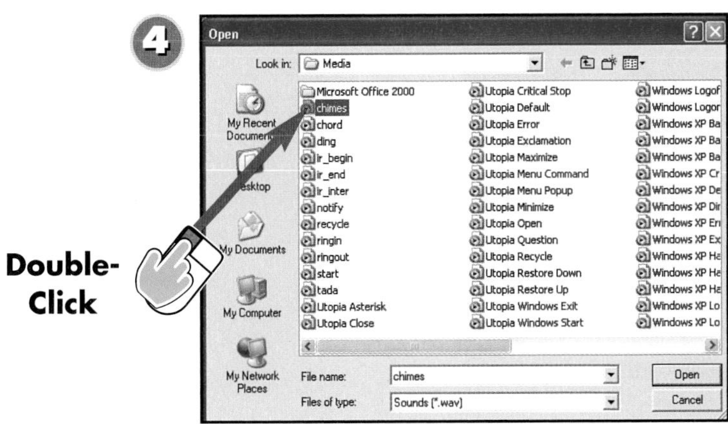

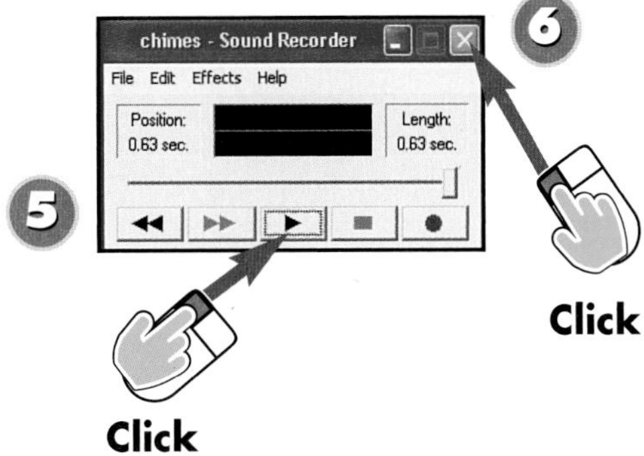

4. Double-click the sound file you want to play.

5. Click the **Play** button to hear the file.

6. When finished, click the **Close** button to close the Sound Recorder window.

TIP

Record a Sound
You can record sounds using Sound Recorder. To do so, you must have an audio input device (microphone) attached to your PC. Click **File**, choose **New**, and then click the **Record** button and record your sound. To stop recording, click the **Stop** button. To save your sound, click **File**, and then choose **Save As**.

TIP

Can't Hear?
If you cannot hear the sound, try adjusting the volume on your speakers or on your keyboard.

Task 4: Playing an Audio CD

1. Insert the CD into the drive. It starts CD Player automatically, and the CD starts playing automatically.

2. To play a different track, double-click it in the track list. The song is played.

INTRODUCTION

In addition to being able to play back sound files, you can play audio CDs using Windows Media Player, enabling you to listen to the background music of your choice as you work. Note that the quality of the playback is determined by the quality of your speakers. Don't expect stereo quality.

TIP

Didn't Start?
If CD Player didn't start automatically, click **Start**, **All Programs**, **Accessories**, and then **Entertainment**. Finally, click **Windows Media Player**.

Start

Task 5: Working with Media Player Controls

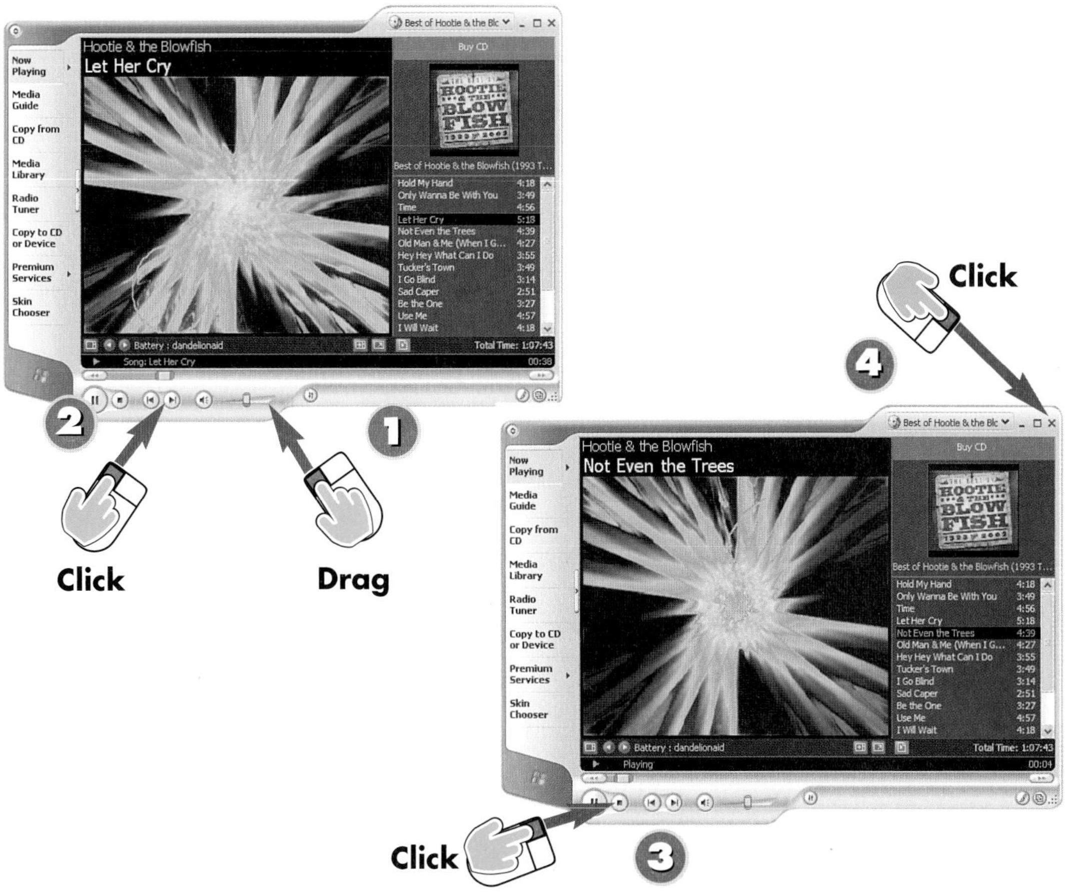

1. To change the volume, drag the volume control.
2. To play a different track, click the **Previous** or **Next** buttons.
3. To stop the playback, click **Stop**.
4. When you're finished, click the **Close** button to close the Media Player window.

INTRODUCTION

When you are listening to your CD, you can use any of the control buttons in the Media Player window to adjust the song, choose a different visualization (moving image), or move to another track.

TIP

Minimized Window
If you don't want the window displayed, but want to listen to the music, minimize the **Media Player** window.

Task 6: Changing the Visualizations

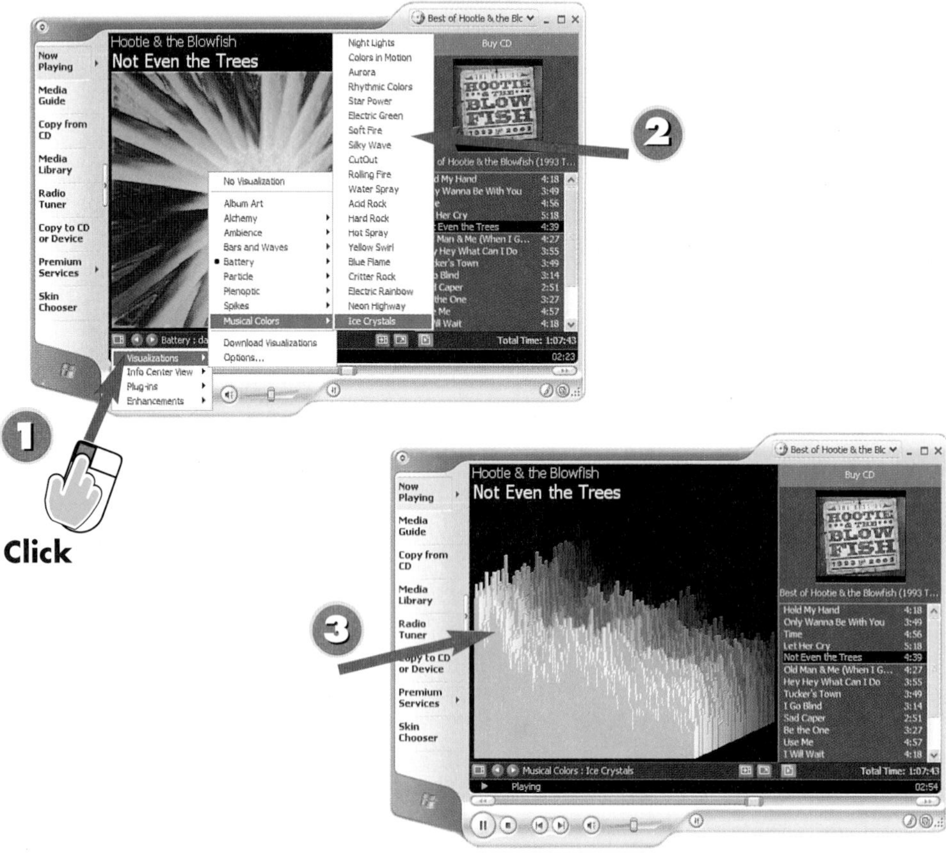

1. To select another style, click the **Select Now Playing Options**, click **Visualizaion**, and click a type.
2. Click the style you want to use.
3. You see the new visualization.

INTRODUCTION

If you like to view a visualization with your music, you can select from several different styles. The visualization only appears in the Now Playing view.

TIP

Use Buttons

Use the **Next visualization** or **Previous visualization** buttons to select a visualization in that style.

Task 7: Copying CD Tracks

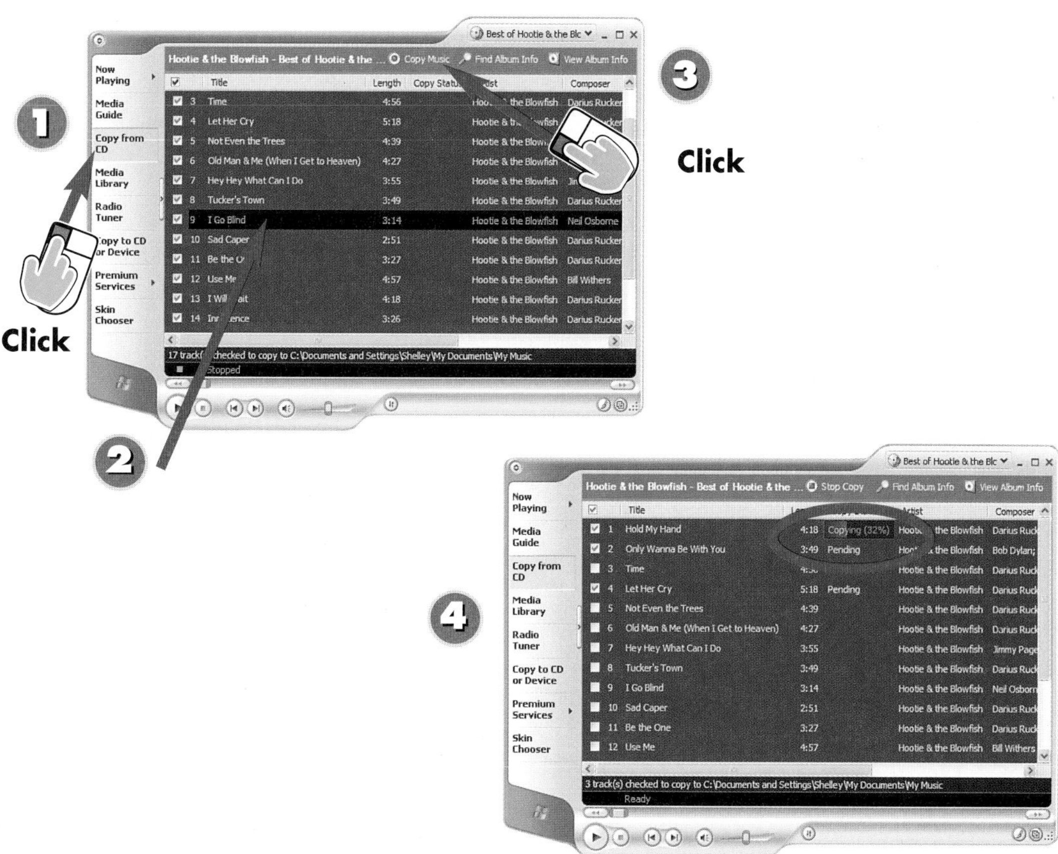

1. Click **Copy from CD**.
2. Check the tracks you want to copy.
3. Click the **Copy Music** button.
4. You see the status of the copy. The copies are displayed in the Media Library and stored in the My Music folder.

INTRODUCTION

You can copy tracks from a CD to your computer. You can then playback the song from the computer rather than the audio CD.

TIP

Copy Protection

When copying audio files, be sure you understand the legal ramifications of copyright protection. The first time you select to copy, you see a warning dialog box. Click **OK** after reviewing this information.

TIP

Copy to CD

You can copy song tracks from your computer to a CD disk or media player if you have one of these devices. Use the Copy to CD or Device button.

Task 8: Using the Media Library

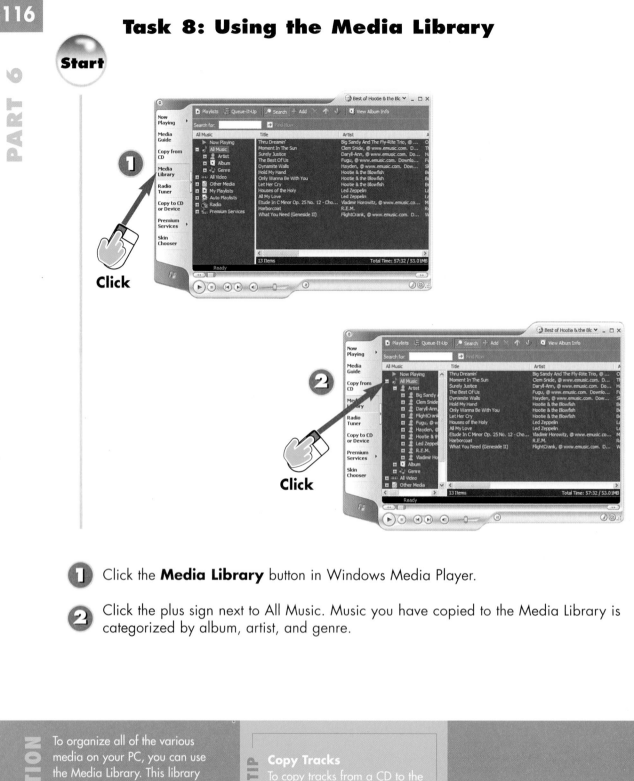

1. Click the **Media Library** button in Windows Media Player.
2. Click the plus sign next to All Music. Music you have copied to the Media Library is categorized by album, artist, and genre.

INTRODUCTION

To organize all of the various media on your PC, you can use the Media Library. This library stores music and videos by several different methods so that you can find a particular file for playback.

TIP

Copy Tracks
To copy tracks from a CD to the Media Library, refer to Task 7 "Copying CD Tracks."

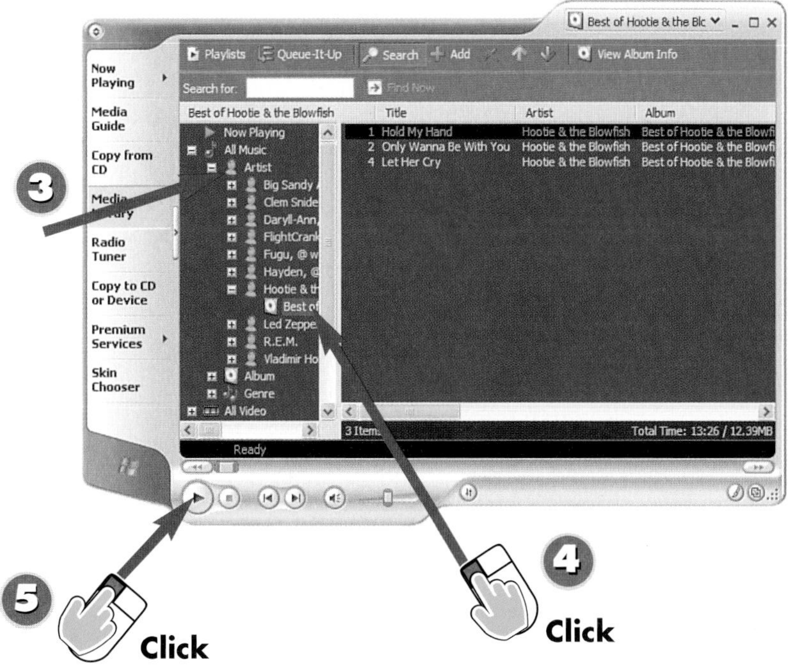

3 Expand the category until you see the song you want to play. For instance, you can expand the Artist category and then select the artist you want.

4 Select the album you want.

5 You see the songs you have copied. Select the song you want to play in the track list. Click the **Play** button. The song is played.

TIP

Search for a Track

If you use the Media Library to store several files, finding the one you want by browsing through the categories may be difficult. To search for a file, click **Search**. Type the word or phrase to find and click **Search**. To display any matches click **View Results**. The matches are listed in the right pane.

TIP

Store Videos

You can also use the Media Library to store and play video files. To display available video files, click the plus sign next to All Video. Then select any of the categories to display the video clips you have stored. See Task 12 "Playing a Video Clip."

Task 9: Creating a Playlist

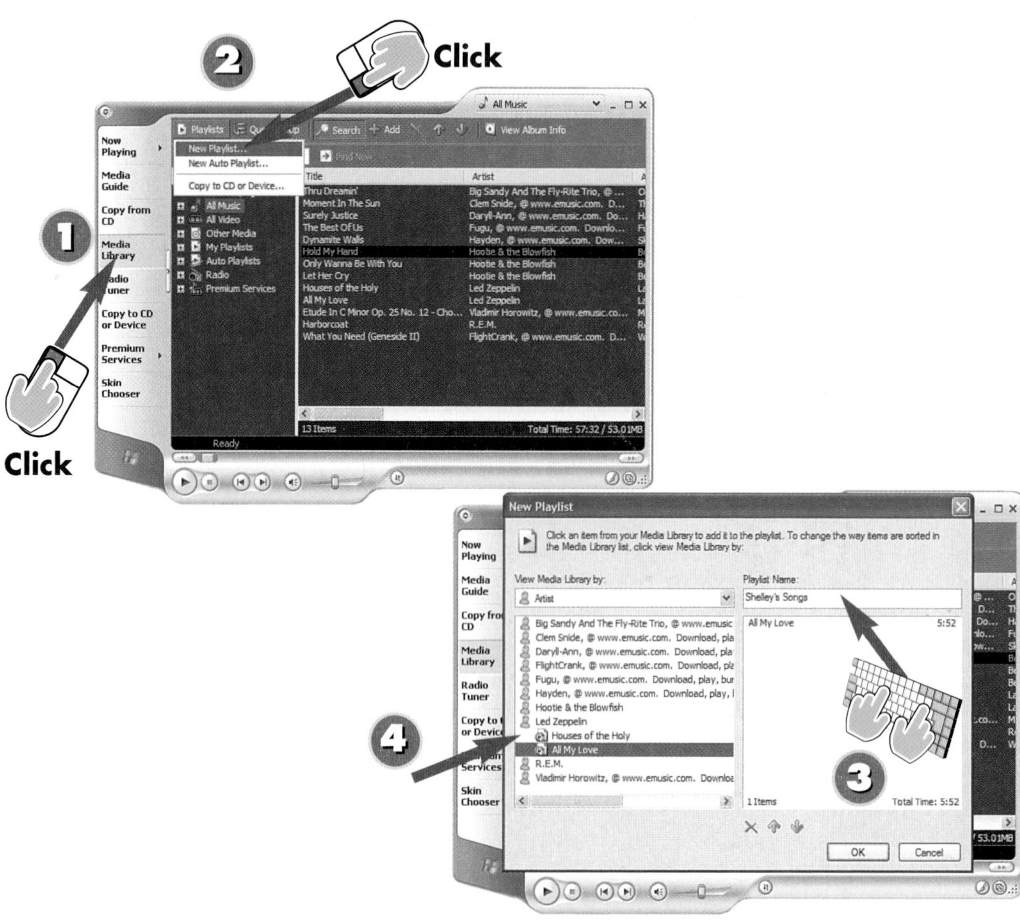

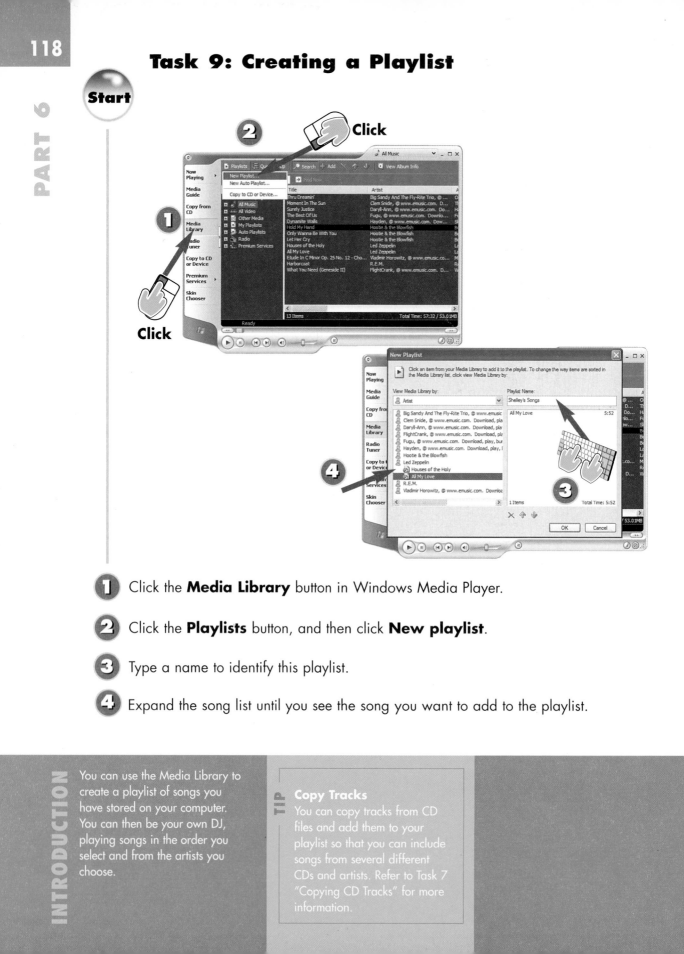

1. Click the **Media Library** button in Windows Media Player.
2. Click the **Playlists** button, and then click **New playlist**.
3. Type a name to identify this playlist.
4. Expand the song list until you see the song you want to add to the playlist.

INTRODUCTION

You can use the Media Library to create a playlist of songs you have stored on your computer. You can then be your own DJ, playing songs in the order you select and from the artists you choose.

TIP

Copy Tracks

You can copy tracks from CD files and add them to your playlist so that you can include songs from several different CDs and artists. Refer to Task 7 "Copying CD Tracks" for more information.

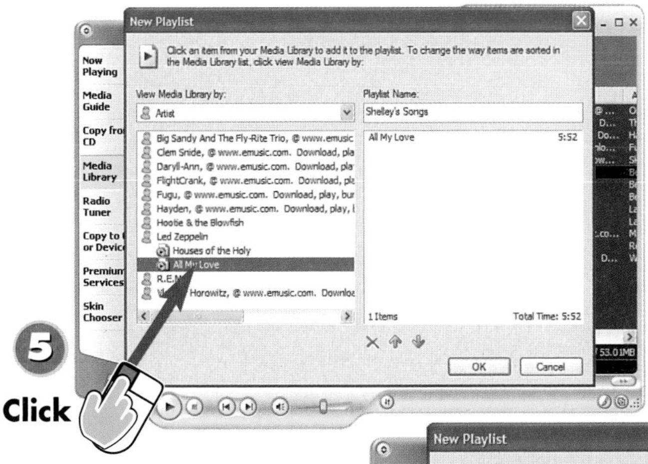

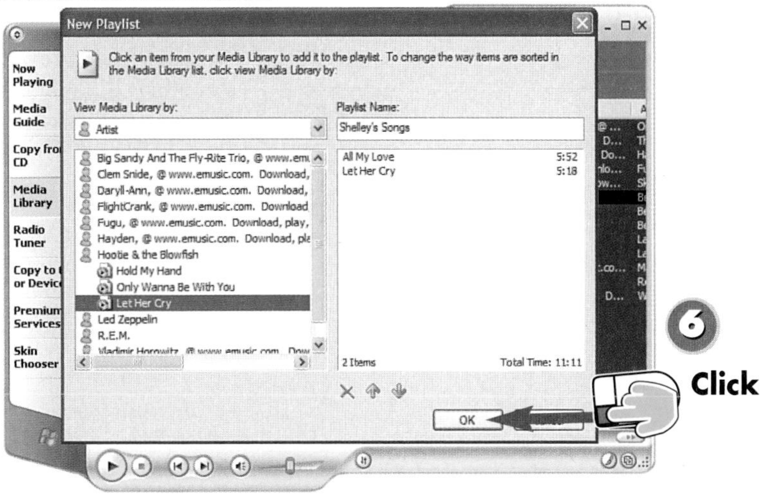

5 Click

6 Click

5 Select the song to add it to the playlist. Do this for all the songs you want to add.

6 Click **OK**.

7 The playlist is added to the Media Library.

TIP

Edit the Playlist

To edit the playlist, select it in the My Playlists category. You can then delete songs by selecting them and clicking the **Delete** button. To rearrange the songs, use the **Move up** or **Move down** buttons.

TIP

Delete a Playlist

To delete a playlist, select it in the list and then click the down arrow next to the **Delete** button and select **Delete Playlist**.

Task 10: Find Music Online

1. Click the **Media Guide** button. Windows Media Player displays the WindowsMedia.com page.
2. Click any of the links to browse for music, videos, or information. For example, you can click **Artists A-Z** to view a list of featured artists.
3. You go to that page. You can continue clicking links to view, play, or download music.

End

INTRODUCTION

You can visit online music sites to sample and even purchase music. You can download songs from a site to your computer. From there, you can copy the songs to a CD. Windows Media Player takes you to its music site. From here, you can use links to browse content and music selections or search for music. To do this, you must be connected to the Internet.

TIP

Navigate with Buttons

You can use the toolbar buttons to navigate backward and forward through the pages you have displayed. You can also select specific media content by clicking Music, Movies, Radio, Entertainment, or Current Events.

Task 11: Changing the Skin for Windows Media Player

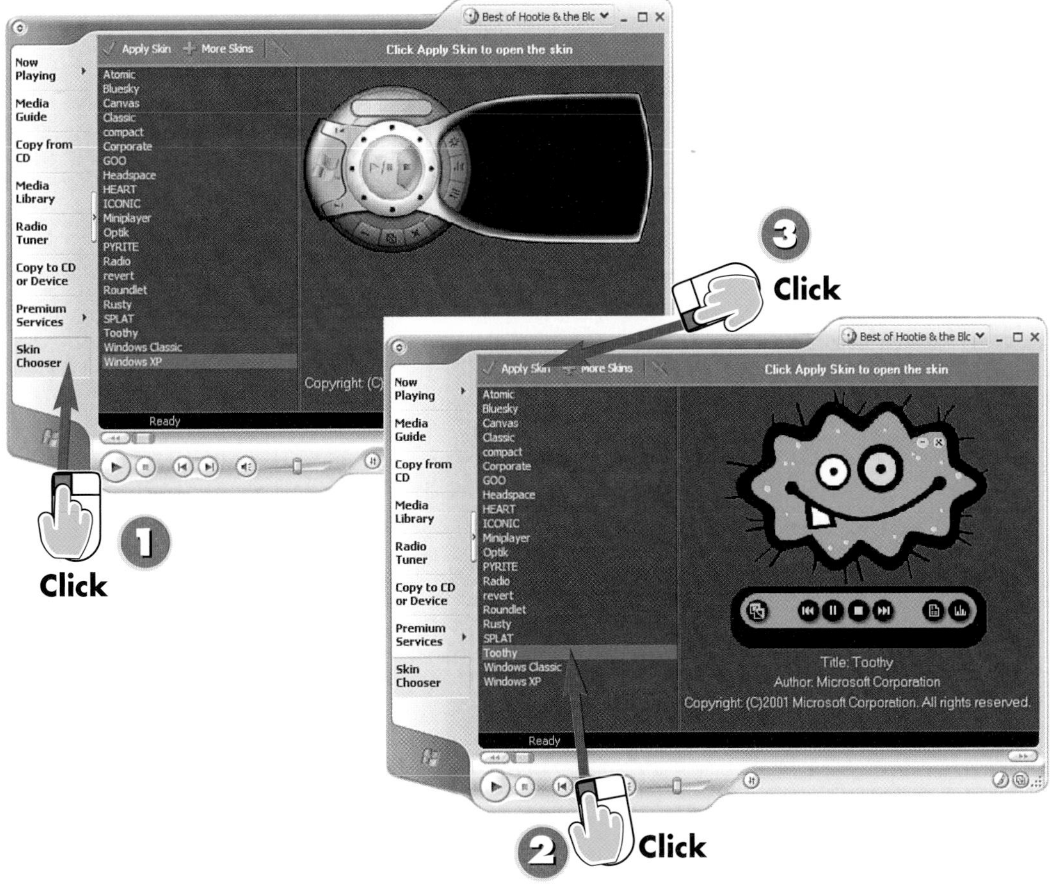

1. Click the **Skin Chooser** button in Windows Media Player. You see a list of the available skins.

2. Select the skin you want to apply. You see a preview.

3. Click the **Apply Skin** button. The skin is applied.

INTRODUCTION

You can change the look of the Windows Media Player, selecting from various *skins*. A skin is like a costume you put over the player interface to change how it looks. You can select from several predesigned skins.

TIP

Return to Full Screen

To go back to the full screen (regular Windows Media Player), click the **Return to Full Mode** button. The button will appear differently depending on the skin. Put the pointer over each of the buttons to pop up the name of the button.

Task 12: Playing a Video Clip

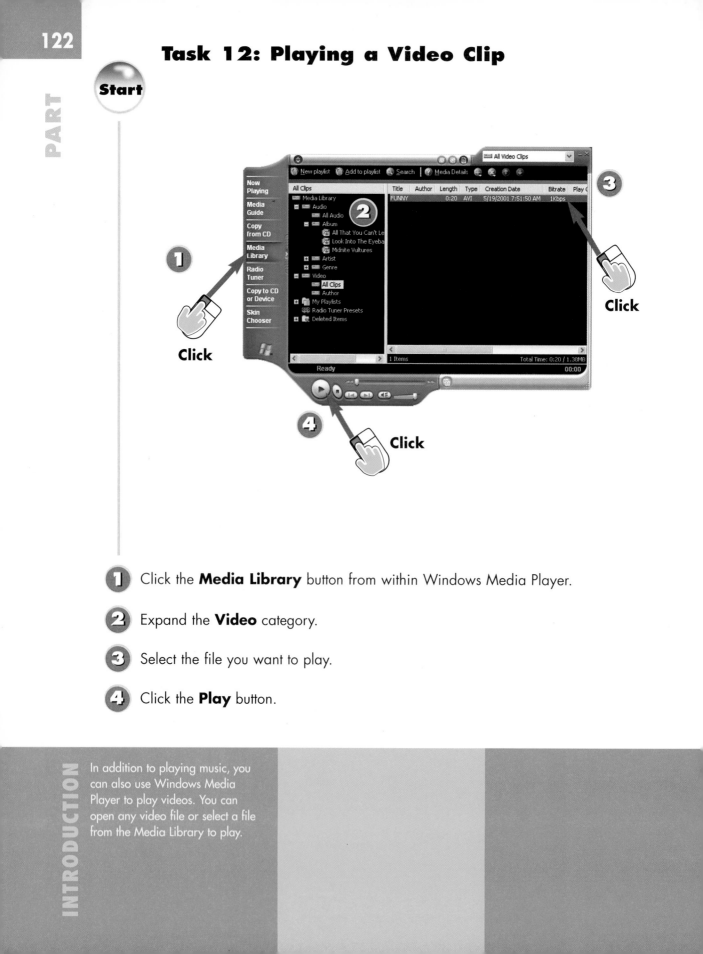

1. Click the **Media Library** button from within Windows Media Player.
2. Expand the **Video** category.
3. Select the file you want to play.
4. Click the **Play** button.

INTRODUCTION

In addition to playing music, you can also use Windows Media Player to play videos. You can open any video file or select a file from the Media Library to play.

5 The video is played.

6 Click the **Close** button to close Windows Media Player.

TIP

View Online Video Clips
You can also find video clips for viewing at many Web sites. For instance, many movie trailers can be viewed online. Select the video clip to playback and then either open it to play it or save it to your hard disk for playback.

Task 13: Importing a Movie with Windows Movie Maker

Start

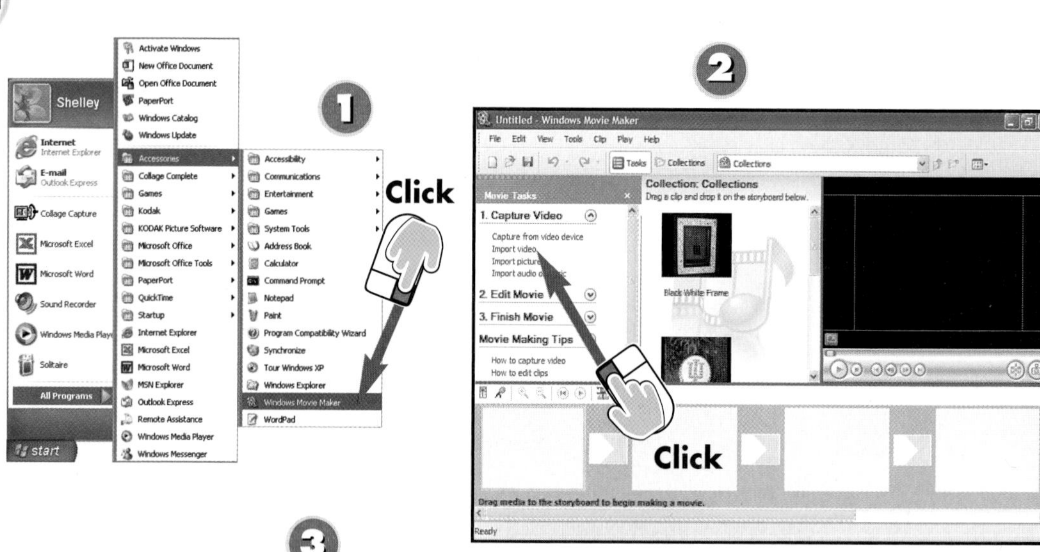

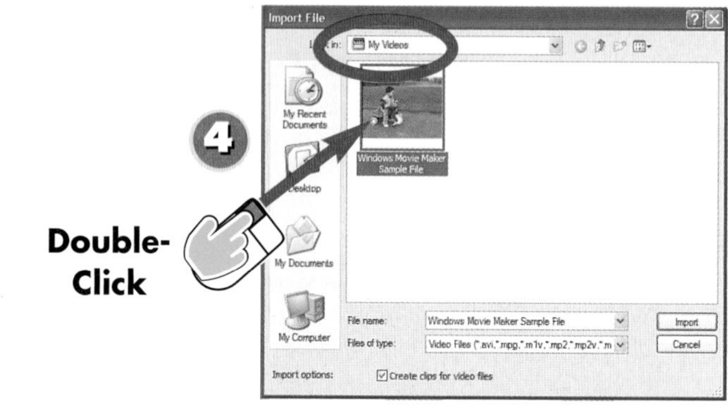

1. Click **Start**, **All Programs**, **Accessories**, and then click the **Windows Movie Maker**.
2. The Windows Movie Maker window appears. Click **Import Video**.
3. Open the folder that contains the movie file.
4. Double-click the file to import.

INTRODUCTION

New with Windows XP is Windows Movie Maker. You can use this accessory program to view and edit movies. To create your own movies, you need a camera capable of recording digital videos. You can then download the video clip from your camera to your computer and use Windows Movie Maker to view and edit it. You can also import other videos or music to use in Windows Movie Maker.

TIP

Record a Movie

You can also record a movie if the video camera is connected to the PC. Use the **File**, **Record** command. Or click the **Record** button. Check your specific video camera for information on connecting the camera and recording movies.

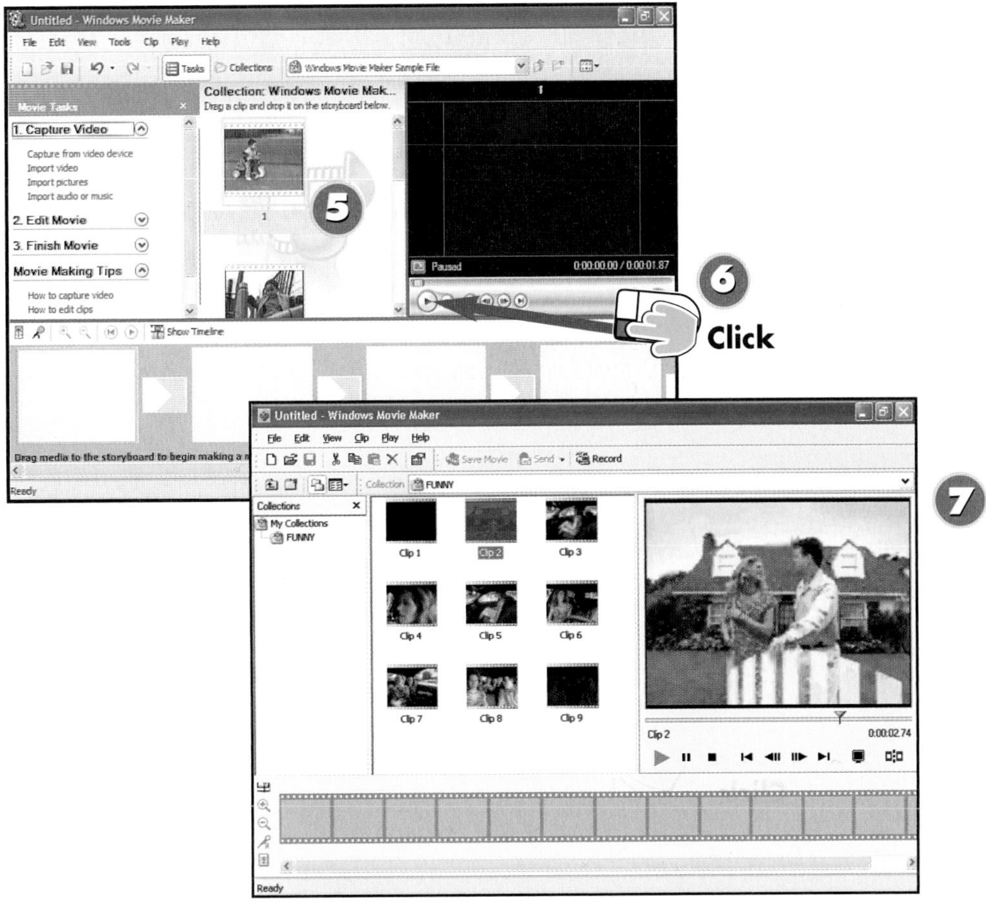

5 You see the clips for this movie file.

6 To play a clip, select it and click **Play**.

7 The clip is played in the preview area.

TIP

Video Clips

When you record or import a movie, Windows Movie Maker divides into separate clips. You can then work with these clips to arrange the sequence of the movie.

TIP

Toolbar Buttons

Use the playback toolbar buttons to pause, stop, and restart the playback of the clip. You can also advance the clip frame by frame by clicking the **Next Frame** and **Previous Frame** buttons.

PART 7

Sending Faxes and Email

Having a PC provides several ways for you to stay in contact. Most PCs include a modem or a fax modem. With a fax modem, you can use the Windows XP accessories programs to send and receive faxes.

With a regular modem or a fax modem and an Internet mail provider, you can send and receive e-mail. To handle this type of correspondence, you can use the mail program, Outlook Express, included with Windows XP. Note that you do not use Outlook Express for faxing.

Tasks

Task 1: Sending a Fax

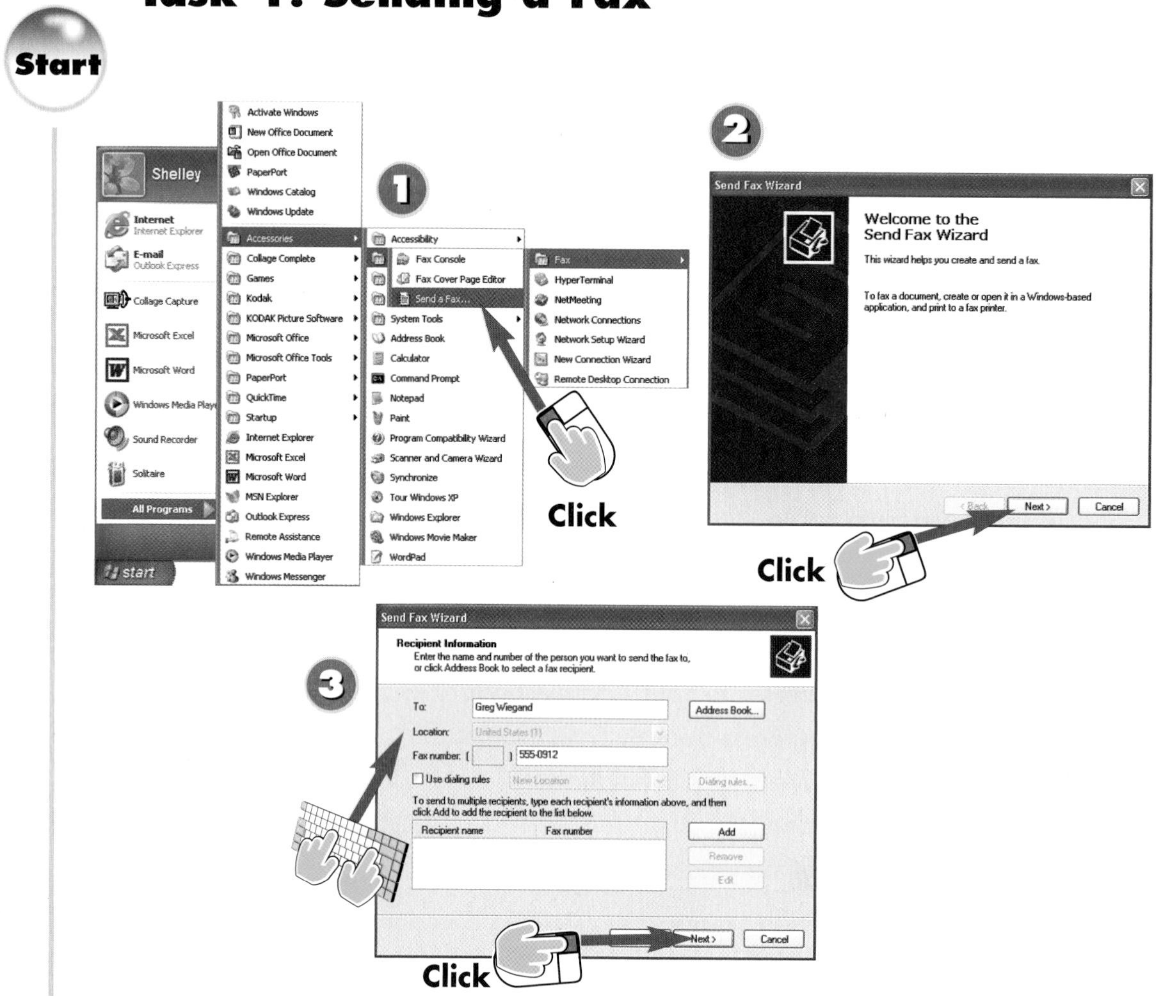

Start

1. Click **Start**, **All Programs**, **Accessories**, **Communications**, **Fax**, and finally **Send a Fax**.

2. Click **Next** to move from the welcome screen to the first step.

3. Enter the name and fax number of the recipient. Click **Next**.

INTRODUCTION

To help you send a fax, Windows XP provides a Fax Send Wizard that leads you through the step of creating and sending a fax cover page. You can also fax documents created in Windows programs by "printing" to the fax; the program will use the fax modem you have set up with the configuration wizard.

TIP

Set Up Fax
To use Windows XP to send a fax, you must configure your fax. If you have a fax modem, Windows should find and set up the hardware. Also, the fax software should be installed. If the fax program is not installed, you can add it. See Part 11, "Setting Up Programs." If you need to change or update the fax configuration, you can do so using the Fax Configuration Wizard. You can start this from the Fax Console, covered in the next task.

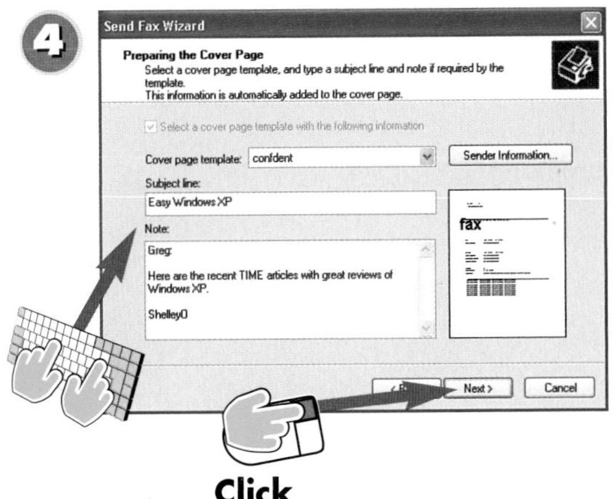

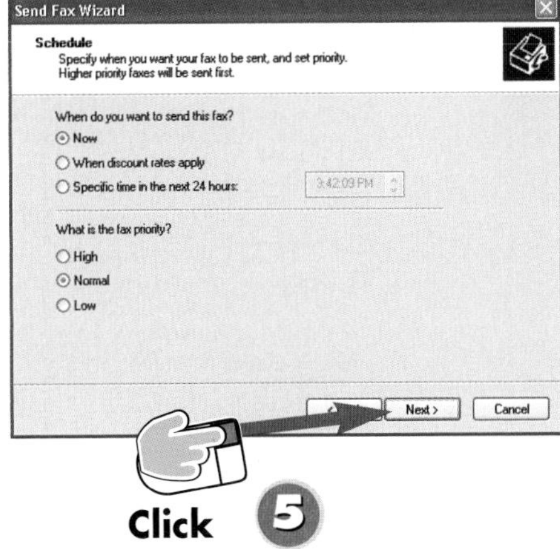

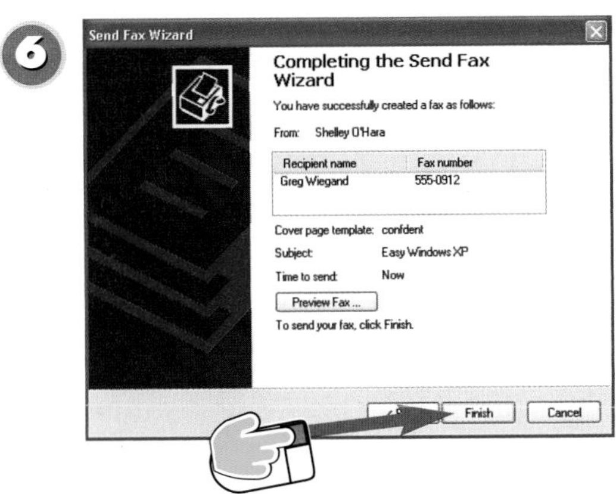

4. Type a subject and the note for the fax cover sheet. Click **Next**.
5. Select when to send the fax and click **Next**.
6. Click **Finish**. The fax is sent at the time you selected for step 5.

TIP

Cover Page Template
You can select from several cover page templates. To select a different template, display the Cover page template drop-down list (see step 4) and select the template to use.

TIP

First Time?
The first time you select this command you are prompted to set up fax and dialing rules. Follow the steps, making choices and clicking **Next**.

TIP

Fax a Document
To fax a document, open the document and then select **File**, **Print**. In the Print dialog box, select **Fax** for the printer. Complete the recipient and other information, clicking **Next** to complete each step in the fax wizard. The document is then faxed to that recipient.

Task 2: Receiving and Viewing Faxes

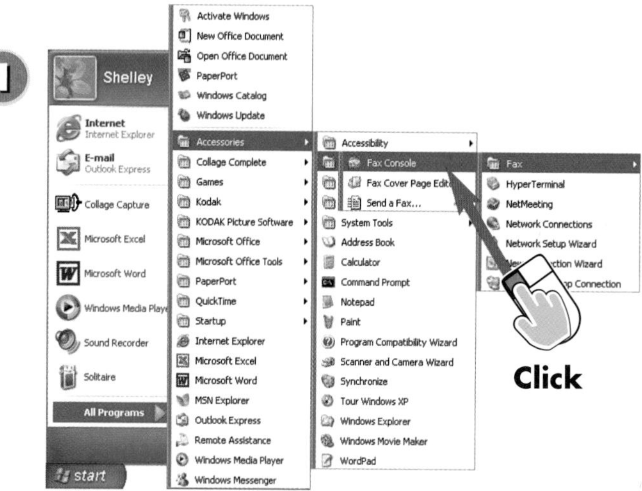

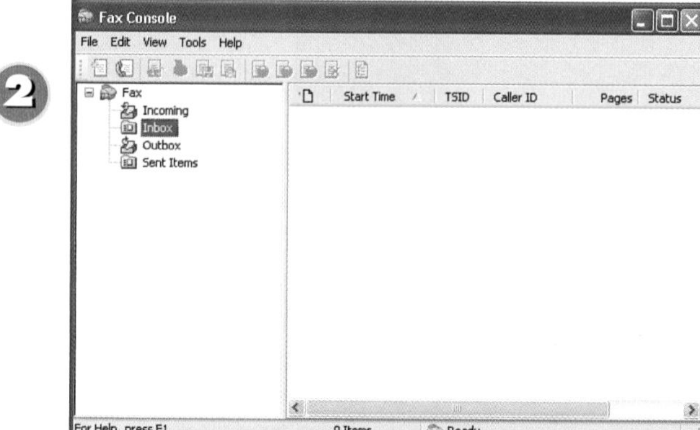

1. Click **Start**, **All Programs**, **Accessories**, **Communications**, **Fax**, **Fax Console**.
2. You see the Fax Console window. Similar to Outlook Express, you see the folders for Incoming faxes, Inbox (received faxes), Outbox (faxes to be sent at a later time), and Sent Items (a copy of sent faxes).

INTRODUCTION

If you have a fax modem, you can receive faxes at any time. They are stored in the Fax Console. To view faxes or make changes to fax settings, you can open the **Fax Console**.

TIP

Problems?
If you have problems receiving faxes, your fax device may not be set up to receive faxes. You can enable send and receive. To do so, click **Start**, **Control Panel**, **Printers and Other Hardware**, and finally, **Printers and Faxes**. Right-click your fax device and click **Properties**. Then click the Device tab. Right-click the fax device, right-click **Receive**, and then click **Auto**.

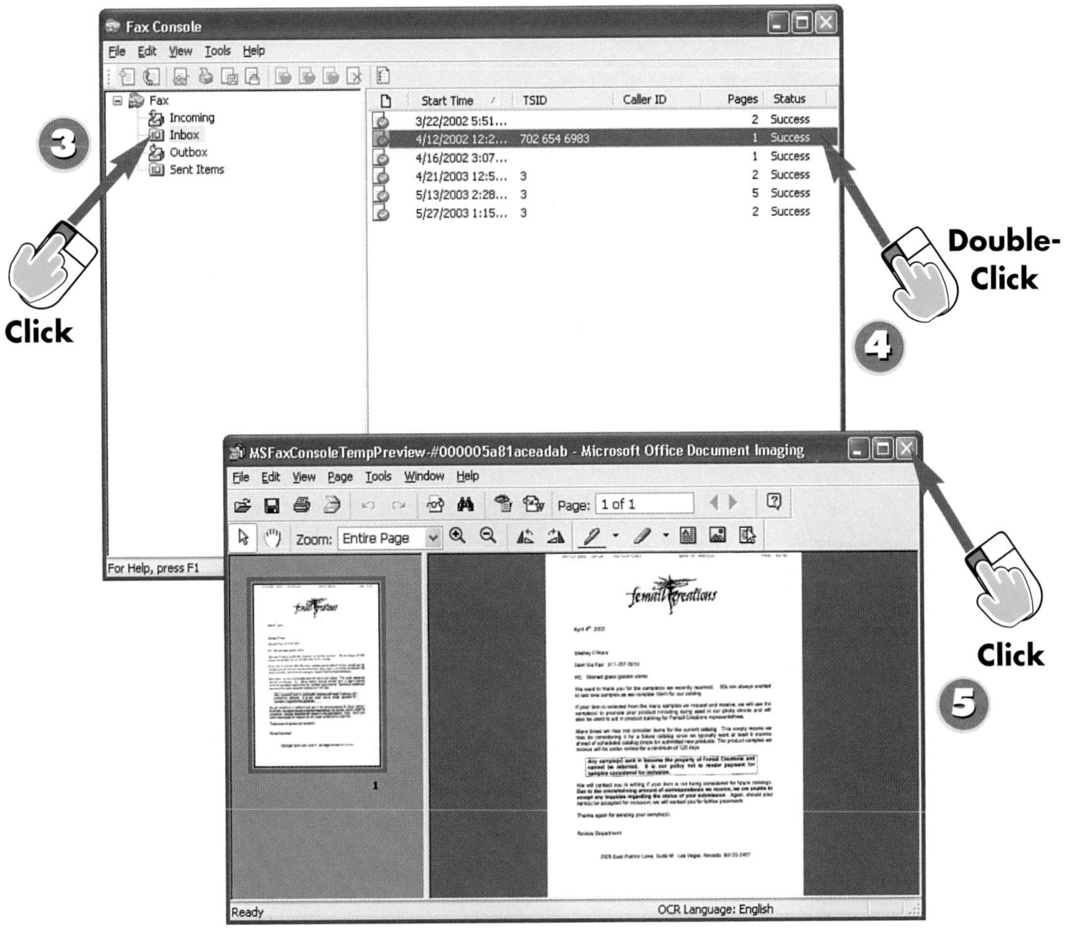

3 To open a fax you have received, click the **Inbox** folder.

4 Double-click the fax you want to open.

5 The fax is displayed onscreen. Click the **Close** button to close the fax.

TIP

Print a Fax
To print a fax, select it and then click the Print button.

TIP

Auto or Manual?
If you set up your fax to automatically receive a fax, your fax device will automatically detect any incoming faxes and place them in your Fax Console Inbox. If you want to manually receive faxes, click **File**, **Receive a fax now**.

TIP

Set Up the Fax
Run the Fax Configuration Wizard to set up a fax from the Fax Console. Click **Tools**, **Configure Fax**. Then follow the instructions in the wizard, clicking **Next** to move from step to step.

Task 3: Starting Outlook Express

Click

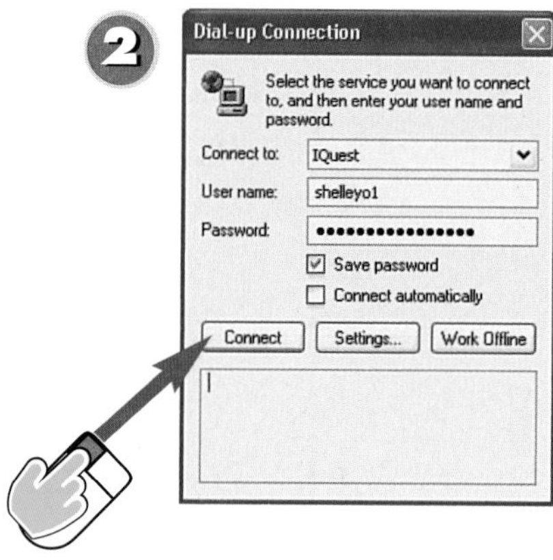

Click

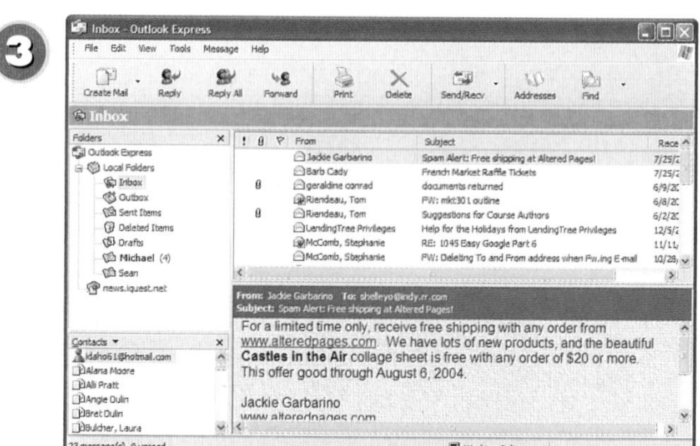

1. Click **Start** and then click **E-mail (Outlook Express)**.
2. If prompted, connect to your Internet service provider.
3. Outlook Express starts.

INTRODUCTION

Before you can use Outlook Express, you need to set up your Internet connection and email account information. Once you have set up a mail account, you can use Outlook Express to create, send, and receive email over the Internet.

TIP

Not Set Up?
To set up your Internet connection, use the Internet Connection Wizard. Follow the onscreen instructions, entering the appropriate user name, password, and mail information from your Internet service provider (ISP).

TIP

Exit and Disconnect
To exit Outlook Express, click the **Close** button for the program window. If you are prompted to log off, select **Yes** or **Disconnect**. If you are not prompted, right-click the connection icon in the taskbar and select **Disconnect**.

Task 4: Reading Mail

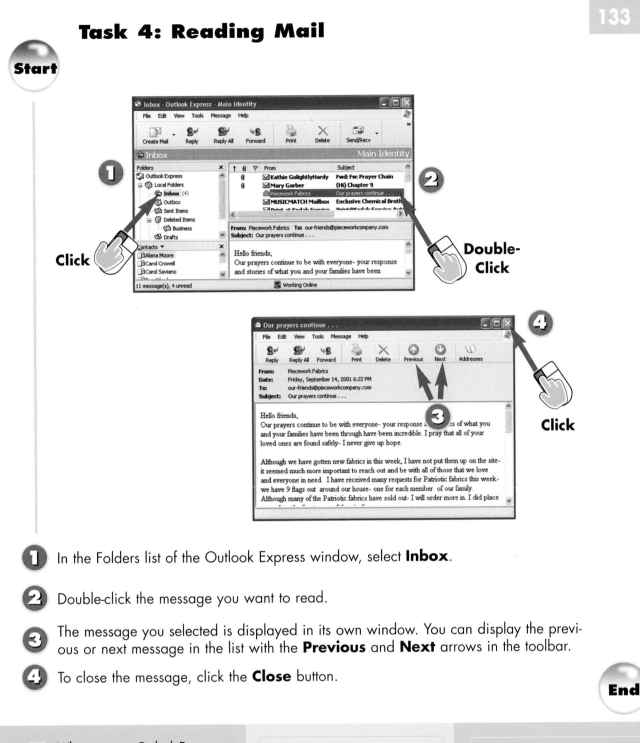

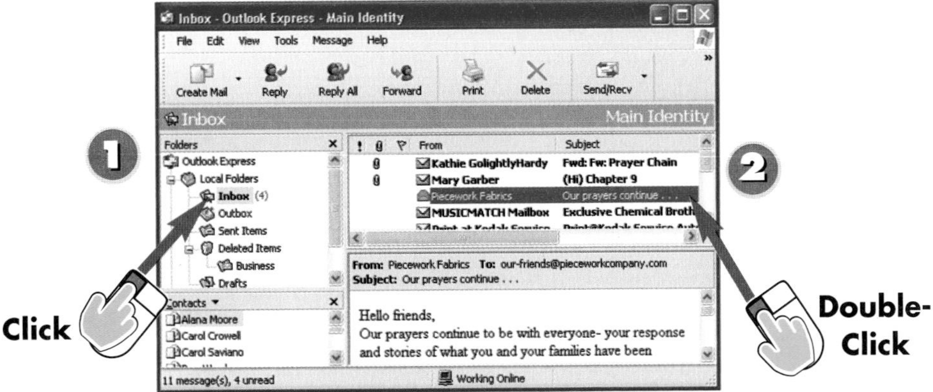

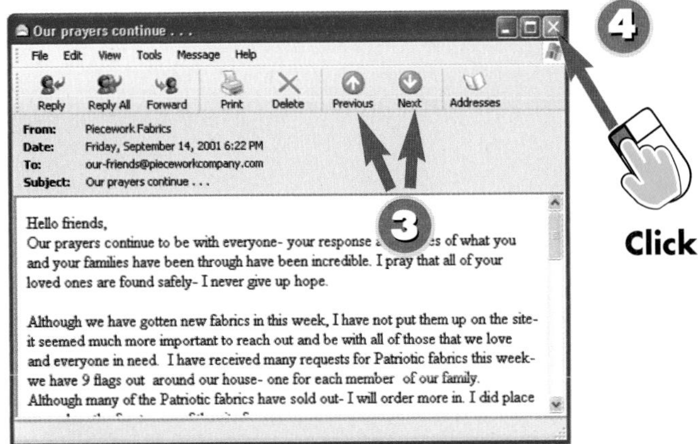

1. In the Folders list of the Outlook Express window, select **Inbox**.
2. Double-click the message you want to read.
3. The message you selected is displayed in its own window. You can display the previous or next message in the list with the **Previous** and **Next** arrows in the toolbar.
4. To close the message, click the **Close** button.

INTRODUCTION

When you start Outlook Express and connect with your ISP, messages are downloaded from your Internet mail server to your computer. The message list lists all messages. Messages appearing in bold have not yet been read.

TIP

Check Mail

To check your mail manually, click the **Send/Recv** button in the Outlook Express window.

TIP

Print a Message

To print an open message, click the **Print** button.

Task 5: Responding to Mail

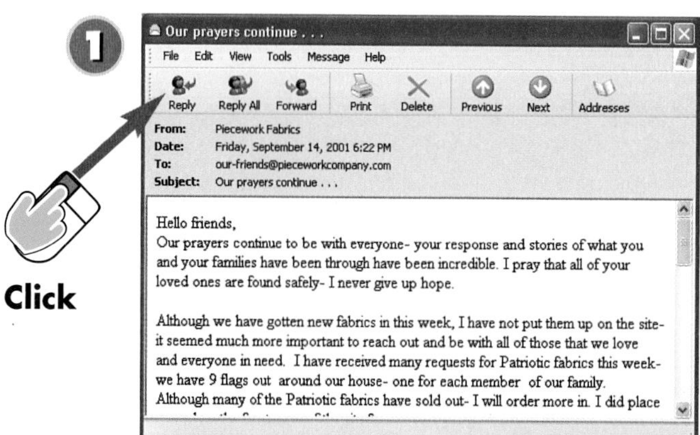

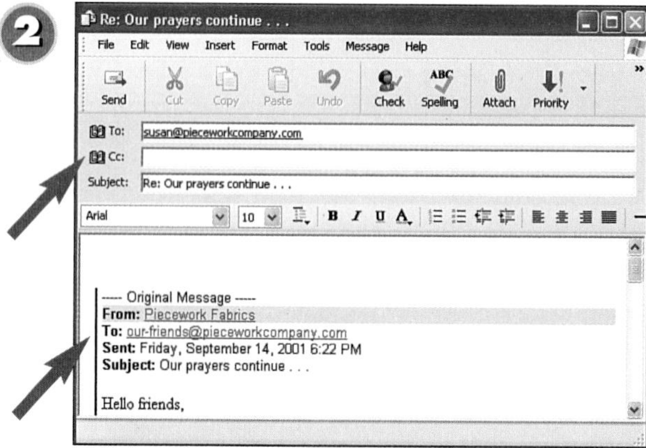

1. Display the message to which you want to reply, and click the **Reply** button in the toolbar.
2. The address and subject lines are completed, and the text of the original message is appended to the bottom of the reply message.

INTRODUCTION

You can easily respond to a message you've received. Outlook Express completes the address and subject lines for you; you can then simply type the response.

TIP

Reply to All

If the message was sent to several people (for example, cc'd to others), you can reply to all the recipients. Click the **Reply All** button, type the message, and then click **Send**.

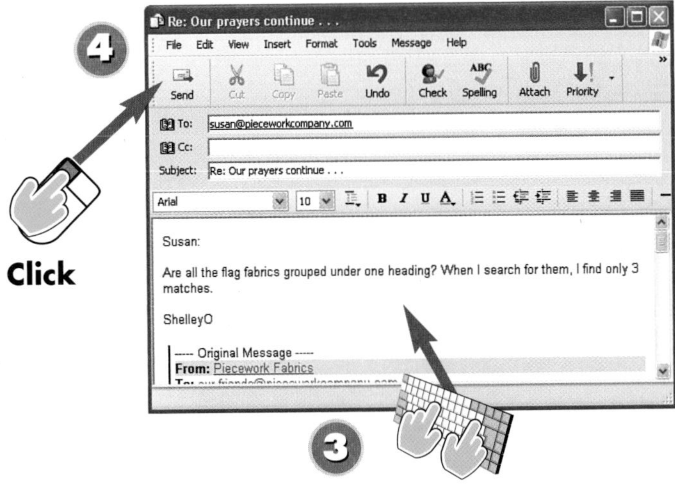

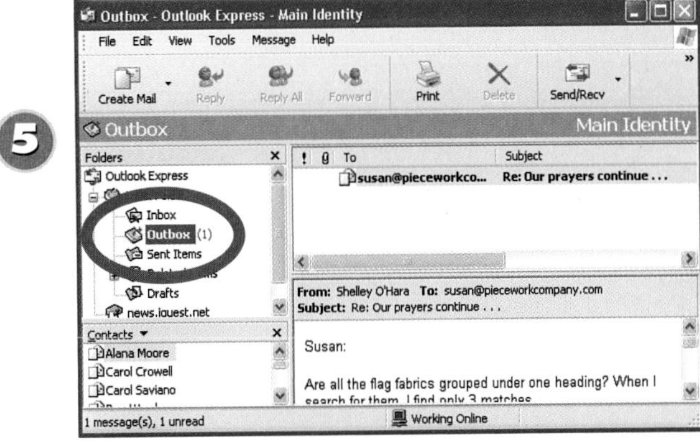

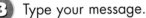

3. Type your message.
4. Click the **Send** button.
5. The message is placed in your **Outbox** and then sent.

TIP

Forward a Message

To forward a message, click the **Forward** button. Type the address of the recipient, and then click in the message area and type any message you want to include. Click the **Send** button to forward the message.

TIP

When Messages Are Sent

Messages are either sent immediately or placed in the Outbox and sent when you click **Send/Rec**. To change your send preferences, see Task 10 "Setting E-mail Options" later in this part.

Task 6: Creating and Sending New Mail

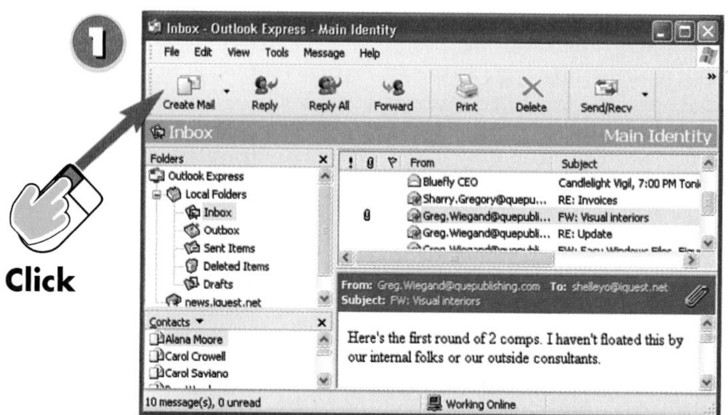

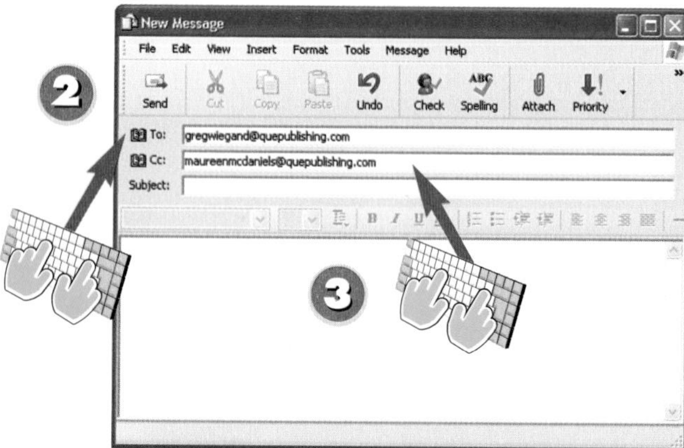

1. In the Outlook Express window, click the **Create Mail** button.
2. Type the recipient's address. Addresses are in the format ***username@domainname.ext*** (for example, **sohara@msn.com**). Press **Tab**.
3. If needed, type an address for the cc (carbon copy) and press **Tab**.

INTRODUCTION

You can send a message to anyone with an Internet email address. Simply type the recipient's email address, a subject, and the message. You can also send a carbon copy (Cc) by entering an address for this field.

TIP

Wrong Address?
If you enter an incorrect address and the message is not sent, you most likely will receive a Failure to Deliver notice. Be sure to type the address in its proper format.

TIP

Select Name from Address Book
Rather than type the address, you can select it from your address book. To do so, click **To** and then select the name. See Task 12 "Using Your Address Book to Enter Names" later in this part.

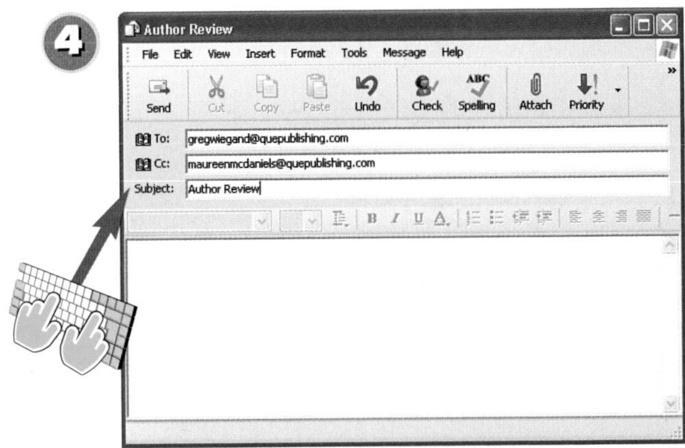

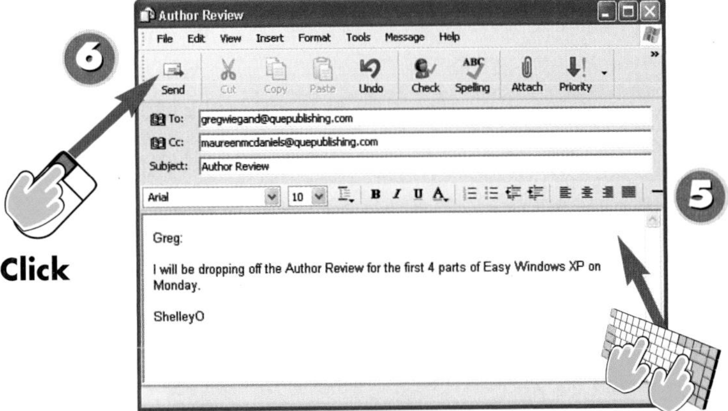

4. Type a subject in the **Subject** text box, and then press **Tab**.
5. Type your message.
6. When you've completed the message, click the **Send** button.

TIP

Check Sent Items
By default, Outlook Express keeps a copy of all messages. To see these messages, click **Sent Items** in the folder list.

TIP

When Sent?
If you are connected to the Internet, the message is sent when you click the **Send** button. If you're not connected to the Internet, Windows places the message in the **Outbox**, where it remains until the next time you connect to your ISP. You can connect and send the message by clicking the **Send/Recv** button.

Task 7: Attaching a File

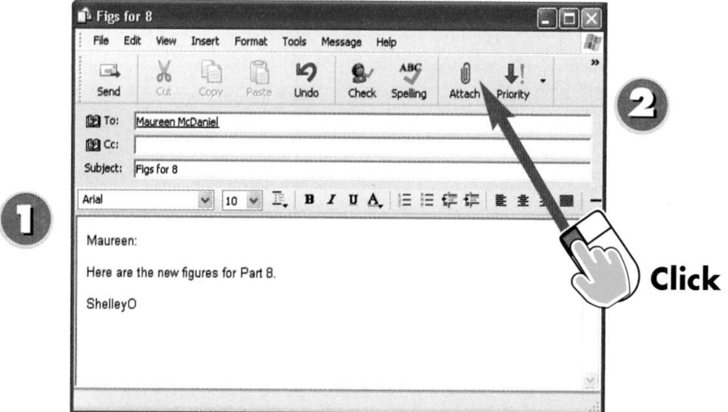

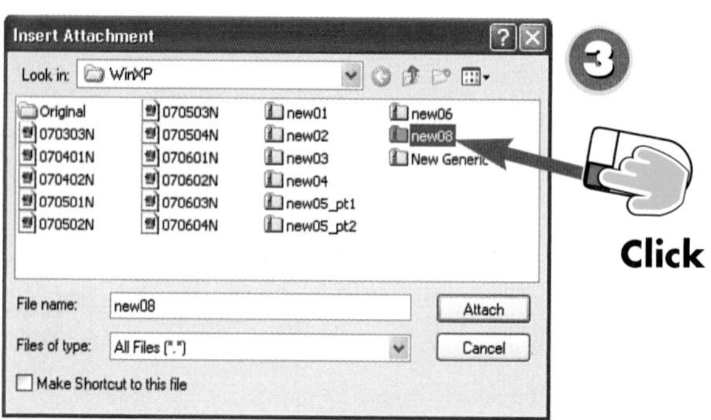

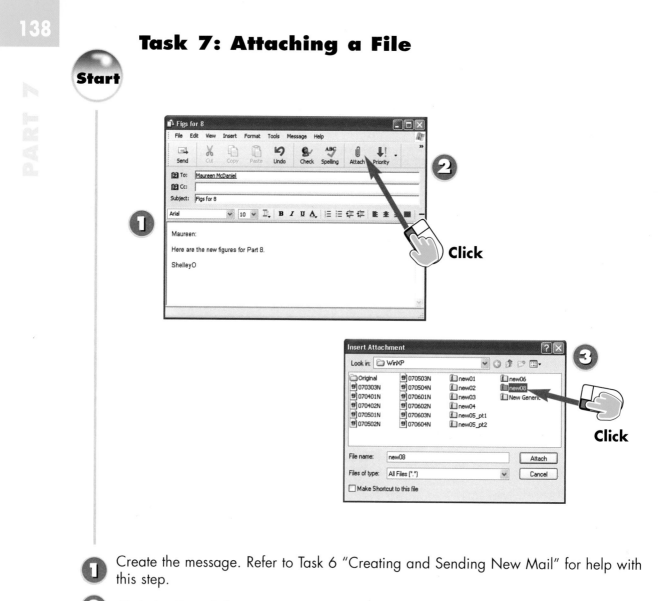

1. Create the message. Refer to Task 6 "Creating and Sending New Mail" for help with this step.
2. Click the **Attach** button.
3. Select the file to attach and click the **Attach** button.

INTRODUCTION

When you create a message, you can also attach a file to send with the message. You may send photographs, for instance, of your child. Or if you work from home, you can attach documents such as a report or an expense worksheet. You can attach any type of file.

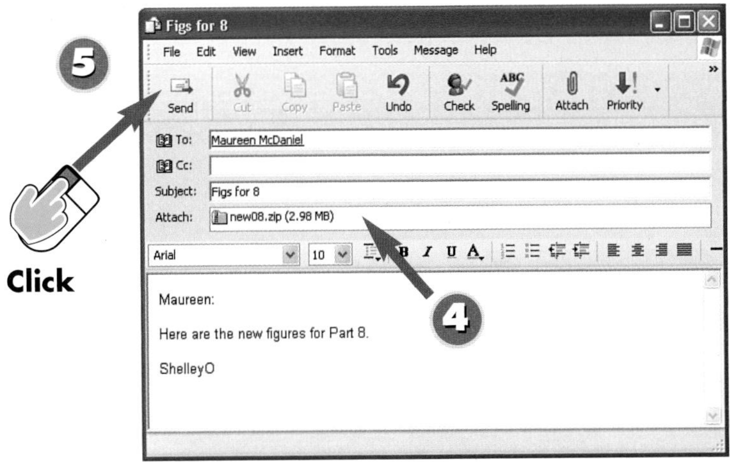

4. The file attachment is listed in the Attach text box.
5. Click the **Send** button to send the message and file attachment.

TIP

Find Attachment
You can display other drives or folders in the Insert Attachment dialog box using the Look in drop-down list. You can also move up through the folder structure by clicking the **Up One Level** button.

TIP

File Sizes
Be careful when sending large files. The mail server or the mail recipient may have limits on the size of attachments. If you need to send large file(s), use a compression program to compress the file before sending.

Task 8: Opening a File Attachment

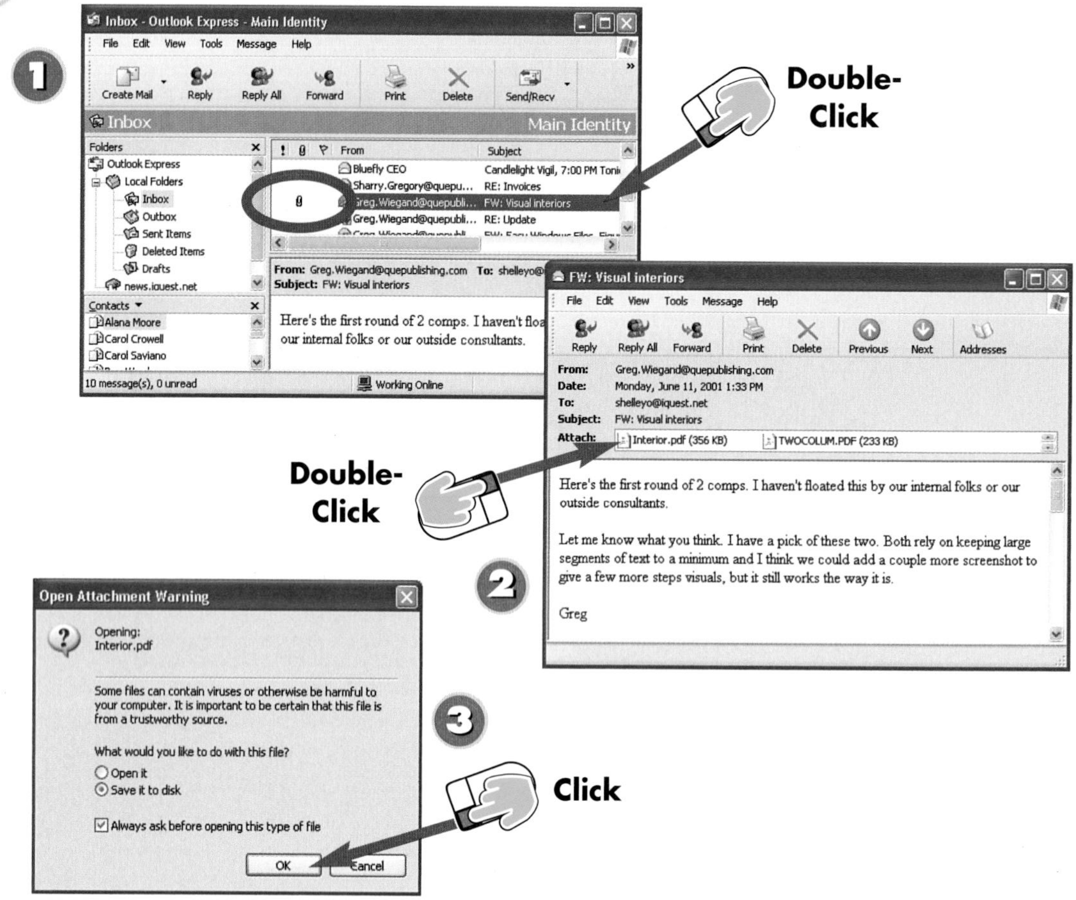

1. Messages with file attachments are indicated with a paper clip icon. Double-click the message to open it.
2. The file attachment(s) are listed in the Attach text box. Double-click the file attachment you want to open.
3. Select to open the attachment and then click **OK**. The file is opened.

INTRODUCTION

If someone sends you a file attachment, you can choose how to handle it. You can save it to your disk or you can open it. To open the attachment, you must have a program that can open and display that particular file type.

TIP

Save Attachment

You can also select to save the attachment to disk. If you choose this option, you see the Save Attachment As dialog box. Select a folder for the file, type a new name or accept the current file name, and then click **Save**.

TIP

WARNING!

Viruses are often sent via email. You should purchase and use a virus protection program and set it up so that it automatically scans any file attachments you receive. See Part 12 for more information on viruses and security.

Task 9: Deleting Messages

1 Click

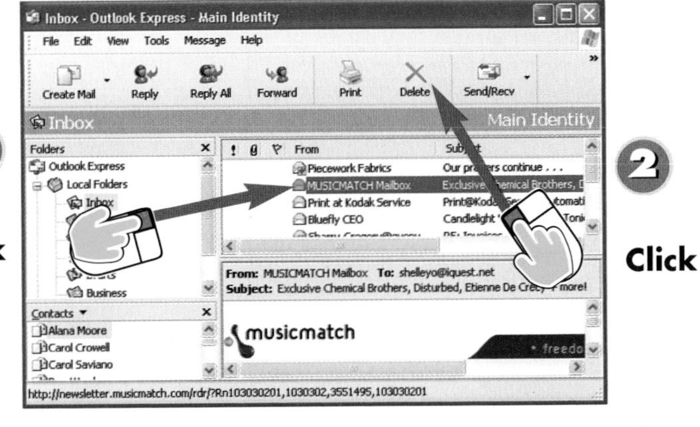

2 Click

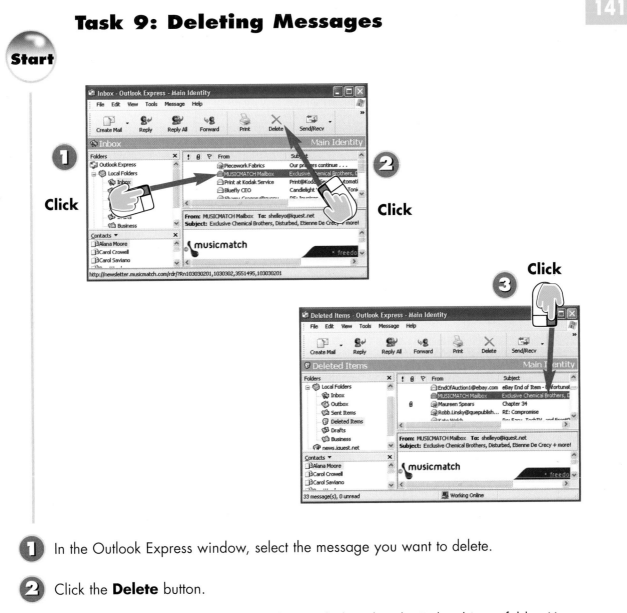

3 Click

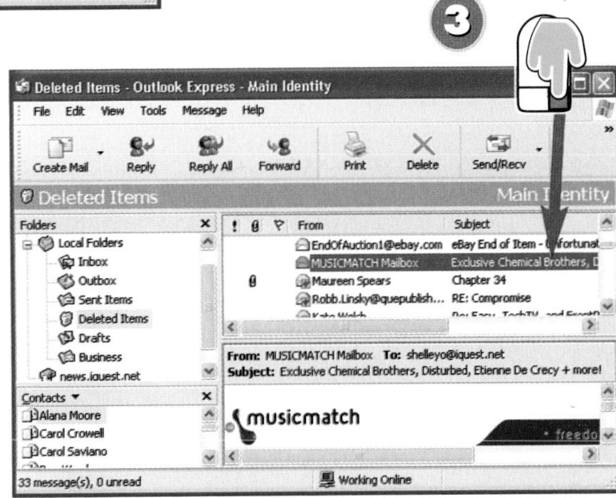

1. In the Outlook Express window, select the message you want to delete.
2. Click the **Delete** button.
3. The message is removed from the Inbox and placed in the Deleted Items folder. You can open this folder by clicking it to confirm the deletion.

INTRODUCTION

As part of keeping your Inbox uncluttered, you can delete messages. When you delete a message, it is not deleted, but moved to the Deleted Items folder. You can retrieve any messages if you accidentally delete them.

TIP

Undelete a Message

To undelete a message, open the Deleted Items folder, select the message, and then move it to another folder. See Task 14, "Moving Messages," for help on moving messages.

TIP

Delete from Mail Window

You can also delete a message after reading it, while the mail window is open. To do so, click the **Delete** button in the mail window.

Task 10: Setting Email Options

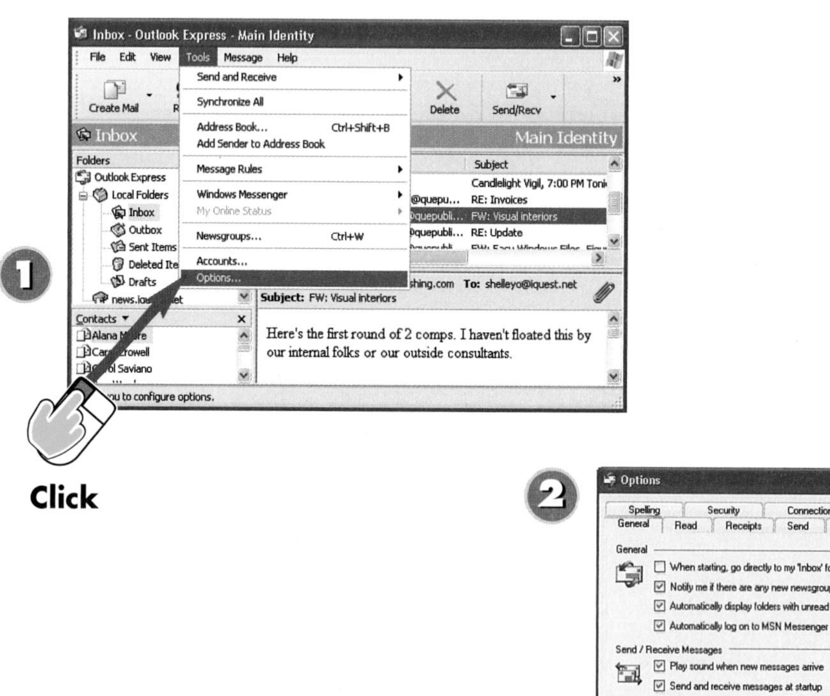

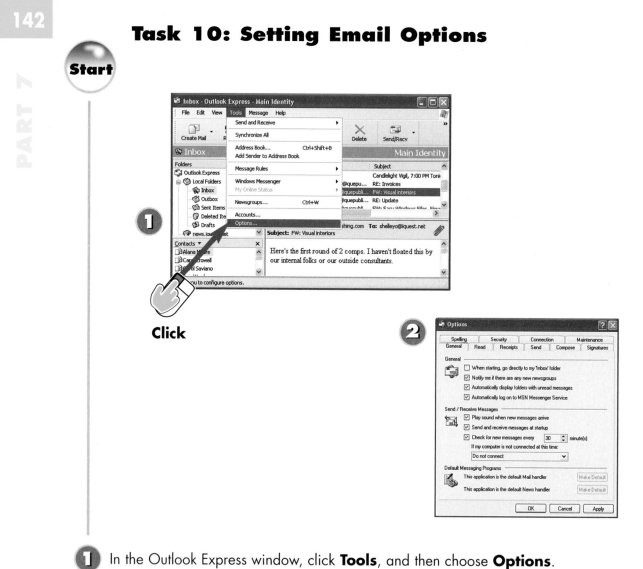

Click

1. In the Outlook Express window, click **Tools**, and then choose **Options**.

2. On the **General** tab, make changes to options such as whether the Inbox is automatically displayed, how often messages are checked, and so on.

INTRODUCTION

Outlook Express uses certain defaults for how messages are handled when you create, send, and receive them. You can check out these settings, and if necessary, make any changes.

TIP

Not Sure About an Option?
If you are unsure what an option does, right-click the option and then select **What's This?** to display a ScreenTip explanation of the option.

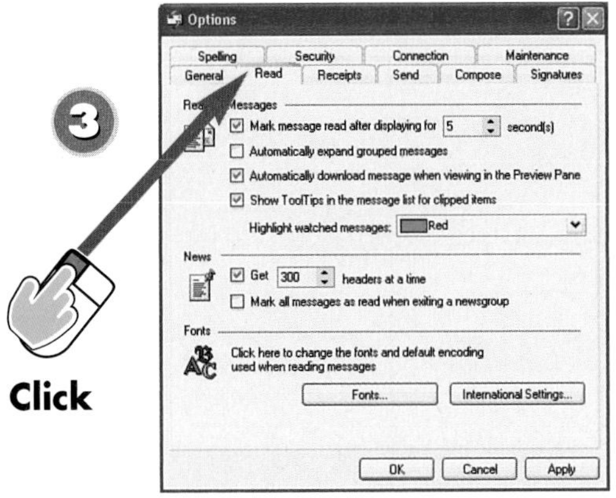

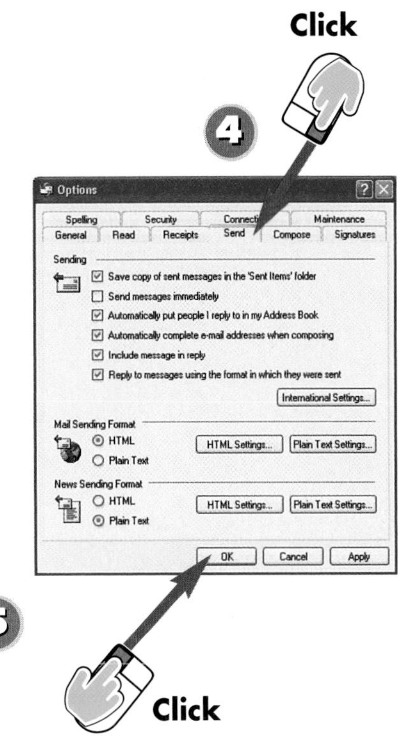

3. Click the **Read** tab and make changes to how new messages are handled.

4. Click the **Send** tab and make changes to how sent items are handled.

5. When you're finished making changes, click the **OK** button.

TIP

Other Tabs

The Options dialog box includes several other tabs for making changes. You can click and review the options on these tabs as well.

Task 11: Adding Addresses to Your Address Book

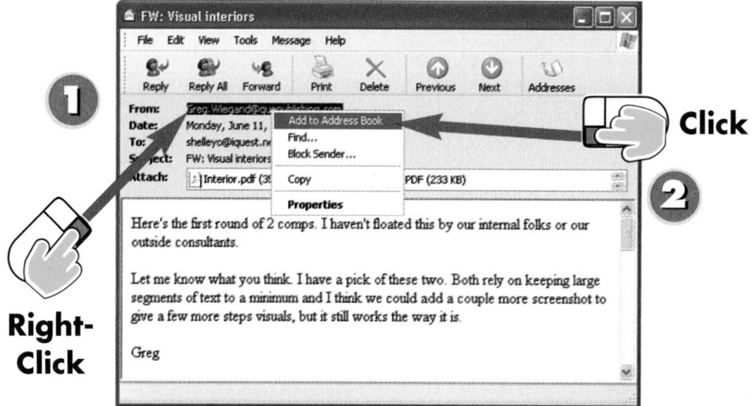

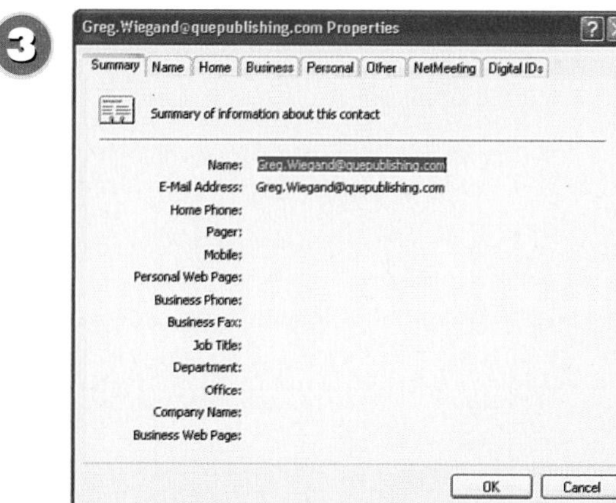

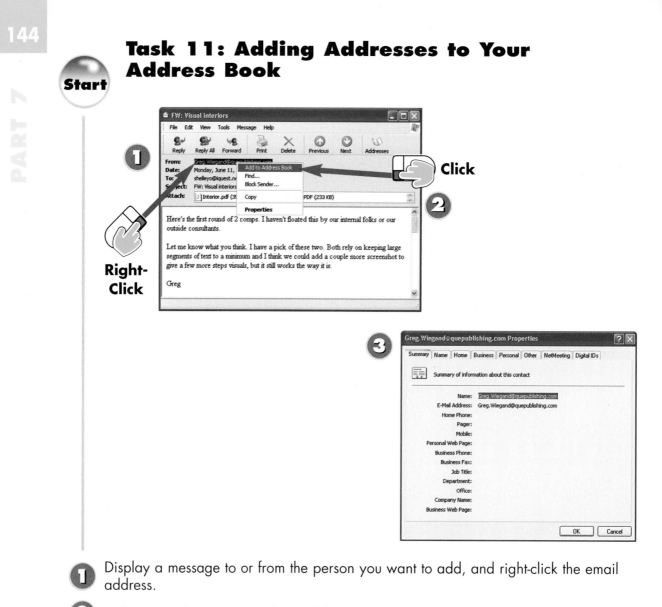

1. Display a message to or from the person you want to add, and right-click the email address.
2. In the menu that appears, click **Add to Address Book**.
3. The Summary tab displays the default name and email address.

INTRODUCTION

If you send email often, you don't want to type the addresses each time. Instead, you can add names to your Address Book. Then you can select the name and address when creating new messages or forwarding messages. The fastest way to add an address is to copy it from an existing message.

TIP

Automatically Add Names
You can automatically add names to the Address Book. To do so, check the **Automatically put people I reply to in my Address Book** on the Send tab of the Options dialog box. See Task 10, "Setting E-mail Options."

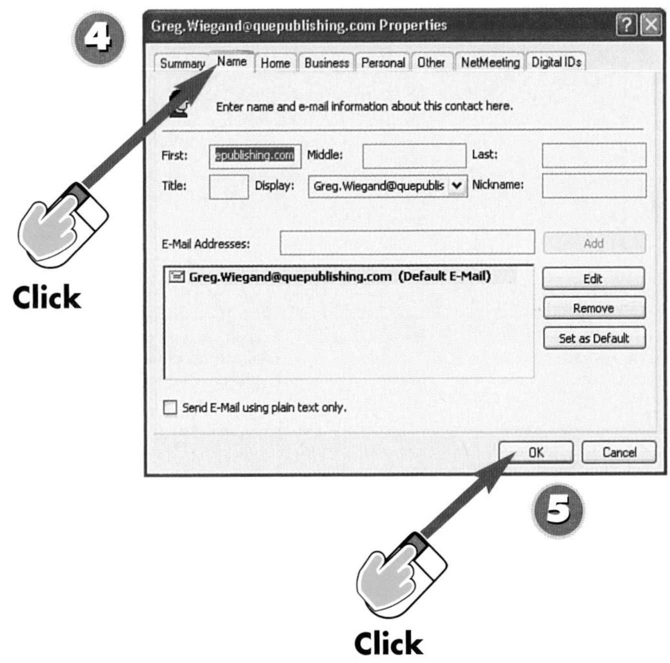

4. Click the **Name** tab and make any changes to the display name (name that appears in the list).
5. Click **OK** to add the name.

TIP

New Address
If you don't have a message, you can manually add a person to the Address Book. Click **Addresses** in the Outlook Express window. Then click **New** and select **New Contact. Complete** the information and click **OK**.

Task 12: Using Your Address Book to Enter Names

Start

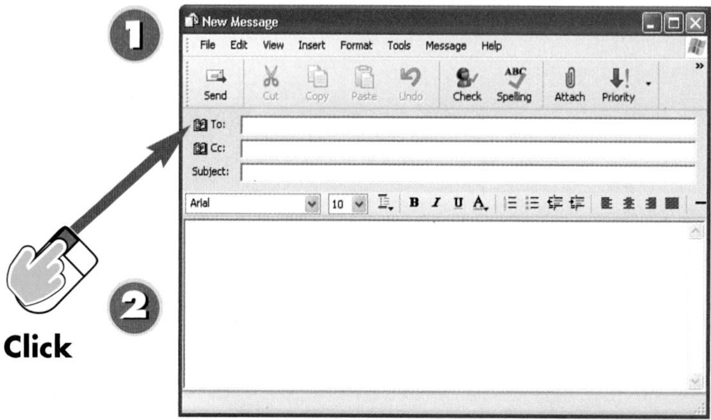

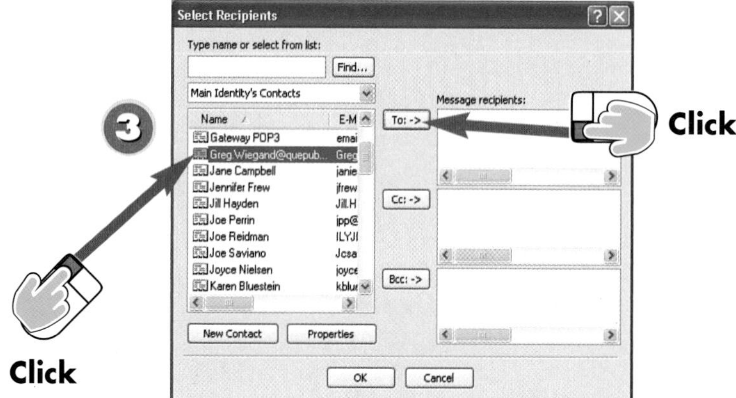

1. Create a new mail message. Refer to Task 6 for help on this step.
2. Click the **To** button in a message window.
3. You see the Select Recipients dialog box listing contacts in your Address Book. Select the person to add and click **To**.

INTRODUCTION

Rather than type a long email name, which can be error-prone, you can create an address book of names and addresses. Then when you create a message, you can select the name from the Address Book rather than type it.

TIP

More Addresses
You can select additional recipients by selecting them and clicking **To**.

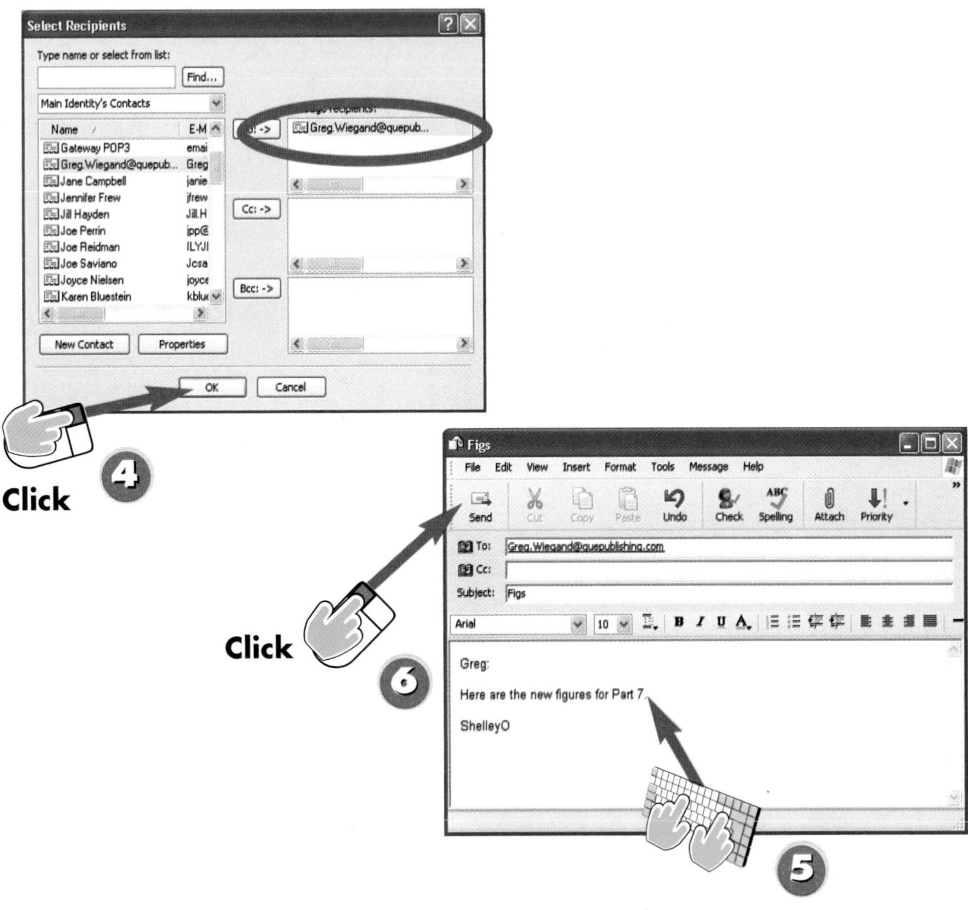

4. That person is added to the Message recipients list. Follow step 3 for each person to which you want to send the message. Click **OK**.

5. Type the subject and message.

6. Click **Send** to send the message.

TIP

Contact List
By default, Outlook Express displays the Contacts list, which is a list of the names in your Address Book. You can double-click any of the listed names to create a new mail message, addressed to the person you double-clicked.

TIP

Cc and Bcc
You can select a name from the Address Book for Cc and Bcc by selecting a name and then clicking the Cc or Bcc buttons.

Task 13: Organizing Messages in Folders

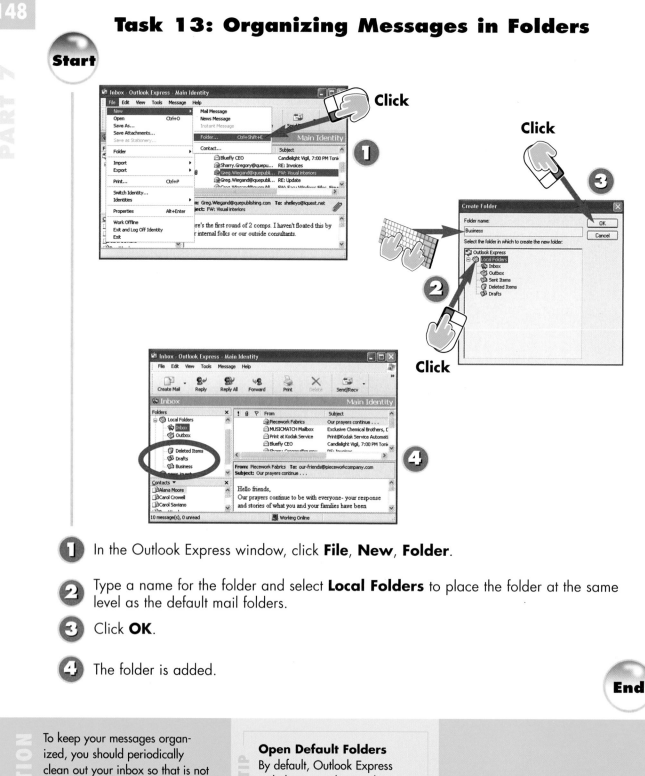

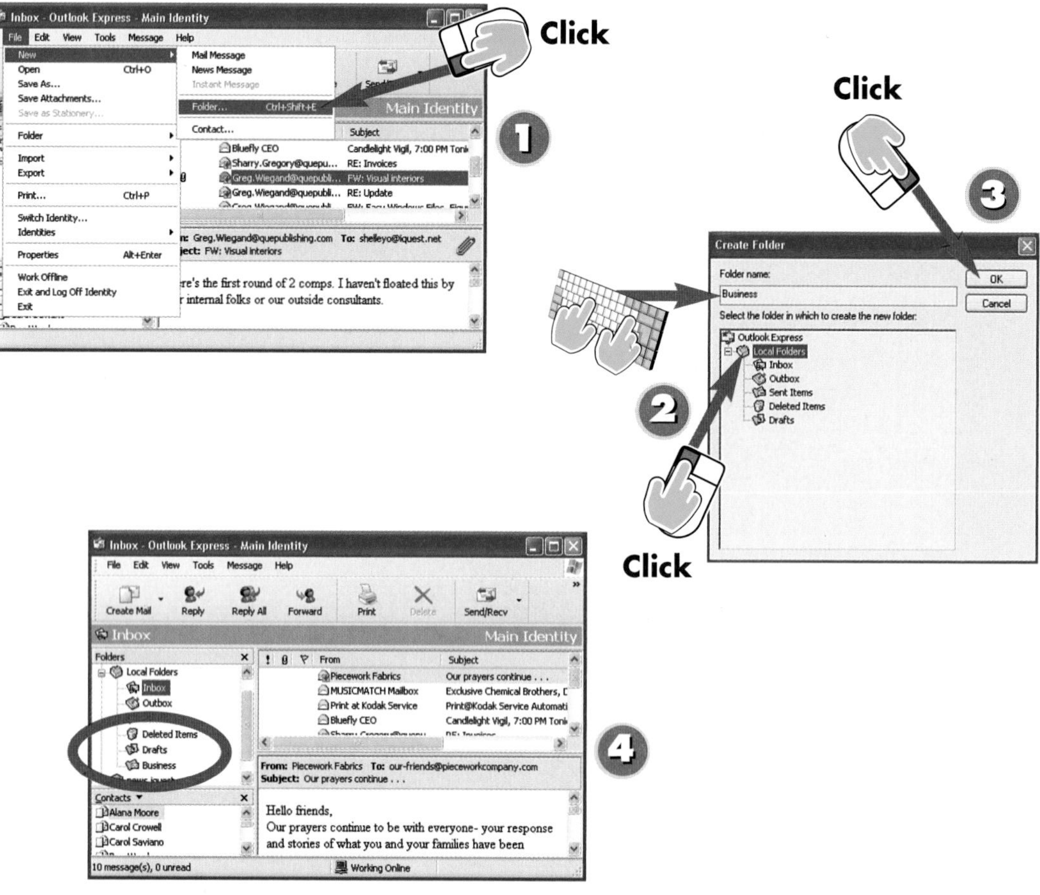

1. In the Outlook Express window, click **File**, **New**, **Folder**.

2. Type a name for the folder and select **Local Folders** to place the folder at the same level as the default mail folders.

3. Click **OK**.

4. The folder is added.

INTRODUCTION

To keep your messages organized, you should periodically clean out your inbox so that is not cluttered. You can set up folders for important messages that you need to keep, but don't want to keep in your Inbox.

TIP

Open Default Folders
By default, Outlook Express includes your Inbox and Outbox as well as folders for Drafts, Sent Items, and Deleted Items. You can view the contents of any of these folders by clicking them in the Folders list.

Task 14: Moving Messages

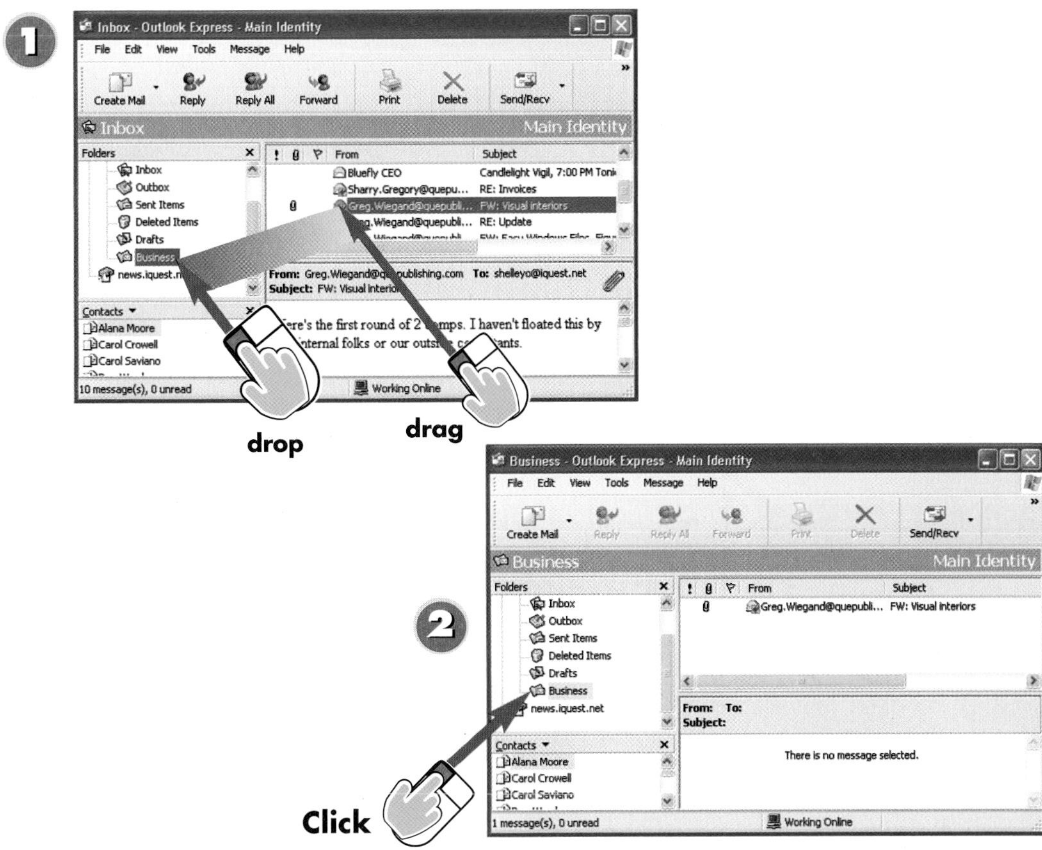

1. In the Outlook Express window, select the message you want to move. Drag the message from the message list to the folder in the Folders list.
2. The message is moved to that folder. You can click the folder in the Folders list to confirm the move.

INTRODUCTION

If you have set up other mail folders, you can move messages you want to keep from your Inbox to these other folders. You can also move folders from any of the default mail folders to another folder.

TIP

Use Commands
If you do not like the drag-and-drop method, you can also select the message and then use the **Edit**, **Move to Folder** command. Select the folder in which to place the message and click **OK**.

Task 15: Cleaning Out the Deleted Items Folder

Start

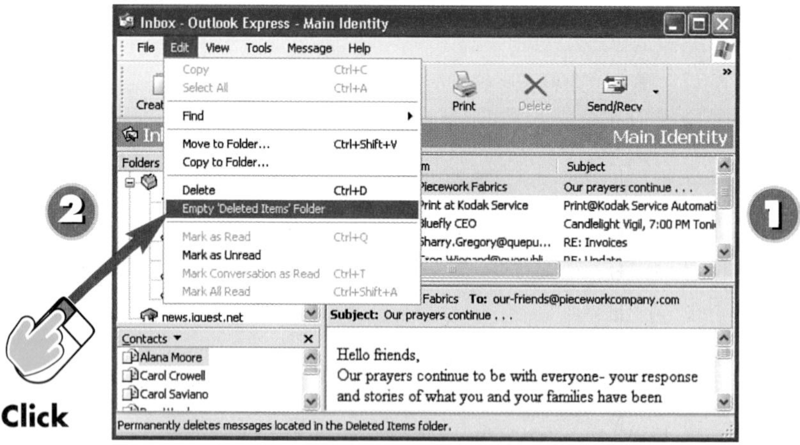

1. Open the Deleted Items folder and make sure it does not contain any messages that you need.

2. Open the **Edit** menu and select **Empty 'Deleted Items' Folder**.

INTRODUCTION

Deleted messages are stored in the Deleted Items folder. To save disk space or to really delete a message, you can clean out this folder.

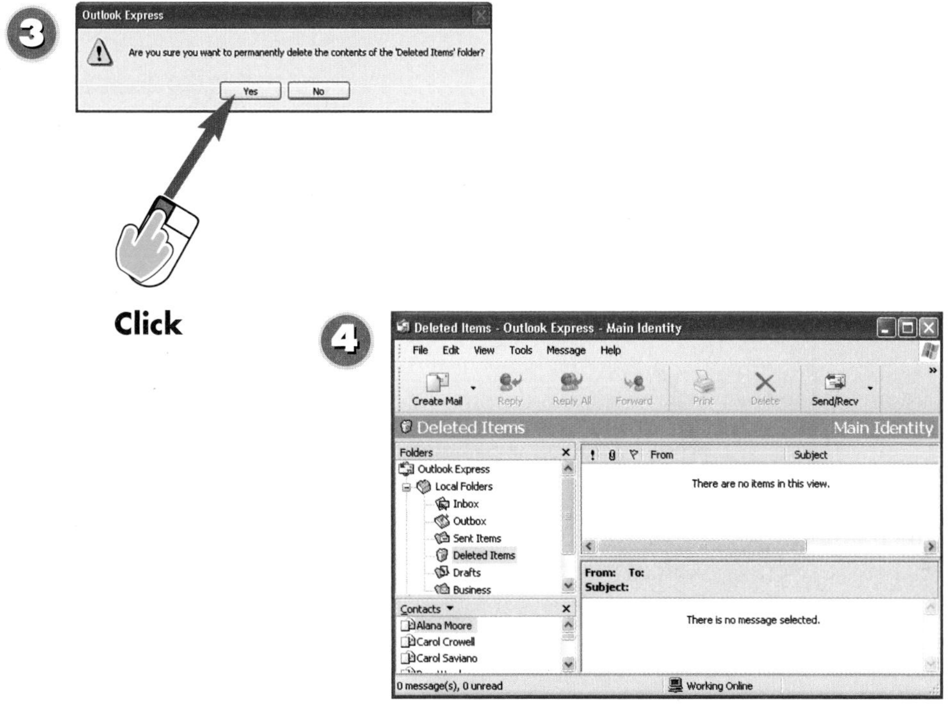

3. Confirm the deletion by clicking **Yes**.

4. The messages are permanently deleted. You can click this folder to confirm it is empty.

TIP

Delete Individual Messages

You can also delete individual messages rather than all of the messages in the folder. To do so, open the folder, select the message(s) you want to delete, and click the **Delete** button. Confirm the deletion by clicking **Yes**.

Task 16: Handling Spam

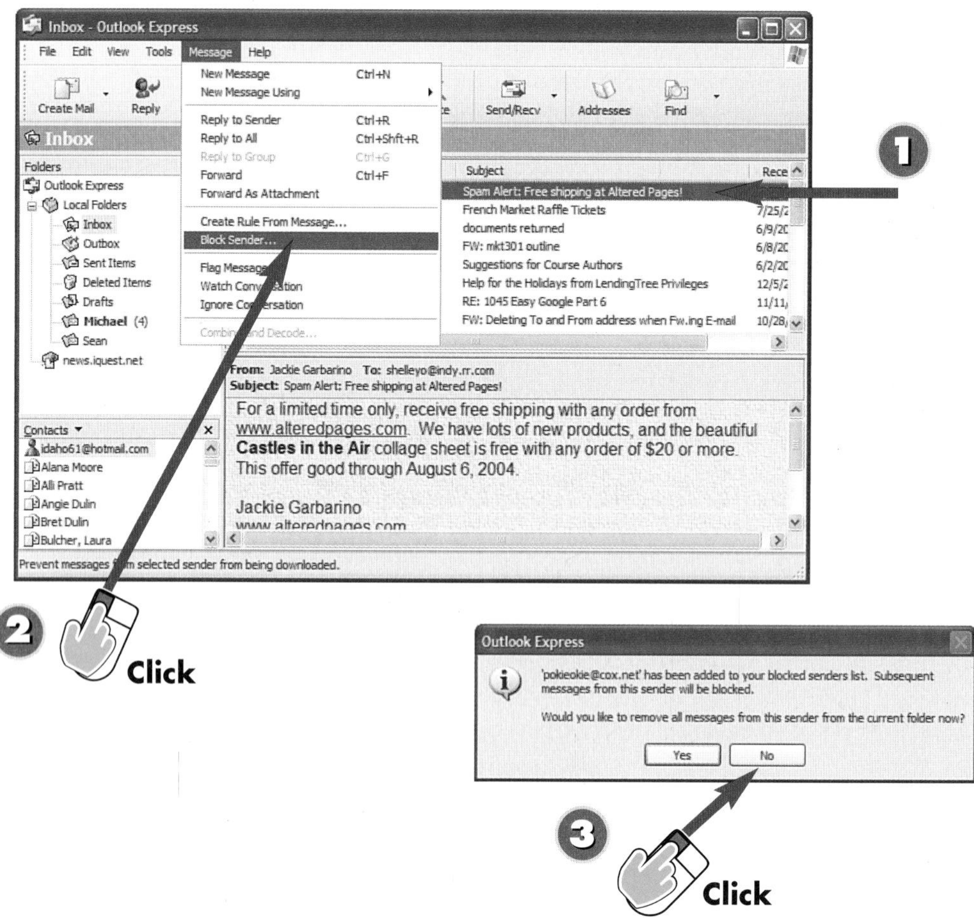

1. To block a particular sender, select a message from the person.
2. Click **Message** and then **Block Sender**.
3. To remove any old messages from this person, click **Yes**. To keep the messages, click **No**.

INTRODUCTION

Junk email is called spam, and you can use Outlook Express to block some spam. When you receive spam, you block that sender so they can no longer send you messages. You can purchase programs that are more effective at blocking spam. Your Internet service provider may include some spam-blocking features.

TIP

WARNING!
You can cut down on the amount of spam by not signing up for free newsletters, product announcements, or contests online.

TIP

To unblock a sender, click **Tools**, **Message Rules**, and then **Blocked Senders List**. Select the person to unblock. Click the **Remove** button. Confirm the removal by clicking **Yes** and then **OK**.

Task 17: Sorting Messages

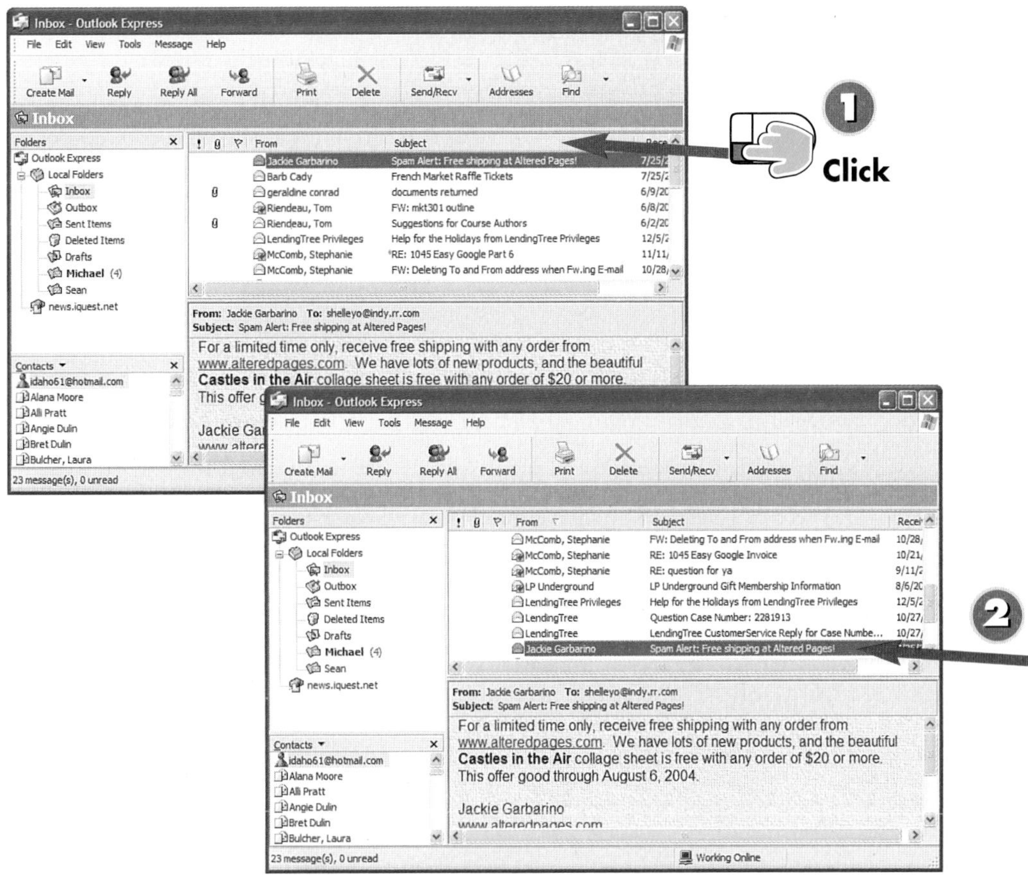

1. Click the column header on which you want to sort. For example, to sort by recipient, click **From**.
2. Messages are sorted in that order.

INTRODUCTION

You'll find that your inbox can quickly become full of messages. One way to find a message is to sort the messages. You can sort by any of the message header columns, including recipient (From), Subject, or Received Date.

TIP

Sort order

You can sort in descending order by clicking the column header again. To return to the default order (sorted by date), click the **Received** column header.

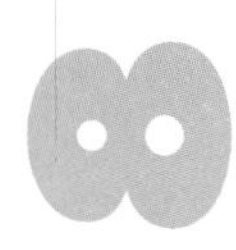

PART 8

Connecting to the Internet

If you have a modem and an Internet connection, you can use Internet Explorer, the Web browser included with Windows XP, to explore the Internet. You can use Internet Explorer to view World Wide Web pages, to search for specific topics, and to set privacy and security features to ensure safe browsing.

To explore the Internet, you must have a modem and an Internet connection. You can get this connection through online providers such as America Online or MSN, or you can get an account from an independent Internet service provider (ISP). Before you can take advantage of all the benefits of the Internet, you must set up your Internet connection. The specifics of setting up depend on your type of connection and your provider, so they are not covered here. Follow the specific instructions you received from your Internet provider to set up your connection and your e-mail account. You can use the Internet Connection Wizard to do so.

Tasks

Task 1: Starting Internet Explorer

1. Click **Start**.
2. Click **Internet**.
3. If needed, enter your user name and password (some information might have been completed for you), and then click the **Connect** button.
4. Windows connects to your ISP (Internet service provider). The Internet Explorer window appears, and you see your start page, usually the MSN home page.

INTRODUCTION

After you've set up your Internet connection, you can start Internet Explorer. Before you start browsing the Web, take a look at the different tools within the Internet Explorer window.

TIP

Trouble Connecting?
If you have problems connecting—the line is busy, for example—try again. If you continue to have problems, check with your ISP.

Button	Name	Click To
Back	Back	Go to the last page you visited
	Forward	Go forward a page, after going back
	Stop	Stop the display of a page
	Refresh	Redisplay the page, refreshing the date
	Home	Return to your home page
	Print	Print the current Web page

5 You can use any of the toolbar buttons to navigate from page to page.

6 When you are done working in Internet Explorer, click its **Close** button to close the program.

TIP

Log Off
When you exit Internet Explorer, you may be prompted to log off your Internet provider. Click **Yes** or **Disconnect Now**. If you are not prompted, be sure to log off. Right-click the connection icon in the status bar and select **Disconnect**.

TIP

Other Buttons
To see the name of a button, put the pointer over the button; the name should appear. Most of the other buttons are covered in this part. For help on the features not covered, consult online help.

TIP

Cable Connection
If you have a different type of connection, for instance, a cable connection, you are always connected to the Internet; this is known as a 24/7 connection.

Task 2: Browsing with Links

1. Click a link. Here you see the MSN start page. Click a link.

2. The page for that link appears (in this case, MSN Sports Page).

INTRODUCTION

Information on the Internet is easy to browse because documents contain links to other pages, documents, and sites. Simply click a link to view the associated page. Links are also called *hyperlinks*, and usually appear underlined and sometimes in a different color.

TIP

Error?

If you see an error message when you click a link, it could indicate that the link is not accurate or that the server is too busy. Try again later.

TIP

Image Links

Images can also serve as links. You can tell whether an image (or text) is a link by placing your mouse pointer on it. If the pointer changes into a pointing hand, the image (or text) is a link.

Task 3: Typing an Address

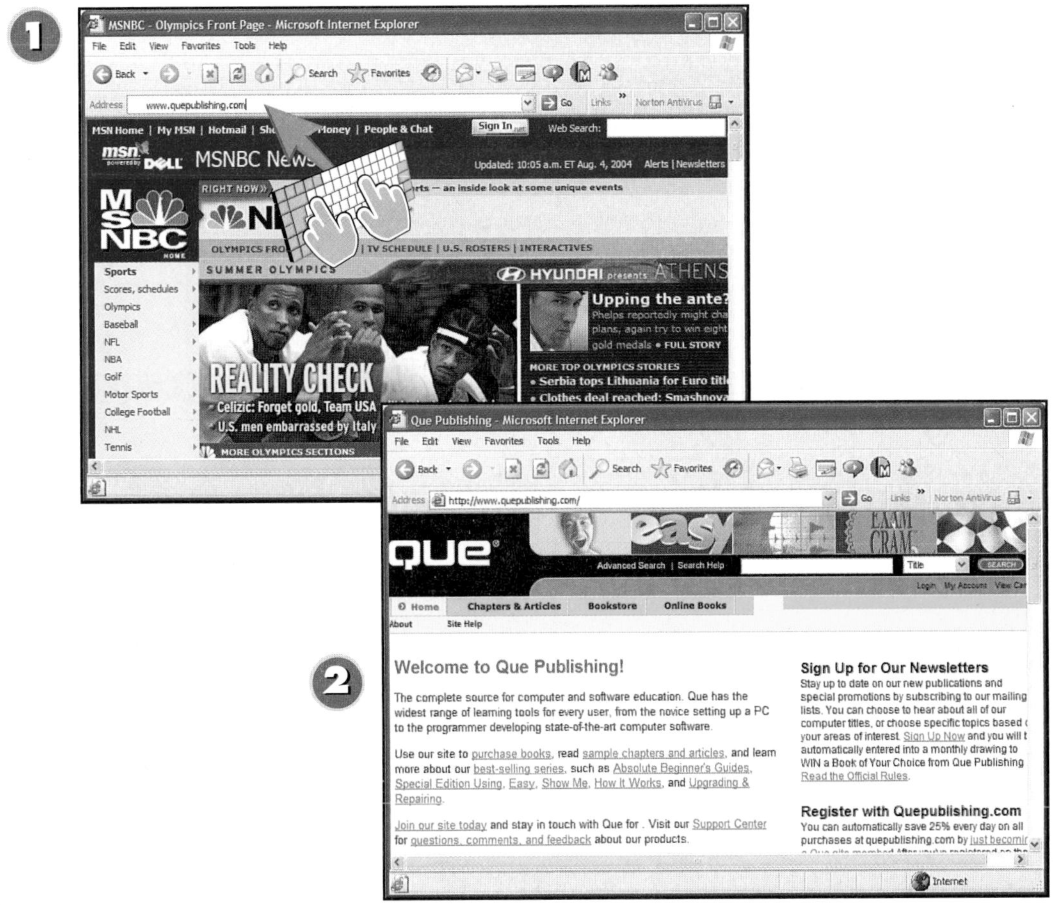

1. Click in the Address bar. Type the address of the site you want to visit, and then press **Enter**.
2. Internet Explorer displays that page.

INTRODUCTION

Typing a site's address is the fastest way to get to that site. An address, or URL (uniform resource locator), consists of the protocol (usually `http://`) www, and the domain name (something like `nba.com`). The domain name might also include a path (a list of folders) to the document. The extension (usually .com, .net, .gov, .edu, or .mil) indicates the type of site (commercial, network resources, government, educational, or military, respectively).

TIP

Address Bar
If the Address Bar is not displayed, click **View**, **Toolbars**, **Address Bar**.

Use AutoComplete
If you have typed a specific address before, you can type only its first few letters; Internet Explorer will display the rest.

Task 4: Searching the Internet

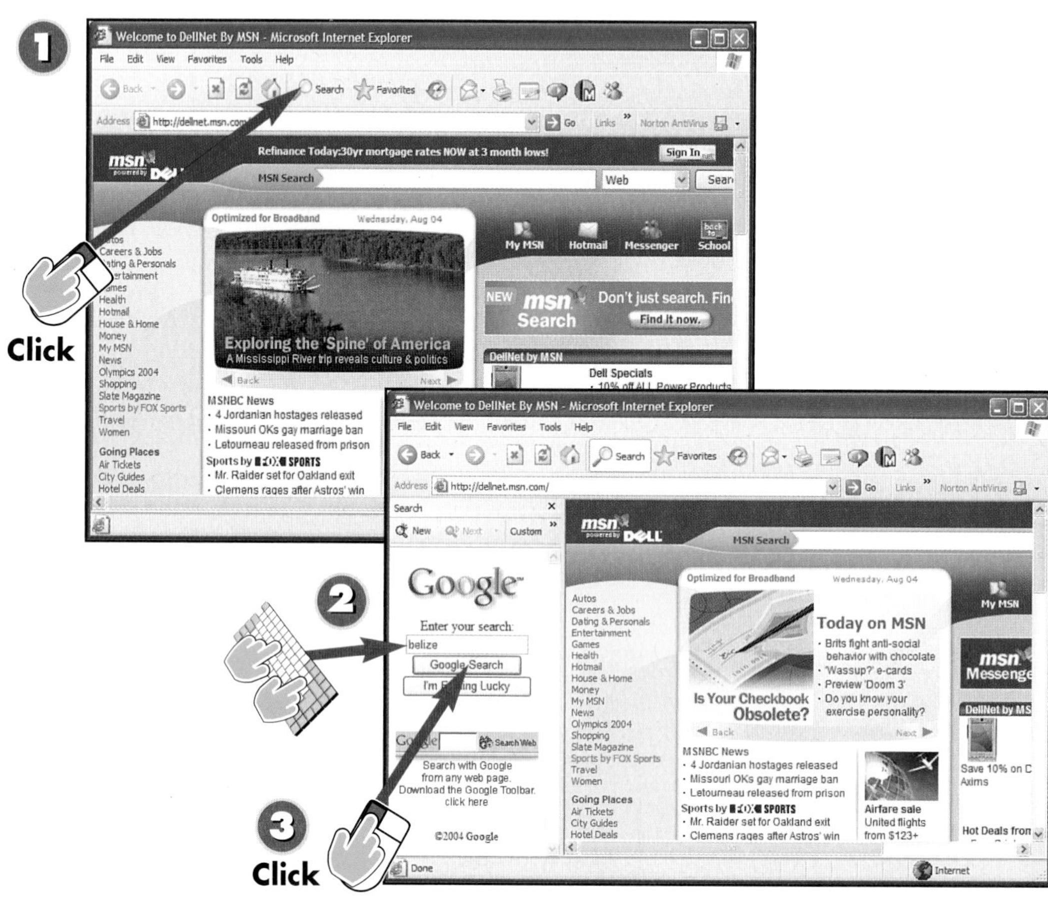

1. Click the **Search** button in the toolbar.
2. You see the Search bar. Type what you want to find.
3. Click the **Google Search** button.

INTRODUCTION

The Internet includes many, many, many different sites. Looking for the site you want by browsing can be like looking for the proverbial needle in the haystack. Instead, you can search for a topic and find all sites related to that topic.

TIP

Google Search

When you click the Search button, Internet Explorer uses Google (a very popular search tool) to perform the search. You can also go directly to Google (or other search sites) and search.

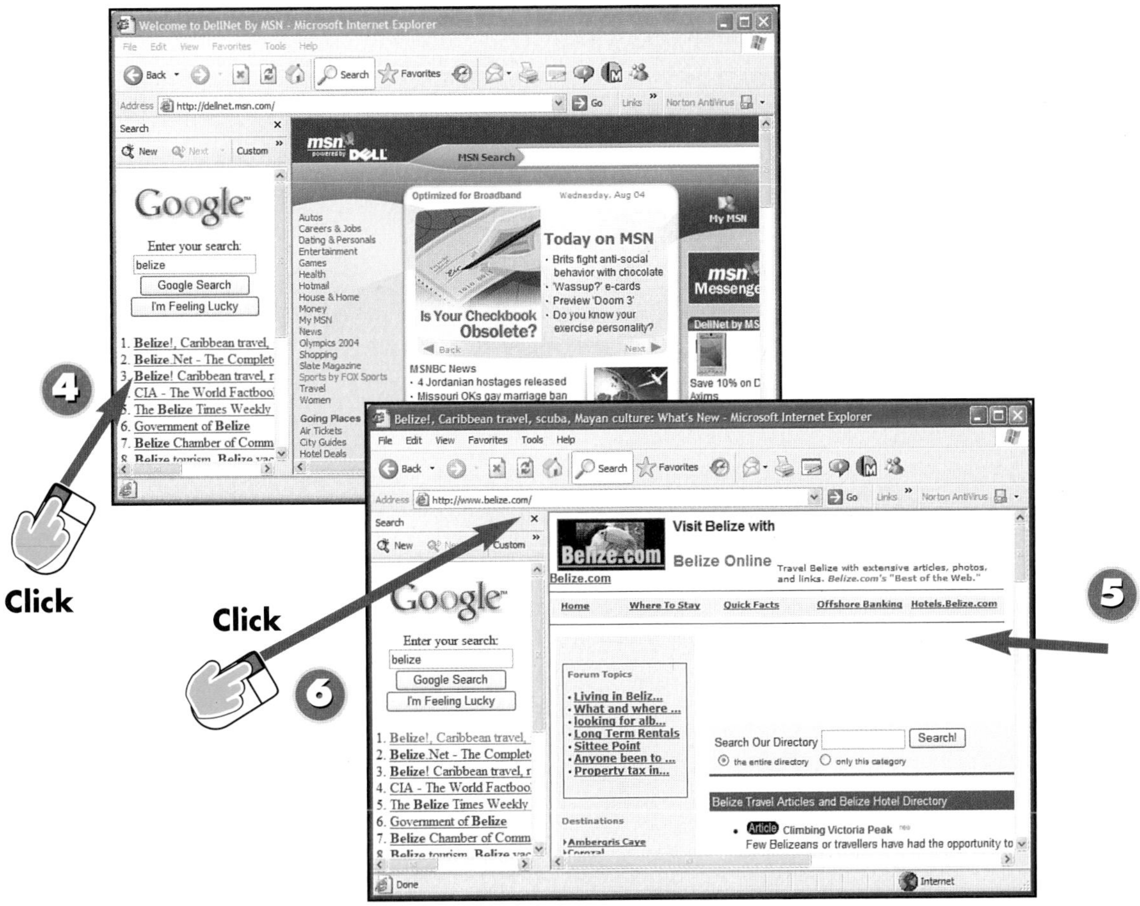

Click

Click

4 You see the results of the search in the window. To go to any of the found searches, click the link in the search results.

5 The page you selected appears in the right pane.

6 Click the **Close** button to close the search bar.

TIP

Home Page

Your home page may include a Search tool. For instance, the MSN home page includes a tool for searching on its opening page. You can also use this feature to search the Internet.

Task 5: Adding a Site to Your Favorites List

Start

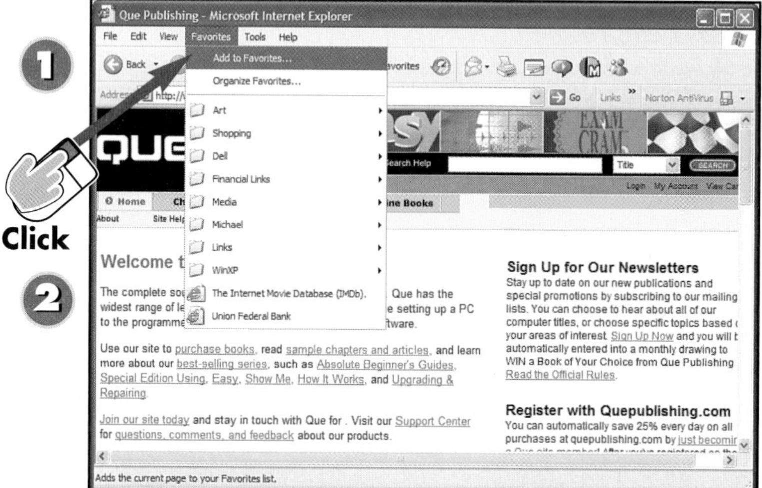

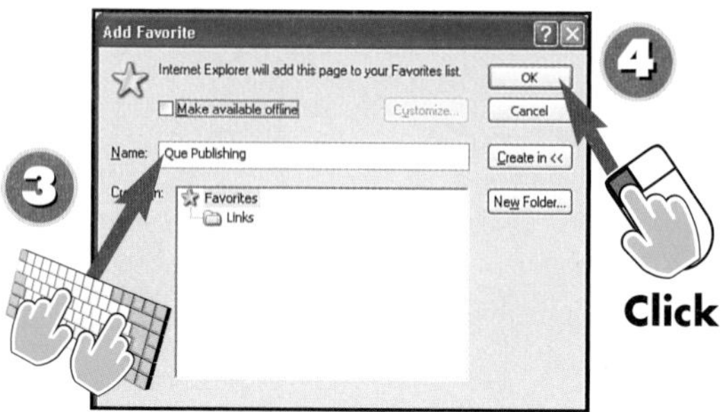

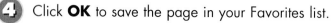

1. Display the Web site that you want to add to your Favorites list.
2. Open the **Favorites** menu and click the **Add to Favorites** command.
3. Type a name for the page (if you're not satisfied with the default name that is provided).
4. Click **OK** to save the page in your Favorites list.

INTRODUCTION

When you find a site that you especially like, you might want a quick way to return to it without having to browse from link to link or having to remember the address. Fortunately, Internet Explorer enables you to build a list of favorite sites and to access those sites by clicking them in the list.

TIP

Add to a Folder

You can add the site to a folder you have set up (covered in Task 7, "Rearranging Your Favorites List"). To do so, click the **Create in** button, and then select the folder in which to place the link.

Task 6: Going to a Site in Your Favorites List

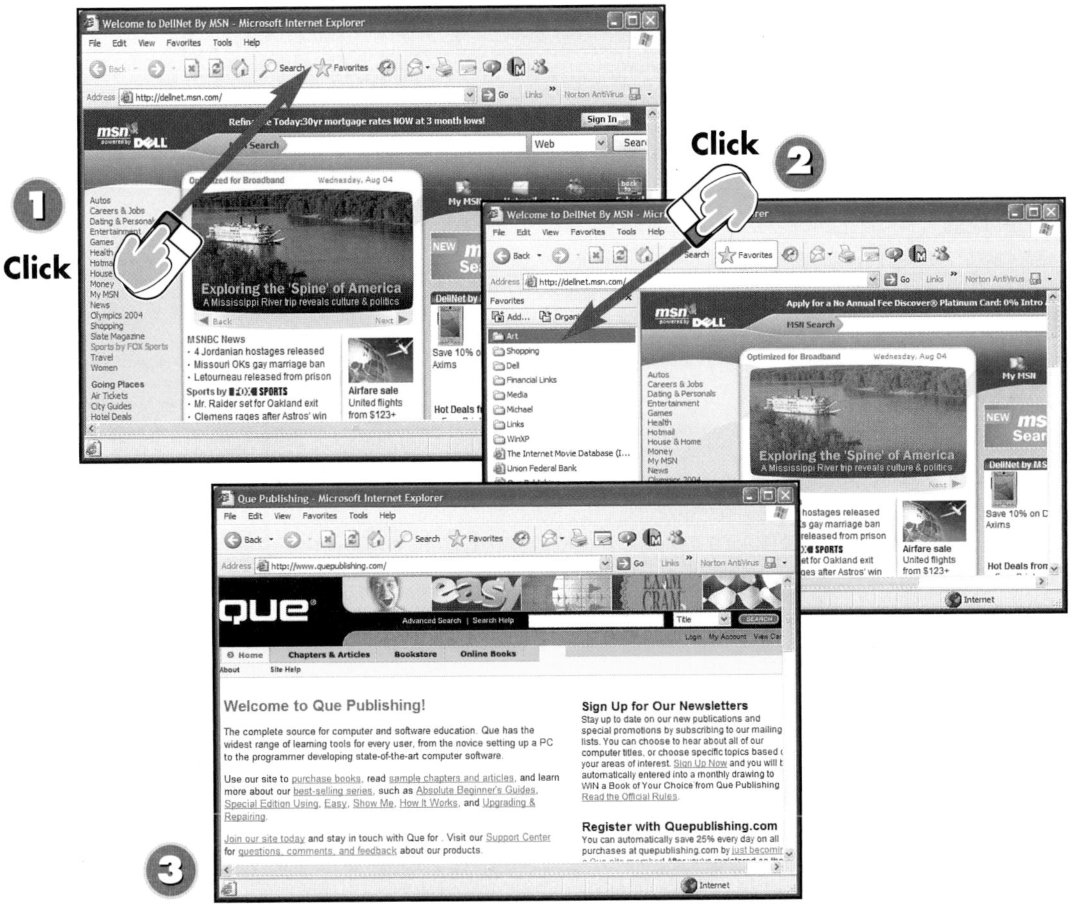

Start

Click

Click

1. Click the **Favorites** button on the toolbar.
2. The Favorites bar is displayed in the left pane. The right pane contains the current page. Click the site you want to visit in the Favorites bar.
3. Internet Explorer displays the site you selected from the Favorites bar.

INTRODUCTION

After you have added a site to your Favorites list, you can easily reach that site by displaying the list and selecting the site.

TIP

Close Bar

To close the Favorites bar, click its **Close** button.

TIP

Use Menu

You can also reach a site by opening the Favorites menu and selecting the site from the list of favorite sites.

Task 7: Rearranging Your Favorites List

Click

Click

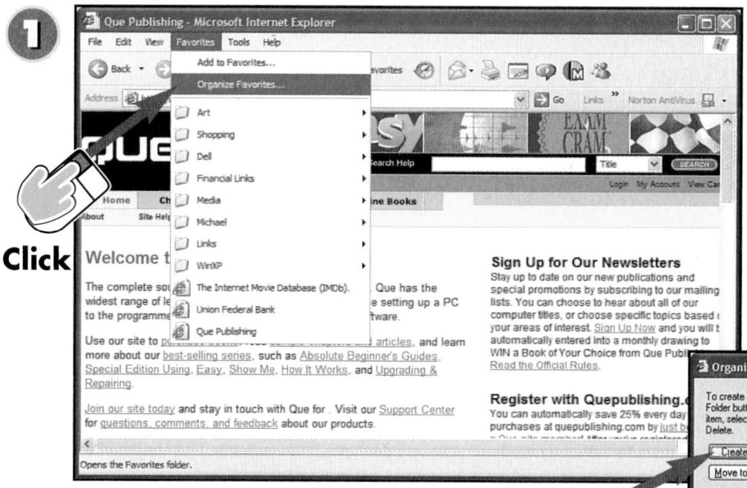

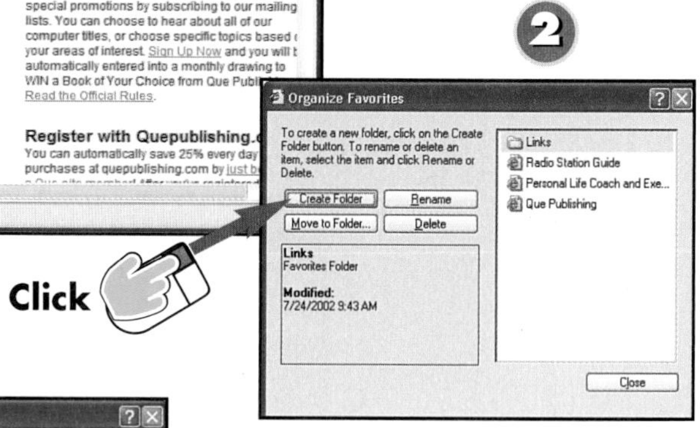

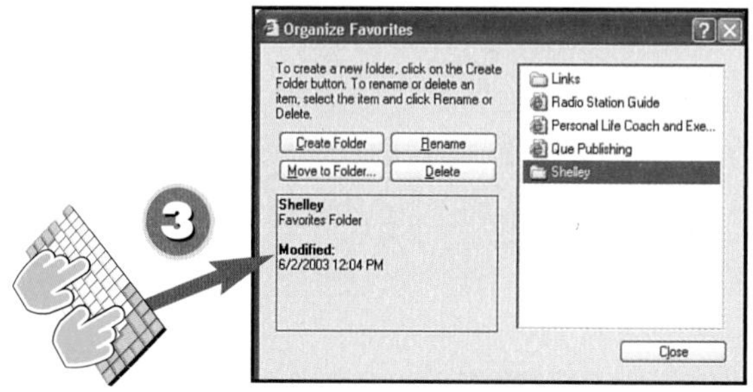

1. Open the **Favorites** menu, and then choose **Organize Favorites**.
2. To create a new folder, click the **Create Folder** button.
3. Type the folder name and press **Enter**. The folder is added.

INTRODUCTION

If you add several sites to your Favorites list, it might become difficult to use. You can organize the list by grouping similar sites together in a folder. You can add new folders and move sites from one folder to another to keep your list from getting cluttered.

TIP

Rename Site
To rename a site, select the site and click the **Rename** button. Type a new name, and press **Enter**.

TIP

Delete Site
To delete a site, select it and click the **Delete** button. Click the **Yes** button to confirm the deletion.

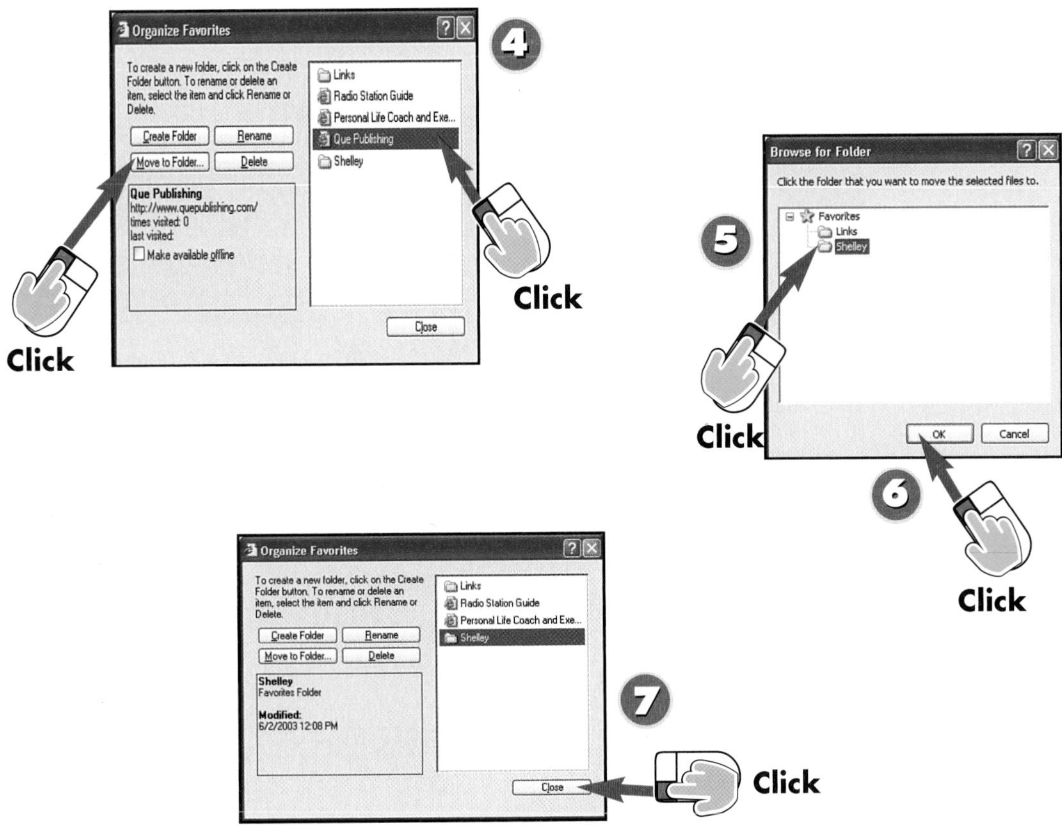

4. To move a site from one folder to another, select the site. Click the **Move to Folder** button.
5. Select the folder to which you want to move the site.
6. Click **OK**. The site is moved to the folder you selected.
7. Click the **Close** button to close the Organize Favorites dialog box.

TIP

Make Changes from Favorites Bar
You can also make changes while the Favorites bar is displayed. Click the **Organize** button in the Favorites bar.

TIP

Folders Added?
Your system may come with default folders and sites already added to your Favorites list. You can move, delete, and rearrange as needed.

Task 8: Using the History List

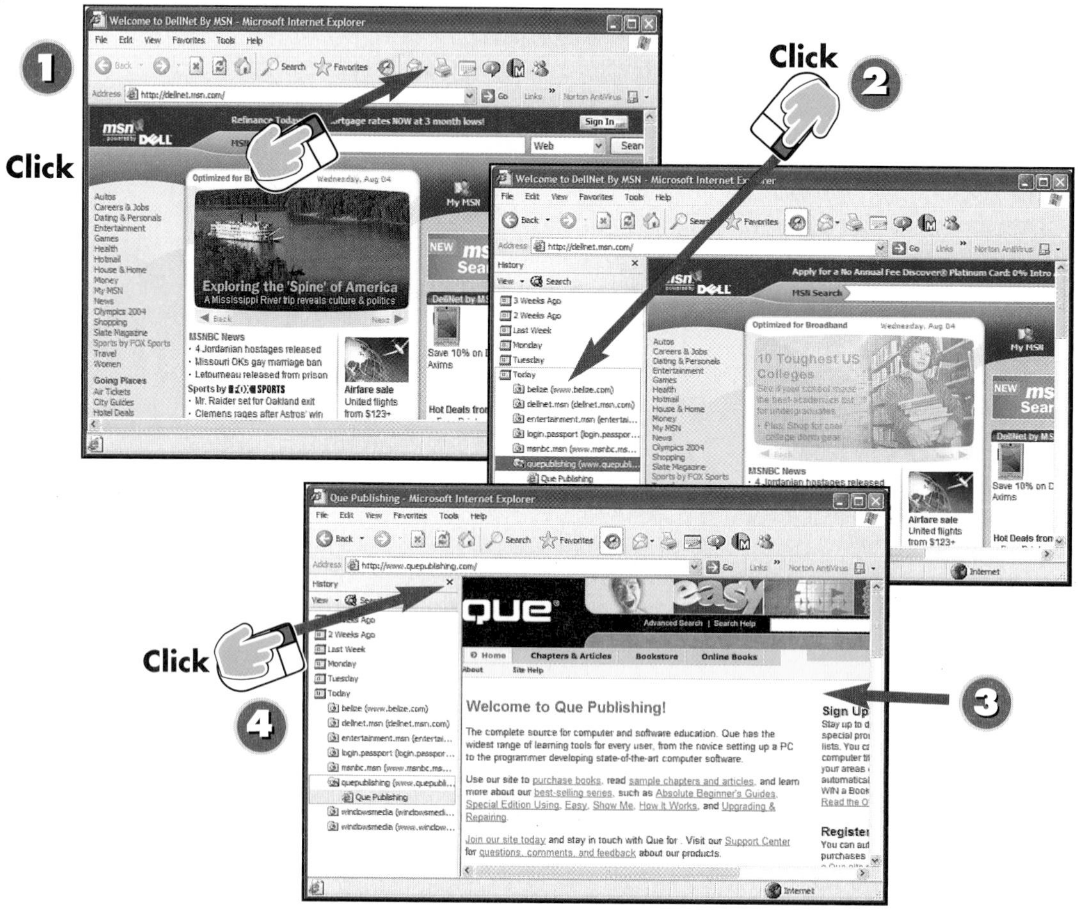

1. Click the **History** button.

2. Internet Explorer displays the History bar. If necessary, select the day or week whose list you want to review, and then click the site and page you want to visit.

3. Internet Explorer displays that site.

4. Click the **Close** button to close the History bar.

INTRODUCTION

As you browse from link to link, you might remember a site that you liked, but not remember that site's name or address. You can easily return to sites you have visited by displaying the History bar. From the list of visited sites, you can select the week and day you want to review, and then the site you want to visit, and finally the specific page at that site.

TIP

Sort the History List

To sort the history list, click the **View** button in the History toolbar and then click the sort order (by date, by site, by most visited, or by order visited today).

Task 9: Clearing the History List

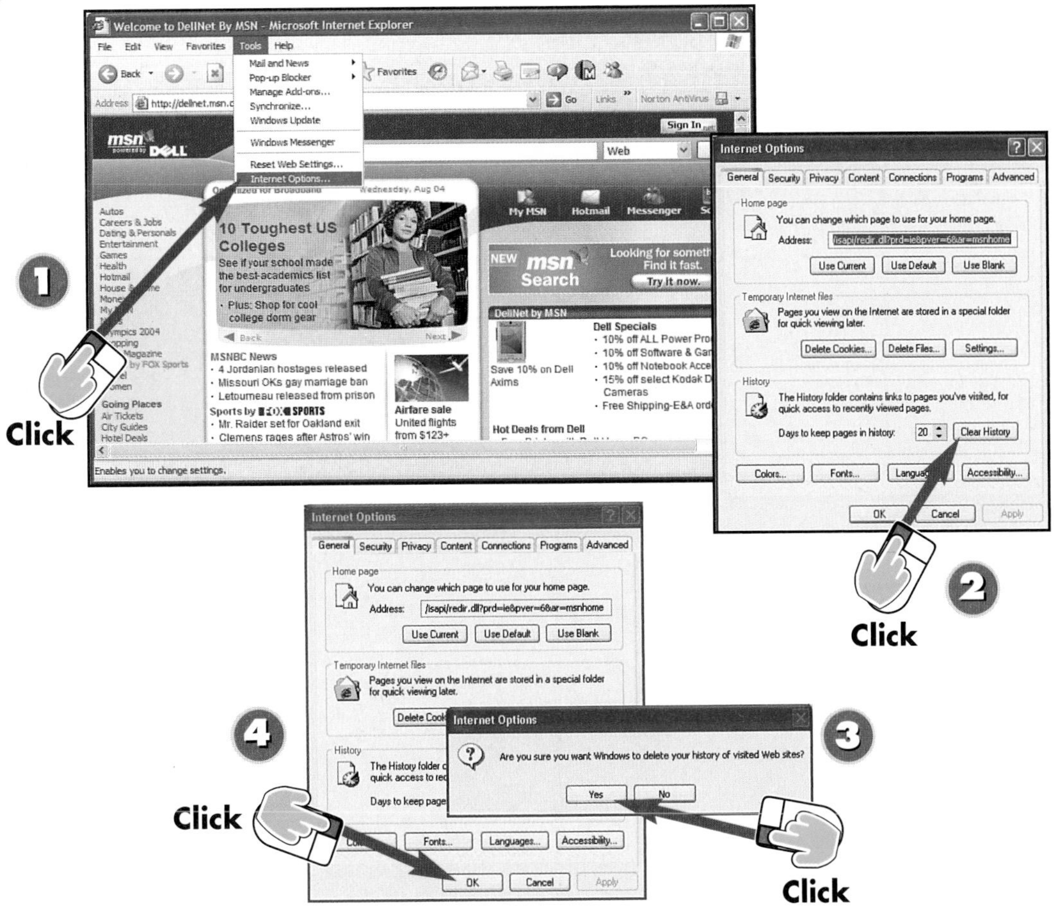

1. Click Tools and then **Internet Options**.
2. To clear the history list, click the **Clear History** button.
3. Confirm the deletion by clicking **Yes**.
4. Click **OK** to close the Internet Options dialog box.

INTRODUCTION

To keep others from browsing through a list of sites you have visited, you can clear your history list. You might also do this to free up the disk space Windows XP uses to store this history list.

TIP

How Long Saved?
You can select how many days the history is kept. Select the number of days the history by typing a value or using the spin arrows to increment the value on the General tab.

Task 10: Emailing a Page or Link

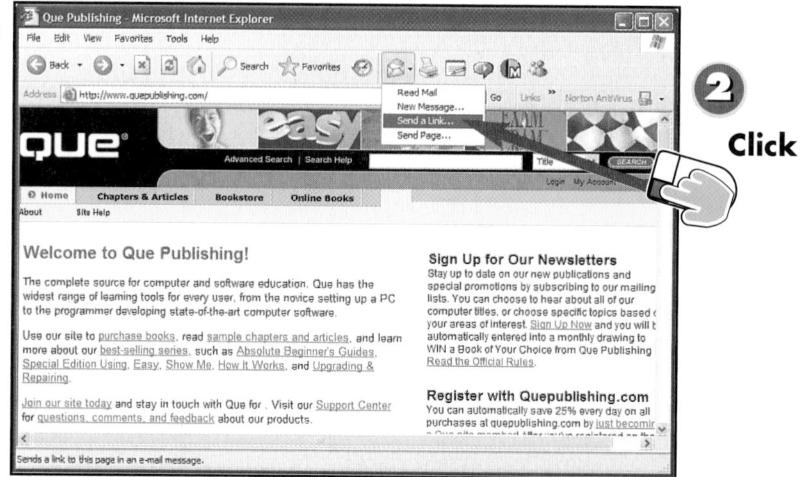

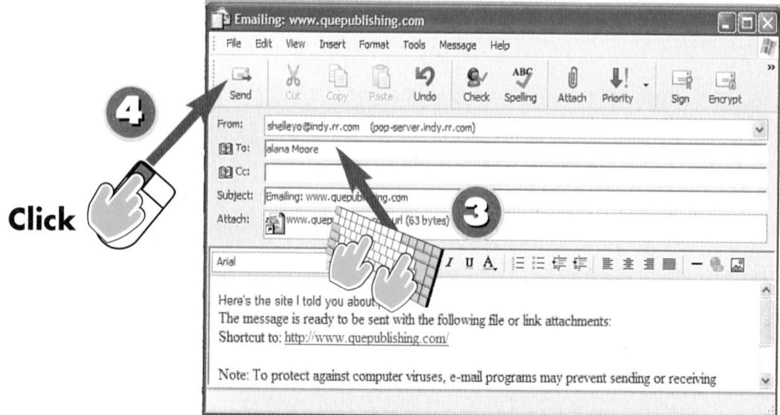

1. Display the page you want to send.
2. Click the down arrow next to the Mail button and select **Send a Link**.
3. You see a mail window with the subject and attach lines completed. The message includes the link to the page. Complete the address.
4. Click **Send**. The message is sent.

INTRODUCTION

If you find a page of interest and want to share it with someone, you can email the page or a link to that page from Internet Explorer. You can either type the recipient's address or select it from your Address Book.

TIP

Research Button

You may also see a Research button in your toolbar. You can use this to look up words or topics in reference books, mostly thesauruses. This button is most commonly added by Microsoft Office.

TIP

Send the Page

To send the page, select this option and follow the same steps.

Help on Email

For more information on sending e-mail messages, see Part 7, "Sending Faxes and Email."

Task 11: Setting Your Home Page

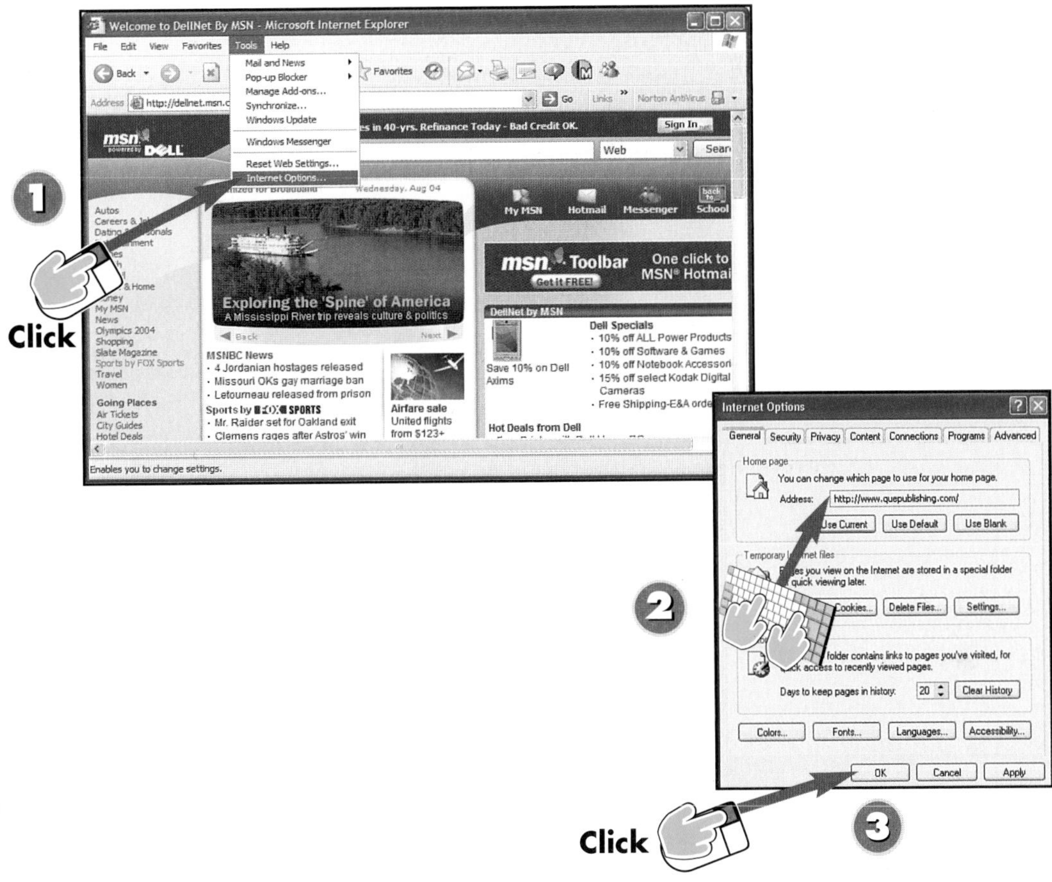

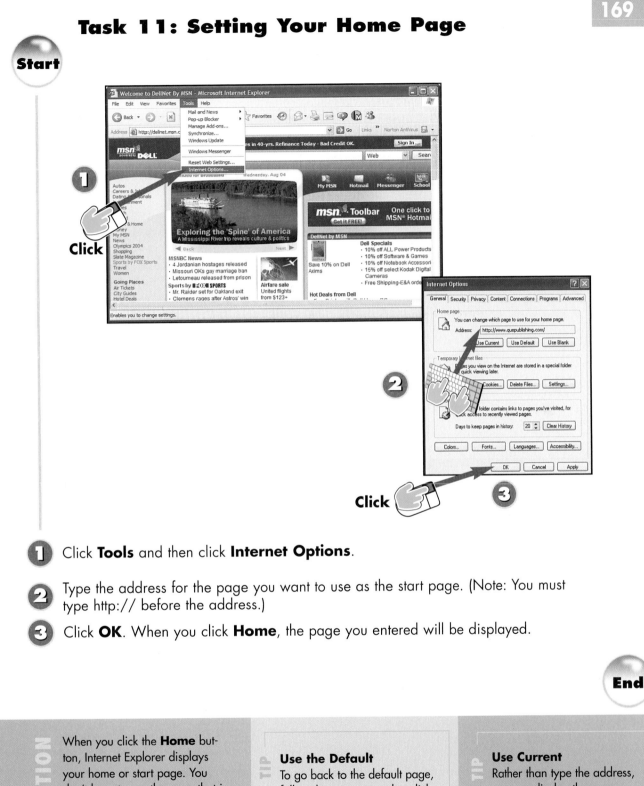

1. Click **Tools** and then click **Internet Options**.
2. Type the address for the page you want to use as the start page. (Note: You must type http:// before the address.)
3. Click **OK**. When you click **Home**, the page you entered will be displayed.

INTRODUCTION

When you click the **Home** button, Internet Explorer displays your home or start page. You don't have to use the page that is selected; you can use any page as your start page.

TIP

Use the Default

To go back to the default page, follow the same steps, but click the **Use Default** button.

TIP

Use Current

Rather than type the address, you can display the page you want to use. Select **View**, **Internet Options**, and then click the **Use Current** button.

Task 12: Setting Privacy Levels and Blocking Pop-Ups

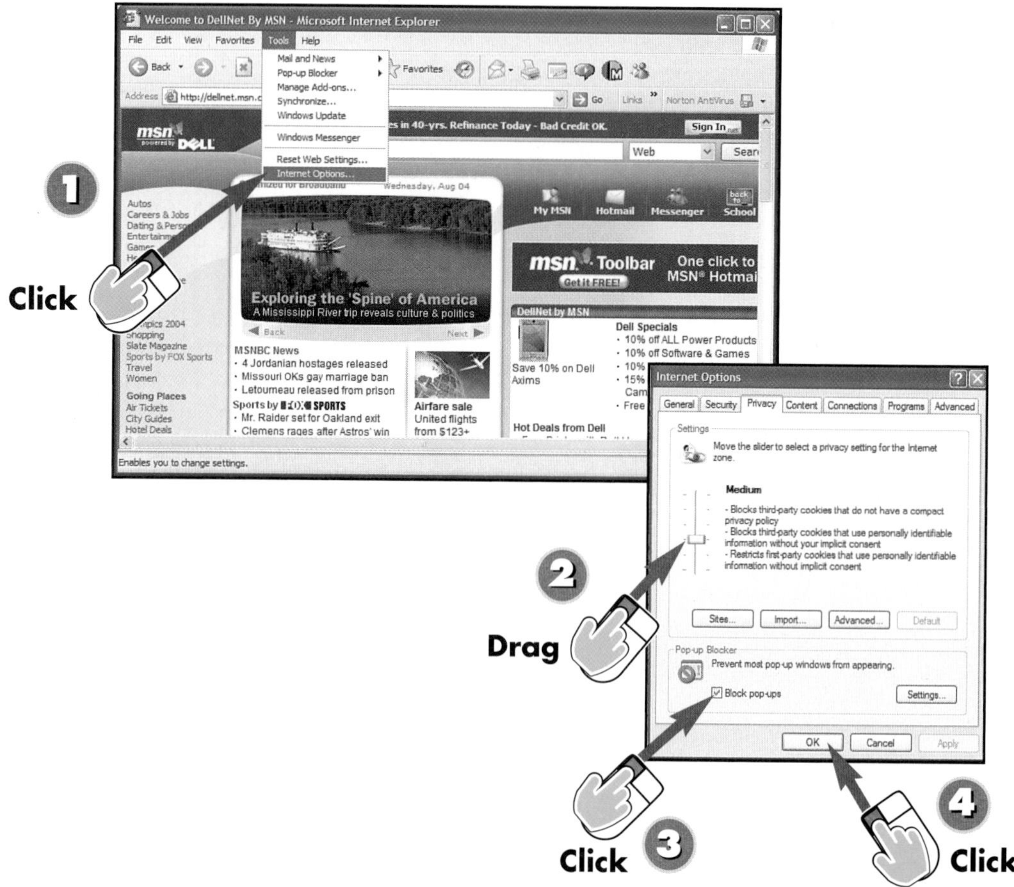

1. Click **Tools** and then choose **Internet Options**.
2. Click the **Privacy** tab. To set the privacy level, drag the slider bar. You can see a description of this setting.
3. Check **Block pop-ups** if needed.
4. Click **OK**.

INTRODUCTION

You can assign various privacy levels for Internet sites. The privacy level controls such options as whether the site can use cookies (temporary files stored on you computer), whether the site has a privacy policy, and other options. You can also block pop-up advertisements.

TIP

Security
For more information on security, review the online help. Internet Explorer devotes an entire section of its help system to security issues.

TIP

Settings
Settings include Accept All Cookies, Low, Medium, Medium High, High, Block All Cookies

Task 13: Turning on Firewall Protection

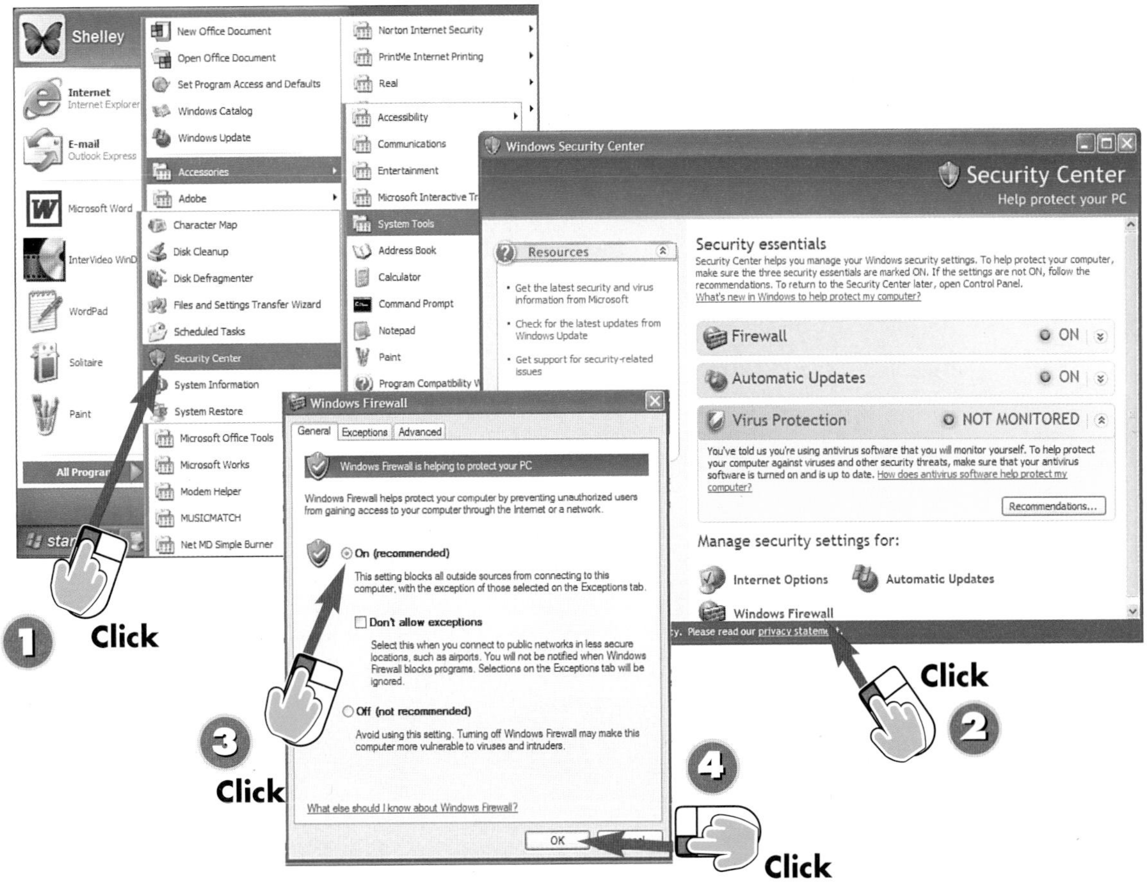

1. Click **Start**, **All Programs**, **Accessories**, **System Tools**, and **Security Center**.

2. Make sure that Windows Firewall is on. If it's not on, click the link for Windows Firewall at the bottom of the window.

3. Click **On (recommended)**.

4. Click **OK** to close this window, and then click the Close button to close the Windows Security Center.

INTRODUCTION

If you use a cable connection, you are connected 24/7. To protect your computer from outside access, you need to use a firewall. You can use the firewall feature of Windows to keep your computer secure.

TIP

Spyware

Another thing to consider when protecting your computer is to protect against spyware. Spyware programs can take monitor where you have been online and then relay this information back to its company site or reset your home page. Most of the time spyware programs are installed without your knowledge or consent. To check for and block this type of program, consider using an anti-spyware program.

PART 9

Using Windows Accessories

Windows XP provides several accessories, or *applications*, that you can use to help you in your work. These accessories are not full-featured programs, but they are useful for specific jobs in the Windows environment. Accessories include a calculator, a painting program, a word processor, a text editor, and Internet applications. (Internet applications are discussed in Part 8, "Connecting to the Internet.")

Tasks

Task 1: Using Calculator

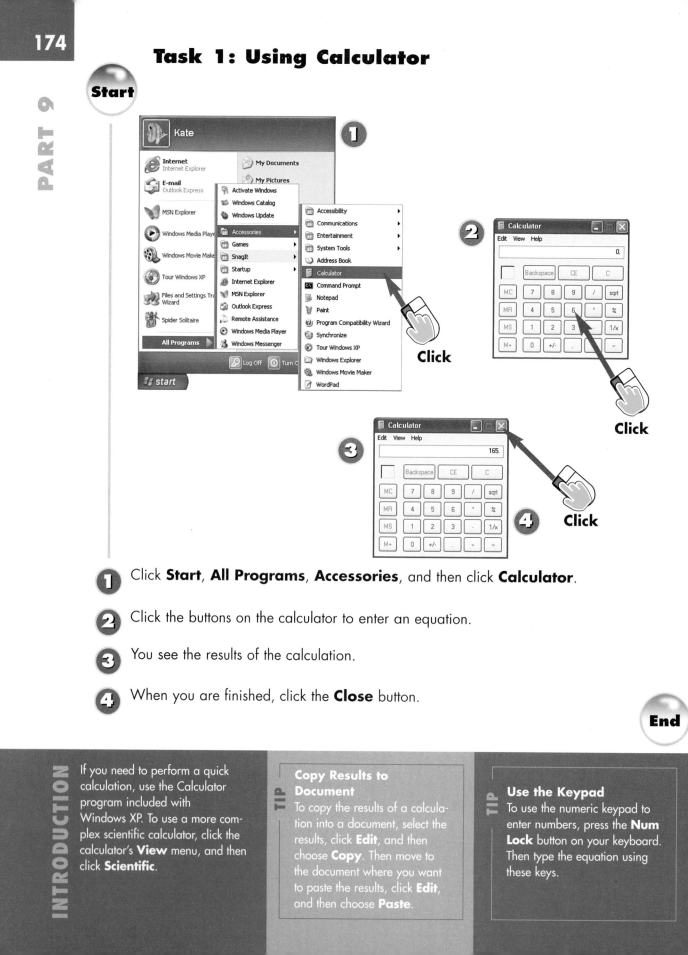

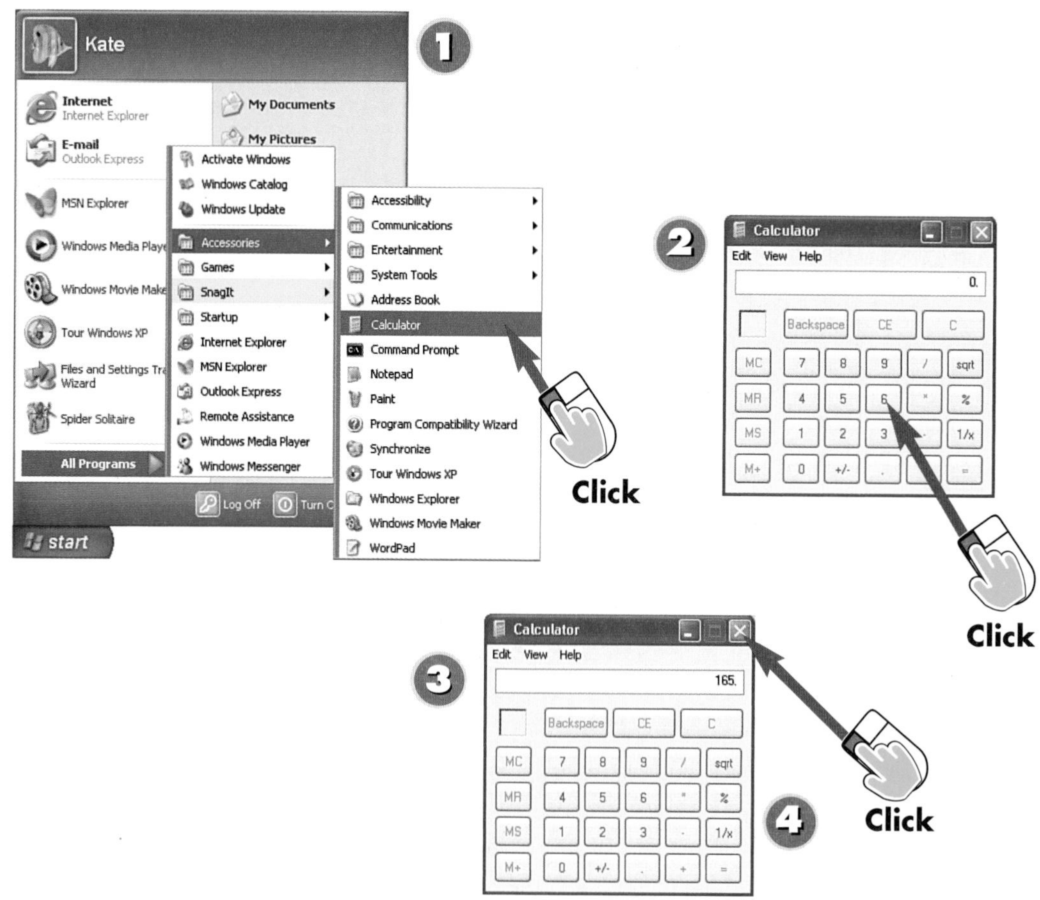

1. Click **Start**, **All Programs**, **Accessories**, and then click **Calculator**.
2. Click the buttons on the calculator to enter an equation.
3. You see the results of the calculation.
4. When you are finished, click the **Close** button.

INTRODUCTION

If you need to perform a quick calculation, use the Calculator program included with Windows XP. To use a more complex scientific calculator, click the calculator's **View** menu, and then click **Scientific**.

TIP

Copy Results to Document

To copy the results of a calculation into a document, select the results, click **Edit**, and then choose **Copy**. Then move to the document where you want to paste the results, click **Edit**, and then choose **Paste**.

TIP

Use the Keypad

To use the numeric keypad to enter numbers, press the **Num Lock** button on your keyboard. Then type the equation using these keys.

Task 2: Using Command Prompt

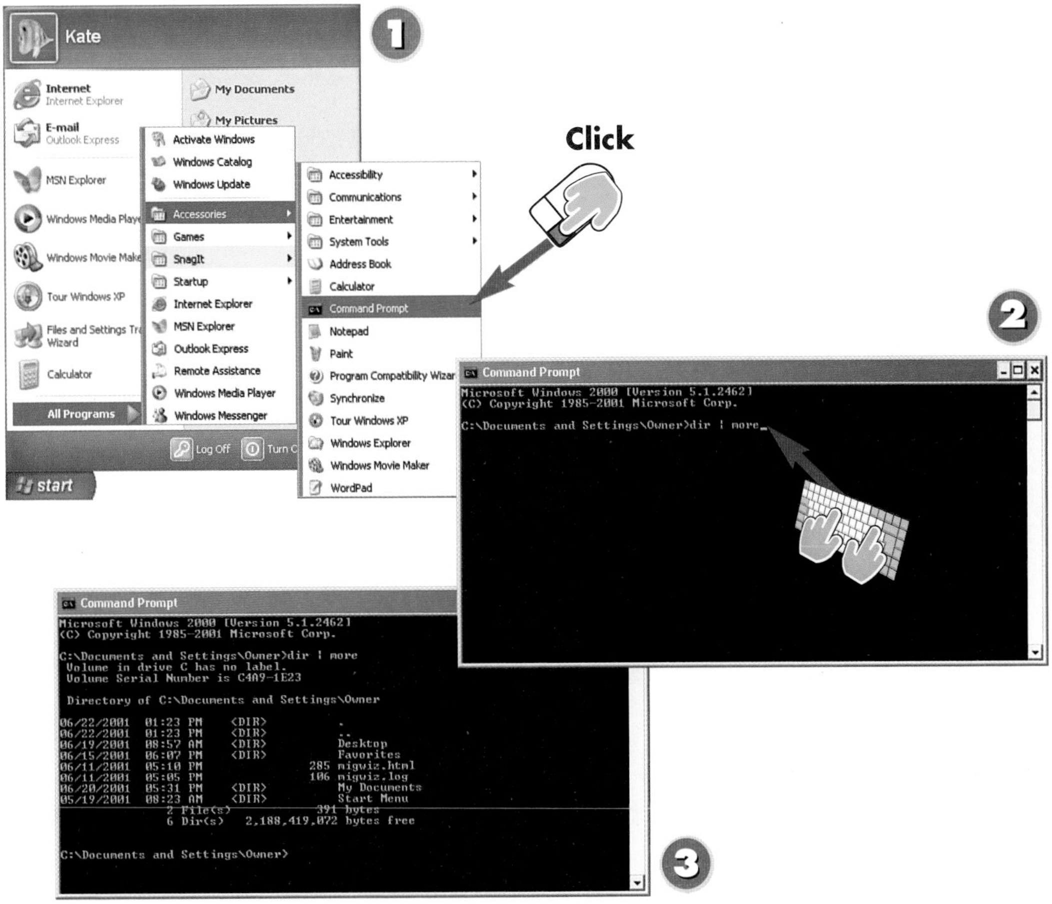

1. Click **Start**, **All Programs**, **Accessories**, and then click **Command Prompt**.

2. Type the desired command and press **Enter**.

3. You see the results of the command you typed.

End

INTRODUCTION

There may be times when you want to access the Command (or DOS) prompt from Windows XP. For example, you might want to run a DOS application or use DOS commands. Alternatively, you might have programs that run in DOS. Windows XP provides a Command prompt window that you can open while working in Windows.

TIP

Enlarge the Window

Press **Alt+Enter** to enlarge the Command window to full screen. Press **Alt+Enter** again to restore the Command window to its original size.

TIP

Close the DOS Prompt

When you are finished working in DOS mode, type `exit` and press Enter to close the Command Prompt window.

Task 3: Using WordPad

Start

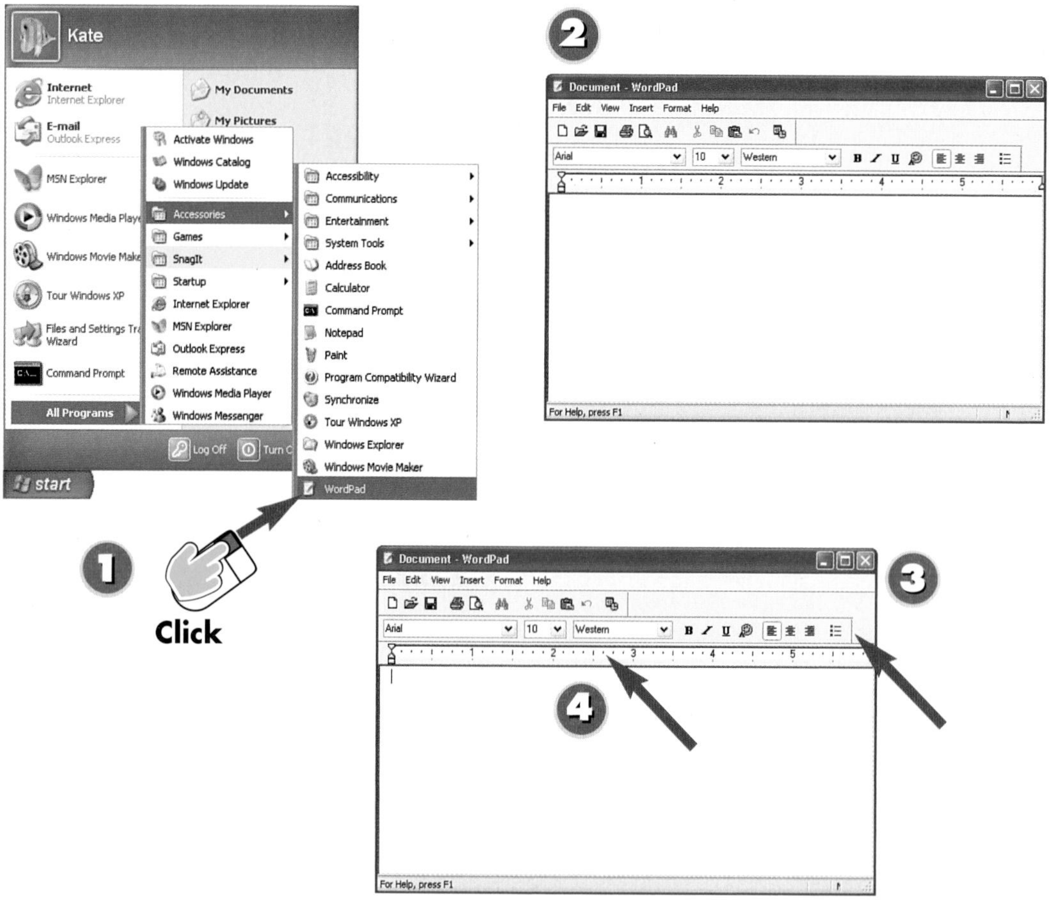

1. Click **Start**, **All Programs**, **Accessories**, and then select **WordPad**.
2. Use the menu bar to select commands. Use the toolbar to select buttons for frequently used commands.
3. Use the format bar to make changes to the appearance of the text.
4. Use the ruler to set tabs and indents.

End

INTRODUCTION

Use WordPad to edit text files or to create simple documents such as notes, memos, fax sheets, and so on. WordPad saves files in Rich Text Format by default, but you can choose to save in a text-only format.

TIP

Hide Toolbars

To hide any of the screen elements in WordPad, open the **View** menu and click the tool you want to hide. A check mark indicates that the tool is showing; no check mark indicates that it is hidden.

Task 4: Typing Text

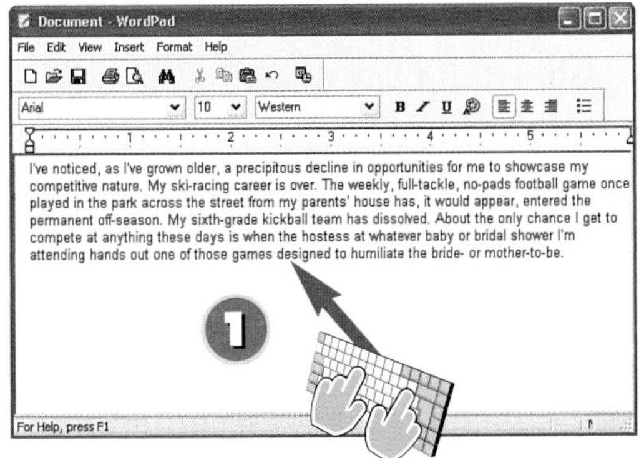

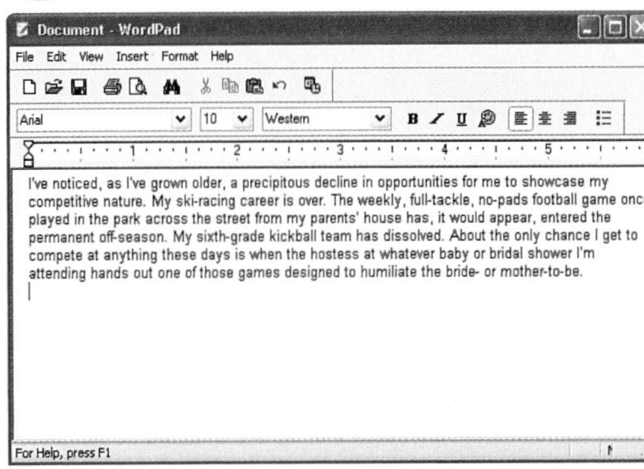

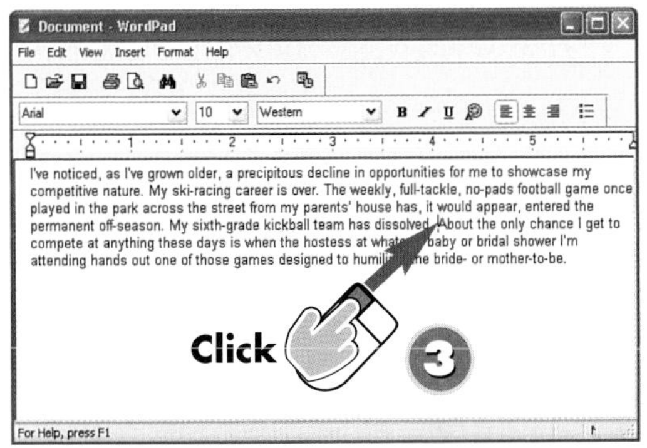

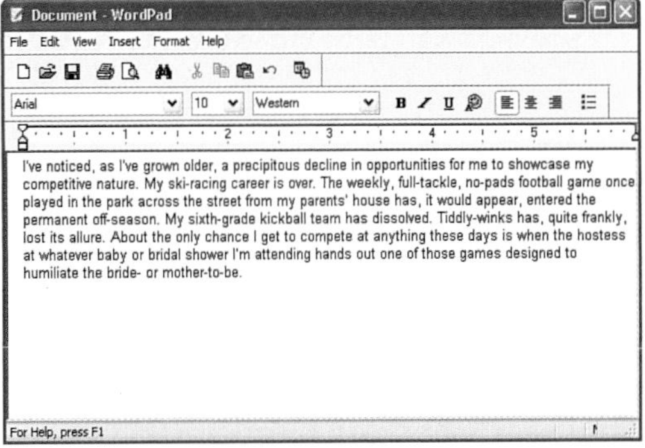

1. Type the text. You don't need to press Enter at the end of each line; WordPad automatically wraps the lines within a paragraph.
2. To end a paragraph and start a new one, press **Enter**. The insertion point moves to the next line.
3. To add text to a paragraph you've already typed, click the spot where you want to make the change, and start typing.
4. The existing text moves over to make room.

INTRODUCTION

To add text to a new document, simply type the text you want to include, much like you do with a typewriter. Unlike a typewriter, though, WordPad enables you to easily change what you've typed.

TIP

Press Backspace to Erase

If you make a mistake while typing, press the **Backspace** key to delete one character at a time. Then retype the text.

Undo a Change

You can undo the last action by clicking the **Edit** menu and choosing **Undo**.

TIP

Save Your Document

Be sure to save your document as you continue to work on it. Click **File** and choose Save (or click the **Save** button on the toolbar) to save your work. For more information, refer to Part 2, Task 5, "Saving and Closing a Document."

Task 5: Selecting Text

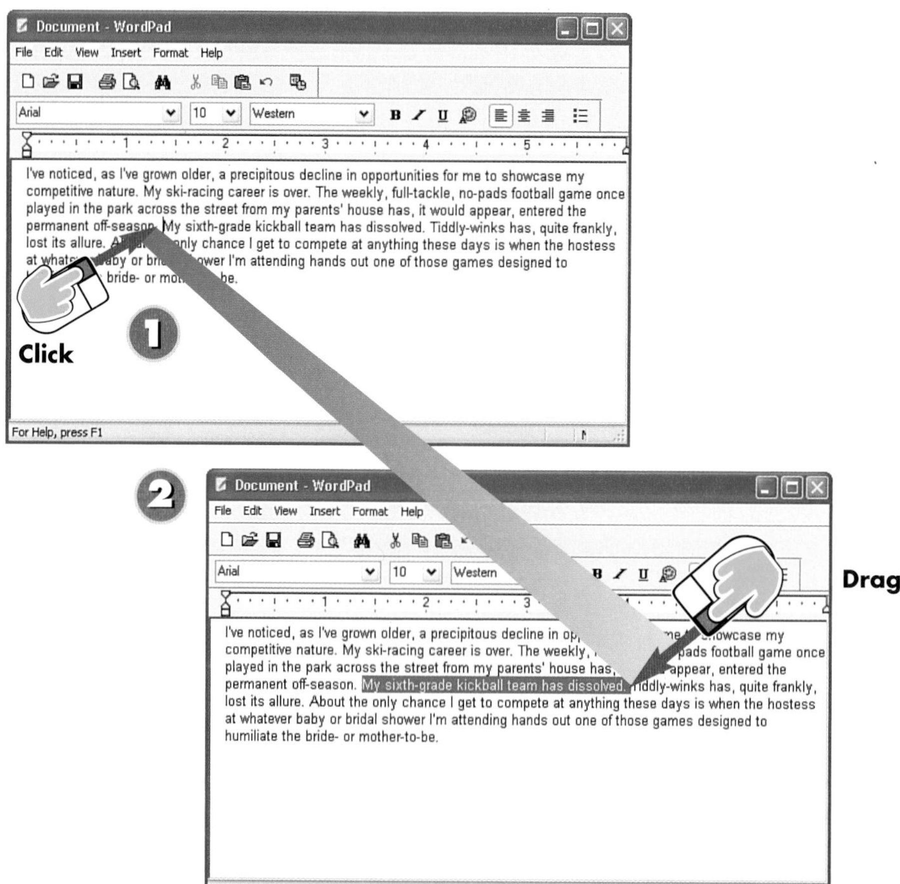

1. Click at the beginning of the text you want to select.

2. Hold down the mouse button and drag across the text, then release the mouse button. The selected text appears highlighted.

INTRODUCTION

Knowing how to select data (text, images, and so on) is very important when using WordPad. For example, you can select text and then delete it, move it, copy it, change its appearance, and more.

TIP

Select an Image
To select an image, click it once.

Use the Keyboard
If you prefer to use the keyboard to select text, hold down the **Shift** key and use the arrow keys to highlight the text you want to select.

TIP

Deselect Text
To deselect text, click outside the selected text.

Task 6: Deleting Text

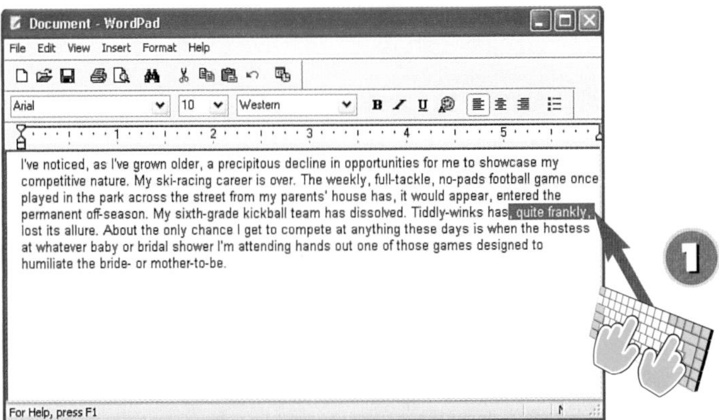

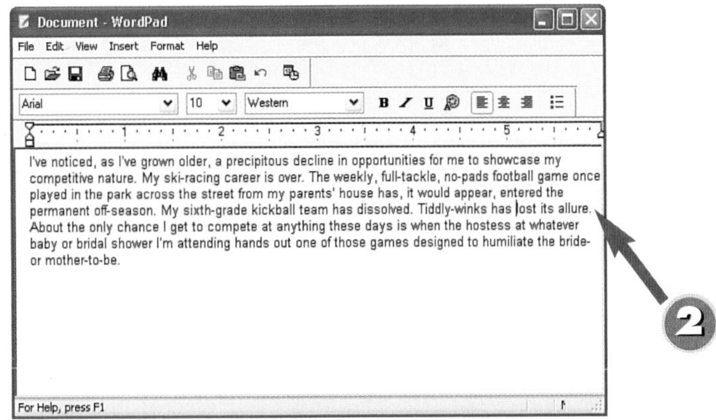

1. Select the text you want to delete, and then press the **Delete** or **Backspace** key on your keyboard.
2. The text is deleted.

INTRODUCTION

Just as you can add text, you can easily delete it. You can delete characters, words, paragraphs, pages, or even all the text in a document.

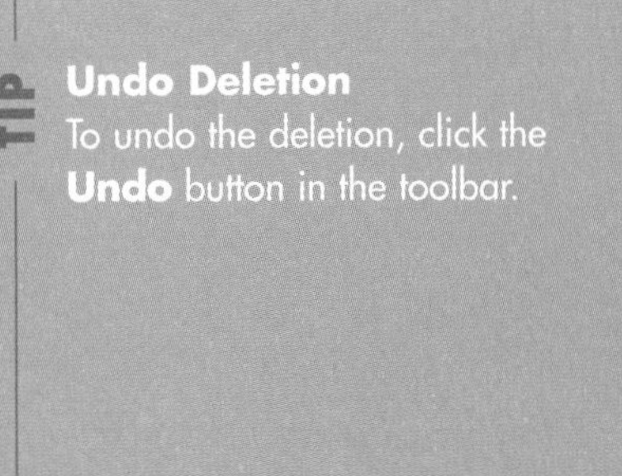

TIP

Undo Deletion

To undo the deletion, click the **Undo** button in the toolbar.

Task 7: Copying Text

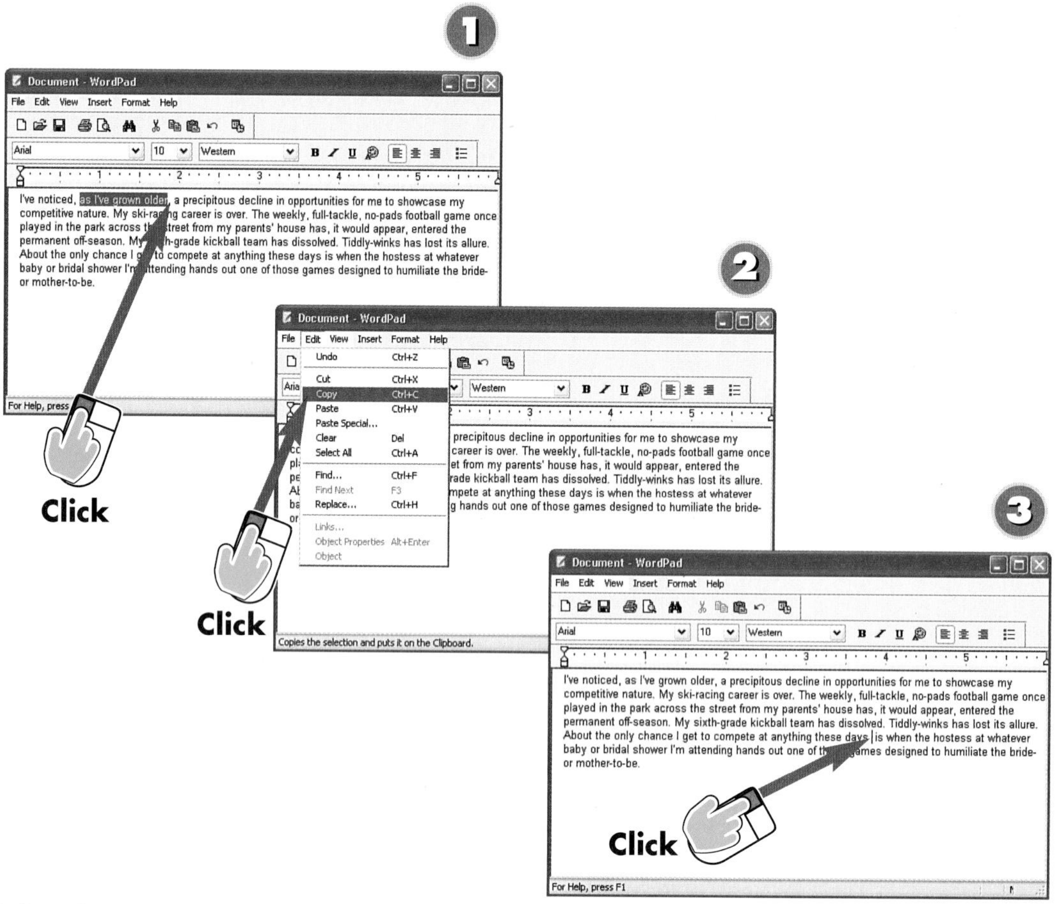

1. Select the text you want to copy.

2. Click **Edit**, and then select the **Copy** command. Windows copies the data from the document and places it in the *Clipboard*, a temporary holding spot.

3. Click the spot in the document where you want to put the copied data.

INTRODUCTION

One of the most common editing tasks is to copy text. You can copy text and paste the copy into the current document or into another document.

TIP

Copy to Another Document

To copy data from one open document to another, select the text and then use the **Window** menu to move to the document where you want to paste the text.

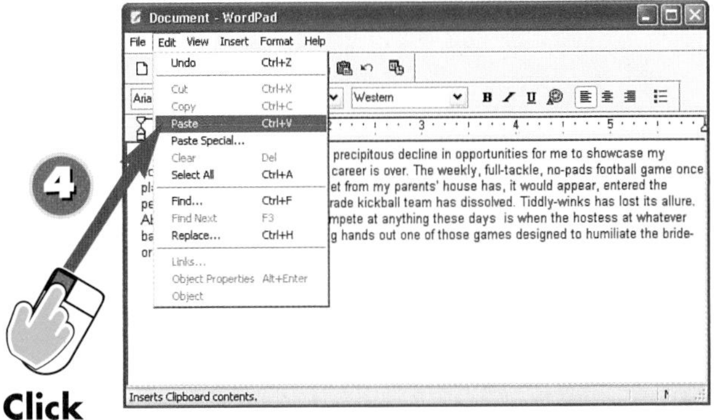

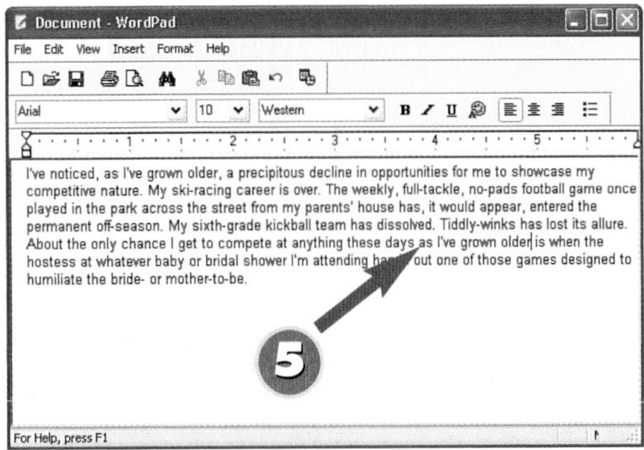

4. Click **Edit** and then select the **Paste** command.

5. The data is pasted into the document.

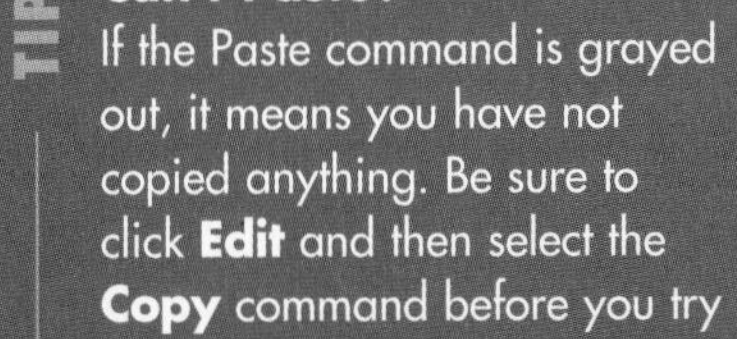

TIP

Can't Paste?

If the Paste command is grayed out, it means you have not copied anything. Be sure to click **Edit** and then select the **Copy** command before you try to paste the text.

TIP

Shortcut Keys

You can also use the shortcut keys **Ctrl+C** for Copy and **Ctrl+V** for Paste. The toolbar also includes a Copy button and a Paste button.

Task 8: Moving Text

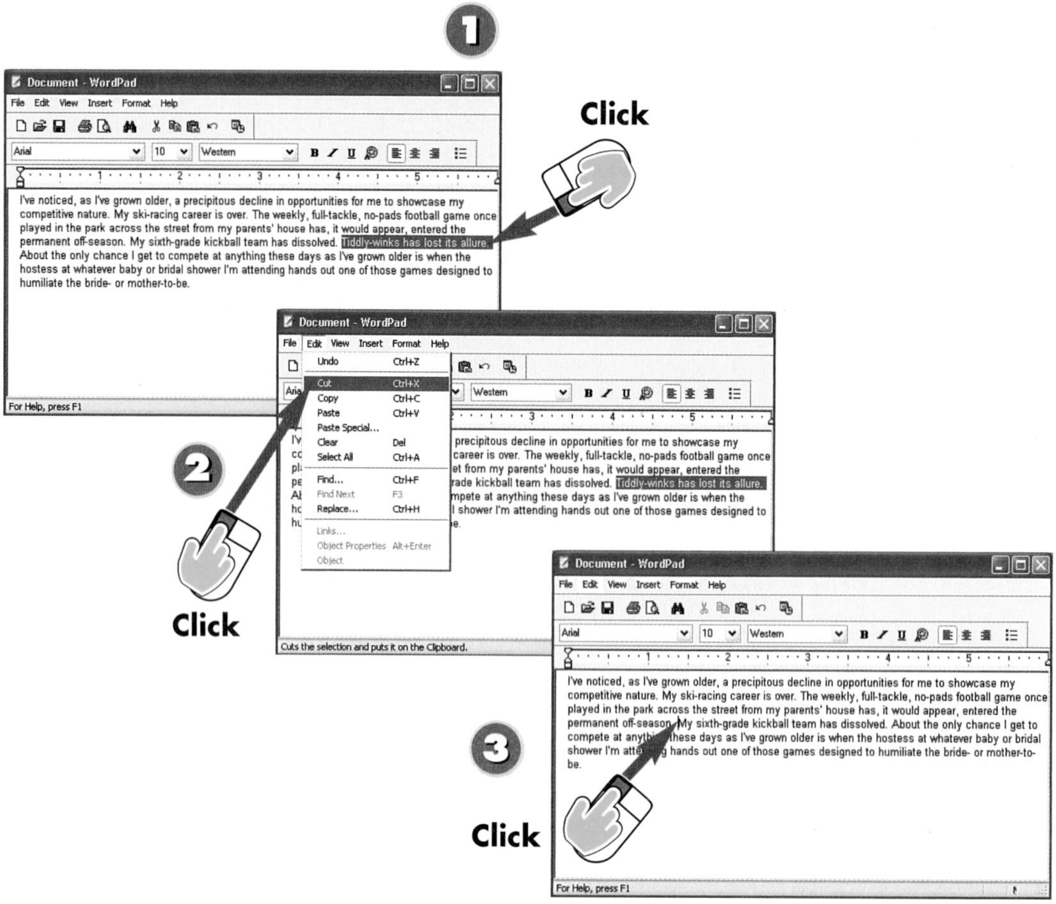

1. Select the text you want to move.
2. Click **Edit**, and then click the **Cut** command. Windows deletes the data from the document and places it in the Clipboard.
3. Click in the document where you want to place the text.

INTRODUCTION

Just as you can copy text, you can move text from one location in a document to another location in the same document. You can also move text from one document to another. Moving text is similar to copying text, except that when you move something it is deleted from its original location.

TIP

Move to Another Application

To move cut or copied data from WordPad to another application, simply switch to the desired application, click the spot where you want the data to be placed, open the **Edit** menu, and select **Paste**.

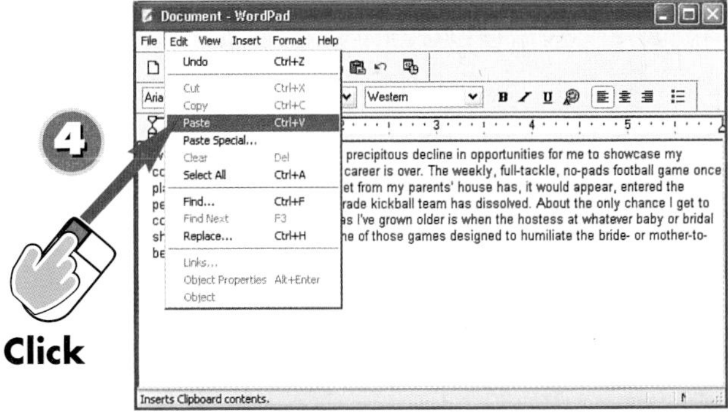

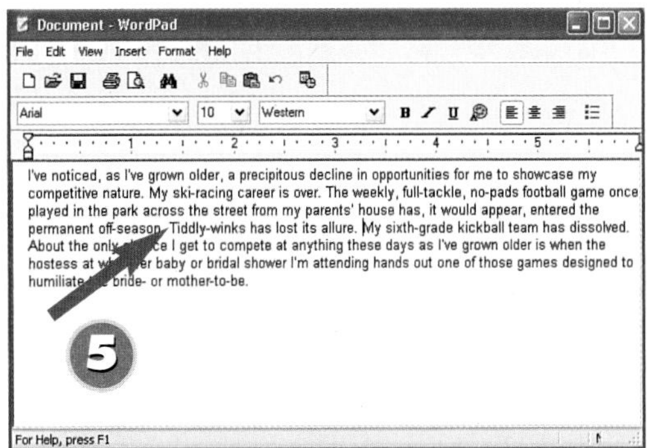

4 Click **Edit** and then select the **Paste** command.

5 The text is pasted into the new location.

TIP

Undo a Move
You can undo a paste operation if you change your mind after performing the action. Simply click **Edit**, and then select the **Undo Paste** command to remove the text you just pasted.

TIP

Shortcuts
WordPad includes toolbar buttons and keyboard shortcuts for Cut, Copy, and Paste operations. The keyboard shortcuts are **Ctrl+X** (Cut), **Ctrl+C** (Copy), and **Ctrl+V** (Paste).

Task 9: Formatting Text

Start

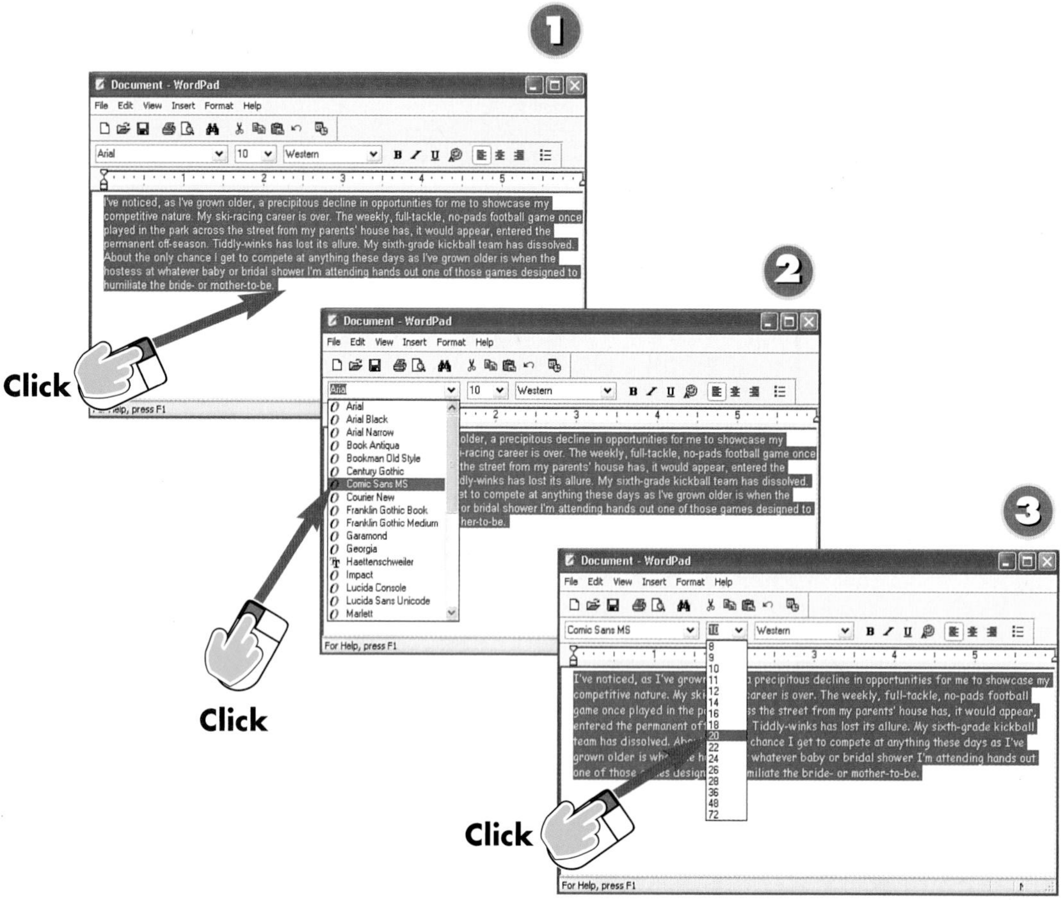

1. Select the text you want to change.

2. To use a different font, click the **Font** drop-down arrow and click the font you want.

3. To use a different font size, select the text you want to change, click the **Font Size** drop-down arrow, and click the size you want to use.

INTRODUCTION

You can easily make simple changes to the appearance of the text. For example, you can change the font or font size, and you can make text bold, italic, or underlined. This task touches on just a few of the formatting changes you can make. Experiment to try out some of the other available formatting features.

TIP

Undoing a Change

To undo a change, click the **Undo** button on the toolbar. The Undo button is the one with a curved arrow pointing to the left.

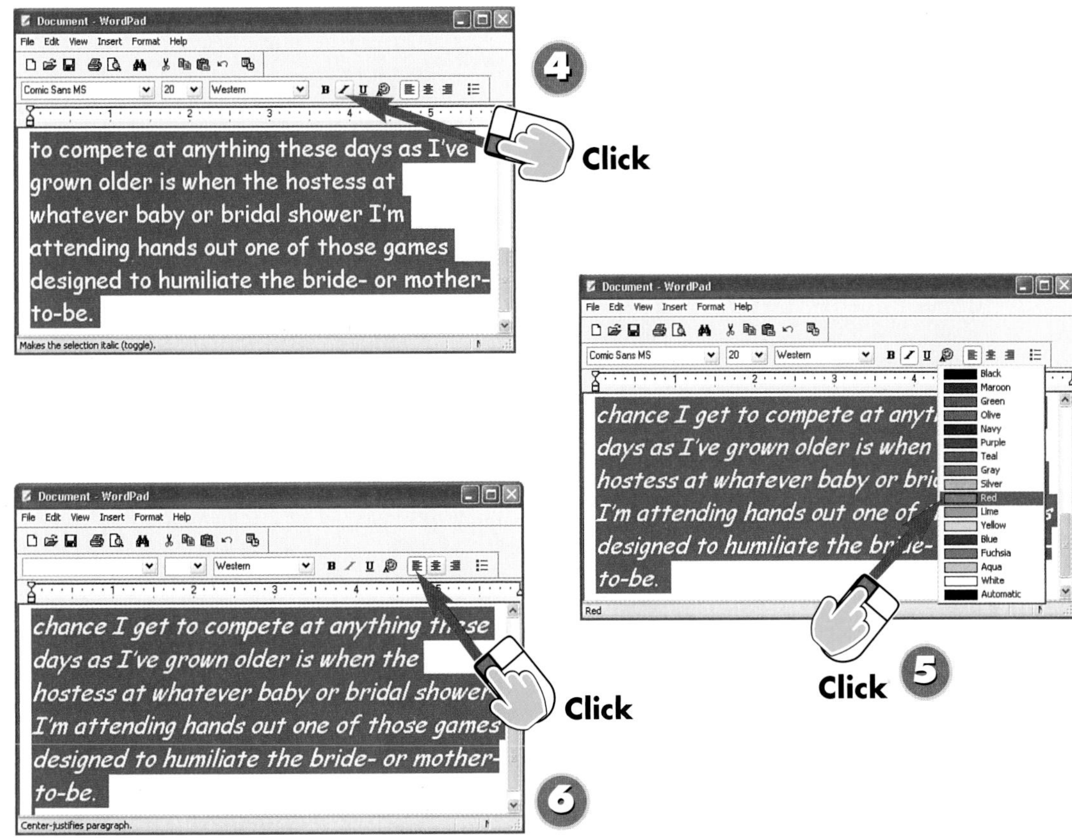

4 To make text bold, italic, or underlined, select the text, and then click the appropriate button in the format bar.

5 To change the font color, select the text you want to change, and then click the **Font Color** button. Select the color you want from the drop-down list that appears.

6 Change the alignment of a paragraph by selecting it and clicking any of the **Alignment** buttons on the toolbar.

TIP

Using the Format Menu

You can use the commands in the **Format** menu to change the appearance of your document. Included on the Format menu are commands to set the font, the bullet style, the paragraph style and the tabs.

TIP

Other WordPad Options

You can also use commands in WordPad's Insert menu to insert the date and time or objects, such as a chart or picture.

Task 10: Using Notepad

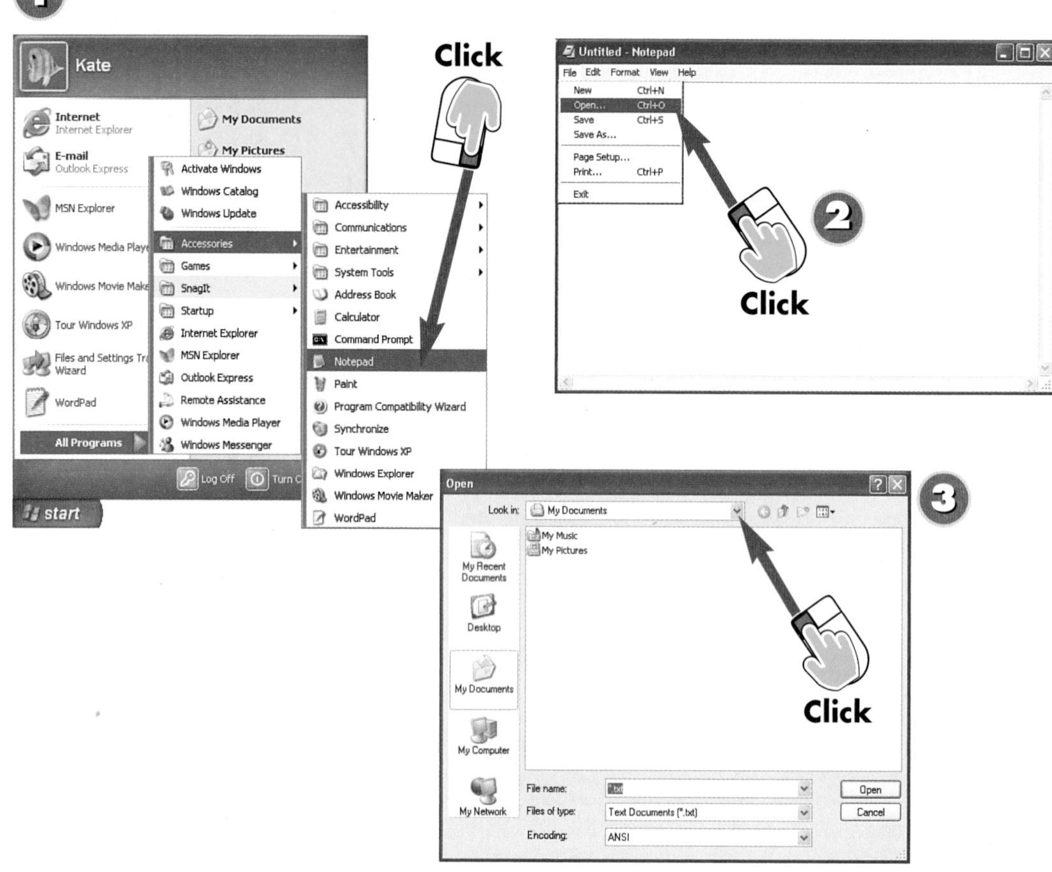

1. Click **Start**, **All Programs**, **Accessories**, and then choose **Notepad**.
2. To open a file in Notepad, click **File**, and then choose **Open**.
3. An Open dialog box appears. Navigate to the folder containing the file you want to open.

INTRODUCTION

The most common type of simple file is a text file, which has the extension .txt. They include instructions on how to install a program, beta notes, and other information. Some configuration files are also text files. To edit and work with this type of file, you can use Notepad, a simple text editor provided with Windows XP.

TIP

NotePad Versus WordPad

NotePad is similar to WordPad, in that both are text-editing programs. WordPad, however, supports more formatting options and other features whereas NotePad does not.

TIP

Navigate the Open Dialog Box

For help navigating the standard Windows Open dialog, refer to Task 6, "Opening a Document," in Part 2, "Working with Programs."

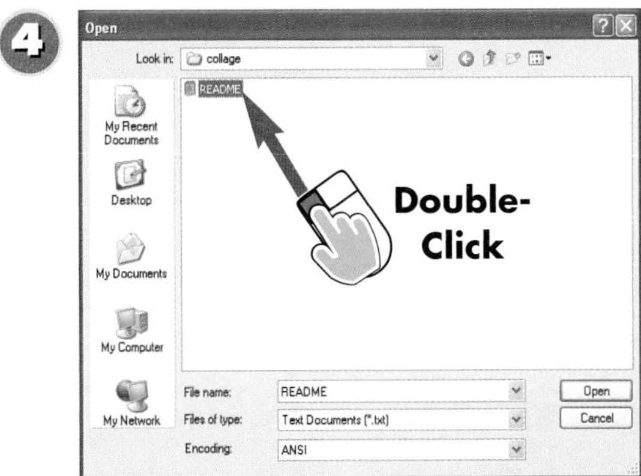

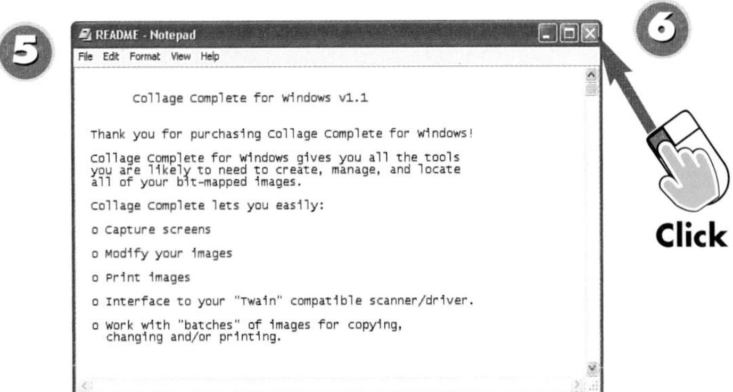

4. When you find the file you want to read, double-click its entry in the Open dialog box.
5. Review the file.
6. To exit Notepad, click the **Close** button.

TIP

Use Scrollbars

Depending on the length of the document, you may need to use the scrollbars to the right of and below the document window. Simply drag the box in the scrollbar up or down depending on your needs.

TIP

Save Text Files

If you want to make changes to the file, do so. Save the changes by opening the **File** menu and choosing **Save**.

TIP

WARNING!

Be careful when making changes to any configuration text file. Be sure you know exactly what you are doing.

Task 11: Using Paint

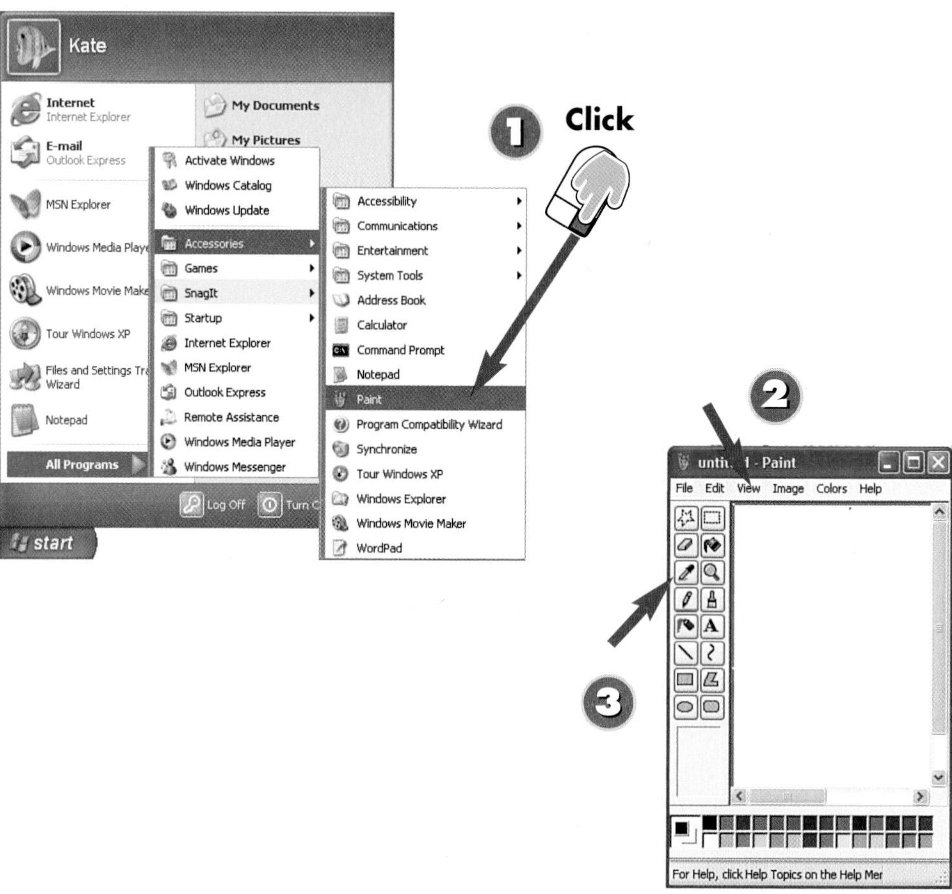

1. Click **Start**, **All Programs**, **Accessories**, and then choose **Paint**.
2. Use the menu bar to select commands.
3. Use the toolbox to select the drawing tool you want to work with.

INTRODUCTION

Use Paint to create art and to edit graphics such as clip art, scanned art, and art files from other programs. You can add lines, shapes, and colors, as well as alter the original components.

TIP

Saving Paint Files

Paint files are saved as bitmap (BMP) files. This is a common graphic file format meaning that you can insert and use your Paint drawings in many other programs.

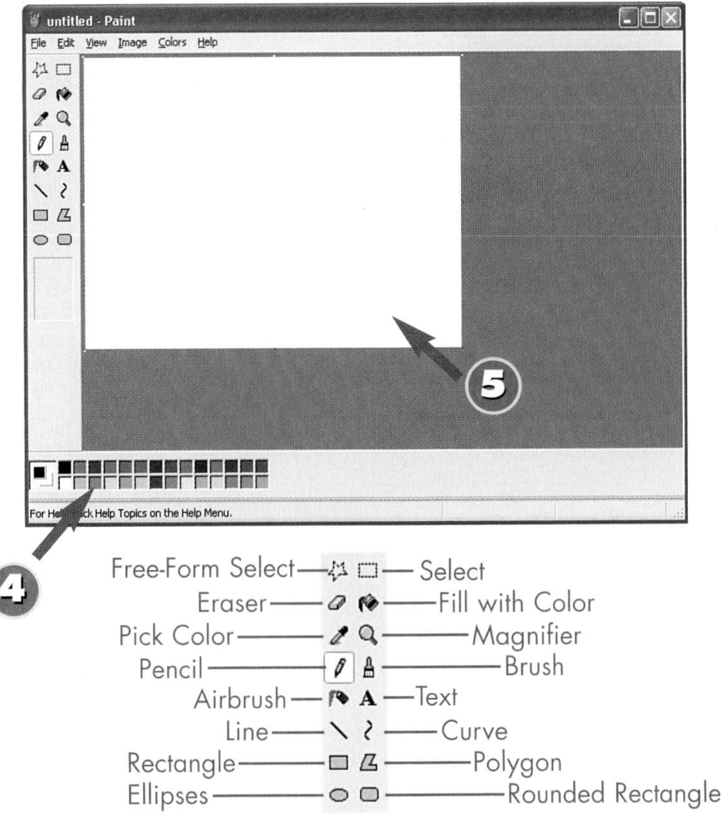

4. Use the color box to select colors for the lines and fills of the objects you draw.

5. Draw in the drawing area.

TIP

Experiment!
You can learn more about Paint by experimenting. Also, use the online help system to look up topics.

TIP

Choose a Color
Click in the color bar at the bottom of the Paint window to choose a color for your shape's lines and borders. Right-click the color you want to use as the fill color.

Task 12: Drawing a Shape with Paint

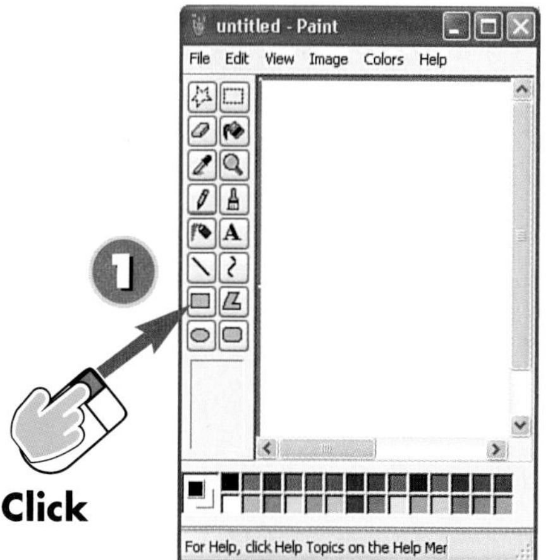

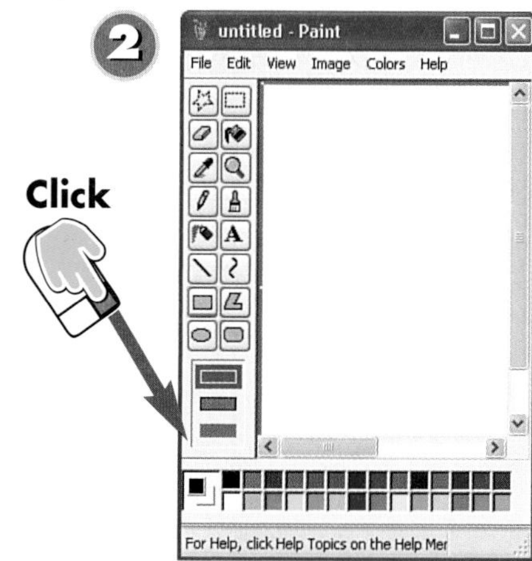

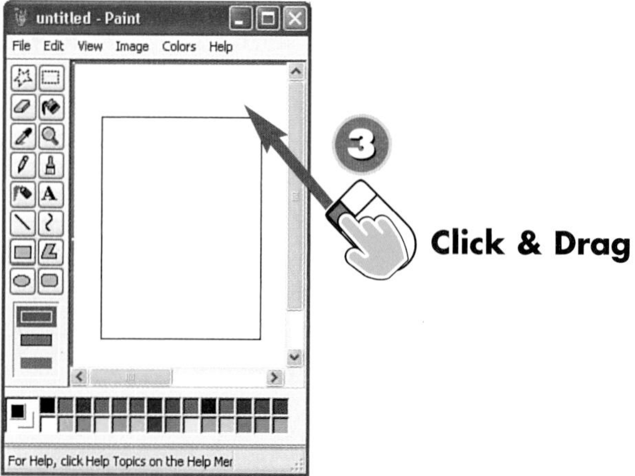

1. Click the tool you want to draw with (in this case, the **Rectangle** tool).
2. Options for the Rectangle tool are displayed. Choose whether you want to draw an empty rectangle, a filled rectangle with a border, or a filled rectangle without a border.
3. Move the pointer into the drawing area. Click and drag in the white canvas area to draw.

INTRODUCTION

Using Paint, you can create lines, curves, rectangles, polygons, ovals, circles, and rounded rectangles. To draw a circle, square, or straight line, hold down the **Shift** key as you use the **Ellipse**, **Rectangle**, or **Line** tool.

TIP

Draw Shapes Freehand

You can draw freehand shapes, much as you would with a pencil or pen. Click the **Pencil** tool, move the pointer into the drawing area, and drag the pencil icon to draw.

TIP

Color an Existing Shape

Select the **Fill with Color** tool, click the color you want to use, and then click inside the shape you want to paint. If color spills outside the area you intended to fill, that probably means you tried to fill an area that was not closed.

Task 13: Adding Text to a Drawing

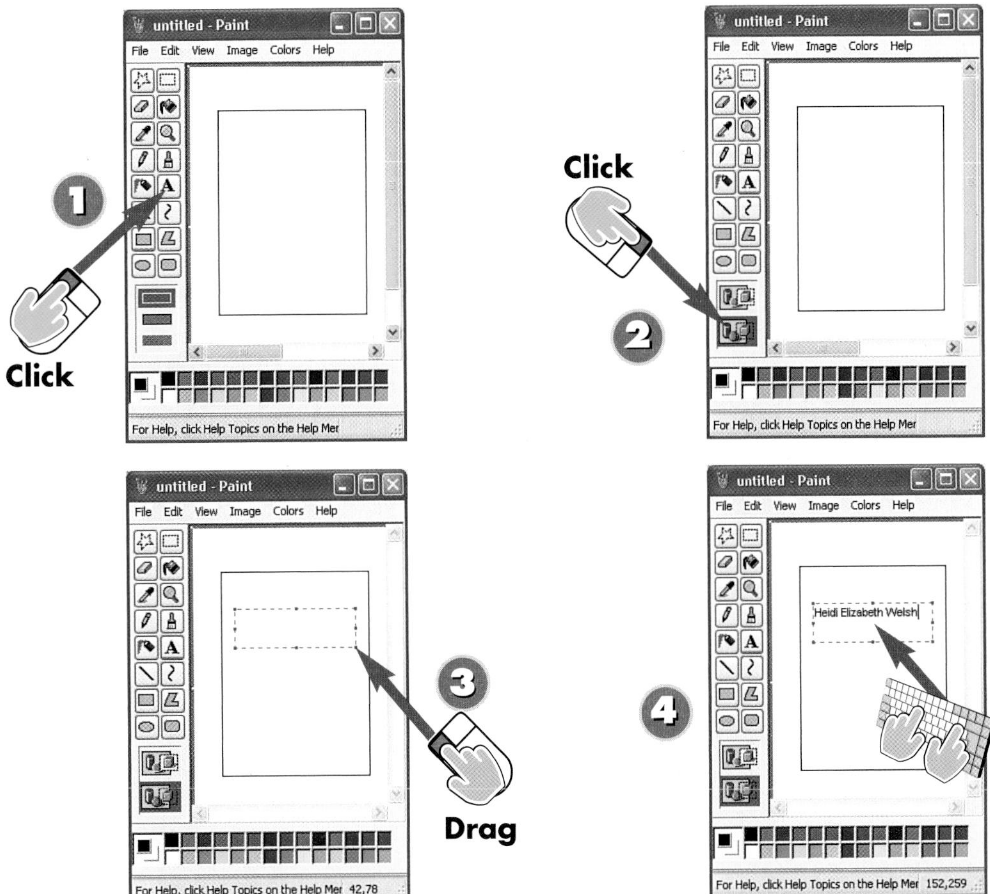

1. Click the **Text** tool.
2. Options for the Text tool are displayed. Choose whether you want to draw a text box that obscures the image beneath it, or one that enables the image beneath it to be seen.
3. Move the pointer into the drawing area. Drag to draw a text box.
4. Type the text you want to add. The text is added to the text box.

INTRODUCTION

You can include text as part of your drawing. To do so, draw a text box, and then type the text you want to include.

TIP

Font Change
You can use the **Fonts** toolbar to select the font, size, and style of the text.

TIP

Undo
If at any time you do not like what you've drawn, open the **Edit** menu and choose **Undo** to undo the last action (or press **Ctrl+Z**).

Task 14: Adding Color to a Drawing

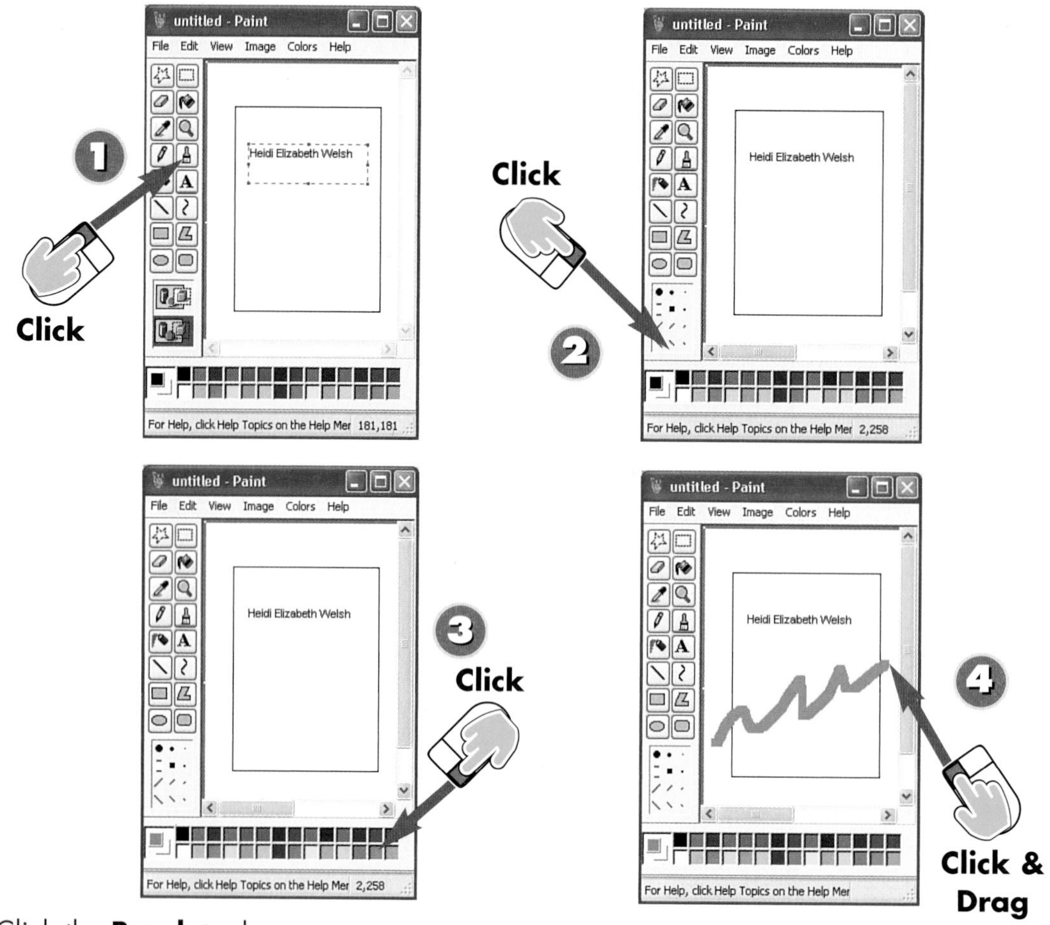

1. Click the **Brush** tool.
2. Click the brush size and shape.
3. In the color box, click the color you want to use.
4. Hold down the mouse button and drag across the page to "paint" with the brush.

INTRODUCTION

There are many ways to add color to a drawing. One way is to use the Brush tool to add paintbrush-style strokes to your image.

TIP

Brush Styles
You can select from different brush styles including angled brushes, pointed brushes, or brushes with squared tips.

TIP

Spray Paint
To get a spray-paint effect on the drawing area, use the **Airbrush** tool.

Task 15: Erasing Part of a Drawing

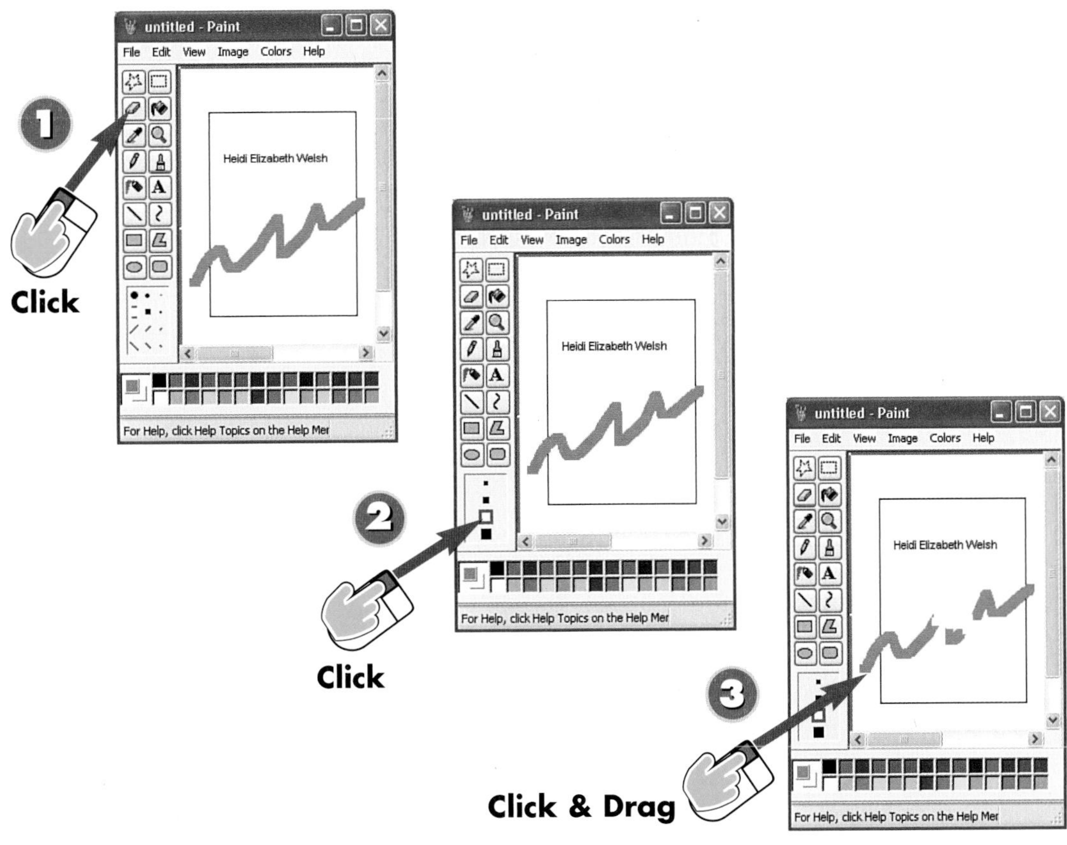

1. Click the **Eraser** tool.
2. Click the size you want the eraser to be.
3. Move the pointer to the drawing area. Hold down the mouse button, and drag across the part you want to erase.

INTRODUCTION

If you make a mistake and want to get rid of something you have added, you can use the Eraser tool.

TIP

Erase Selected Area
To erase a selected part of a drawing, click the **Select** tool (the top-right button on the toolbar) and drag the mouse across part of your drawing. Press the **Delete** key to remove the selected part of the drawing.

TIP

Clear the Whole Page
To clear everything on the page, open the **Image** menu, and then choose **Clear Image**.

PART 10

Personalizing Windows

Windows XP includes many options for setting up your work environment just the way you want. You can move and resize the taskbar, placing it where you want on the desktop. You can adjust the colors used for onscreen elements such as the title bar. You can change how the mouse works, when sounds are played, and more. This part shows you how to customize Windows XP.

Tasks

Task 1: Customizing the Taskbar

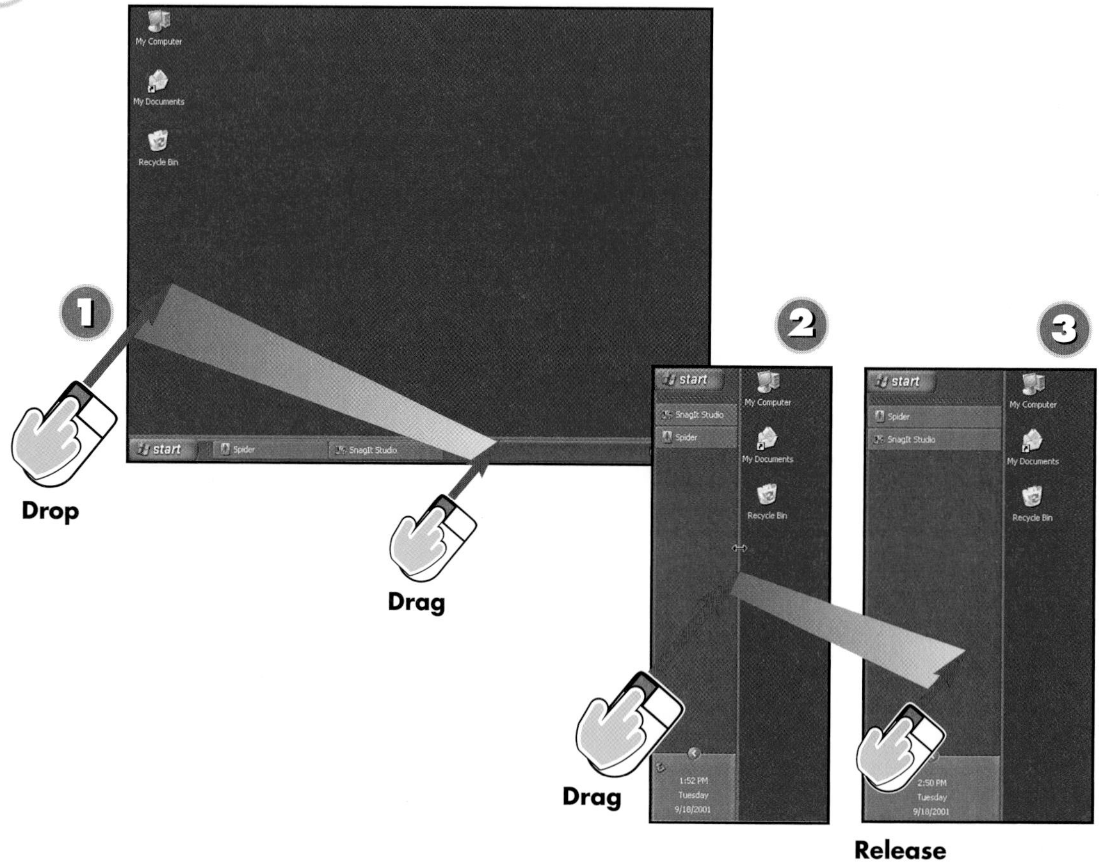

1. Place the mouse pointer anywhere on the taskbar except on a button or on the clock. Then press and hold the left mouse button and drag the taskbar to the location you want.

2. When you release the mouse button, the taskbar jumps to the new location. To resize the taskbar, drag the Taskbar's border until the taskbar is the size you desire.

3. When you release the mouse button, the taskbar is resized.

INTRODUCTION

You can resize the taskbar and place it on the top, left, right, or bottom of the screen. Addtionally, you can hide the taskbar so that you have more room on the desktop for other windows, folders, and programs. When you do, the taskbar disappears until you move the mouse to the portion of the screen where the taskbar normally resides.

TIP

Move Taskbar Back

To move the taskbar back to the bottom of the screen, drag it to that area.

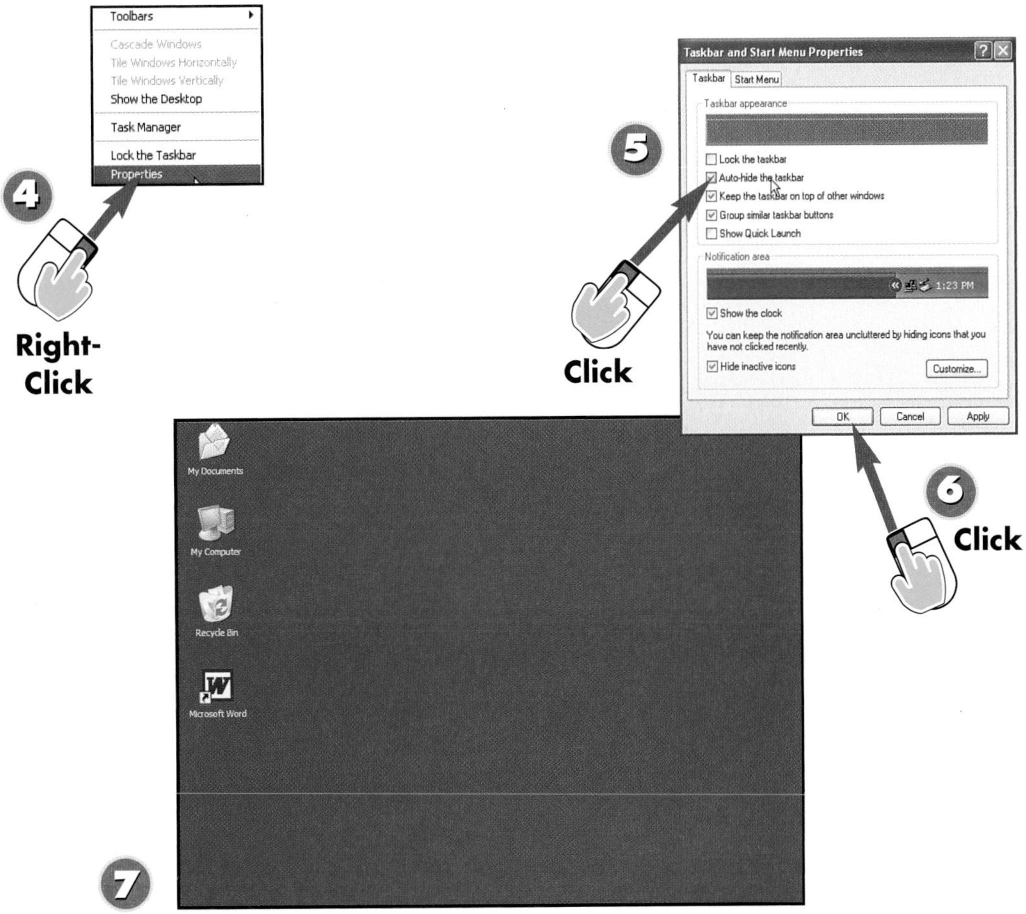

4 To instruct Windows XP to hide your taskbar anytime you aren't using it, right-click the taskbar and select **Properties** from the pop-up menu that appears.

5 Click the **Auto-hide the taskbar** check box.

6 Click the **OK** button.

7 The dialog box closes and the taskbar disappears.

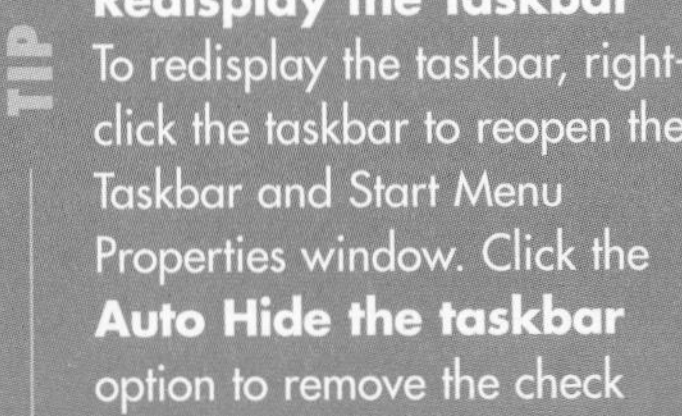

TIP

Redisplay the Taskbar
To redisplay the taskbar, right-click the taskbar to reopen the Taskbar and Start Menu Properties window. Click the **Auto Hide the taskbar** option to remove the check mark. Then click **OK**.

TIP

Use Small Icons
You can use Taskbar and Start Menu Properties dialog box to specify that small icons be displayed and to enable or disable the clock. To do so, check or uncheck these options.

TIP

Display Other Toolbars
You can display toolbars in the taskbar. To do so, right-click a blank part of the taskbar and then select **Toolbars**. Then check the toolbar you want to turn on.

Task 2: Selecting a Desktop Theme

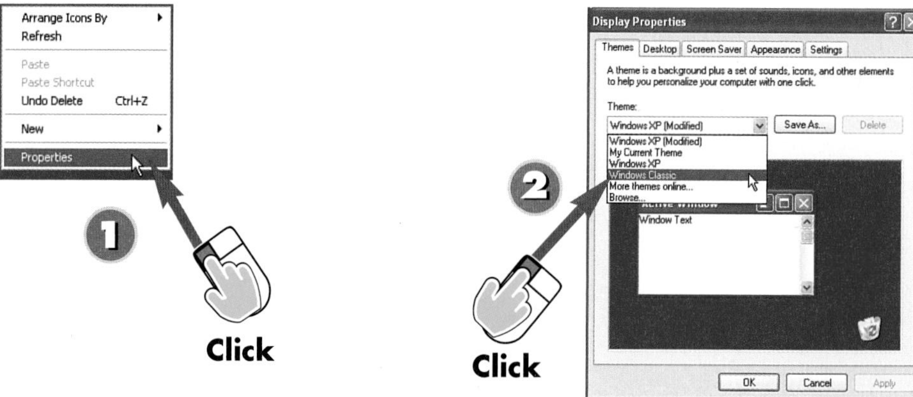

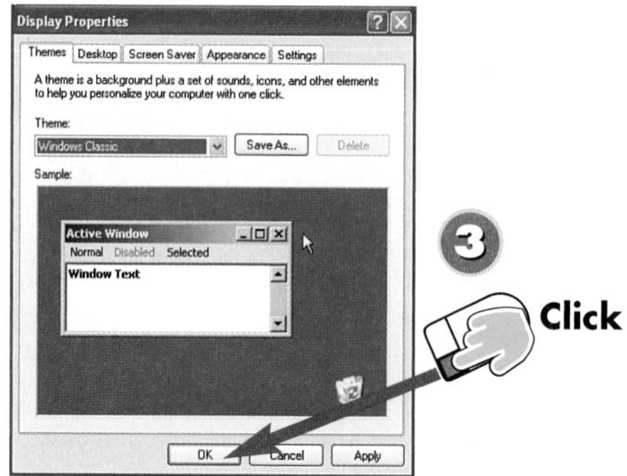

1. Right-click an empty spot on your desktop, and select **Properties** from the pop-up menu that appears.
2. The Display Properties dialog box appears, with the Themes tab displayed. Open the **Themes** drop-down list, and select a theme.
3. The theme you selected is previewed in the Sample window. To apply the theme, click the **OK** button.

INTRODUCTION

Windows XP enables you to personalize your workspace by selecting a desktop theme. Desktop themes consist a background, sounds, icons, and other elements. Windows XP offers numerous color-coordinated themes to choose from; alternatively, you can create your own.

TIP

Saving Your Changes

If you modify the chosen theme, you can save it as a new theme. To do so, click the **Save As** button on the **Themes** tab in the Display Properties dialog. A Save As dialog box opens; give the theme a name, specify where you want it saved, and click the **Save** button. The theme is saved, and its name is added to the **Themes** drop-down list.

Task 3: Applying a Background Image

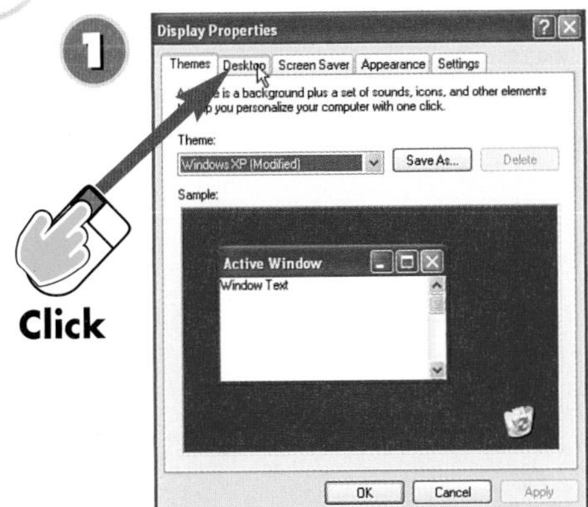

1. In the Display Properties dialog box, click the **Desktop** tab. (Refer to the preceding task if you need help opening the Display Properties dialog box.)
2. In the **Desktop** tab, click one of the entries in the **Background** list.
3. The selected background image appears in the sample monitor on the Desktop tab. To apply the image to your desktop, click the **OK** button.
4. The background image is added to your desktop.

INTRODUCTION

You can personalize your desktop in Windows by applying a background image. Windows offers many colorful image options, including a tropical island, an arid desert, and bubbles.

TIP

Desktop Not Covered?
If you see only one small image in the center of your screen when selecting a background image, click the **Position** drop-down list and choose **Tile**. Click **Apply**, and then click **OK** to accept the changes.

TIP

Display Your Own Photo
To display one of your own digital photos click the **Browse** button on the **Desktop** tab. Then double-click the image you want to use. That file will appear at the bottom of the **Desktop** tab's **Background** list; select it as you would any other background.

Task 4: Customizing Desktop Icons

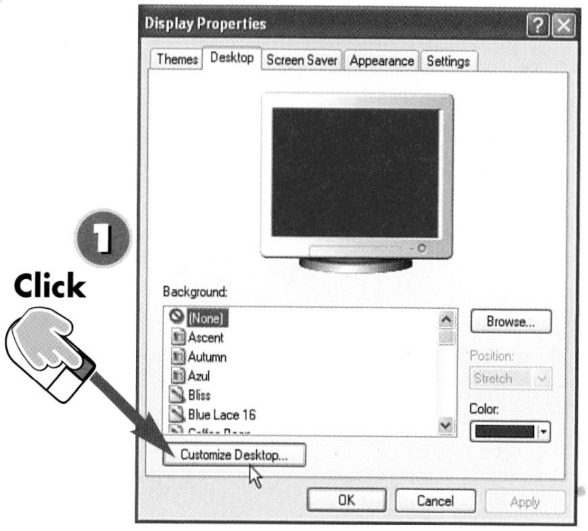

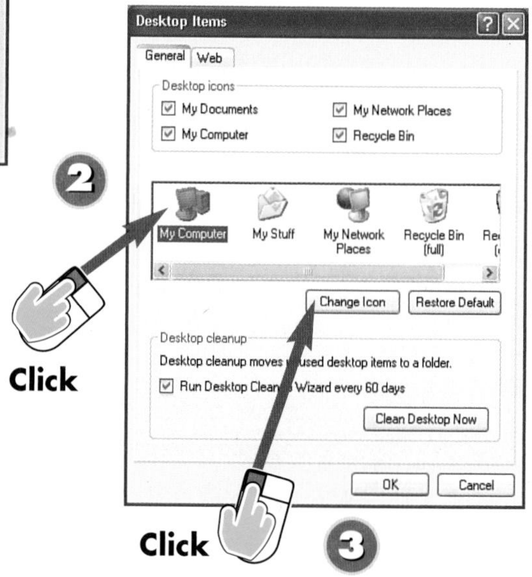

1. In the Desktop tab of the Display Properties dialog box, click the **Customize Desktop** button. (For help navigating to the Display Properties dialog, refer to Task 2.)
2. The Desktop Items dialog box opens, with the General tab displayed. In the middle of the General tab, click the icon you want to change.
3. Click the **Change Icon** button.

INTRODUCTION

Another way to experiment with the appearance of the desktop is to change how the icons are displayed. You can select a different picture for any of the default icons. Windows XP comes with several icons to choose from.

TIP

Add or Remove Icons from the Desktop

If you want only certain icons to appear on your desktop, open the Desktop Items dialog box and, in the Desktop icons area, check those folders that you want to appear on your desktop.

TIP

Enlarge Icons

To enlarge the icons displayed on your desktop, open the **Appearance** tab on the Display Properties dialog, and click the **Effects** button. The Effects dialog opens; click the **Use large icons** check box, and then click the **OK** button.

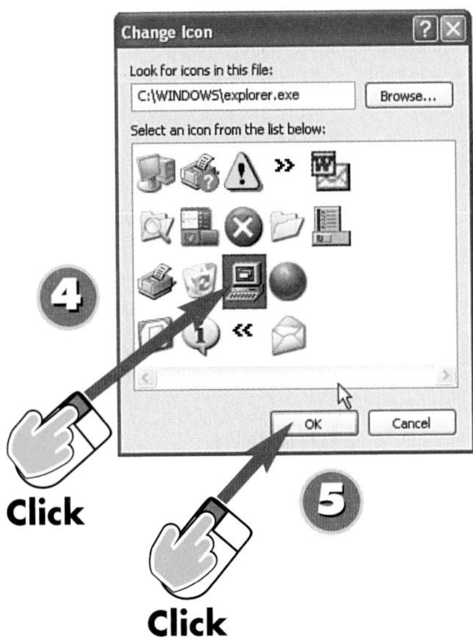

4 Select the picture you want to use for the selected icon.

5 Click the **OK** button in the Change Icon dialog box, click the **OK** button in the Desktop Items dialog box, and click the **OK** button in the Display Properties dialog box.

6 The icon on your desktop reflects the change you made.

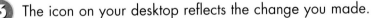

TIP

Display Your Own Icon
If you've created or obtained pictures that you would like to apply to your icons, simply click the **Browse** button in the Change Icon dialog box. In the screen that appears, locate and then double-click the image you want to use.

TIP

Revert to Original Icons
To revert to an icon's original image, display the Desktop Items dialog box and select the icon. Click the **Restore Default** button, and then click the **OK** button.

Task 5: Adding Desktop Content

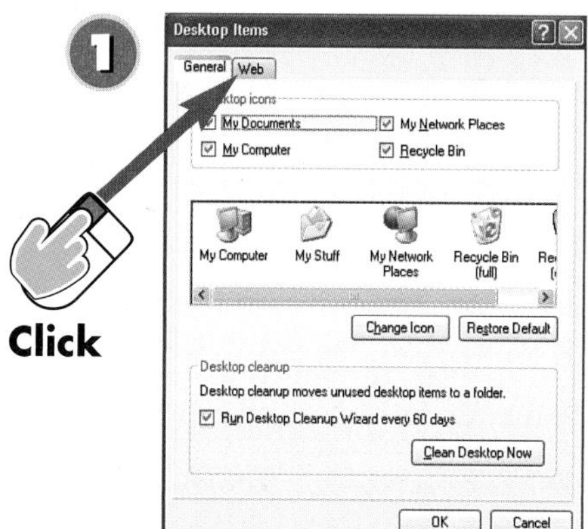

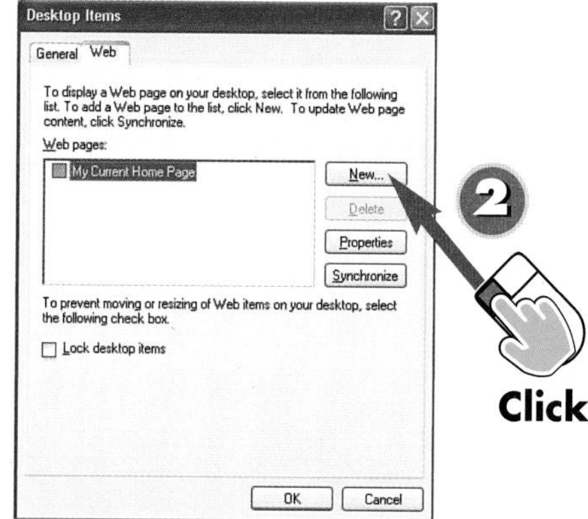

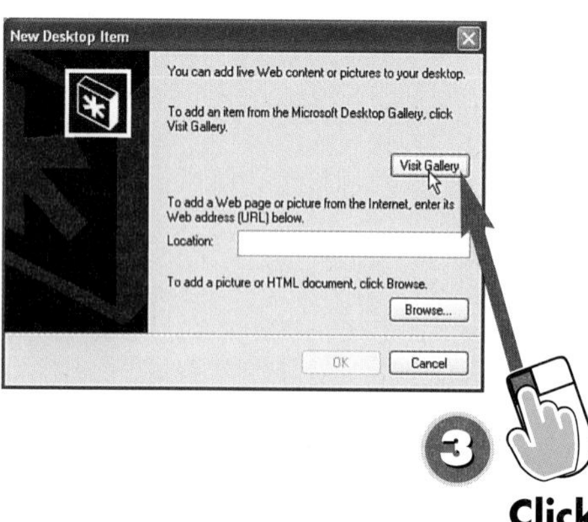

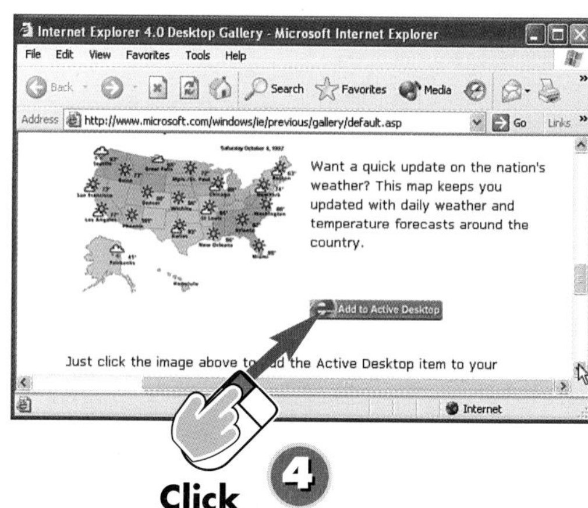

1. In the Desktop Items dialog box, click the **Web** tab. (For help opening the Desktop Items dialog box, refer to the preceding task.)
2. On the Web tab, click the **New** button.
3. The New Active Desktop Item dialog box opens. To add a stock ticker, weather map, or similar item, click the **Visit Gallery** button.
4. A Web browser window displays items you can add to your desktop. Click the **Add to Active Desktop** button by the item you want to add.

INTRODUCTION

Using Windows XP, you can exhibit any of a number of Web-related items on your desktop, including a stock ticker, a listing of sports scores, a weather map, and a satellite tracker. To add active desktop items (stock tickers, weather maps, and the like), you must be connected to the Internet.

TIP

Display Your Home Page

In addition to active desktop items, you can display your Internet home page on your desktop. (See Task 11, in Part 8 for information on selecting the page you want displayed when you open your Web browser.) To do so, check the **My Current Home Page** check box on the **Web** tab of the Desktop Items dialog box. Then, click the **OK** button in the Desktop Items dialog box, and click **OK** in the Display Properties dialog box.

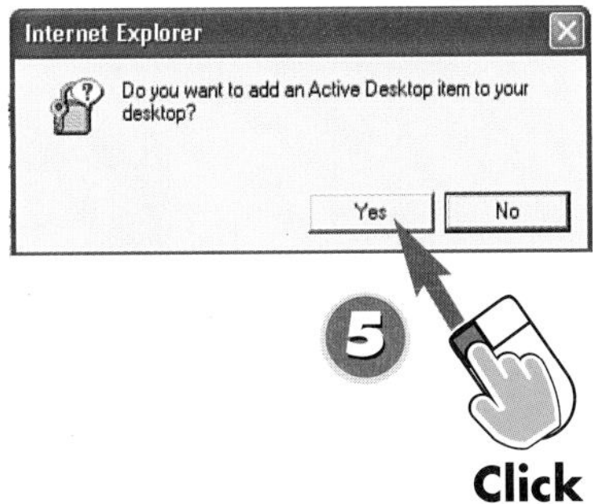

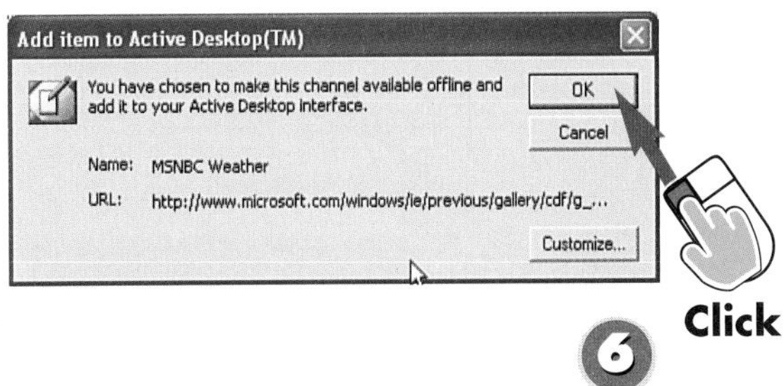

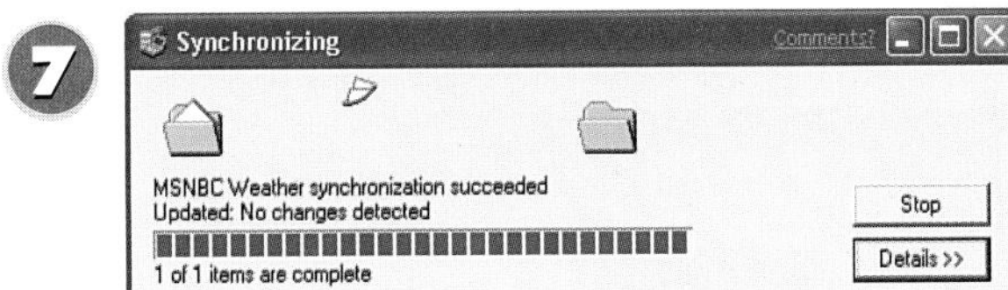

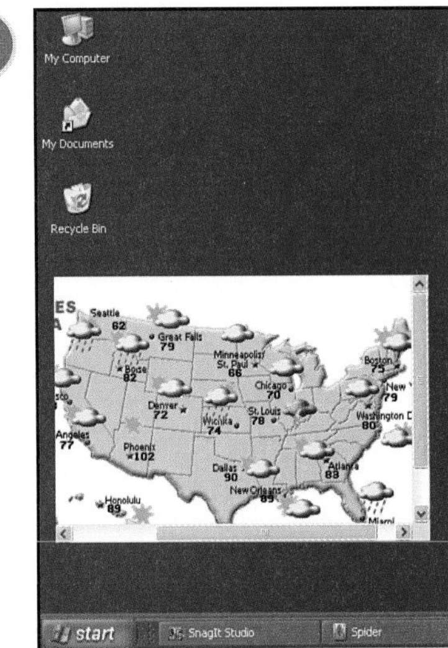

5 When asked whether you want to add the Active Desktop item you selected to your desktop, click the **Yes** button.

6 The Add item to Active Desktop dialog box appears, noting the item you have chosen to add to your desktop (in this case, a weather map from MSNBC). Click the **OK** button.

7 A dialog box indicates the progress of the installation process. Wait until the installation is complete; the dialog box will close on its own.

8 The item is added to your desktop. (You may need to minimize any open windows to see it.)

TIP

Click the Custom Button

Clicking the **Custom** button in the Add item to Active Desktop dialog box starts a wizard that enables you to specify how often you want to synchronize the stock ticker, sports ticker, weather map, or satellite tracker.

TIP

Resize the Page

You can resize the page displayed on your desktop (whether it's your home page, as discussed in the tip on the preceding page, or one of the items shown on the page in step 4) by using the buttons in the title bar, or by dragging the page's border. If you don't see the title bar at the top of the page displayed on your desktop, try moving the mouse pointer so that it hovers at the top of the page until the title bar appears.

Task 6: Choosing a Screen Saver

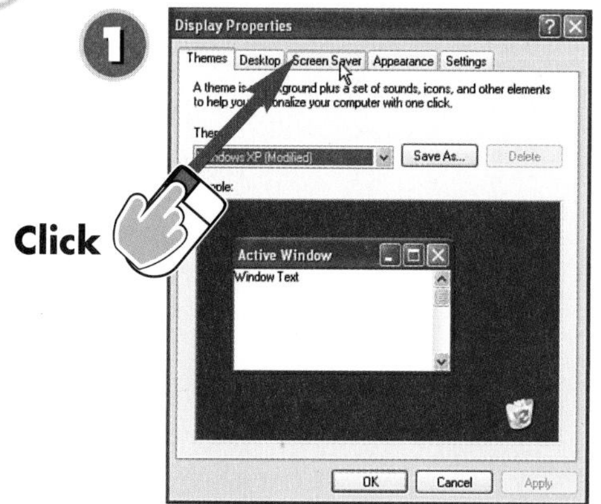

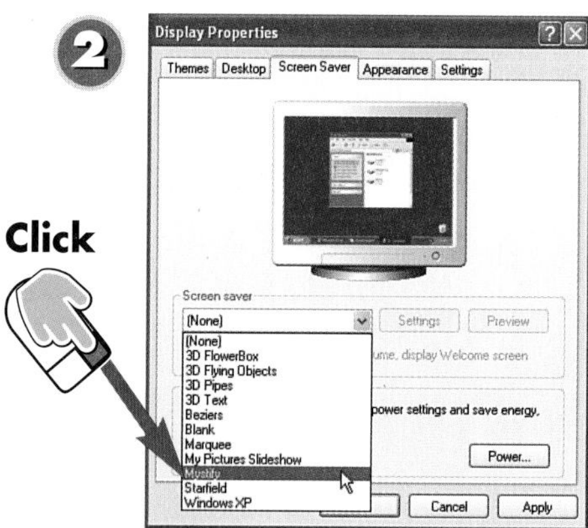

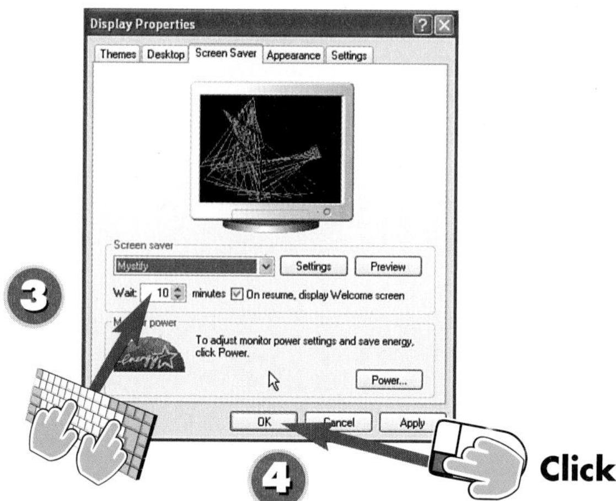

1. In the Display Properties dialog box, click the **Screen Saver** tab. (Refer to Task 2 if you need help opening the Display Properties dialog box.)
2. Click the **Screen saver** drop-down list box arrow to display the list of available screen savers, and then select the screen saver you want to use.
3. The selected screen saver appears on the sample monitor. Type in the **Wait** text box the number of minutes you want Windows to wait before it starts the screen saver.
4. Click the **OK** button. The next time your computer is idle for the amount of time specified in step 3, the screen saver will be activated.

INTRODUCTION

In the past, screen savers helped prevent your monitor's screen from burn-in, in which a "ghost" of the Windows screen was still visible, even after you turned off your computer. Although modern monitors do not suffer from burn-in, many people still use screen savers for fun.

TIP

Set Screen Saver Options

Click the **Settings** button to select options for how the screen saver is displayed; these options vary depending on the screen saver.

Deactivate Screen Saver

When the screen saver is displayed, move the mouse or press the spacebar to return to the normal view.

Task 7: Changing the Color Scheme

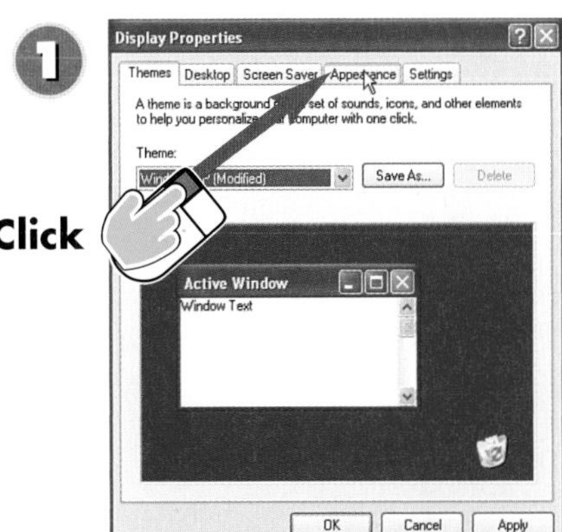

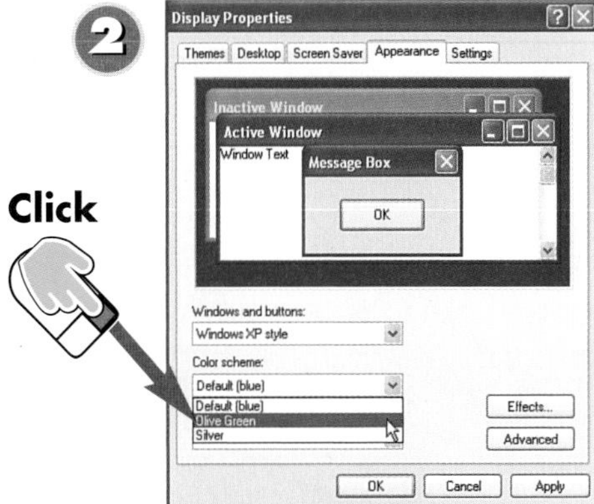

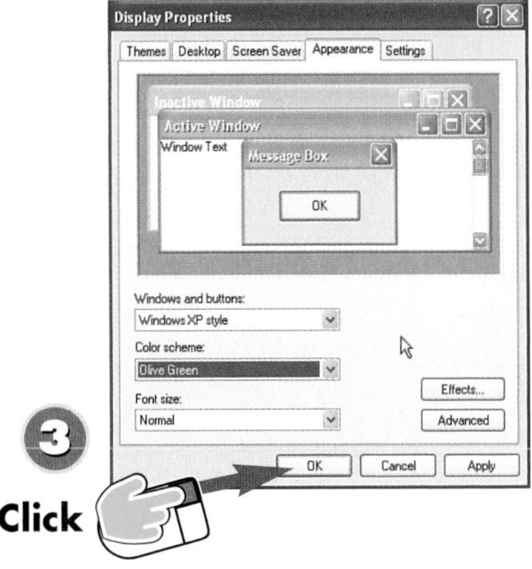

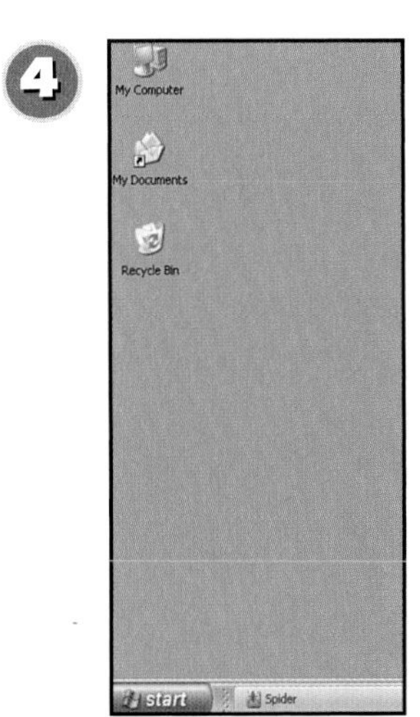

1. In the Display Properties dialog box, click the **Appearance** tab. (Refer to Task 2 if you need help opening the Display Properties dialog box.)
2. Open the **Color scheme** drop-down list and select the scheme you want to apply.
3. The scheme you selected is previewed in the Sample window. To apply the scheme, click the **OK** button.
4. The scheme is applied.

INTRODUCTION

Windows XP enables you to change the sets of colors used for certain onscreen elements such as the title bar, background, and so on. These sets of colors are called schemes, and you can select colors that work best for you and your monitor.

TIP

Additional Effects

For additional customization options, click the **Effects** button on the **Appearance** tab to open the Effects dialog box. From there, you can apply transition effects to menus and tooltips, indicate the method used to smooth font edges.

TIP

Original Colors

To revert to the original colors, select the Windows Standard scheme from the list.

Task 8: Setting Resolution and Color Quality

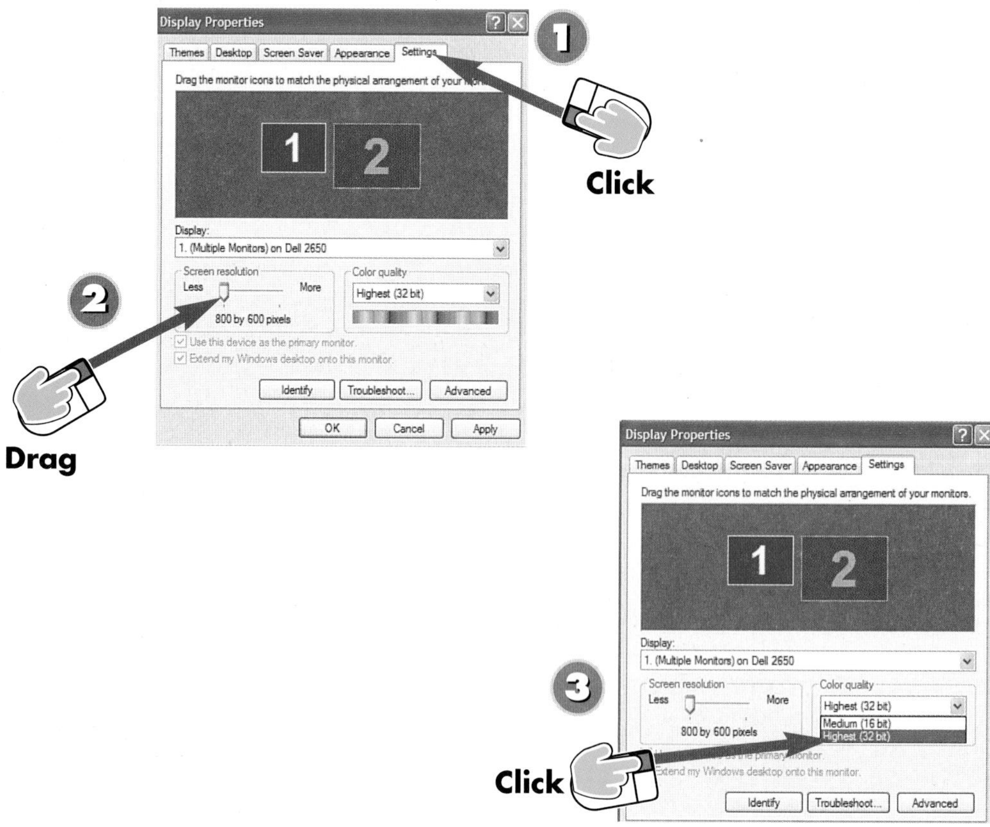

1. In the Display Properties dialog box, click the **Settings** tab. (Refer to Task 2 if you need help opening the Display Properties dialog box.)
2. To change the resolution, drag the **Screen resolution** bar to the desired setting.
3. To change the number of colors used for the display, click the **Color quality** drop-down list and choose the number you want.

INTRODUCTION

You may be able to select certain options about how your monitor operates, such as the number of colors it displays or its resolution. (Resolution measures the number of pixels or picture elements displayed. An example of a common resolution is 800x600.)

TIP

Choices Vary

The available choices will depend on your equipment. If the settings you select don't look right, revert to the original ones.

TIP

Other Options

You can use the Identify button to display a number that corresponds with the icons shown above. Also, you can set up your computer to use multiple monitors; the check boxes in this dialog box help you set up how these monitors work.

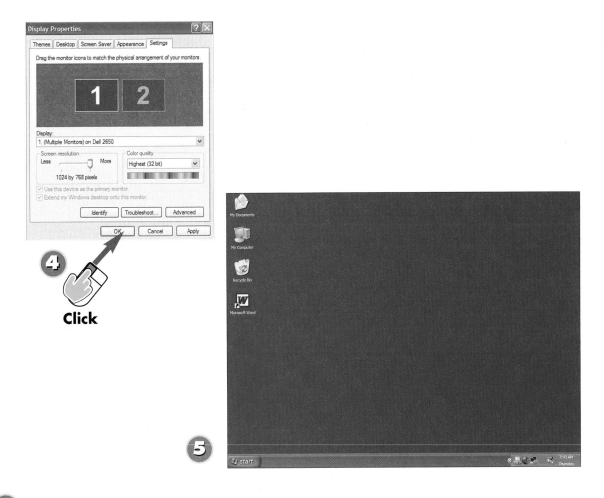

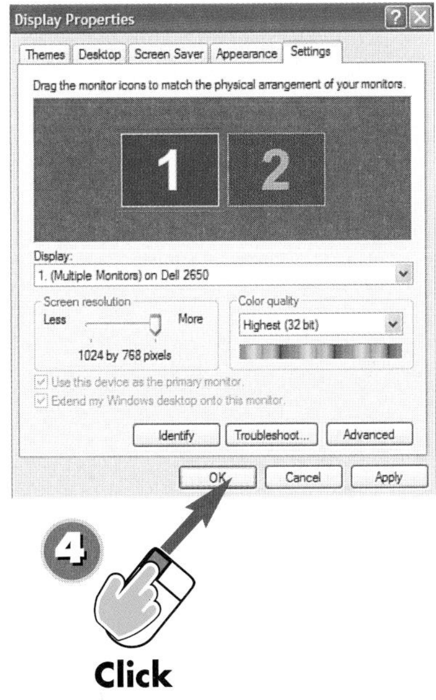

4. Click the **OK** button.

5. Windows uses the new settings, here a higher resolution.

TIP

Troubleshoot
Clicking the **Troubleshoot** button on the Settings tab of the Display Properties dialog box opens the Video Display Troubleshooter, which steps you through the troubleshooting process in the event your monitor is experiencing difficulties.

TIP

Additional Information and Settings
For additional information about your monitor, as well as more settings, click the **Advanced** button. This opens a dialog box containing information about your display adapter and your monitor, as well as settings for font size, compatibility, and more.

Task 9: Changing How the Mouse Works

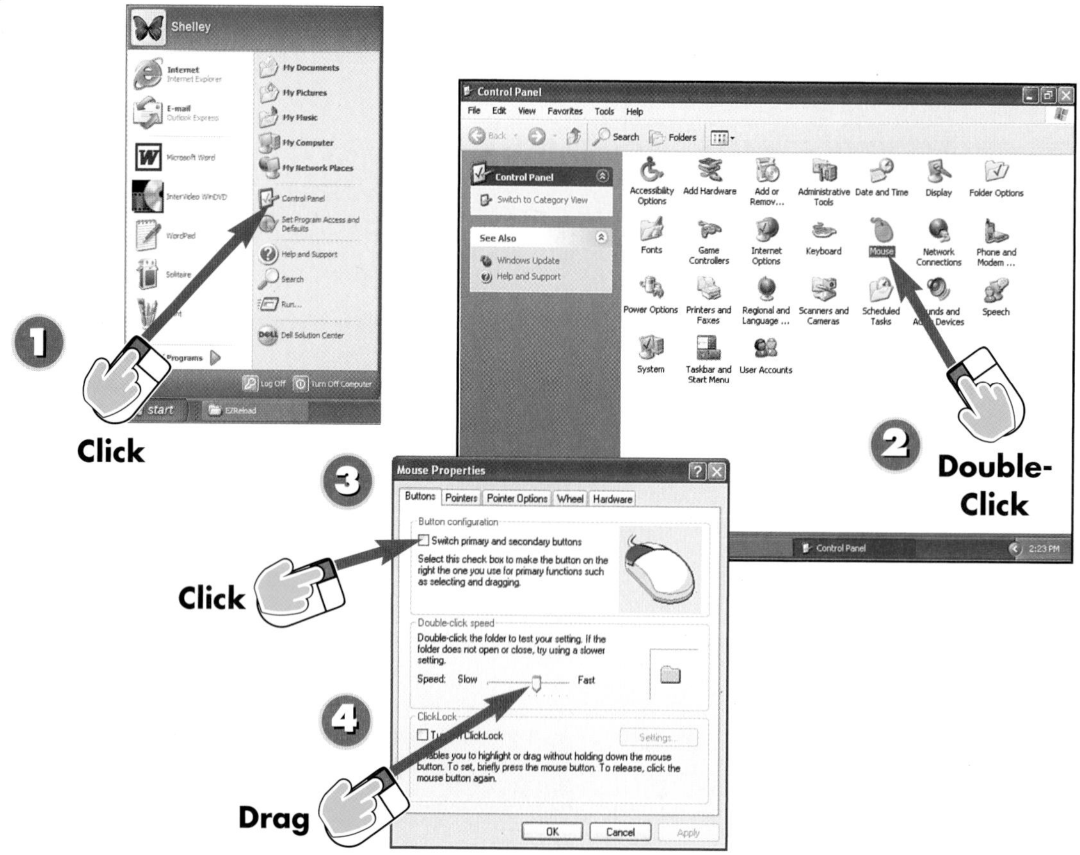

1. Click the **Start** button and choose **Control Panel**.
2. Double-click the **Mouse** icon in the **Control Panel** window. (You may need to click the Switch to Classic View link in the left-most pane in order to reveal the Mouse icon.)
3. In the Buttons tab of the Mouse Properties dialog box click the **Switch primary and secondary buttons** check box to make the button on the right the one you use for clicking and dragging.
4. Adjust the **Double-click speed** slider to make the double-click speed faster or slower, depending on your needs.

INTRODUCTION

You can adjust your mouse to make it work the way you want. For example, if you are left-handed, you can switch the mouse buttons. If you have trouble double-clicking, you can adjust the double-click speed. If you're not crazy about the way your mouse pointer looks onscreen, you can change it. In addition, you can slow your pointer speed to make it easier to see your mouse pointer when you move it onscreen.

TIP

ClickLock
Click the **Turn on ClickLock** check box to enable ClickLock, which allows you to highlight or drag without holding down the mouse button.

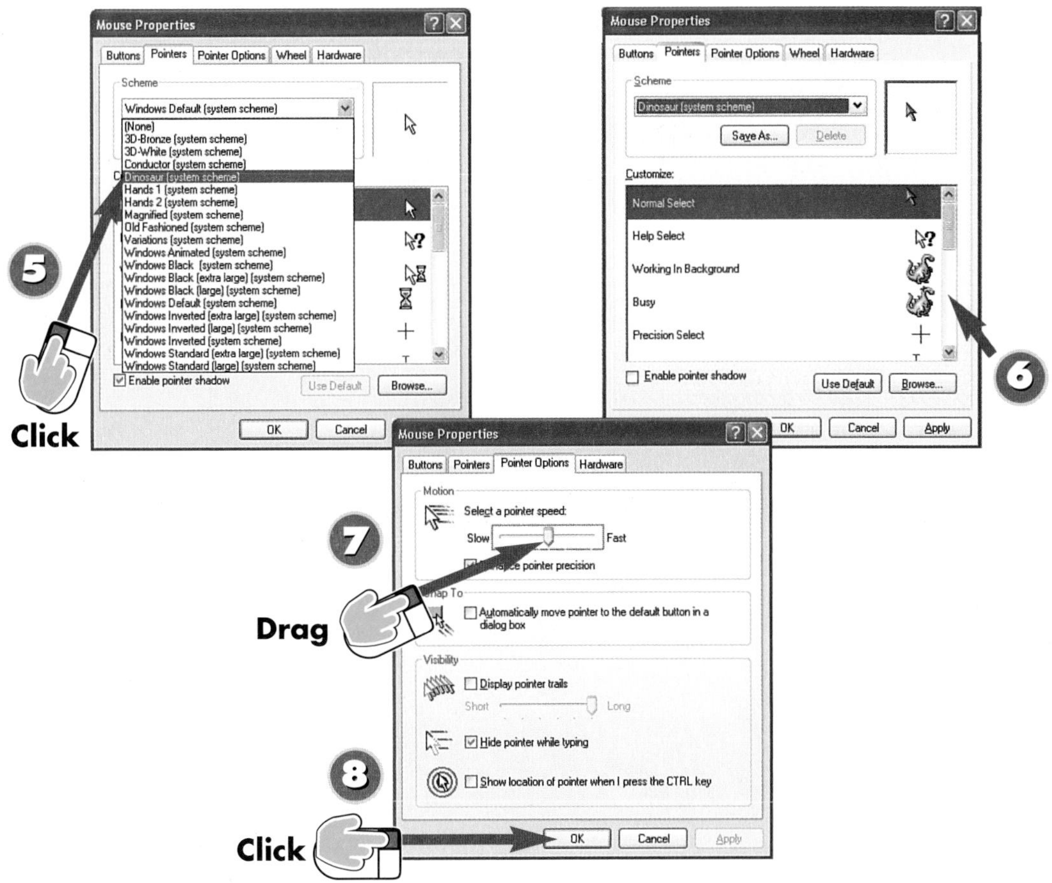

5 In the **Pointers** tab, display the **Scheme** drop-down list and choose the scheme you want to use.

6 A preview of each pointer in the chosen scheme (in this case, Dinosaur) is displayed.

7 In the **Pointer Options** tab, drag the **Select a pointer speed** slider to the right or the left to make the pointer speed faster or slower.

8 Click **OK** to accept the changes and to close the dialog box.

TIP

Use Original Pointers

To go back to the default scheme, display the **Pointers** tab of the Mouse Properties dialog box, and then select **None** from the **Scheme** drop-down list.

TIP

Intellimouse Settings

If you use an Intellimouse (the kind with the wheel in the middle), you can adjust how many lines are scrolled each time you notch the wheel. Simply display the **Wheel** tab, and select either the **Scroll this many lines** or **Scroll one screen at a time** radio button. If you select **Scroll this many lines**, enter the number of lines you want each notch of the wheel to scroll in the accompanying spin box.

Task 10: Changing the Sound Scheme

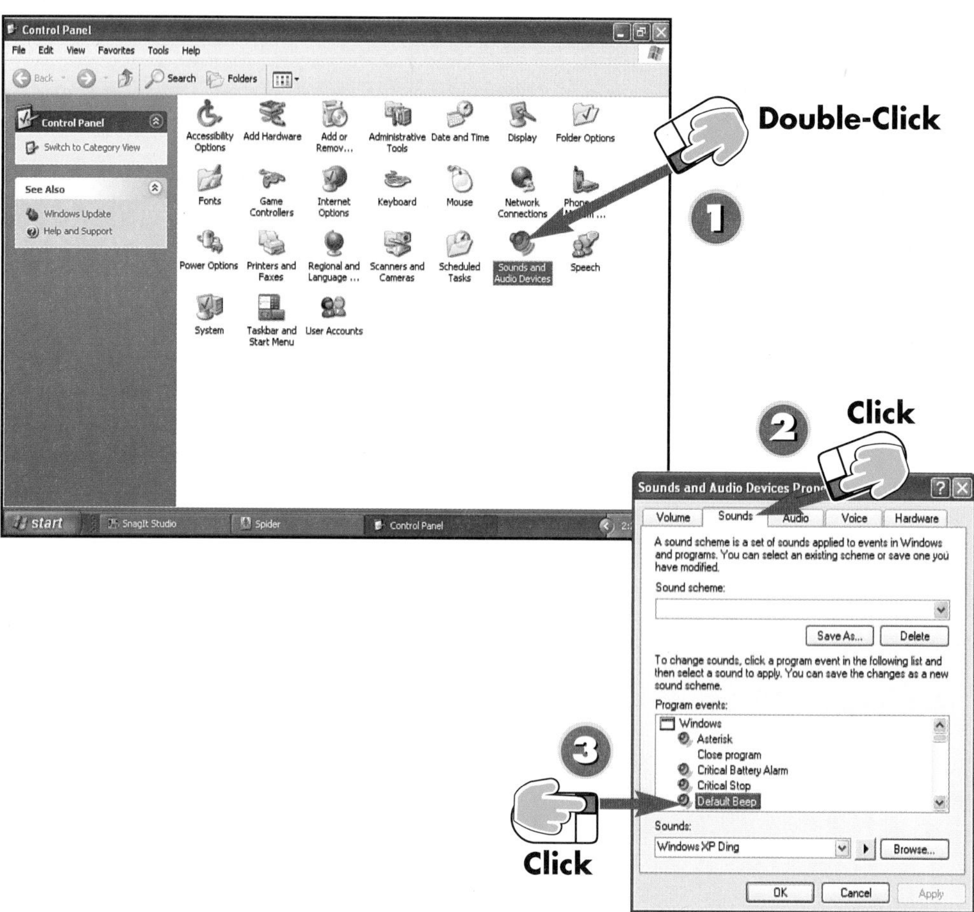

1. Double-click the **Sounds and Audio Devices** icon in the Control Panel window (refer to Task 9, "Changing How the Mouse Works," if you need help opening the Control Panel window). Also you need to change to Classic view.
2. Click the **Sounds** tab. The Sounds and Audio Devices Properties dialog box opens.
3. In the **Program events** list, click the sound event you want to change.

INTRODUCTION

When you perform certain actions in Windows XP, you might hear a sound. For example, you hear a sound when Windows XP is started. You might hear a sound when an alert box is displayed. You can stick with the default sounds, or you can select a different sound to use for each key Windows event.

TIP

Select a Scheme

If you have sound schemes, you can select a set of sounds by displaying the **Schemes** drop-down list in the Sounds tab of the Sounds and Audio Devices dialog box. Select the scheme you want, and then click **OK**.

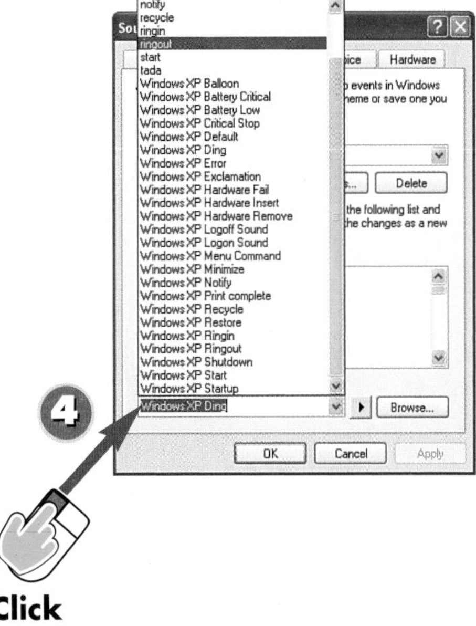

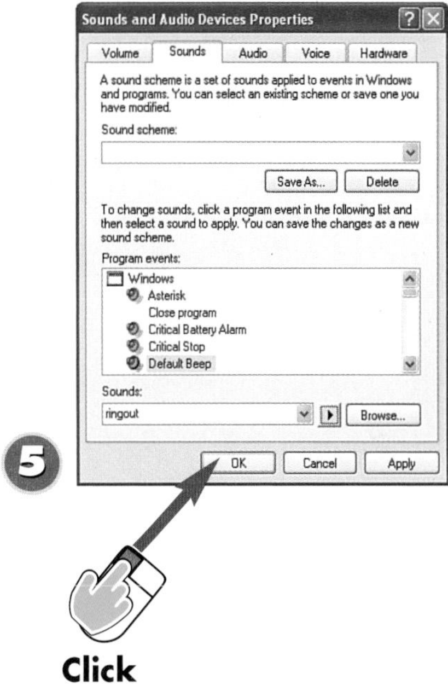

4 Display the **Sounds** drop-down list to select the sound that you want to assign to that event.

5 Click **OK** to accept the changes and to close the dialog box.

TIP

Preview the Selected Sound

To hear a preview of the sound, click the **Play** button to the right of the **Sounds** drop-down list.

TIP

Browse for Sounds

If the sound you want to use is not listed in the **Sounds** list, click the **Browse** button. A standard Browse dialog box opens, enabling you to locate the sound file you want to use.

TIP

No Sound?

If you don't want a sound played for an event, select that event and choose **None** from the **Sounds** list.

Task 11: Changing the System Date and Time

Start

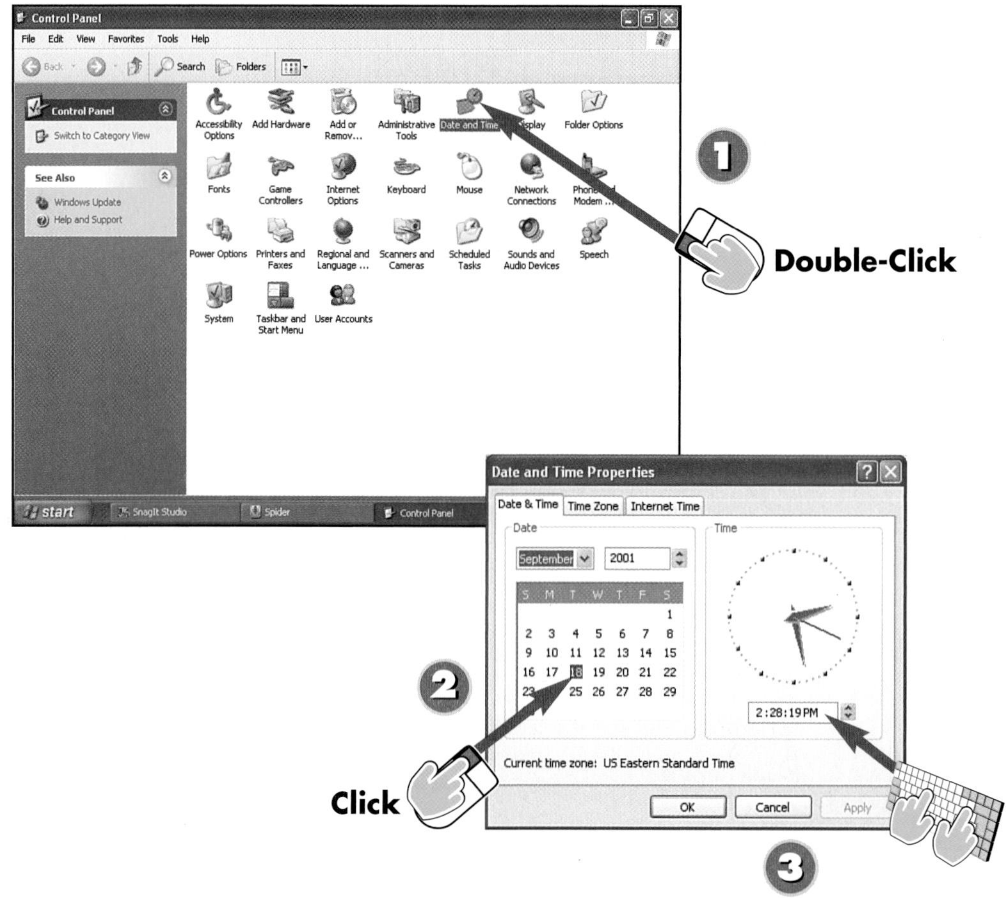

1. Double-click the **Date and Time** icon in the Control Panel window (refer to Task 9 if you need help opening the Control Panel window). Also switch to Classic view.
2. The Date and Time Properties dialog box opens, displaying the Date & Time tab. Click the correct date in the calendar.
3. If the time is wrong, enter the correct time in the **Time** spin box.

INTRODUCTION

You can place the pointer over the time in the taskbar to display the current date. If your system clock is wrong, you should correct it because Windows stamps the time and date on every file you save.

TIP

Date Wrong?

If the date is wrong, it could indicate that you have a dead battery. If so, you must replace your computer's internal battery (check your system manual).

TIP

Correcting the Date

If the month is wrong, display the **Month** drop-down list and select the correct month. If the year is incorrect, type the correct one in the appropriate text box or use the up and down arrows to adjust it. If the date is wrong, click the correct date on the calendar.

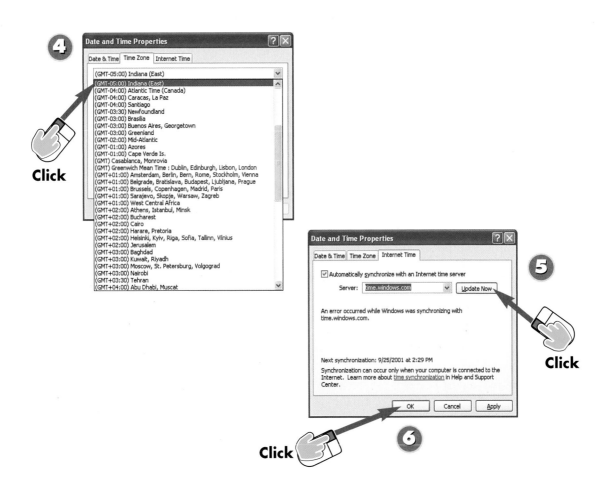

4. Click the **Time Zone** tab and then display the drop-down list. Select your time zone from this list.

5. If you want your computer to automatically synchronize with a time clock on the Internet, make sure the check box on the **Internet Time** tab is checked. Alternatively, click the **Update Now** button on this tab to synchronize your time clock immediately.

6. Click the **OK** button.

TIP

Internet Time

In order for your computer to synchronize its clock with a time clock on the Internet, you'll need to be connected. If your computer resides behind a firewall or connects to the Internet via a proxy server, however, you may not be able to take advantage of this feature.

TIP

Choose Time Server

You can choose a different time server to synchronize with by selecting one from the Server drop-down list in the Internet Time tab.

Task 12: Setting Up Windows for Multiple Users

Start

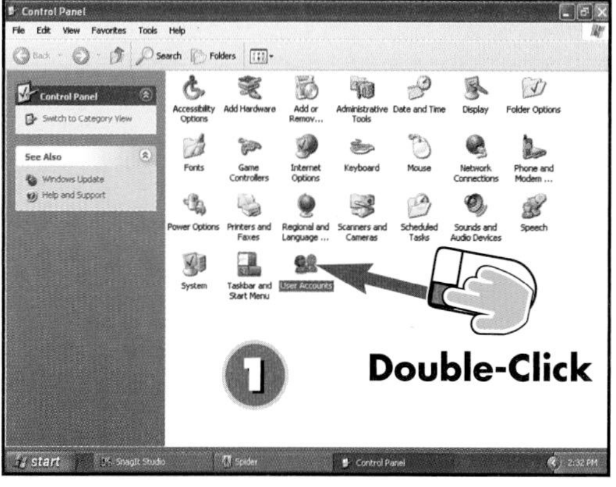

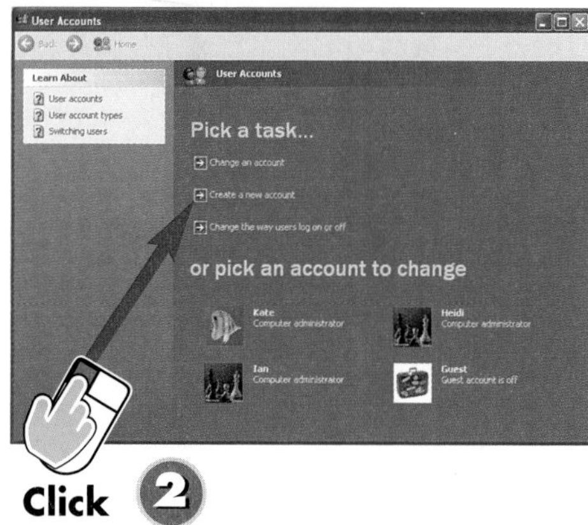

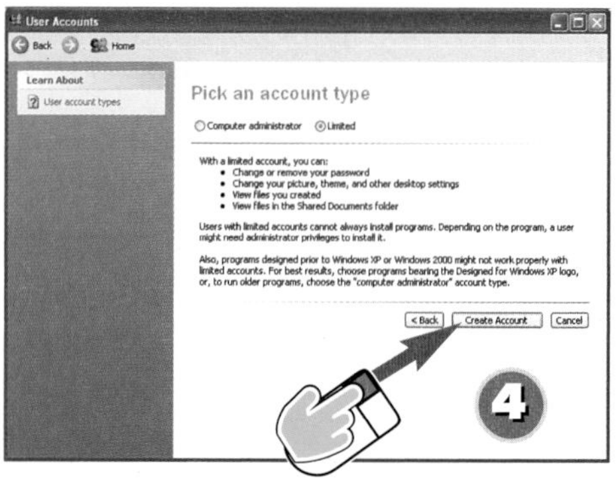

1. After you've set up Windows the way you like it, double-click the **User Accounts** icon in the Control Panel window. (If you need help opening the Control Panel window, refer to Task 9.)
2. Click the **Create a new account** link.
3. Type the name of the person whose account you are setting up, and then click the **Next** button.
4. Specify what type of account you want to create by selecting either the **Computer administrator** or **Limited** radio button, and then click **Create Account**.

INTRODUCTION

If more than one person uses your PC, each person can set up Windows the way he or she wants and then create a user profile. Each time that person logs on, all those settings will be used.

TIP

Types of User Accounts

Create a computer administrator account if you want the person for whom you are creating the account to be able to create and delete user accounts on the computer; and to change other people's account names, pictures, passwords, and account types. Otherwise, create a limited account.

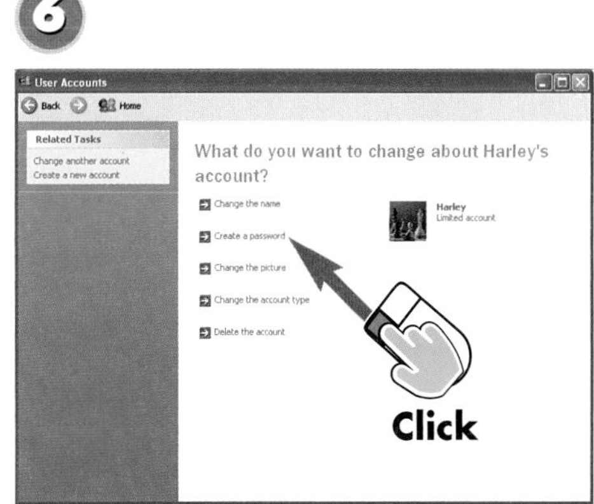

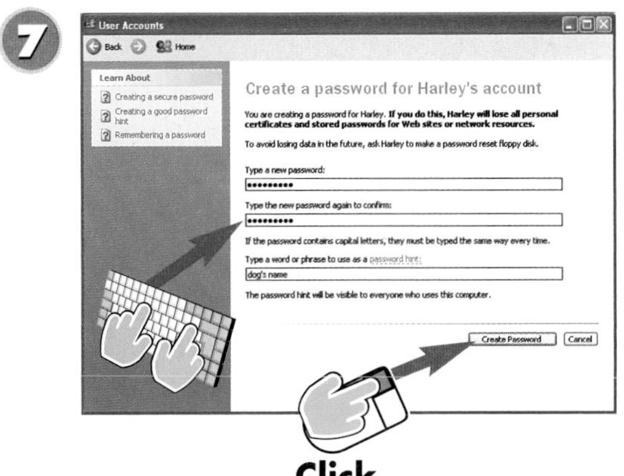

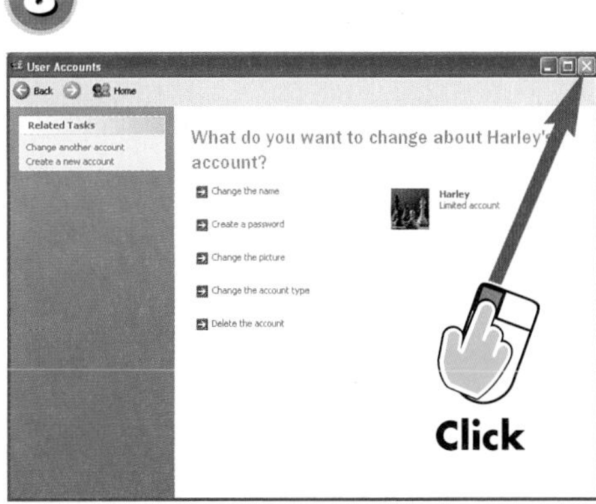

5 The account is created. Click the account to modify it, for example, to create a password for the account.

6 Click the **Create a password** link.

7 Type the password you want to use, and type it again to confirm. Type a hint to help you remember the password, and then click the **Create Password** button.

8 Click the **Close** button to close the User Accounts window.

TIP

Modify the Account

When you select to change the name or the account type in the screen shown in step 6, the appropriate window from the User Accounts wizard appears.

TIP

Delete Account

To delete an account, display the User Accounts screen and select the account you want to change. Click **Delete the account**. Select to keep the files associated with this account (the contents of that user's My Documents folder) or to delete them. Click **Delete Account** to complete the deletion. Then close any open User Accounts windows. To delete an account, note that the user must be logged out. Also, only administrator accounts can make this change.

Task 13: Changing the Account Image

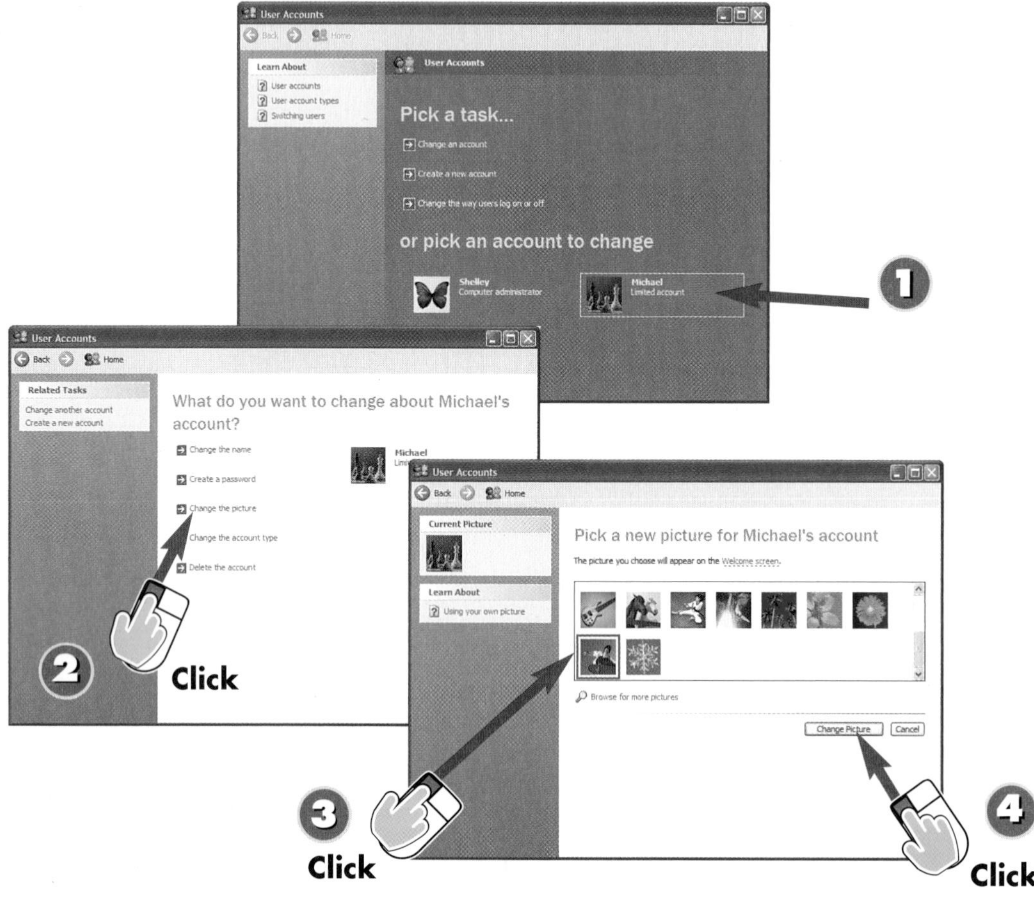

1. From the User Accounts Control Panel, select the account whose image you want to change. (See the preceding task for help on displaying this screen.)
2. Click the **Change the picture** link.
3. Select the image you want to use.
4. Click **Change Picture**.

INTRODUCTION

Windows XP includes images that you can use to represent each user's account. You can choose to use these images, or you may customize the image by using another picture—perhaps an actual photo of that person. You can select from any of Windows XP images as well as any images you have.

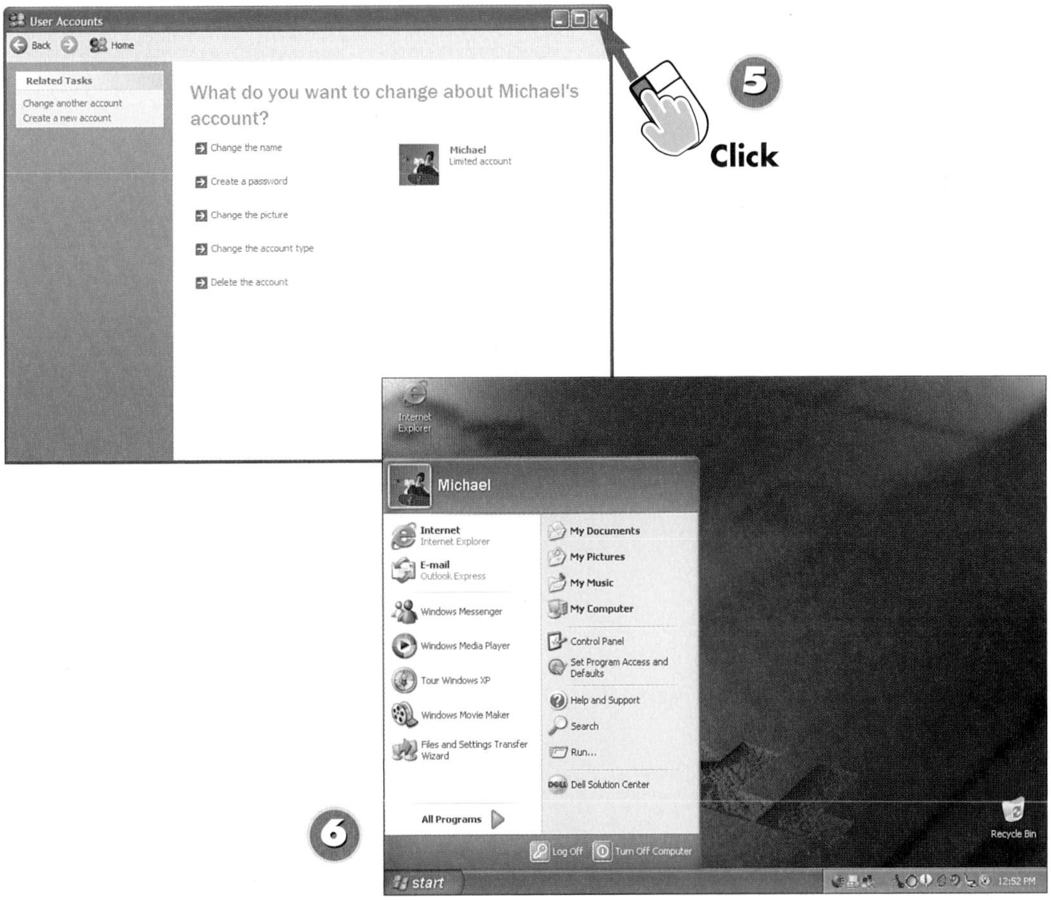

5 You are returned to the User Accounts window. Click the **Close** button to close this window. Click **Close** again to close the Control Panel window.

6 Windows uses the new image. This image appears on the logon screen as well as at the top of the Start menu.

TIP

Use a Picture

To select another picture file of your own, click **Browse for more pictures**. Then navigate to the drive and folder that contains your image and select it. Click **Open**. This image is then used to identify the account.

Task 14: Logging Off

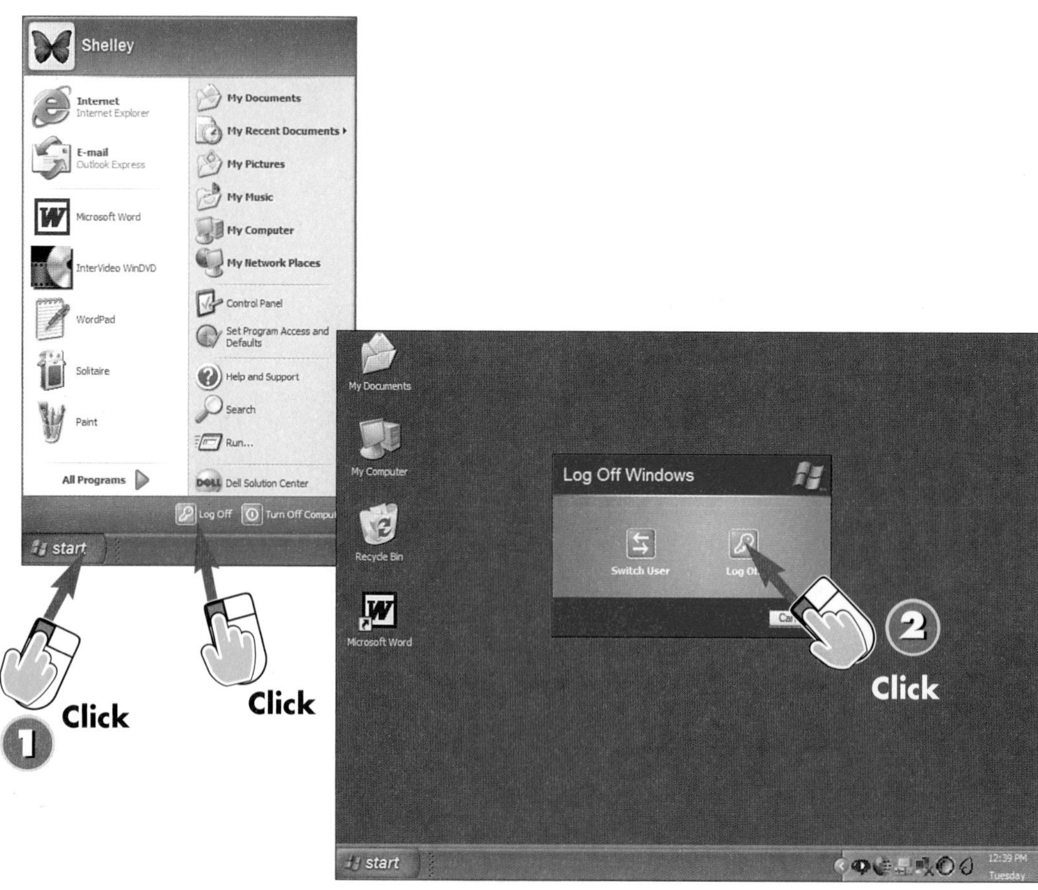

1. Click the **Start** button, and then click **Log Off**.

2. Click **Log Off**. You are returned to the Windows logon screen.

INTRODUCTION

When you set up user accounts, each user can log on to access their own personal Windows set up. Once they are done, they can log off.

TIP

Log Back On

To log back on from the Windows logon screen, click the icon for your account. If it's password protected, type the password.

Task 15: Switching Users

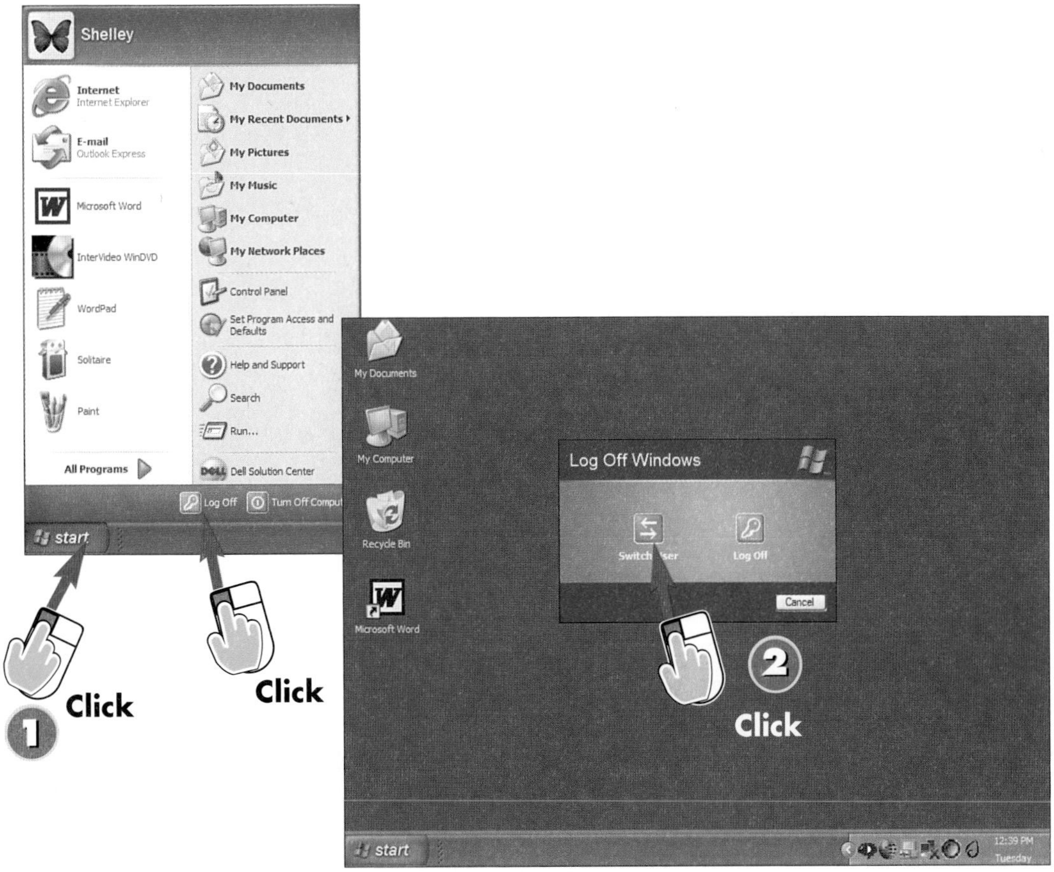

1. Click the **Start** button, and then click the **Log Off** button.

2. Click **Switch User**. You are returned to the Windows logon screen. You can then log on to a different account by clicking its icon.

INTRODUCTION

If someone else is logged on, rather than log off and let the new user log on, you can simply switch users.

TIP

Turn Off Computer
If you want to turn off the computer, you can do so from the Windows logon screen. Click **Turn off computer**.

Task 16: Using Accessibility Options

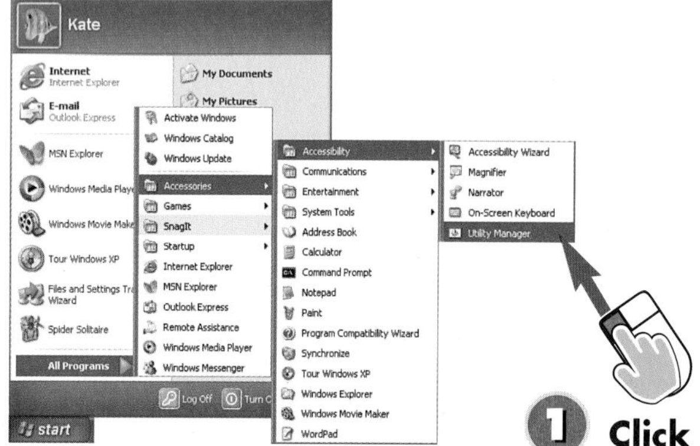

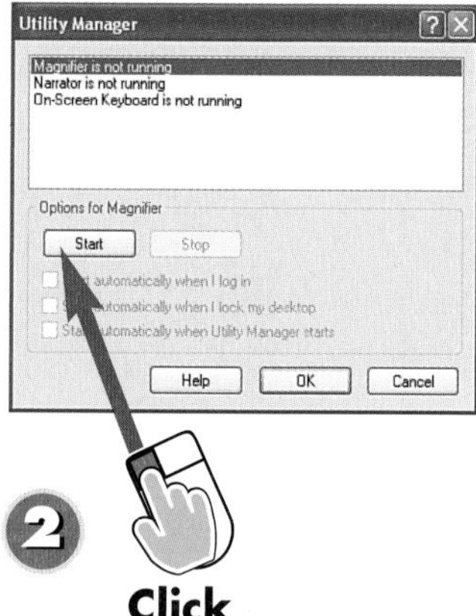

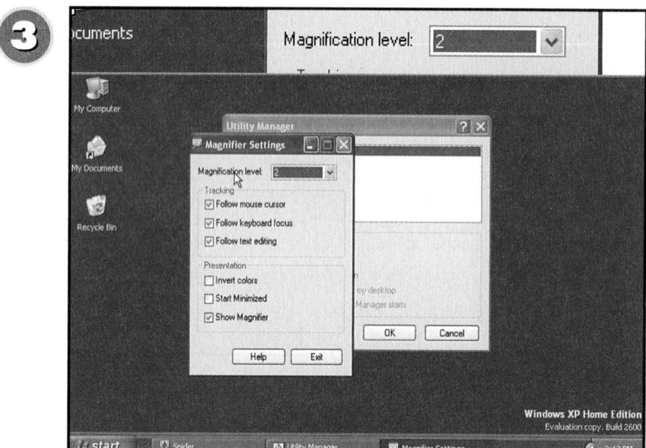

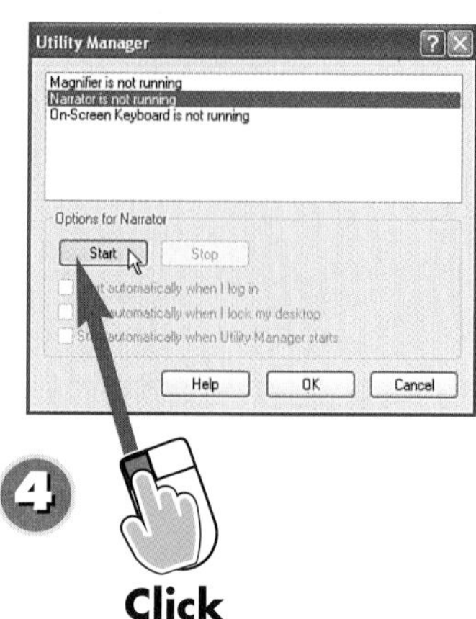

1. Click the **Start** button, select **All Programs**, choose **Accessories**, click **Accessibility**, and select **Utility Manager**.
2. The Utility Manager dialog box opens. To start Magnifier, click **Magnifier is not running**, and then click **Start**.
3. Magnifier starts, magnifying part of your screen. In the Magnifier Settings dialog box, adjust the **Magnification level**, **Tracking**, and **Presentation** settings as desired.
4. In the Utility Manager dialog box, click **Narrator is not running**, and then click **Start**.

INTRODUCTION

Windows XP offers programs that make it easier for those with disabilities to use the operating system. Magnifier magnifies the contents of your screen, Narrator reads the contents of your screen aloud, and On-Screen Keyboard enables users who have limited mobility to type onscreen using a pointing device.

TIP

Informational Dialog Boxes

You may notice the appearance of a dialog box when you start each program that provides information about the program you opened. Simply read the contents of the dialog box, and click **OK** to close it.

TIP

Exit Accessibility Programs

Clicking the **Exit** button on the Magnifier Settings, Narrator, or On-Screen Keyboard dialog boxes closes the program. To keep the program open, but remove its dialog box from view, click the **Minimize** button in the top-right corner of the dialog box.

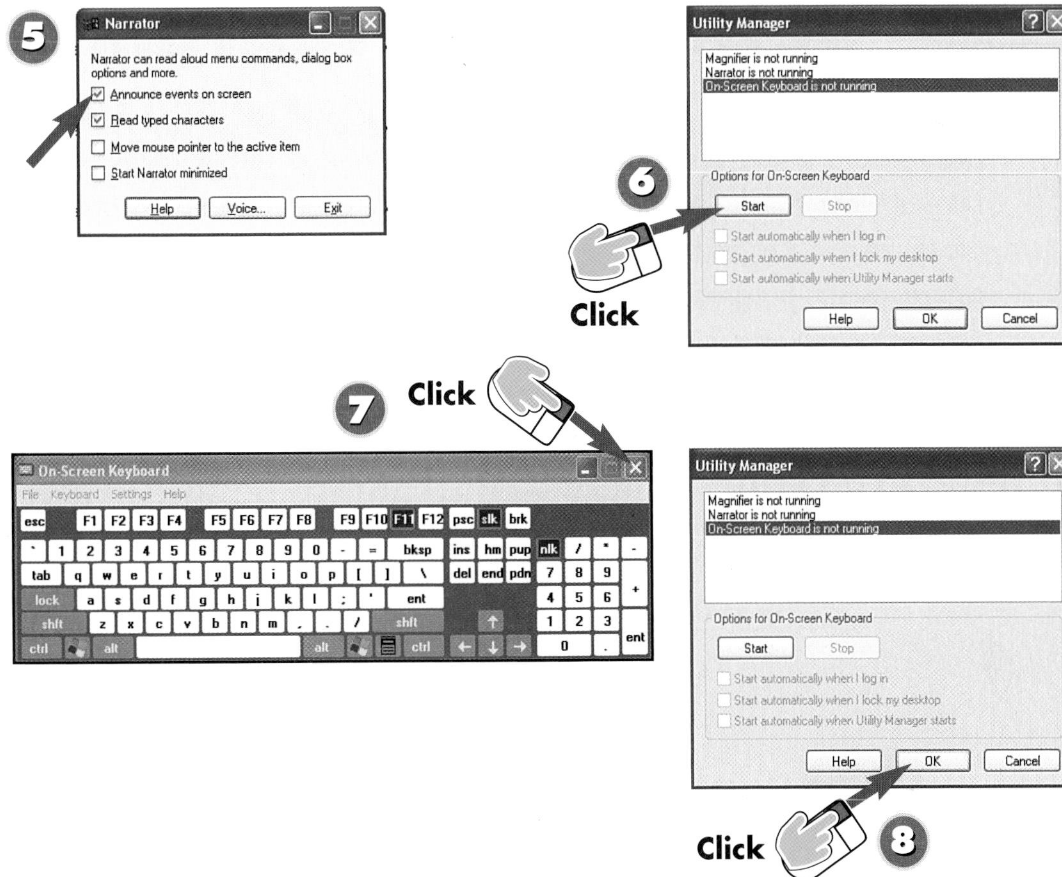

5 Narrator starts, displaying the Narrator dialog box. Check any of the desired options.

6 In the Utility Manager dialog box, click **On-Screen Keyboard is not running**, and then click **Start**.

7 On-Screen Keyboard opens on your screen. To close this program, click the **Close** button in the upper-right corner.

8 Click the **OK** button to close the Utility Manager window.

TIP

Select a Narrator Voice
You can select a voice you want to use for Narrator, as well as the speed, volume, and pitch of that voice. To do so, click the **Voice** button in the Narrator dialog box. A Voice Settings dialog box opens; select your settings, and then click **OK**.

TIP

Type with On-Screen Keyboard
On-Screen Keyboard has three typing modes. In clicking mode, you click the onscreen keys with your mouse pointer to type text. In scanning mode, On-Screen Keyboard scans the keyboard, highlighting letters; you press a hot key or use a switch-input device whenever On-Screen Keyboard highlights the character you want to type. In hovering mode, you use a mouse or joystick to hover the pointer over a key; the selected character is then typed.

PART 11

Setting Up Programs

Most of the time you spend using your computer will be using some type of application. To make it as easy as possible, Windows XP enables you to set up several ways to start programs. You can create shortcuts to a program and place the shortcut on the desktop to make it more accessible. You can rearrange the programs on the Start menu so that they are more suited to how you work. You can install new programs and remove programs you no longer use. There is no right or wrong way to set up your programs; you can select the style and organization that most suit you.

Tasks

Task 1: Creating a Shortcut Icon

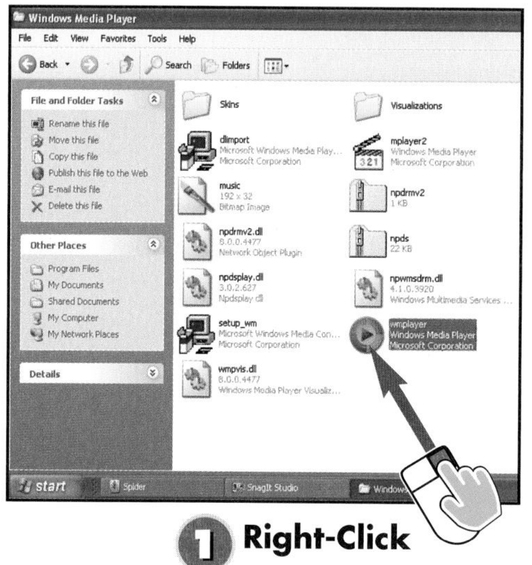

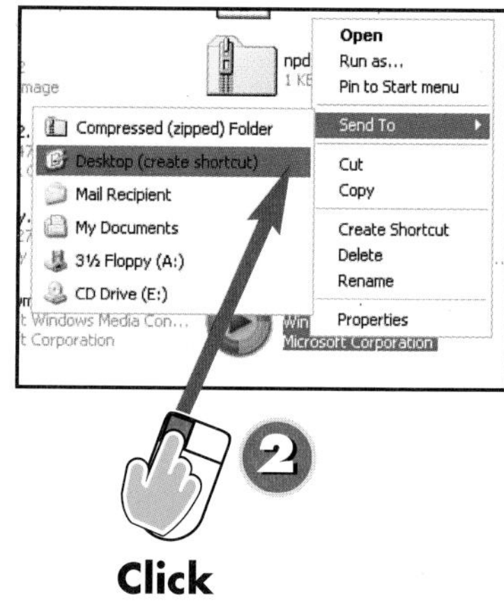

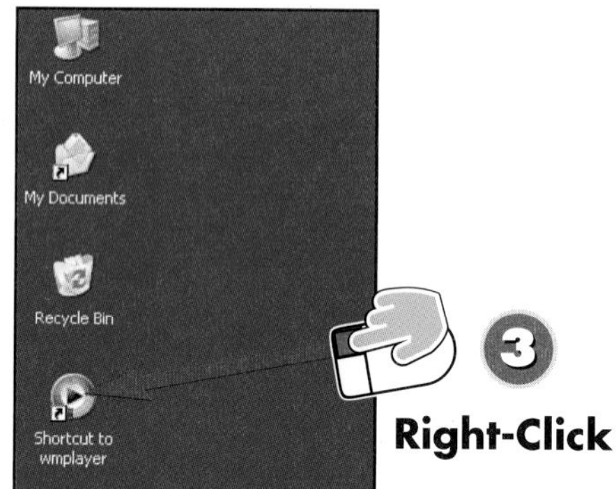

1. After you've located the program file for which you want to create a shortcut icon, right-click it.
2. In the menu that opens, choose **Send To**, and then select **Desktop (create shortcut)**.
3. Windows adds the shortcut to your desktop. (You might have to minimize any open windows to see it.)

INTRODUCTION

You can create shortcuts and place them on the desktop to provide quick access to programs. You can then double-click a shortcut to quickly start that program or open that file—without having to open menus and folders.

TIP

Shortcut to File or Printer
In addition to creating shortcuts to programs, you can create them to files or folders or to your printer.

TIP

Search for a File
If you can't find the program file for which you want to create a shortcut icon, try searching for it. Finding a particular file is covered in Part 4, "Working with Files."

Task 2: Deleting a Shortcut Icon

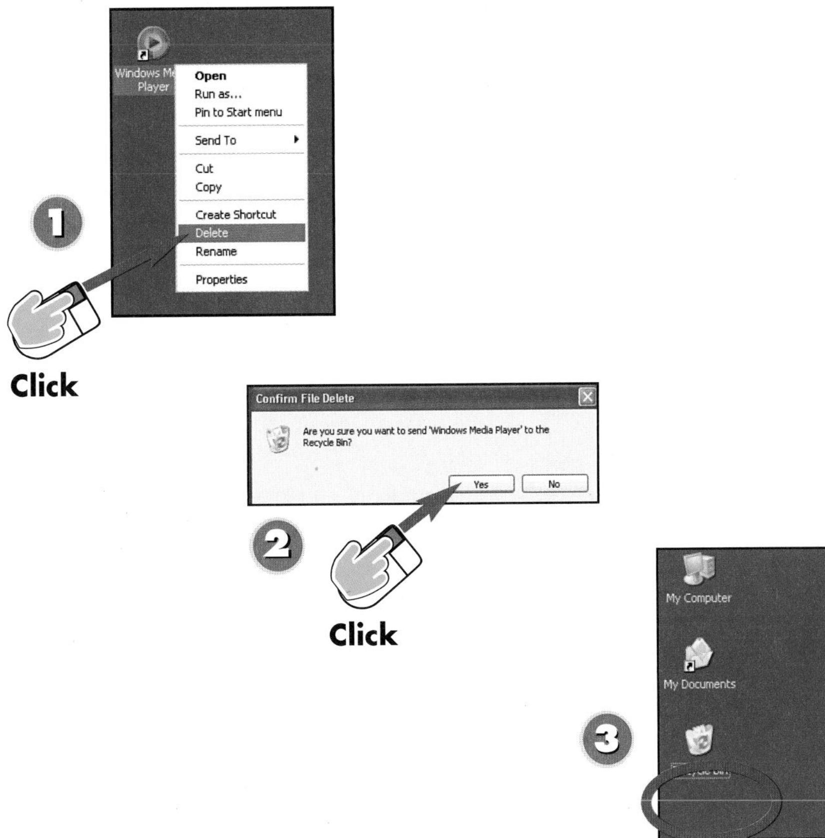

1. To delete a shortcut icon, right-click it, and choose **Delete** from the menu that appears.
2. In the Confirm File Delete dialog box, click **Yes** to delete the shortcut.
3. The shortcut is deleted from your desktop.

INTRODUCTION

If you have shortcut icons that you don't need, you can delete them. Doing so can keep your desktop uncluttered. Note that when you delete the shortcut icon, you are not deleting the program. (To delete the program, uninstall it. Uninstalling is covered later in this part.)

TIP

Rename an Icon
You can rename an icon if needed. Right-click the shortcut icon, click **Rename**, and type a new name. Press Enter.

Start

Task 3: Pinning a Program to the Start Menu

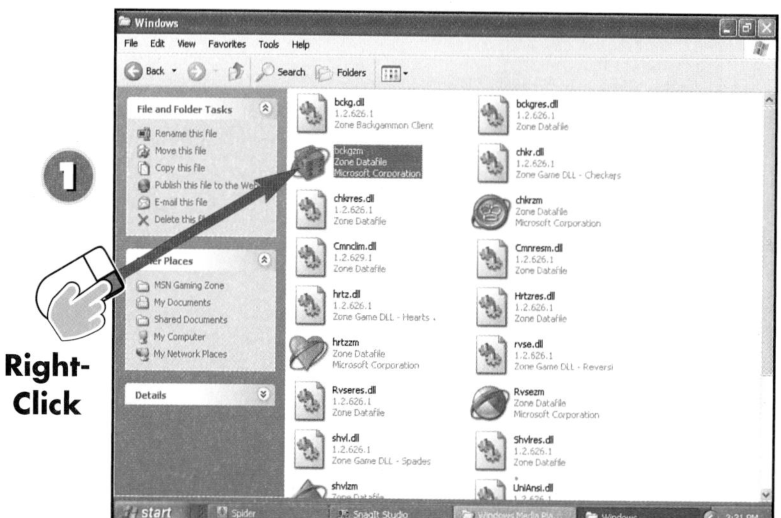

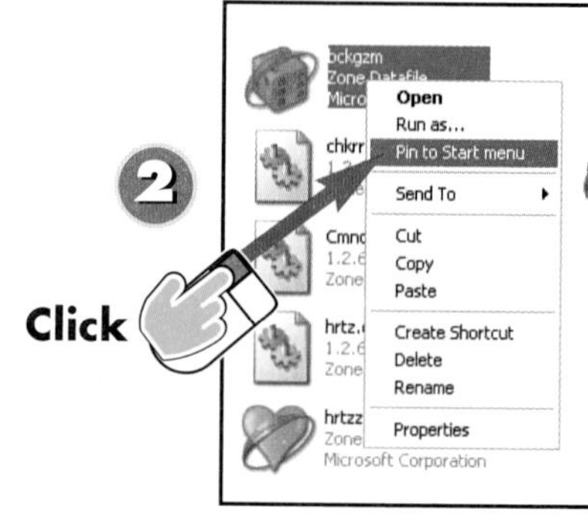

1. Navigate your folder structure to locate the program you want to pin to your Start menu and right-click the program icon.
2. Choose **Pin to Start** menu from the menu that appears.

INTRODUCTION

The Start menu includes on the opening menu commands for accessing the Internet and email. It also lists programs you frequently use. If you want a program to always appear in this first list, you can pin it to the Start menu. Then you can simply click Start and then click the program without having to display all programs and select program folders.

TIP

Shortcut

You can also display the program name in the Start menu. Right-click the name and select **Pin to Start** menu.

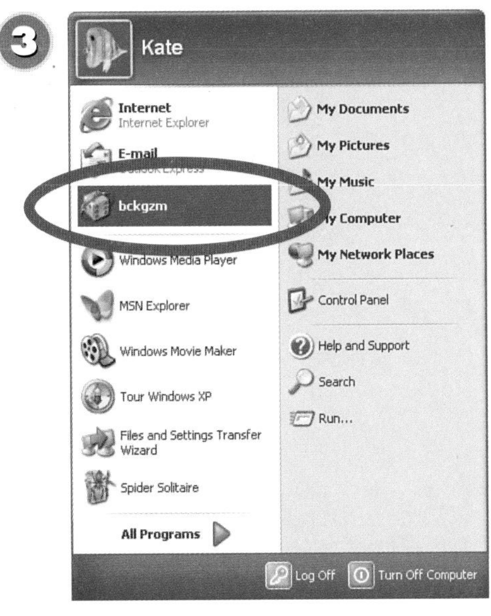

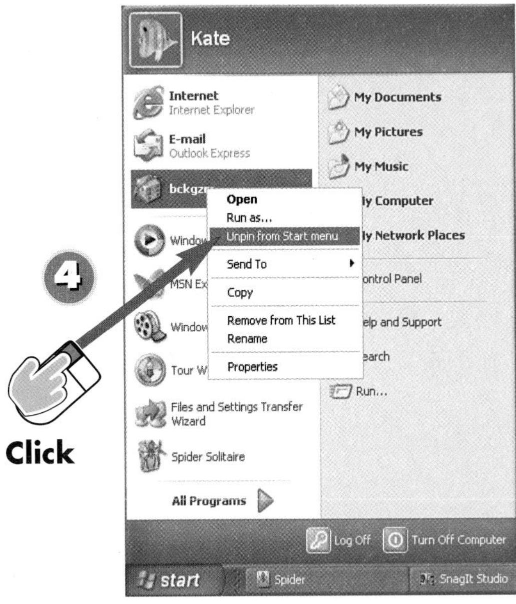

3 The program is added to the top of your Start menu.

4 To unpin the program from your Start menu, open the menu, right-click the program entry, and choose **Unpin from Start** menu.

TIP

Move the Program

When you pin a program to your Start menu, it is placed in the left column of the menu. You can drag the pinned program to the My Documents, My Pictures, or My Music folder, but nowhere else within the Start menu. If you want to organize your Start menu in a certain way, with specific applications in specific folders, you'll need to switch to Classic view. Several tasks in this chapter cover managing the Start menu in Classic view.

Task 4: Customizing the Start Menu

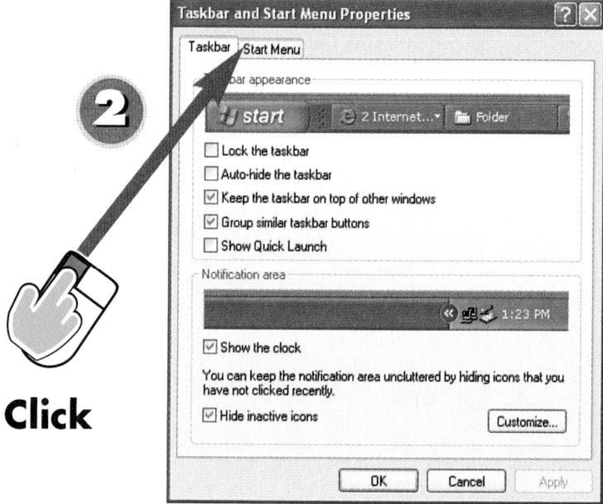

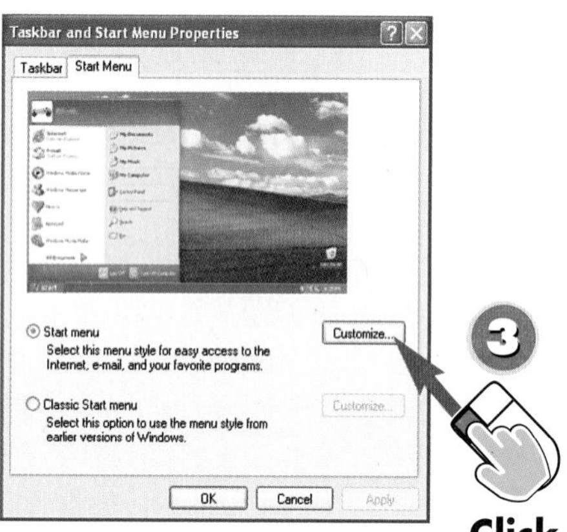

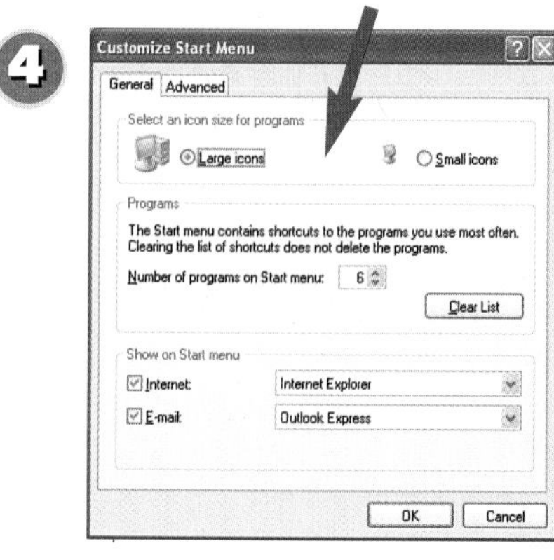

1. Right-click the taskbar, and choose **Properties** from the menu that appears.
2. The Taskbar and Start Menu Properties dialog box opens. Click the **Start Menu** tab.
3. In the Start Menu tab, click the **Customize** button next to the Start menu option.
4. The Customize Start Menu dialog box opens. Select either **Large icons** or **Small icons** in the Select an icon size for programs area.

INTRODUCTION

In addition to enabling you to pin programs to the Start menu, Windows XP allows you to make other customizations. You can specify whether the icons in the Start menu are small or large, how many of your most recently used programs are displayed, and whether your Internet and e-mail programs appear on the menu.

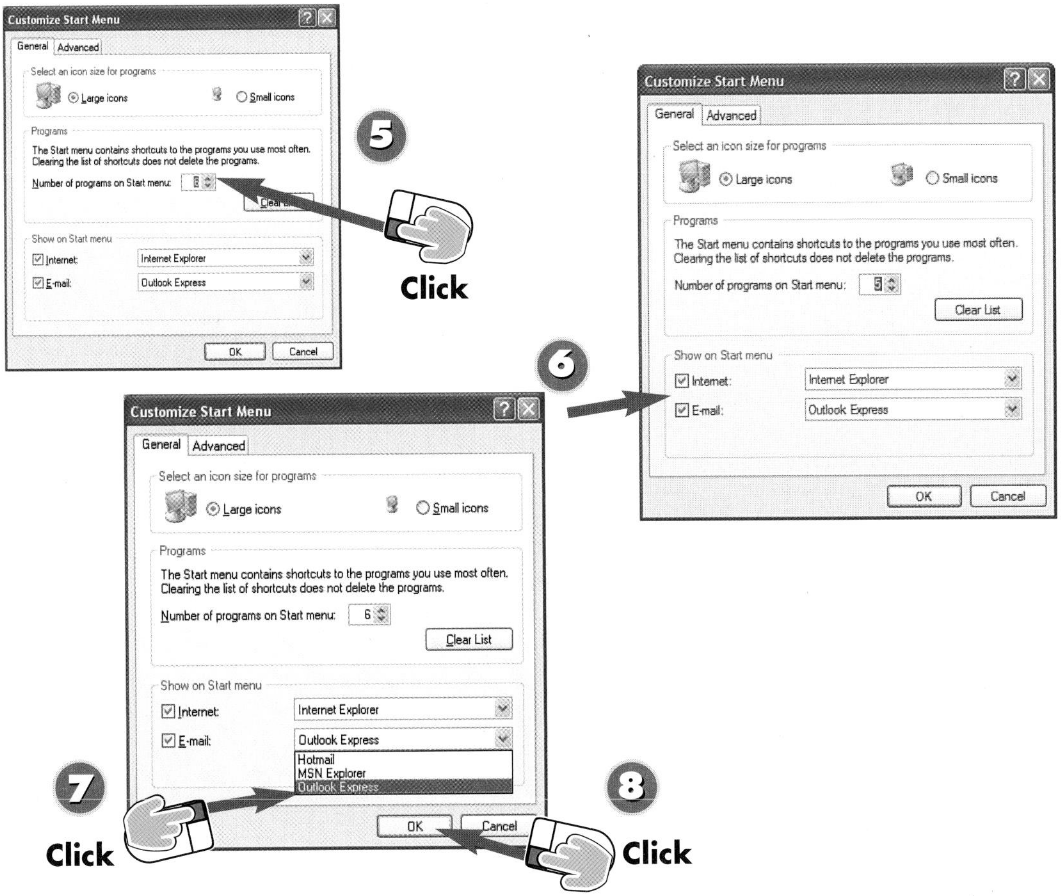

5 Select how many recently used programs you want the Start menu to display.

6 Specify whether you want the Start menu to prominently display your Internet browser and e-mail programs, and specify which programs you use by ckecking the check-boxes.

7 To select which program you use to access the Internet or e-mail, click the down arrow next to the current program. Select the program you want to use.

8 Click **OK** to close all open dialog boxes.

TIP

Display Recent Documents
If you want to display a command that lists your most recently opened documents, click the **Advanced** tab and then check **List my most recently opened documents**. Click **OK** to close all open dialog boxes.

TIP

More Advanced Options
You can also select whether new programs are highlighted and any other Start menu items to include from the Advanced tab. Click **Advanced** and make any changes. Click **OK** to close the dialog box.

Task 5: Adding Programs to the Classic Start Menu

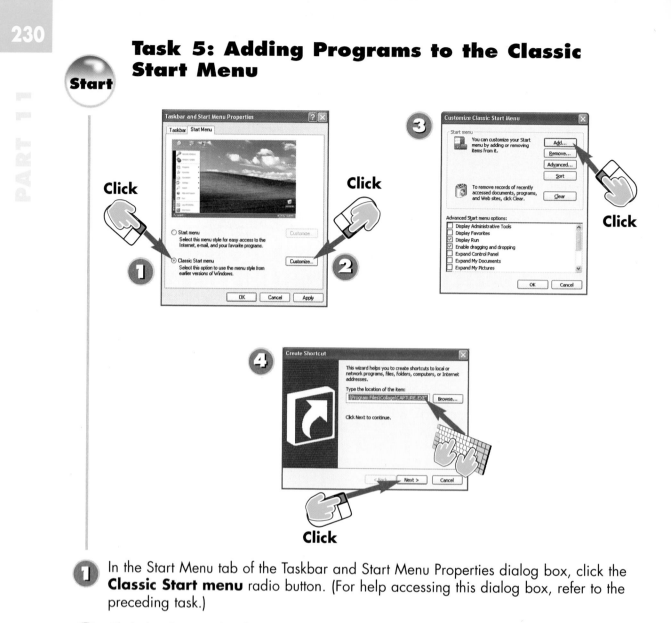

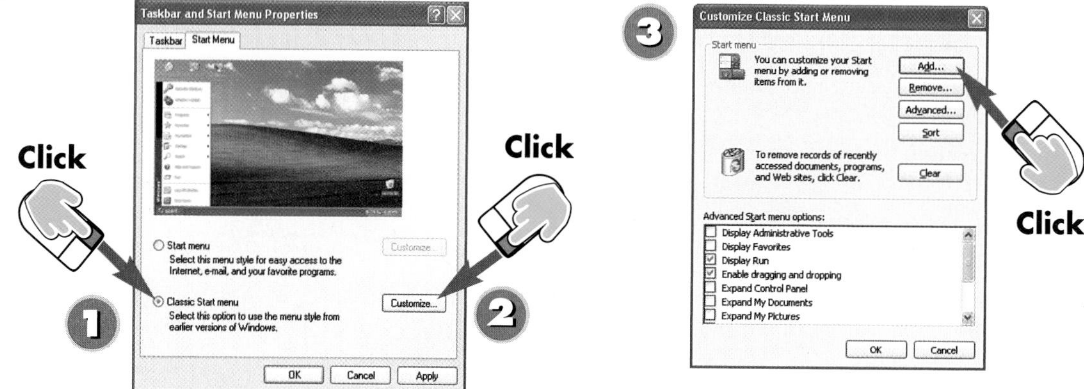

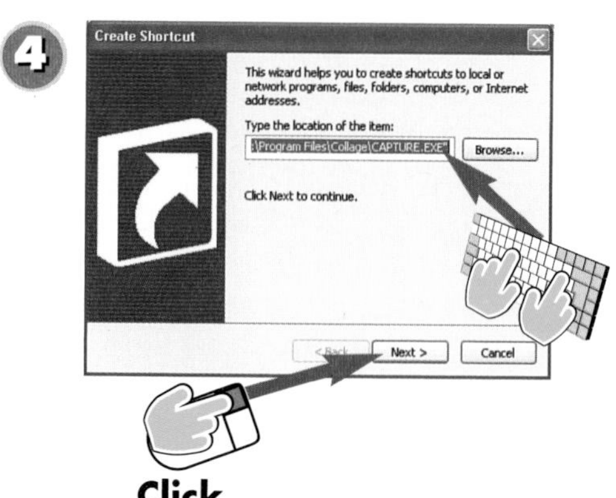

1. In the Start Menu tab of the Taskbar and Start Menu Properties dialog box, click the **Classic Start menu** radio button. (For help accessing this dialog box, refer to the preceding task.)
2. Click the **Customize** button.
3. The Customize Classic Start Menu dialog box opens. To add a program, click the **Add** button.
4. Type the location of the program you want to add, and click the **Next** button.

INTRODUCTION

Although Windows XP enables you to pin programs to your Start menu (as described in Task 3, "Pinning a Program to the Start Window"), it is the Classic view that offers users the most control and flexibility when it comes to organizing the Start menu. In order for you to add programs to specific folders on the Start menu, to delete programs from the Start menu, to create new folders on the Start menu, and to move programs from one folder to another on the Start menu, you must switch to the Classic-style menu.

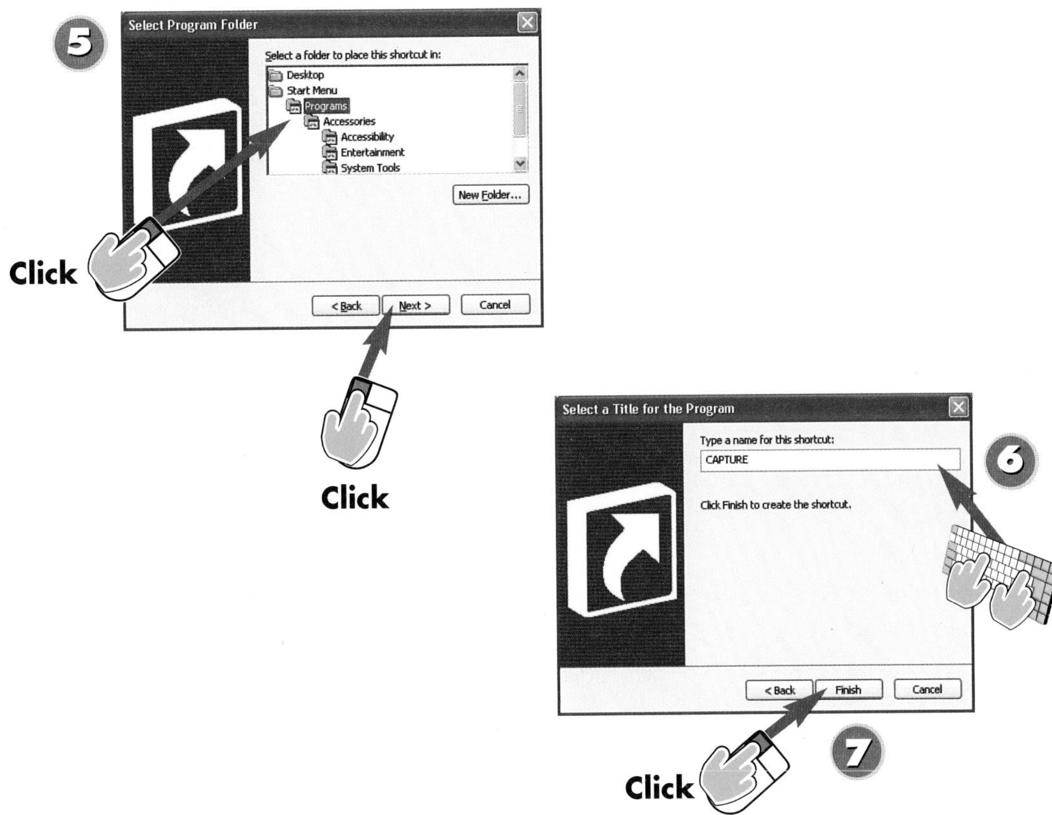

5. Click the folder in which you want to place the program, and click the **Next** button.
6. Type a name for menu entry.
7. Click the **Finish** button. The program is added to the Start menu.

TIP
Use the Browse Button
If you don't know where the location of the program you want to add (refer to step 6), click the **Browse** button, and then select the folder and the program name from the Browse dialog box.

TIP
Add New Folder
You can click the **New Folder** button in step 5 to add a new folder to your Start menu structure.

TIP
Close the Dialog Boxes
Click the OK button to close the Customize Classic Start Menu dialog box. Then click **OK** to close the Taskbar and Start Menu Properties dialog box.

Start

Task 6: Removing Programs from the Classic Start Menu

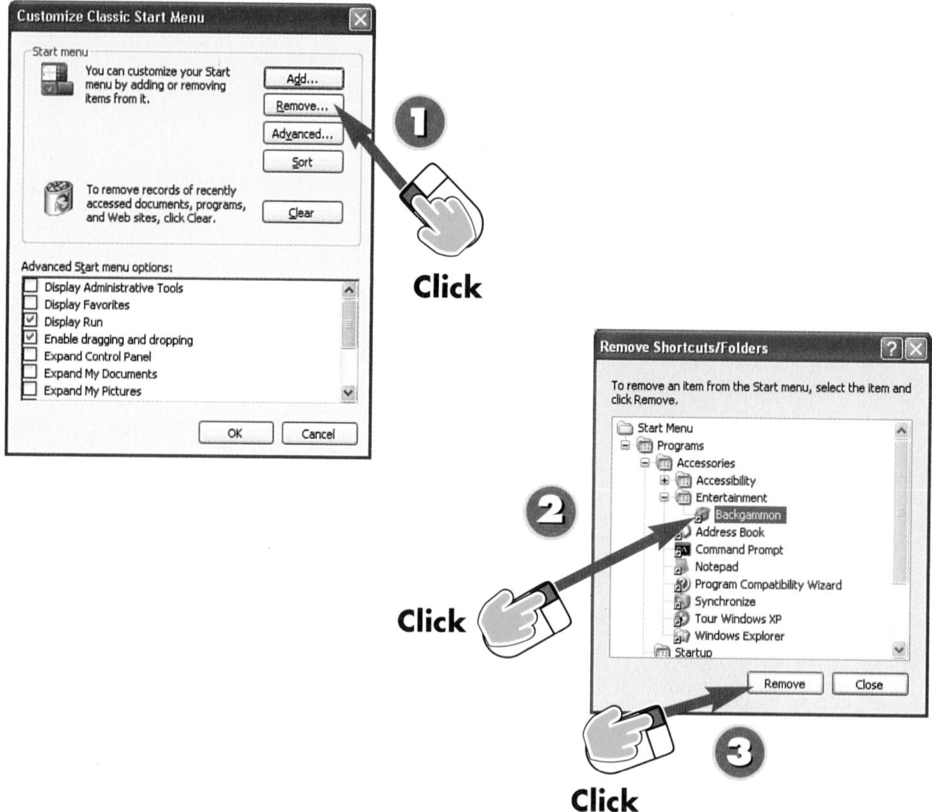

1. In the Customize Classic Start Menu dialog box, click the **Remove** button. (Refer to the preceding task if you need help reaching this dialog box.)
2. The Remove Shortcuts/Folders dialog box opens. Locate and click the program you want to remove.
3. Click the **Remove** button.

INTRODUCTION

At first, you might go a little crazy and add all kinds of icons to your Start menu. But after you use the computer more and more, you might want to streamline the Start menu and weed out programs that you don't use.

TIP

Expand the Listing

To display and select the program you want to remove, you might need to expand the folder listings. Click the plus sign next to the folder that contains the desired program.

TIP

WARNING!

Keep in mind that removing a program from the Start menu does not remove the program and its files from your hard disk. To do this, you must uninstall the program or manually delete it and its related folders and files (see Task 13).

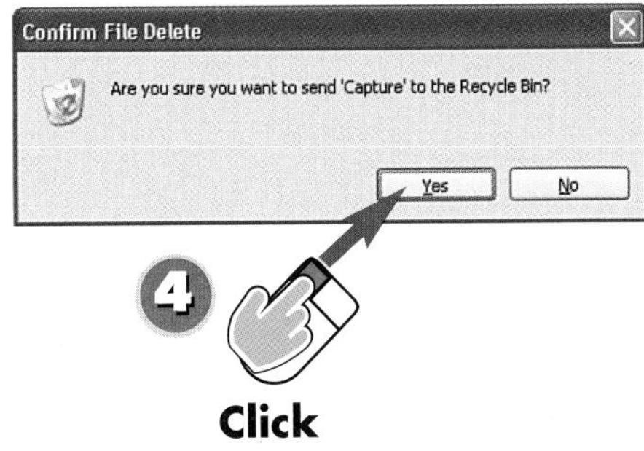

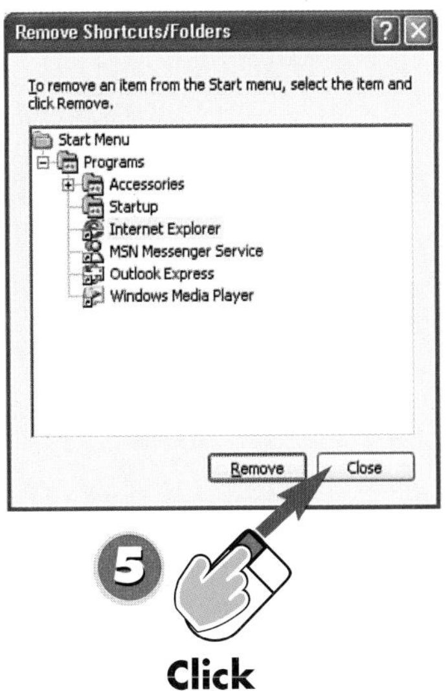

4 The Confirm File Delete dialog box opens, asking whether you're sure you want to delete the shortcut. Click the **Yes** button.

5 The program is removed. Click the **Close** button to close the Remove Shortcuts/Folders dialog box.

TIP

Remove a Folder

You can follow this procedure to remove a folder from the Start menu. Simply select the folder, and then click the **Remove** button. You are prompted to confirm the removal before the folder and all its contents are removed.

TIP

Close the Dialog Boxes

Click the **OK** button to close the Customize Classic Start Menu dialog box. Then click **OK** to close the Taskbar and Start Menu Properties dialog box.

Task 7: Adding Folders to the Classic Start Menu

Start

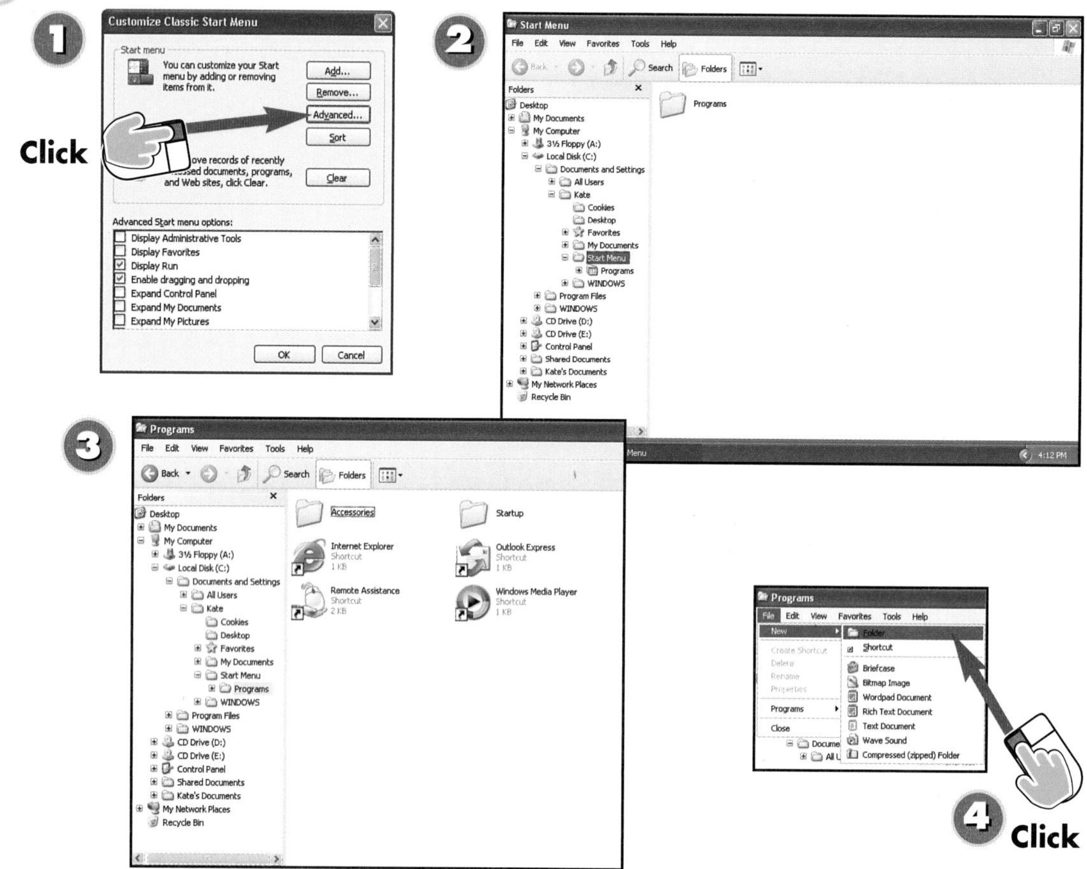

1. In the Customize Classic Start Menu dialog box, click the **Advanced** button. (Refer to Task 5, "Adding Programs to the Classic Start Menu," if you need help reaching this dialog box.)
2. Windows Explorer opens, displaying the contents of the Start Menu folder in the right-hand pane.
3. Open the folder in which the new folder should be placed. For this example, the new folder will be placed within the Programs folder, so that folder is open.
4. Click **File**, select **New**, and then click **Folder**.

INTRODUCTION

When you install a new program, that program's installation process sets up program folders and icons for itself. If you don't like the arrangement of the folders and icons, you can change it. For example, if more than one person uses your PC, you might set up folders for each person and then add the programs that a certain person uses to his or her folder.

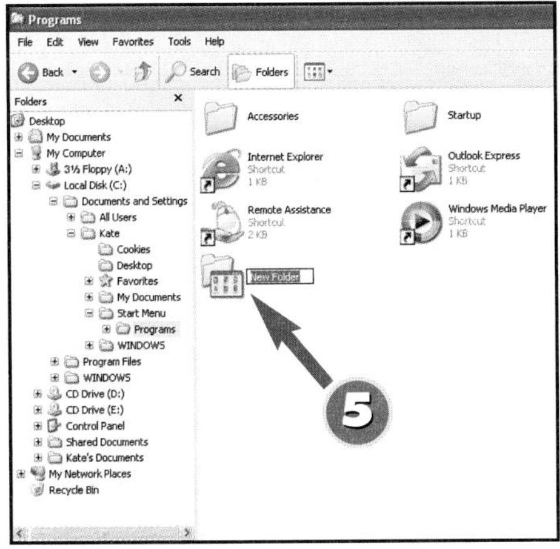

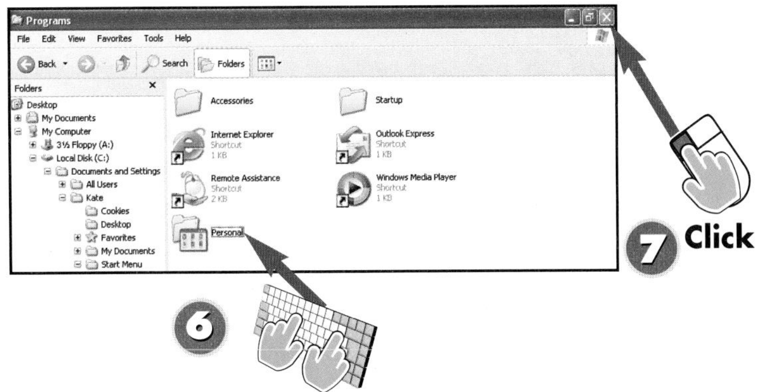

5 The new folder is added to the Start menu in the Programs folder.

6 Type a descriptive name for the folder, and press the Enter key on your keyboard. The folder is added.

7 Click the **Close** button to close Windows Explorer.

TIP

Delete Folders
You can delete folders. To do so, simply right-click the folder and select the **Delete** command from the shortcut menu. Click **Yes** to confirm the deletion.

TIP

Move Programs to the New Folder
You'll learn how to move programs into the folder you just created in the next task.

TIP

Close the Dialog Boxes
Click the **OK** button to close the Customize Classic Start Menu dialog box. Then click **OK** to close the Taskbar and Start Menu Properties dialog box.

Start

Task 8: Rearranging the Classic Start Menu

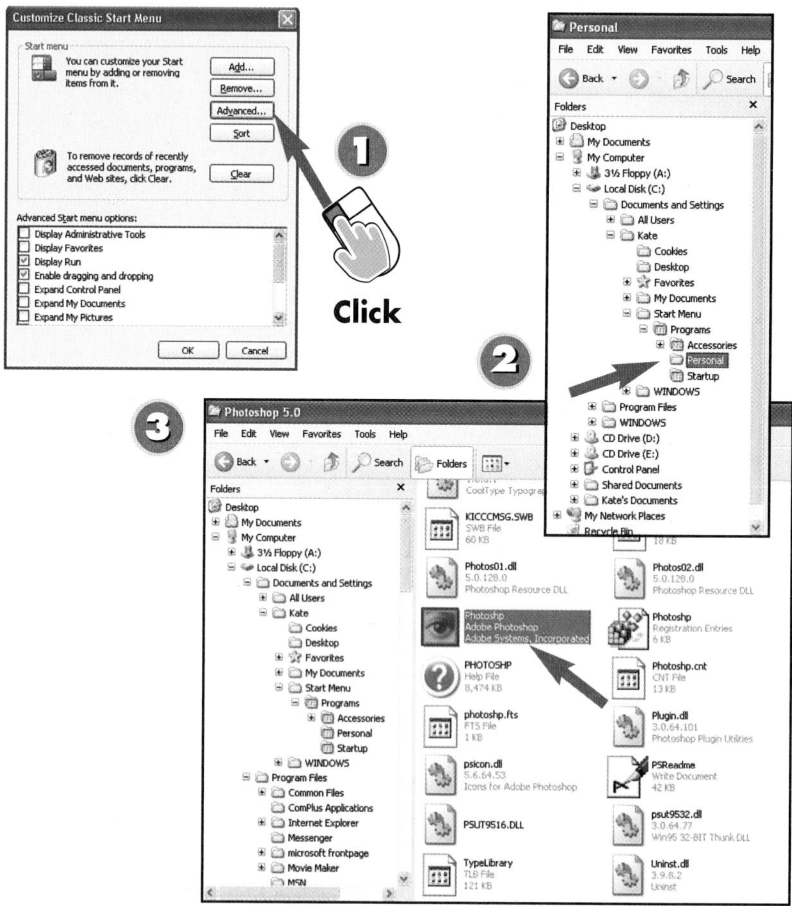

1. In the Customize Classic Start Menu dialog box, click the **Advanced** button. (Refer to Task 5 if you need help reaching this dialog box.)
2. Windows Explorer opens. Expand the folder listing in the left pane until you see the folder where you want to place a program (in this case, the **Personal** folder).
3. In the right-hand pane, open the folder that contains the program you want to move (in this example, **Adobe Photoshop**).

INTRODUCTION

After you set up folders, you can organize your Start menu, putting the program icons in the folder and order you want.

TIP

Advanced Customization Options

The Customize Classic Start Menu dialog box offers several advanced customization options. In the **Advanced Start menu options** area, you can specify that various features, such as Favorites, be displayed in the Start menu. You can also choose to expand various folders within the menu, such as Control Panel, My Documents, and more.

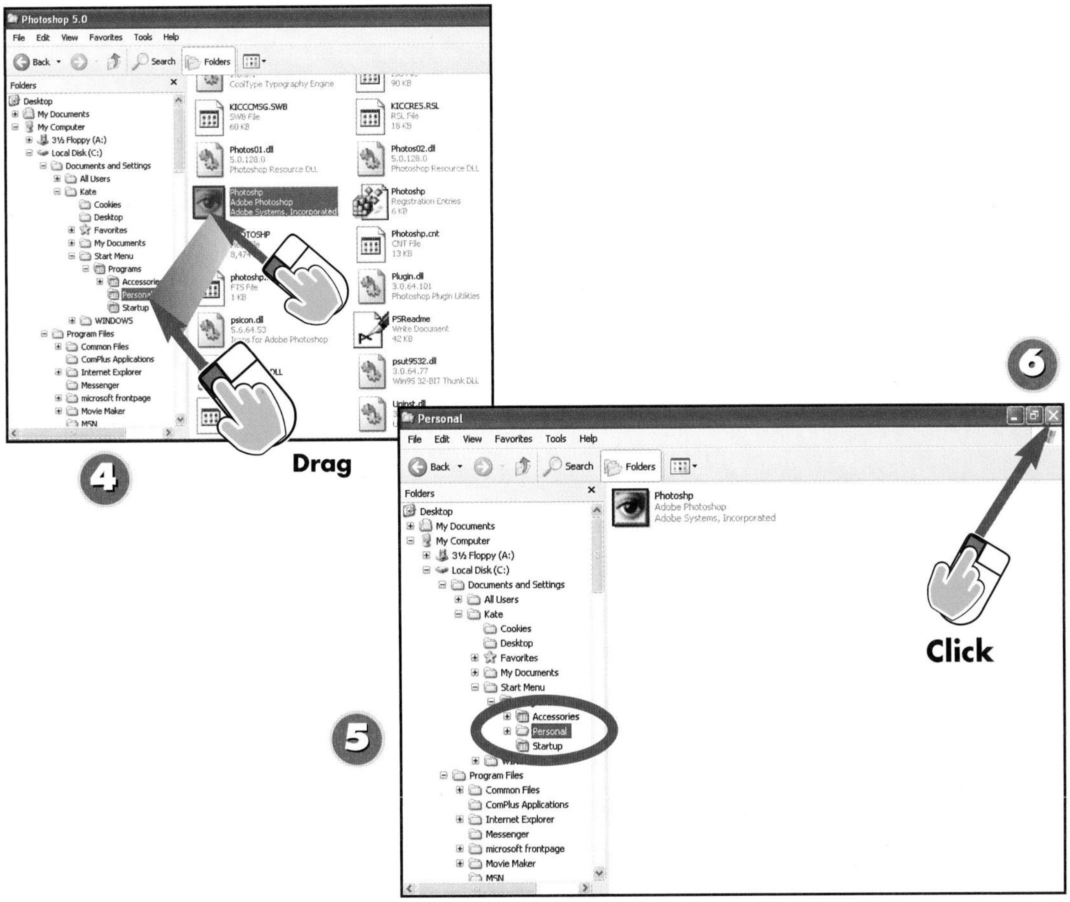

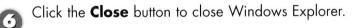

4 Drag the program icon from the right pane to the folder in the left pane.

5 The program is moved to the folder.

6 Click the **Close** button to close Windows Explorer.

TIP

Sort

You can revert to the default order of the folders and icons by clicking the **Sort** button in the Customize Classic Start Menu dialog box.

TIP

Copy, Not Move

To copy a program to a different folder rather than moving it, right-click the program shortcut, and choose **Copy** from the menu that appears. Then, right-click the folder in which you want to place a copy of the program shortcut, and choose **Paste** from the menu that appears.

TIP

Close the Dialog Boxes

Click the **OK** button to close the Customize Classic Start Menu dialog box. Then click **OK** to close the Taskbar and Start Menu Properties dialog box.

Task 9: Starting an Application When You Start Windows

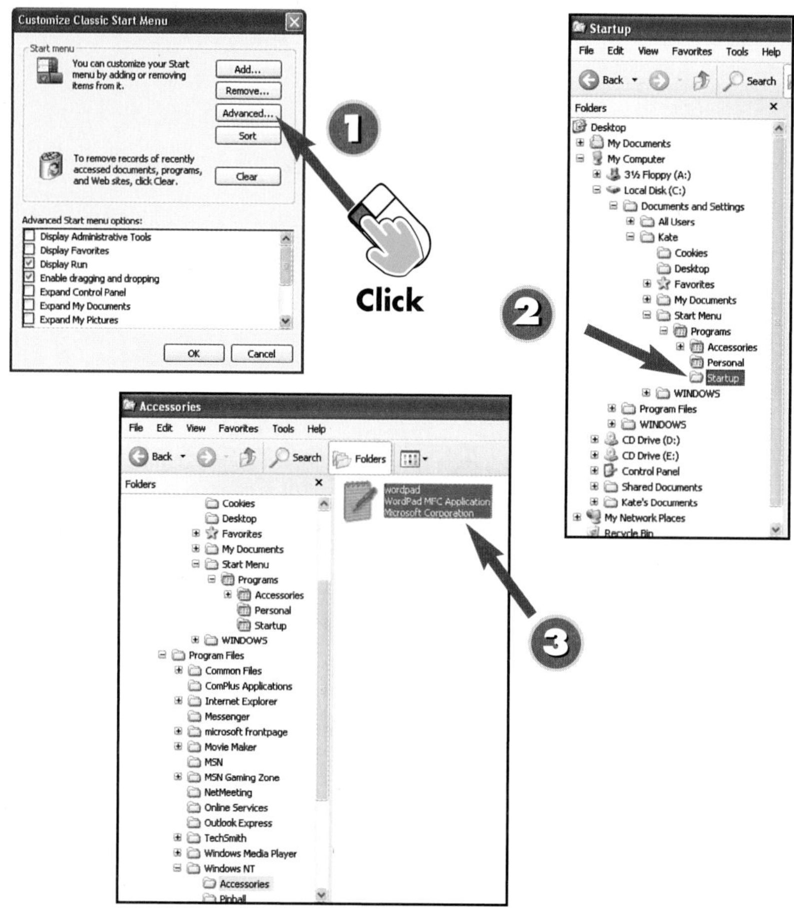

1. In the Customize Classic Start Menu dialog box, click the **Advanced** button. (Refer to Task 5 if you need help reaching this dialog box.)
2. Windows Explorer opens. Expand the folder listing in the left pane until you see the **Startup** folder.
3. In the right-hand pane, open the folder that contains the program you want to move to the Startup folder (in this example, **Wordpad**).

INTRODUCTION

Windows XP enables you to start one or more programs at the same time that you start Windows by turning your computer on. You must use Classic style for the Start menu.

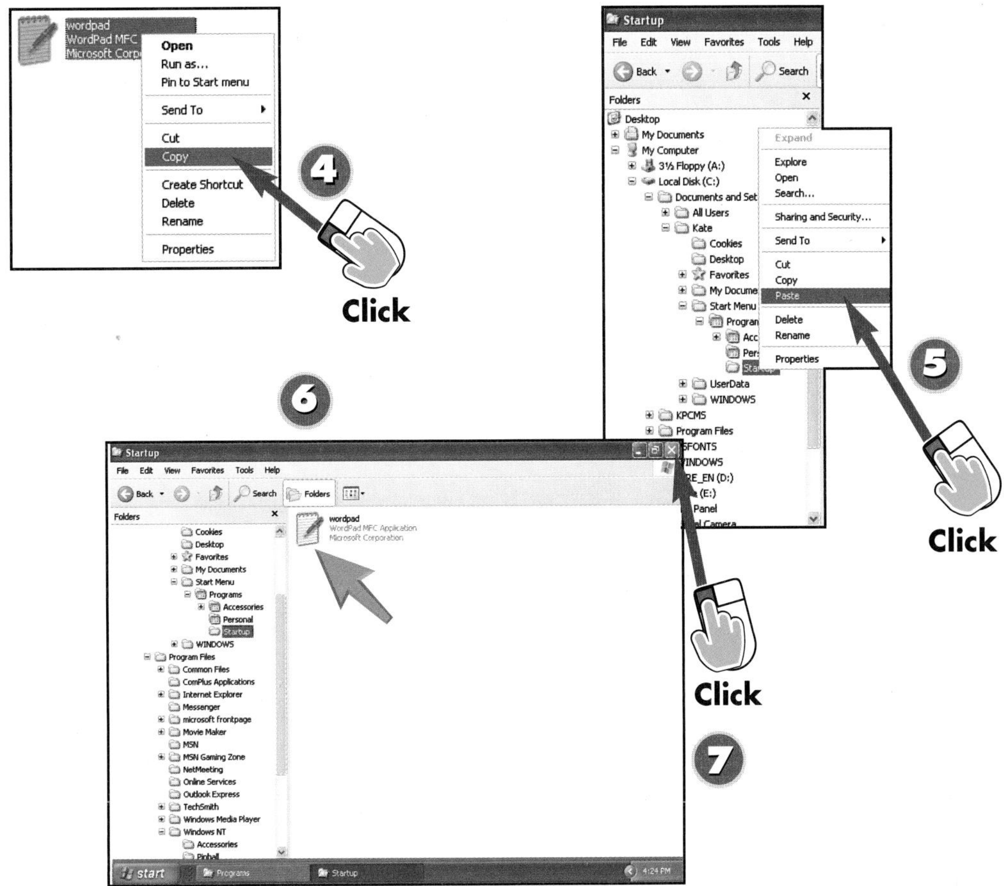

4 Right-click the icon for the program you want to add to the Startup folder, and choose **Copy** from the menu that appears.

5 Right-click the Startup folder in the left-hand pane, and select **Paste** from the menu that appears.

6 The program is copied to the Startup folder.

7 Click the **Close** button to close Windows Explorer.

TIP

Close the Dialog Boxes
Click the **OK** button to close the Customize Classic Start Menu dialog box. Then click **OK** to close the Taskbar and Start Menu Properties dialog box.

TIP

WARNING!
If you don't turn off your computer each night and then turn it on again when you begin work, programs in the Startup folder will not start each morning. They are started only when you start Windows.

TIP

Remove a Program
To remove a program from the Startup folder, follow the steps in this task to open the folder. Then, right-click the icon for the program you want to remove, and select **Delete** from the menu that appears.

Task 10: Installing Software

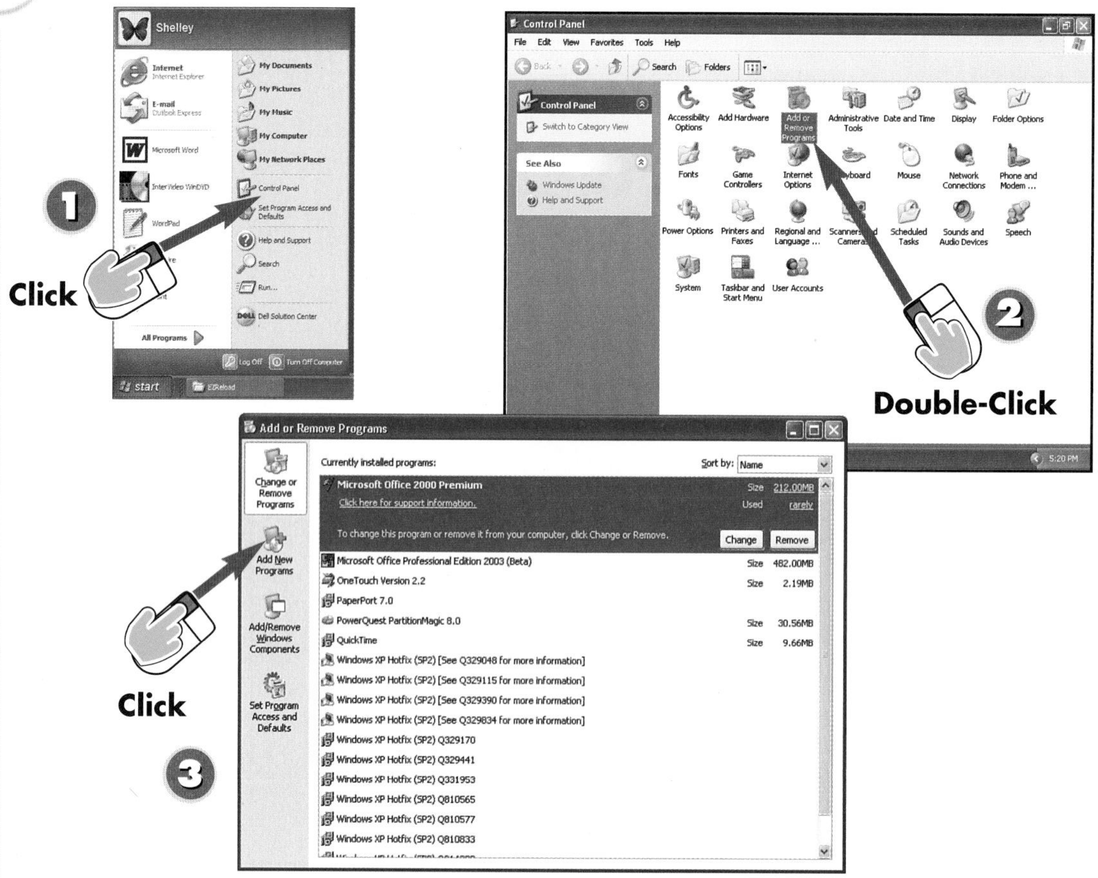

1. Click the **Start** button and choose **Control Panel**.
2. Double-click the **Add or Remove Programs** icon. (You may need to switch to Classic view first.)
3. The Add or Remove Programs window opens. Click the **Add New Programs** button.

INTRODUCTION

When you bought your computer, it might have come with certain programs already installed. If you want to add to these, you can purchase additional programs and then install them on your system. Different programs employ different installation processes. That is, the steps you take to install one program will differ from the steps you'll take to install another. Windows XP's Add or Remove Programs function enables you to begin the process of installing programs from a CD-ROM, a floppy disk, a network, or Microsoft Windows Update.

TIP

Install Automatically

Some programs have an automated installation process. Once you insert the disk, the installation program may start automatically. In this case, you don't need to use the Add New Programs Control Panel utility.

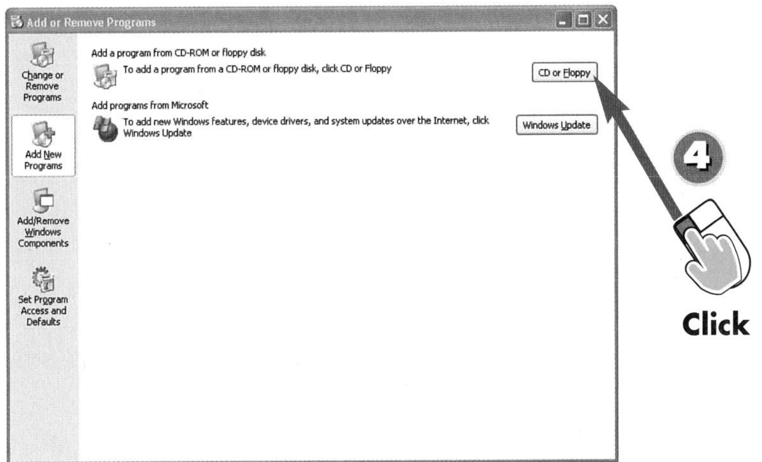

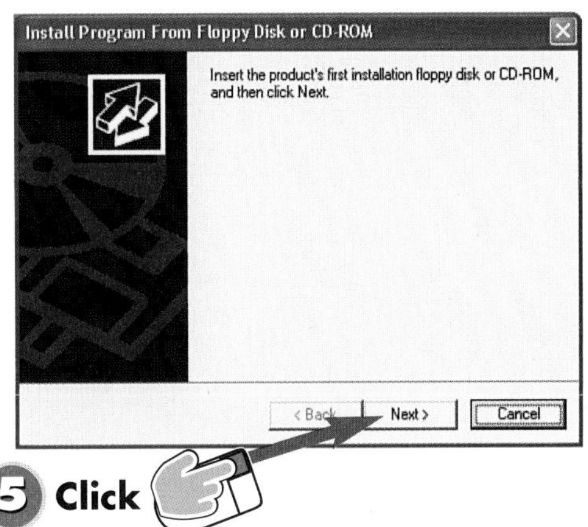

4. To add a program from a CD or floppy disk, click the **CD or Floppy** button.

5. Insert the program's CD-ROM or floppy disk, and click the **Next** button. What happens next depends the software you are installing; follow the onscreen directions.

TIP

Add Icons

The installation program usually adds an icon to your Start menu so that you can easily start the program. If it does not, you can add one for the program. Refer to Task 3 or Task 5 in this part.

TIP

Use the Run Command

If this procedure does not work, you can use the Run command to run the installation program. Insert the CD-ROM or disk into the appropriate drive, and then click the **Start** button and choose **Run**. Enter the path and program name to run the installation program, and click **OK**. (If you don't know the name of the program or its path, click the **Browse** button and use the Browse dialog box to find the file.) Follow the onscreen instructions.

Task 11: Controlling Windows Updates

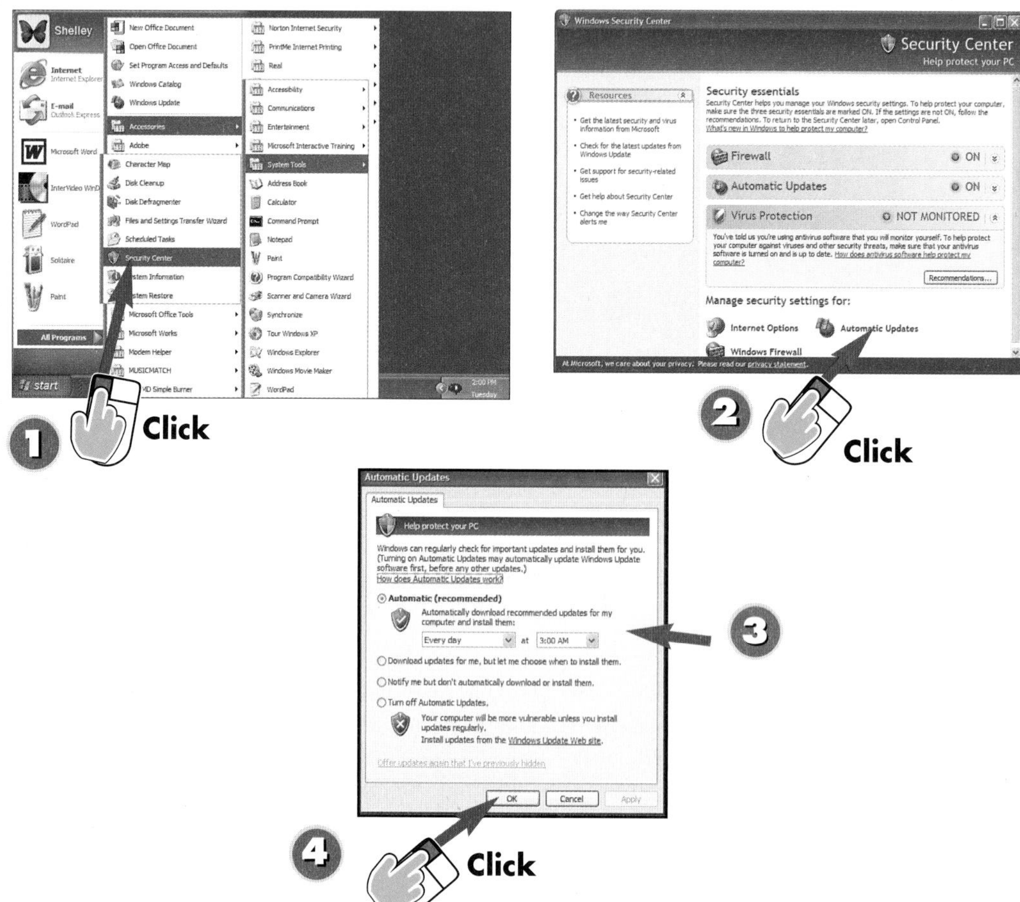

1. Click **Start**, **All Programs**, **Accessories**, **System Tools**, and finally **Security Center**.
2. You see the new Windows Security Center. At the bottom of the screen, click **Automatic Updates**.
3. Select how you want to handle updates.
4. Click **OK**.

INTRODUCTION

You can have Windows check for and automatically install new updates. Updates include fixes for problems and holes in security (usually called patches). The updates are free. To start, you can control how Windows XP handles updates.

TIP

Automatic Installation

If you have set up Windows to automatically install updates, you'll see an Automatic Windows Update icon in the system tray prompting you to install the new updates. Click **Install**. When the installation is complete, restart your system, as directed.

More Information?

For more information about how Automatic Updates work, click the **How does Automatic Updates work**? link.

Task 12: Updating Windows

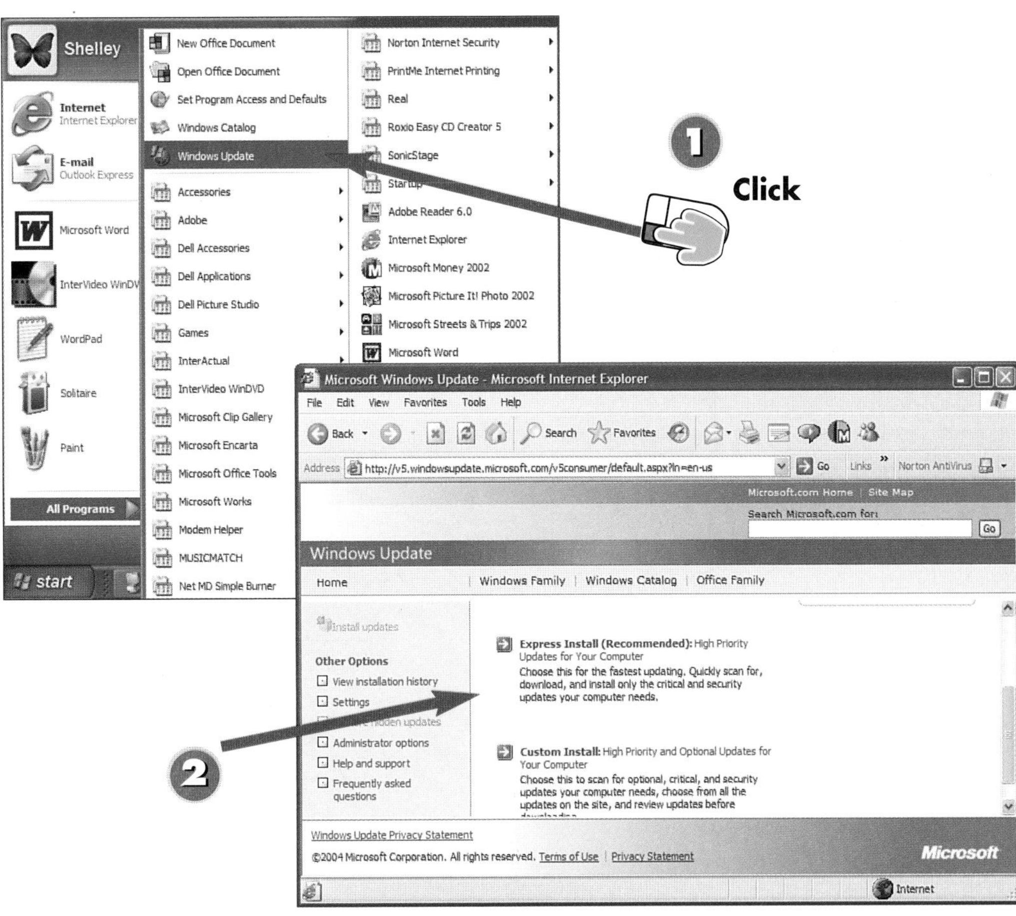

1. Click **Start**, **All Programs**, **Windows Update**.

2. Use the links at this site to check for and install any new updates. Follow the onscreen instructions.

INTRODUCTION

When new updates are available you can install them. Installation varies depending on how you have set up Windows to handle automatic updates (see the preceding task). You can manually check for and install updates also (as covered here). To access the update site, you must be connected to the Internet.

TIP

What to Install?

You should install any critical updates because these updates fix serious problems (often with security). For other updates, you can decide whether to install by reading a description of the update and its purpose.

Task 13: Uninstalling Applications

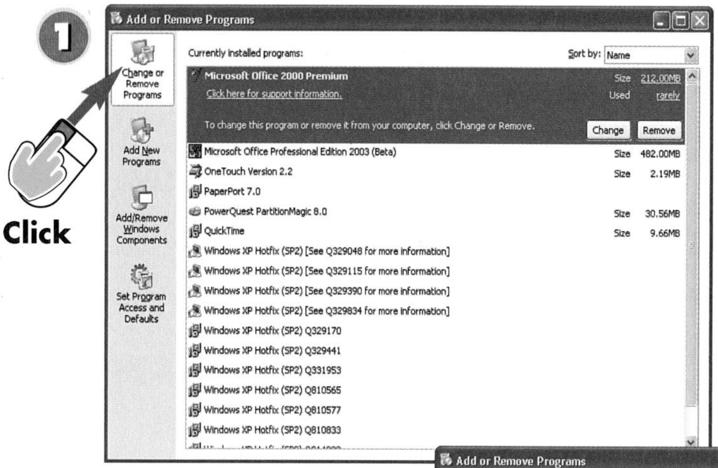

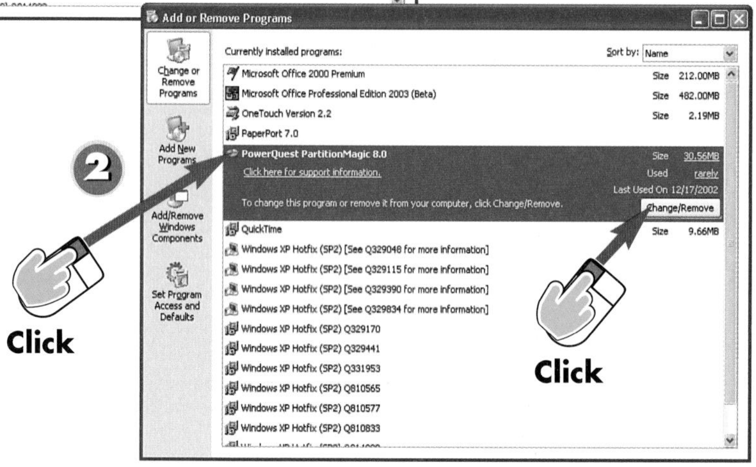

1. In the Add or Remove Programs window, click **Change or Remove Programs**. (Refer to the Task 10, "Installing Software," for help finding the Add or Remove Programs window.)
2. Select the program you want to remove. Click **Change or Remove Programs** button.
3. Follow the on-screen instructions, which vary from program to program.

INTRODUCTION

You can remove a shortcut icon or an item from the Start menu, but doing so leaves that program on your hard disk. When you want to get rid of the program and its files entirely, you must uninstall it. (You should move any data files from your program folders if, for example, you plan to use them in another program.)

TIP

WARNING!

With some programs, simply clicking the **Remove** button is all it takes to delete the program from your system. You won't be prompted as to whether you really, really want to delete it.

TIP

Program Not Listed?

Some programs can't be uninstalled via the Add or Remove Programs dialog box. If your program is not listed, you must use a different procedure. Check your program documentation for specific instructions.

Task 14: Setting Program Access and Defaults

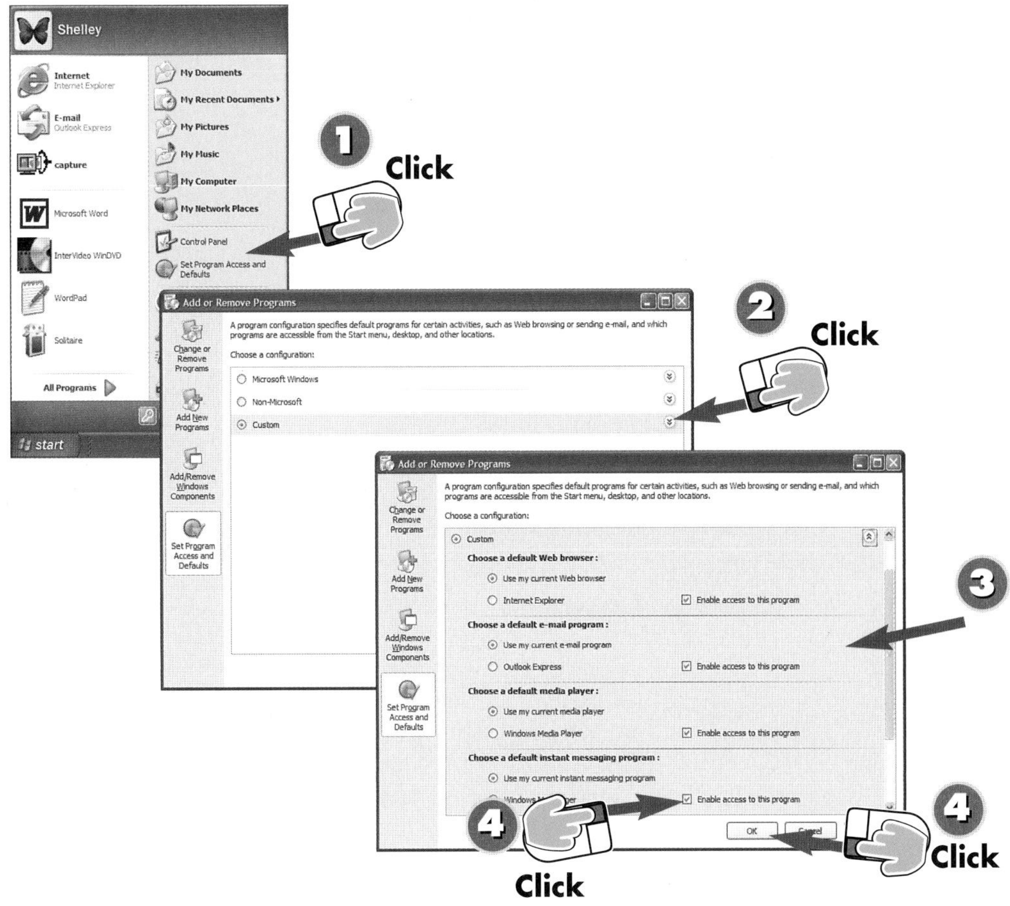

1. Click the Start button, and then click **Set Program Access and Defaults**.

2. Click the **Custom** button, and then click the down arrow at the far right part of the screen.

3. You see a list of program types. For each one, select to use your current program or the Microsoft program.

4. If you want this item included on your Start menu, check **Enable access to this program**. Click **OK** when you have finished your changes.

INTRODUCTION

You can select which programs are used for certain activities such as Web browsing and e-mail. You can choose all Microsoft programs, non-Microsoft programs, or Custom (a mix). With Custom, you can individually select the programs for each option (covered here).

TIP

Program Types

You can select a default Web browser, email program, media player, and instant messaging program. If you cannot see all the options, click the scroll arrows to scroll to the bottom and view all program types.

TIP

Use Current

If you select Use my current for the program, the current default program for that category will be used.

Task 15: Removing Windows Components

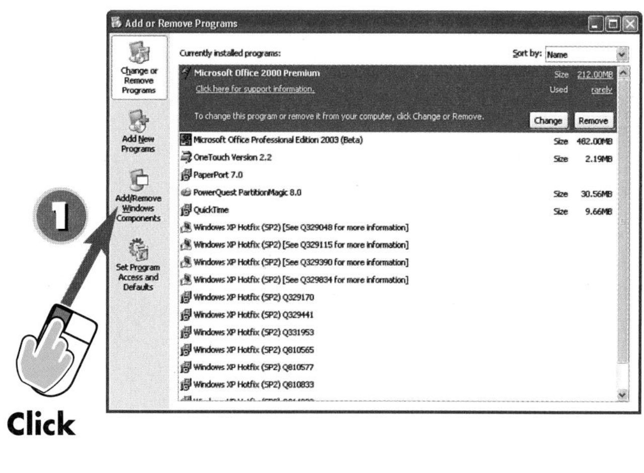

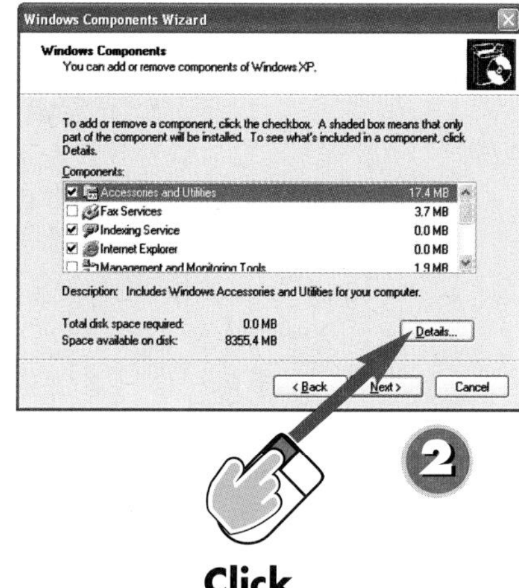

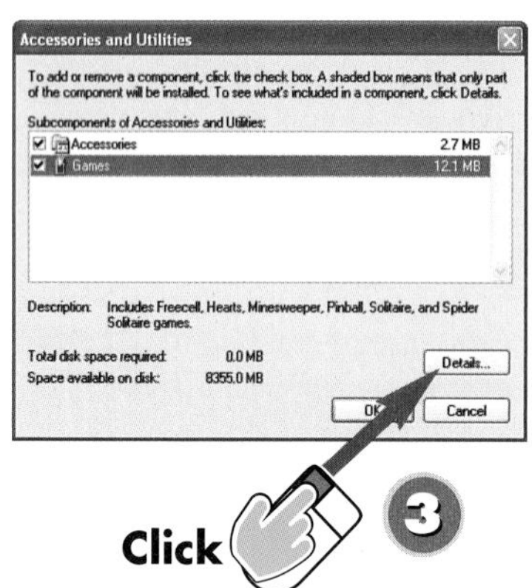

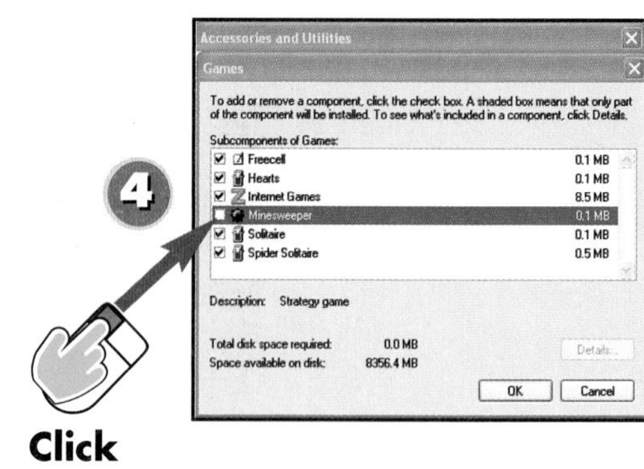

1. In the Add or Remove Programs window, click **Add/Remove Windows Components**. (Refer to Task 10 for help finding the Add or Remove Programs window.)
2. Select the **Accessories and Utilities** entry in the Components list, and click the **Details** button.
3. A dialog box, listing subcomponents of Accessories and Utilities, opens. Select the **Games** entry, and click the **Details** button.
4. The games included with Windows XP are listed in the dialog box that appears. Click the **Minesweeper** check box to uncheck it, and then click the **OK** button.

INTRODUCTION

If you have a new PC, it probably came with Windows already installed—which means that it probably features several components that you might not want or need. For example, you might wish to remove one or all of the games included with Microsoft XP to eliminate the temptation to waste time playing them. This task shows you how to delete Minesweeper.

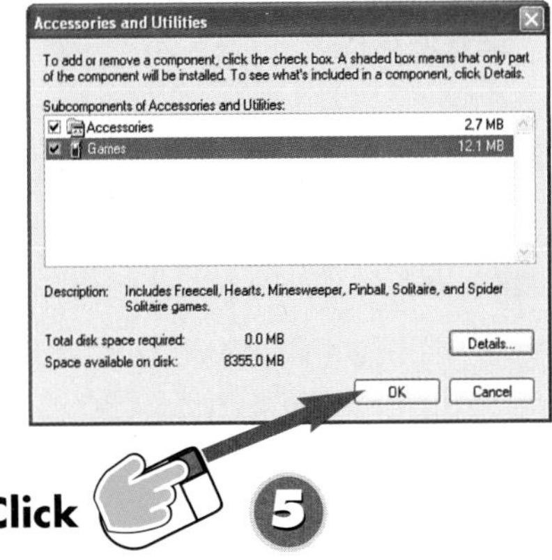

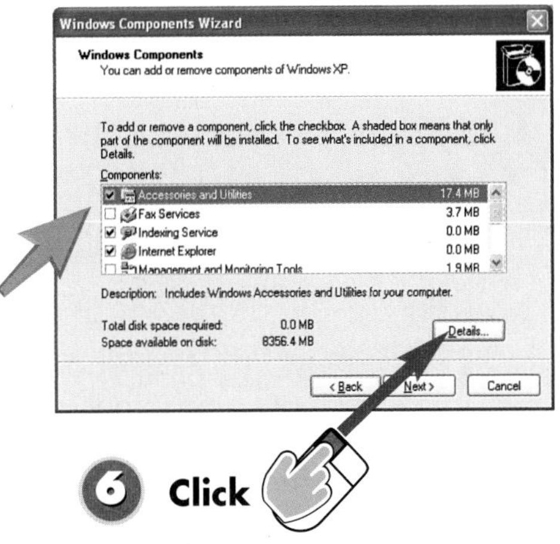

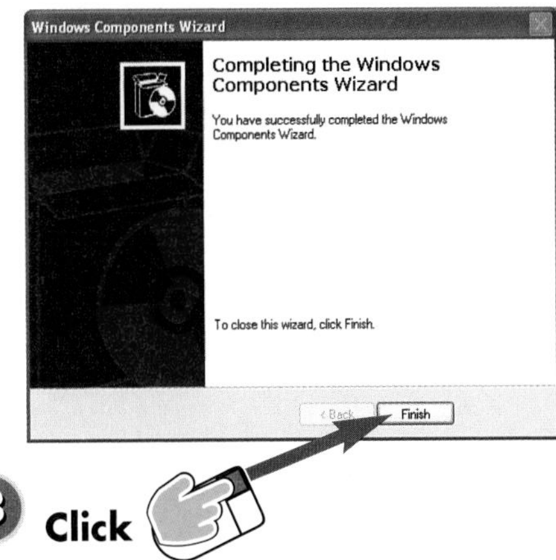

5. The dialog box shown in step 3 reappears, with the **Games** checkbox grayed out. Click the **OK** button.
6. The dialog box shown in step 2 reappears, with the **Accessories and Utilities** checkbox grayed out. Click the **Next** button.
7. A dialog box with progress bar indicates the progress of the component removal.
8. A window appears, indicating that the process is complete. Click the **Finish** button.

TIP

Gray Versus Checked
If an item is checked, it is installed. Items that are gray and checked have some, but not all, of the items installed.

TIP

Add Windows Components
Adding a Windows component is rather like removing one. The difference is that when you see the screen like the one in step 4, where you unchecked the component you wanted to remove, you check the component you want to add. Windows XP asks you to insert your Windows XP CD-ROM; do so, and the component will be added!

PART 12

Maintaining Your System

This part of the book introduces some techniques that are useful for maintaining your system: defragmenting a disk, scanning a disk for damage, restoring your system, and others. Although you don't have to do these tasks every day, you should periodically do some system housecleaning. For example, if your PC performance has been slow, you might defragment your disk. Check this section for these and other system enhancements and maintenance.

Tasks

Task 1: Displaying System Information

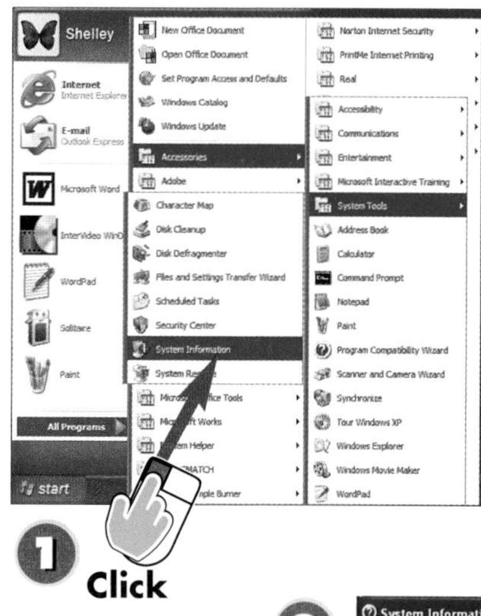

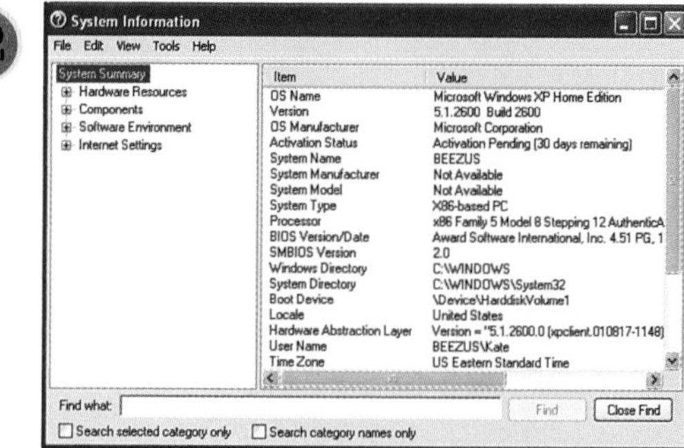

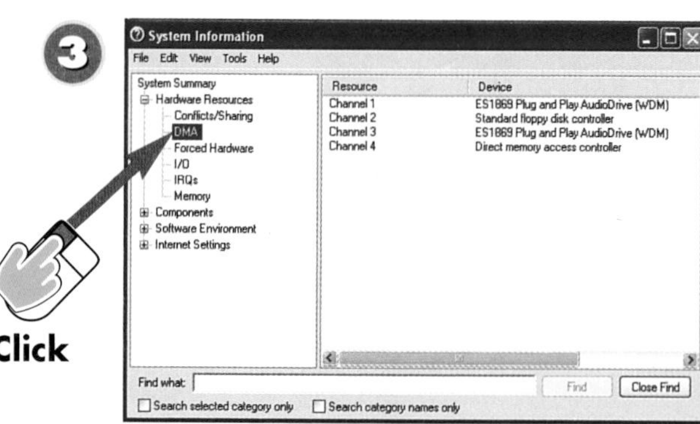

1. Click the **Start** button, choose **All Programs**, select **Accessories**, click **System Tools**, and choose **System Information**.
2. System Information opens, displaying general information about your operating system, BIOS, processor type, and memory.
3. Double-click the **Hardware Resources** entry in the left-hand pane to open the Hardware Resources folder. This folder includes several subcategories; select one to view information about it.

INTRODUCTION

When you are troubleshooting, you sometimes need to display information about your system. Windows XP displays all system information—including information about hardware configurations, computer components, and software—in one convenient spot: System Information.

TIP

Technical Information

Most of the device information in System Information is technical, and you will need to review or make changes only if you are having a problem. In that case, consider getting help from your technical support resource, who will lead you through the steps to make a change based on the hardware experiencing problems.

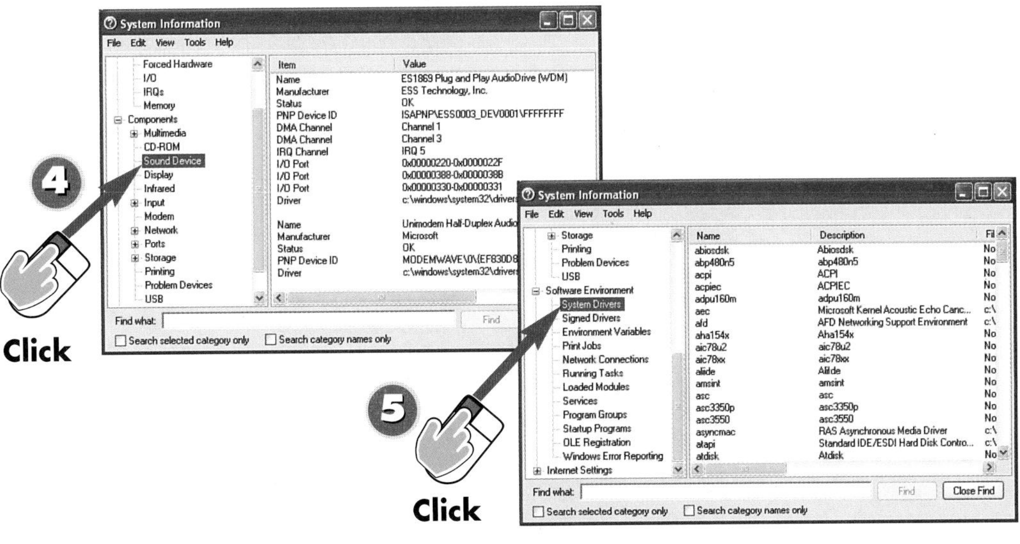

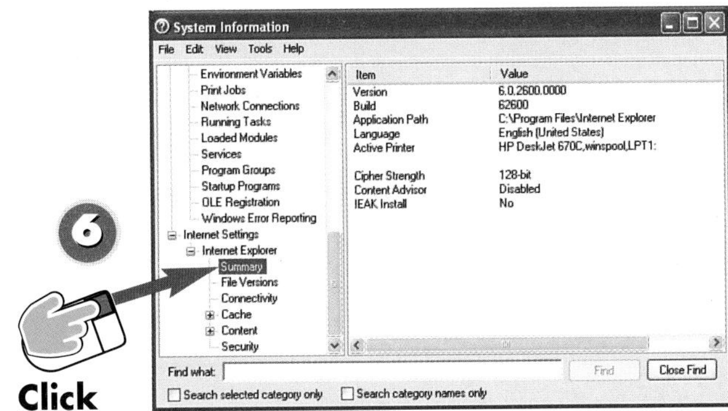

4. Double-click the **Components** entry in the left-hand pane to open the Components folder, and then select one of the subcategories to view information.

5. Double-click the **Software Environment** entry to open the Software Environment folder, and then select one of the subcategories to view information.

6. Double-click the **Internet Settings** entry to open the Internet Settings folder, and then select one of the subcategories to view information.

TIP

Finding System Data

If you don't want to open all the folders and subfolders to find the information you seek, type a word or words corresponding to the information you seek in the **Find what** text box at the bottom of the dialog box. (If this box is not visible, open the **Edit** menu, and uncheck the **Hide Find** entry.) Then, select a search option (you can search the selected category, search category names only, or search all categories), and click the **Find** button.

TIP

Running a System Tool

System Information's **Tools** menu enables you to run many system tools without exiting System Information.

Task 2: Displaying Disk Information

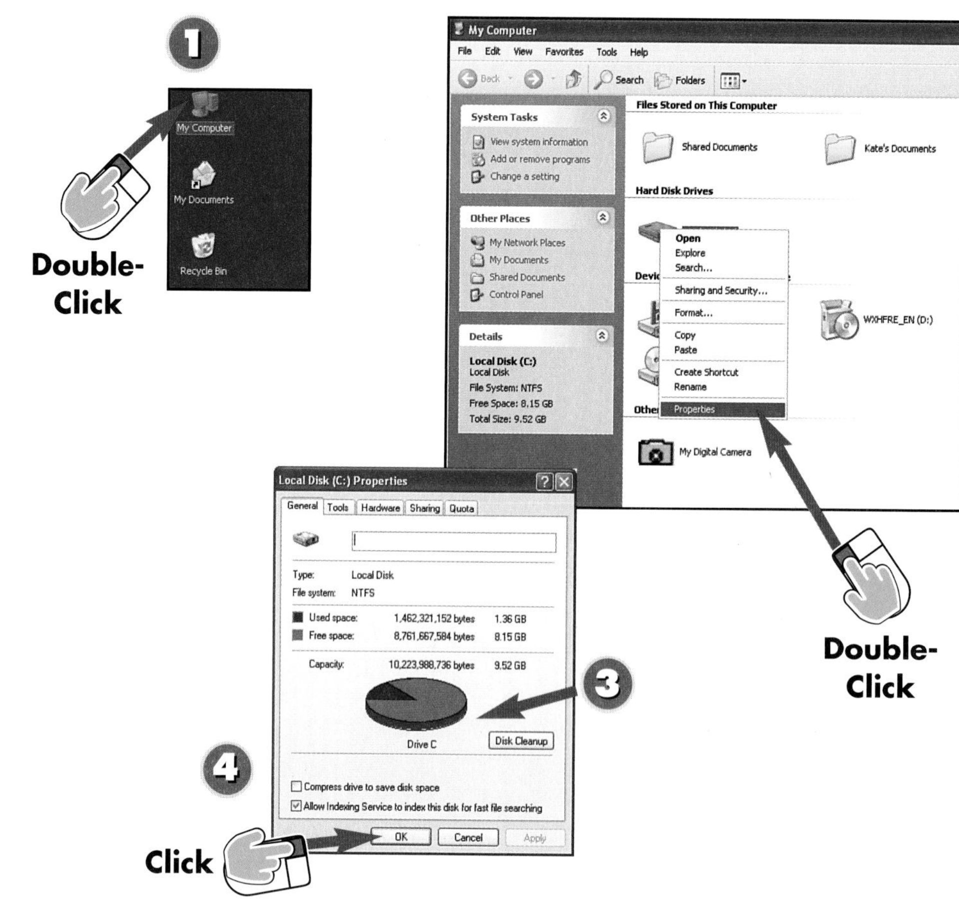

1. Double-click the **My Computer** icon on the desktop.
2. In the My Computer window, right-click the disk for which you want information, and choose **Properties** from the menu that appears.
3. The disk's Properties dialog box opens, with the General tab displayed. View information about used and free space.
4. Click the **OK** button to close the dialog box.

INTRODUCTION

You can display information about your disks, such as the size, the amount of occupied space, and the amount of free space.

TIP

Using the Hardware Tab
Use the **Hardware** tab to view the properties of attached hardware devices, and to troubleshoot those devices.

TIP

Using the Tools Tab
Use the **Tools** tab to select various programs for maintaining your system. This part covers most of the tools found under this tab.

Task 3: Cleaning Up Unnecessary Files

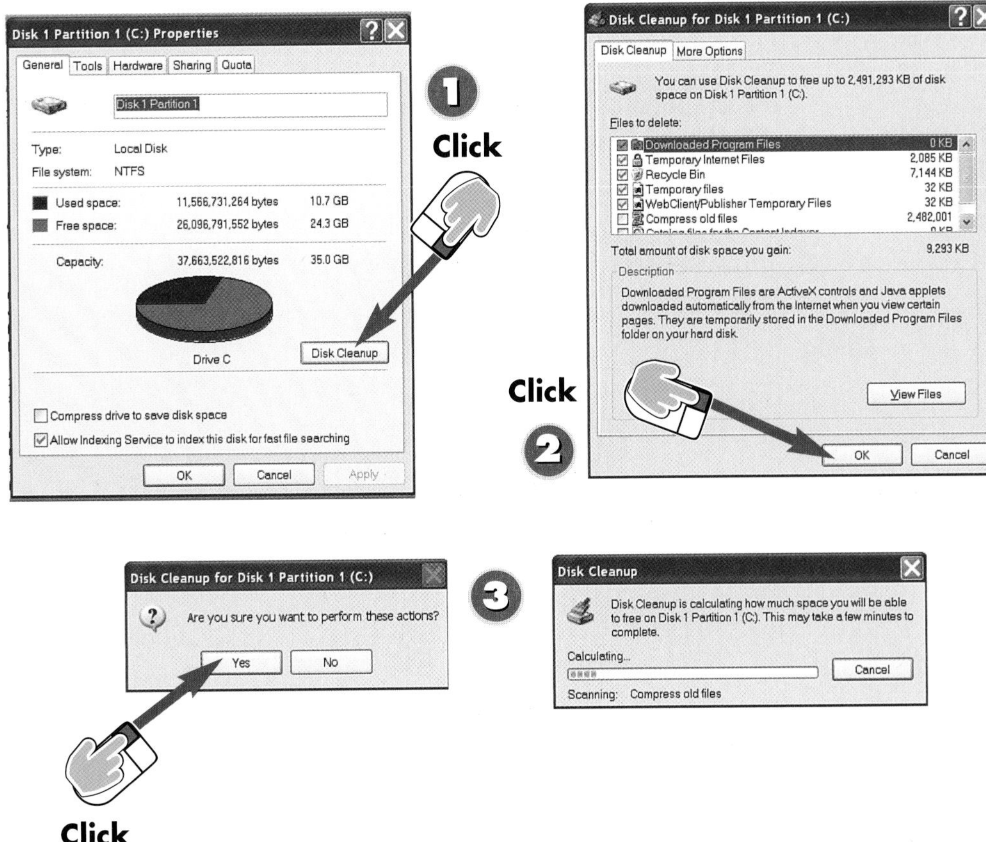

1. In the Properties dialog box for the disk you want to clean, click the **Disk Cleanup** button in the General tab. (Refer to the preceding task for help opening the Properties dialog box.)
2. The Disk Cleanup dialog box opens. Check options in the **Files to delete** list to specify which files are deleted, and click the **OK** button.
3. When prompted to confirm the removal, click the **Yes** button. A dialog box will indicate Disk Cleanup's progress.

INTRODUCTION

Unnecessary files might be hogging your disk space. For example, the Recycle Bin houses files that you have deleted but are still kept in case you need them. You can easily get rid of these and other files and gain some disk space by using Disk Cleanup.

TIP

Review Files
You can view the files that are recommended for removal. Select the files you want to view, and then click the **View Files** button.

TIP

WARNING!
Be sure you don't need any of these files. You cannot get them back after they are removed.

Task 4: Scanning Your Disk for Errors

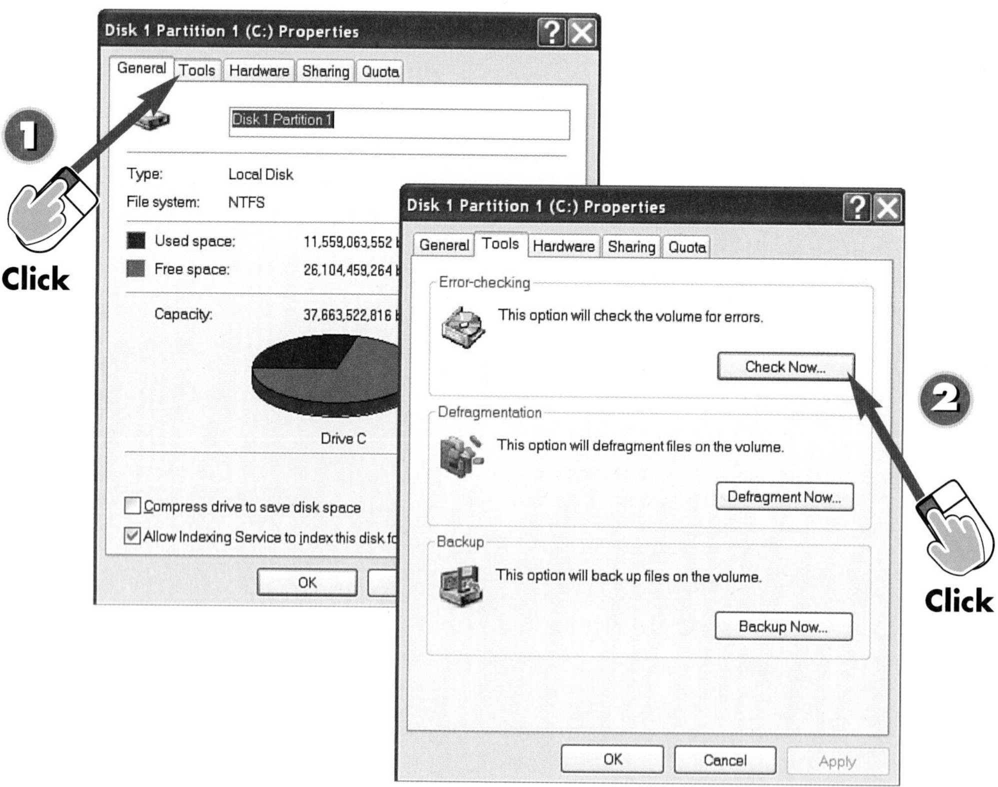

1. Click the **Tools** tab in the Properties dialog box for the disk you want to scan. (Refer to Task 2, "Displaying Disk Information," for help opening the Properties dialog box.)
2. The Tools tab opens. Click the **Check Now** button in the tab's Error-checking area.

INTRODUCTION

Sometimes parts of your hard disk get damaged, and you might see an error message when you try to open or save a file. You can scan the disk for damage using the ScanDisk program and fix any problems. You must also run ScanDisk before you can defragment a hard disk (covered in the next task).

TIP

Restarting Your PC
Windows may display a dialog box notifying you that the disk check could not be performed because the utility needs exclusive access to certain files, and that those files can be accessed only by restarting Windows. To schedule the disk check to occur the next time you restart your computer, click **Yes**.

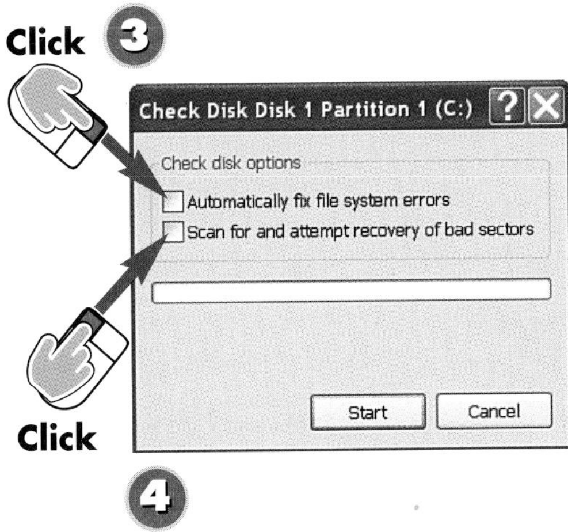

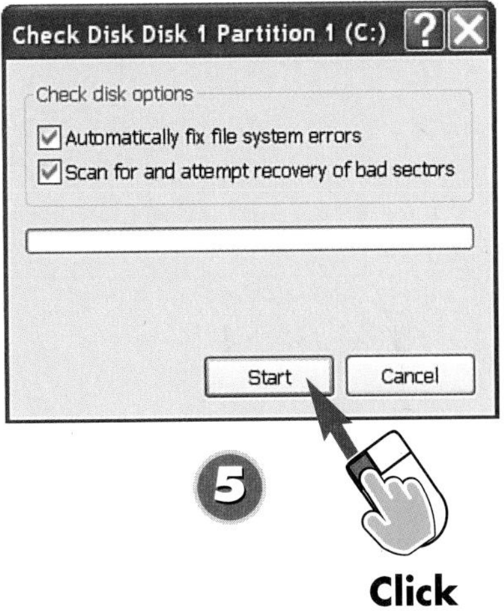

3. Click the **Automatically fix file system errors** check box.
4. Click the **Scan for and attempt recovery of bad sectors** check box.
5. Click the **Start** button. ScanDisk performs the scan.

TIP

Errors Found?
If ScanDisk finds an error, a dialog box appears explaining the error. Read the error message and choose the option that best suits your needs. Click **OK** to continue. Do this for each message.

TIP

Scanning After Rebooting
If you don't properly shut down Windows, you might be prompted to run ScanDisk when you reboot. You can then check for errors before your system is restarted.

TIP

Periodically Scan
It's a good idea to periodically run ScanDisk, even if you aren't having problems. Doing so helps keep your system running efficiently.

Task 5: Defragmenting a Disk

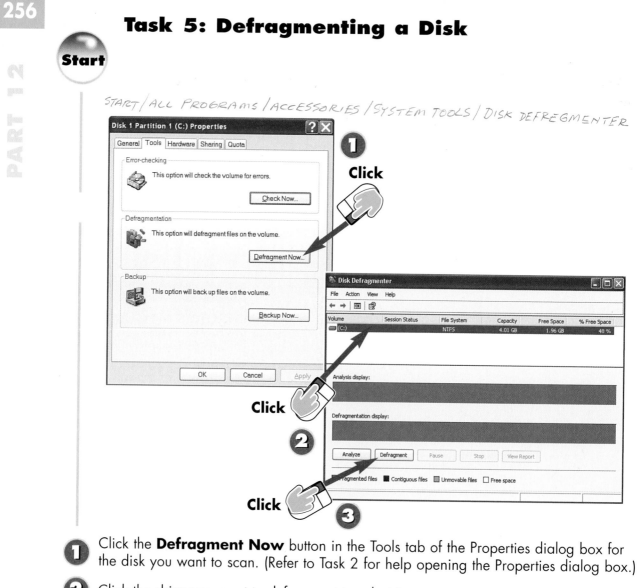

START/ALL PROGRAMS/ACCESSORIES/SYSTEM TOOLS/DISK DEFREGMENTER

1. Click the **Defragment Now** button in the Tools tab of the Properties dialog box for the disk you want to scan. (Refer to Task 2 for help opening the Properties dialog box.)
2. Click the drive you want to defragment to select it.
3. Click the **Defragment** button.

INTRODUCTION

When a file is stored on your hard drive, Windows places as much of the file as possible in the first available section (called a *cluster*), and then goes to the next cluster to put the next part of the file. Over time, your disk files may become fragmented. To help prevent potential problems with fragmented files, you can defragment your disk, putting files in clusters as close to each other as possible. Defragmenting your disk is a general-maintenance job that you should perform every few months for best results.

TIP

Creating a Restore Point
Be careful when defragmenting. You might want to create a restore point first so that you can restore your system to its pre-defragment state in the event of a problem. See Task 10 in this part about creating restore points.

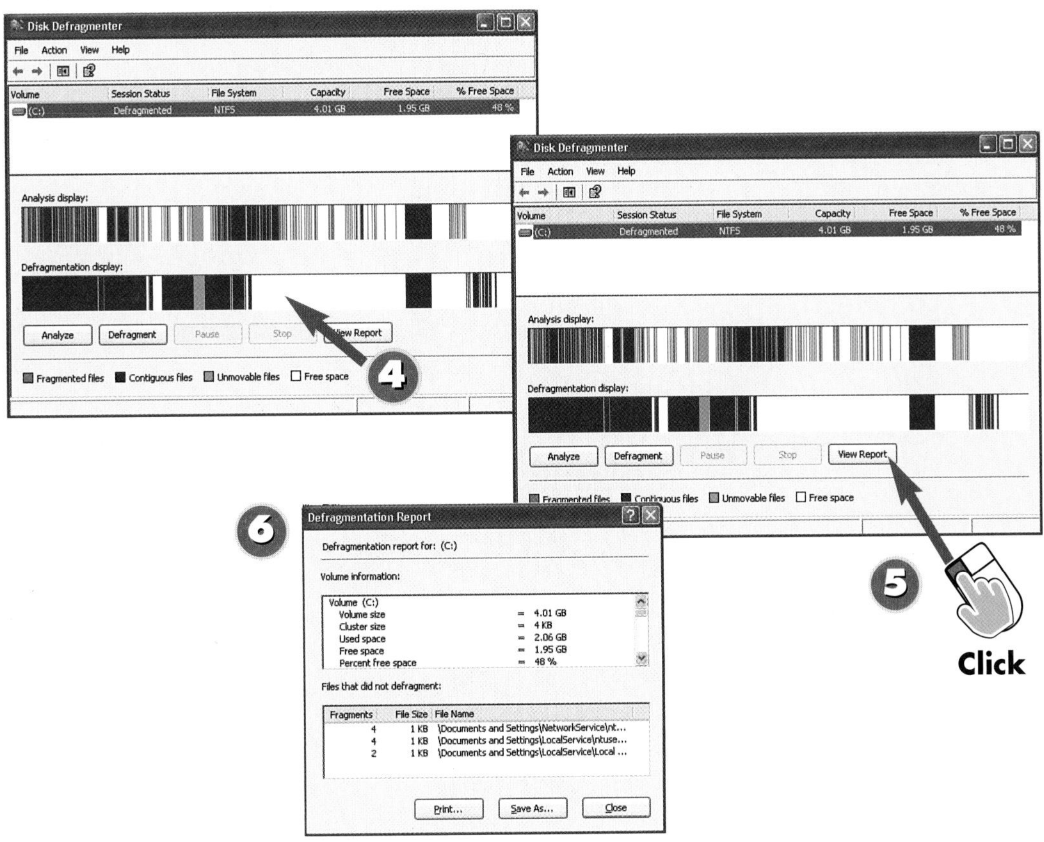

4 Disk Defragmenter's progress is indicated by the progress bar in the Disk Defragmenter window.

5 When the process completes, Disk Defragmenter displays the results. Click **View Report**.

6 The Defragmentation Report dialog box displays detailed information about the disk that was defragmented.

TIP

Analyzing First

It's a good idea to analyze your disk before defragmenting it. Doing so enables you to see how fragmented the disk is, so you can decide whether you want to defragment.

TIP

Free Disk Space

In order for Disk Defragmenter to completely defragment your disk, the disk should have at least 15% free space. If the disk has less free space, it will be only partially defragmented.

TIP

Logging On As Administrator

You must be logged on as an administrator or a member of the Administrators group in order to complete this procedure.

Task 6: Scheduling Tasks

Start

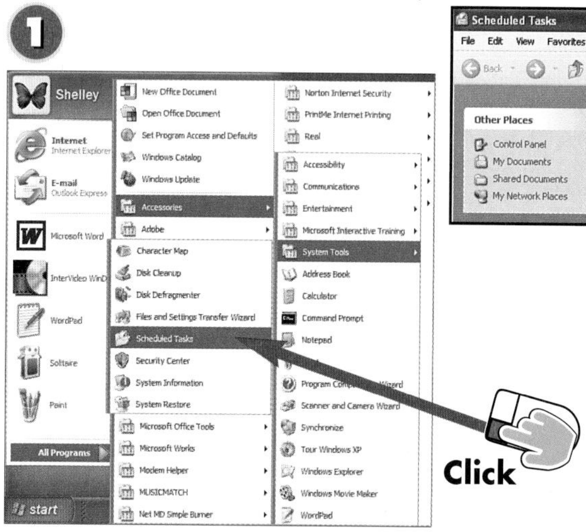

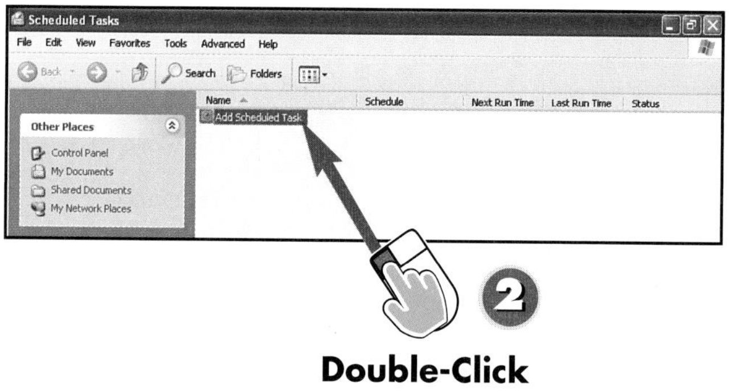

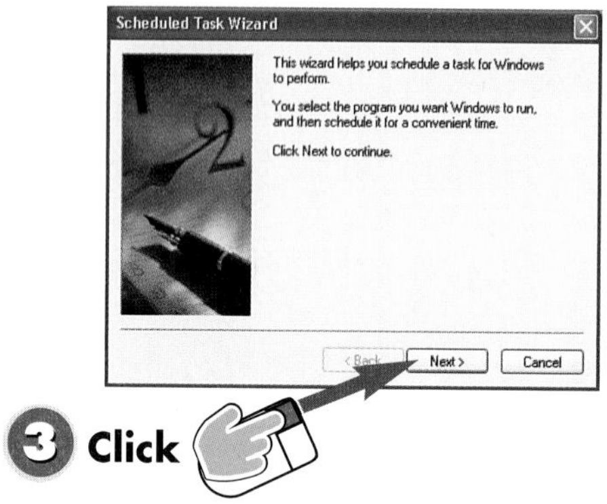

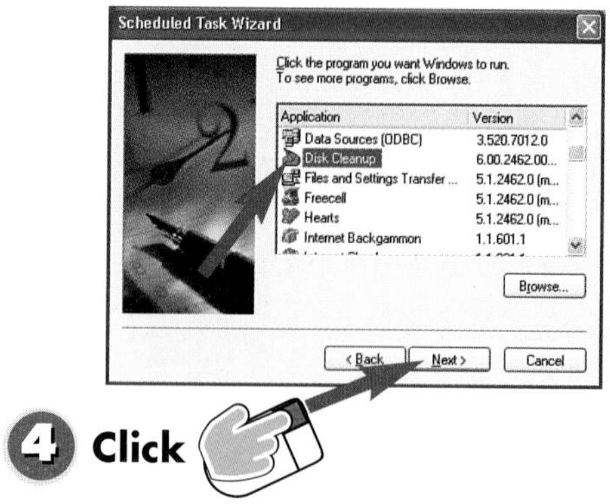

1. Click **Start**, **All Programs**, **Accessories**, **System Tools**, and then choose **Scheduled Tasks**.
2. The Scheduled Tasks window opens. Double-click the **Add Scheduled Task** list item.
3. The Schedule Task Wizard starts. Click the **Next** button.
4. Select the name of the program that you want Windows to run, and then click the **Next** button.

INTRODUCTION

If you perform the same tasks repeatedly, or if you often forget to perform routine maintenance tasks, you can set up a schedule that instructs Windows to perform these tasks automatically.

TIP

Browsing

If the program you want to schedule is not listed in the dialog box shown in step 4, click the **Browse** button and locate the program on your hard drive.

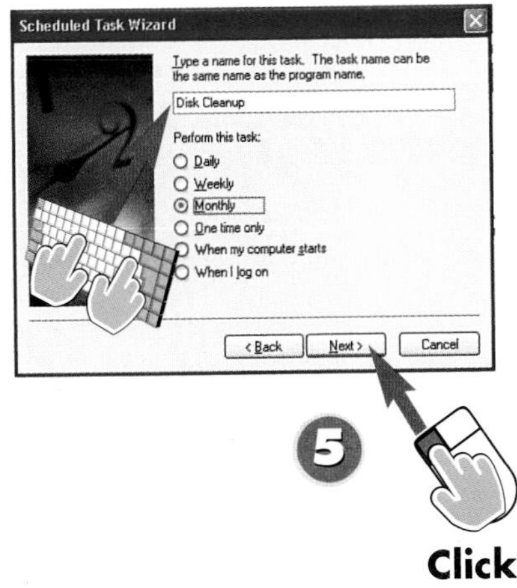

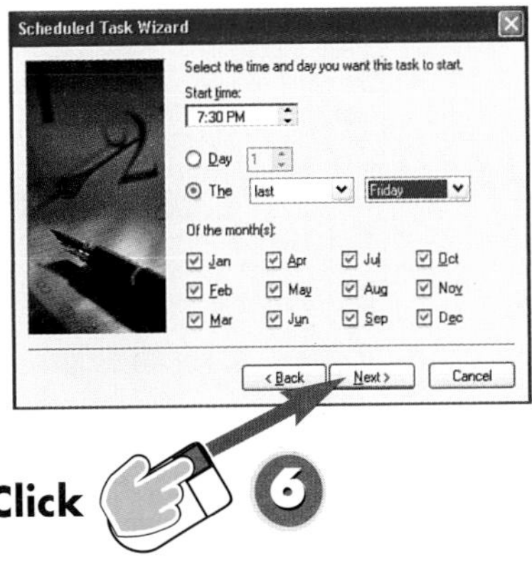

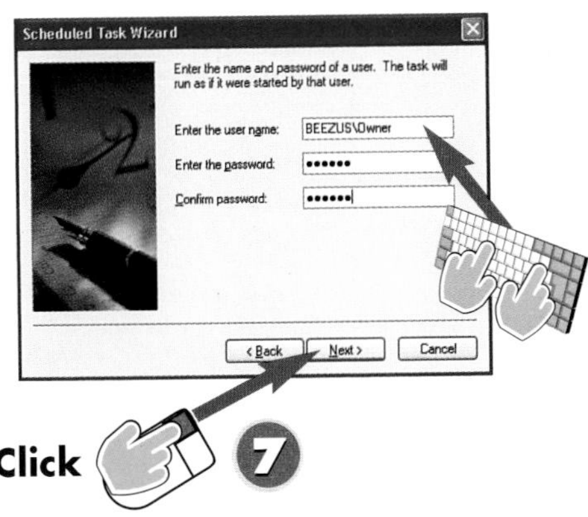

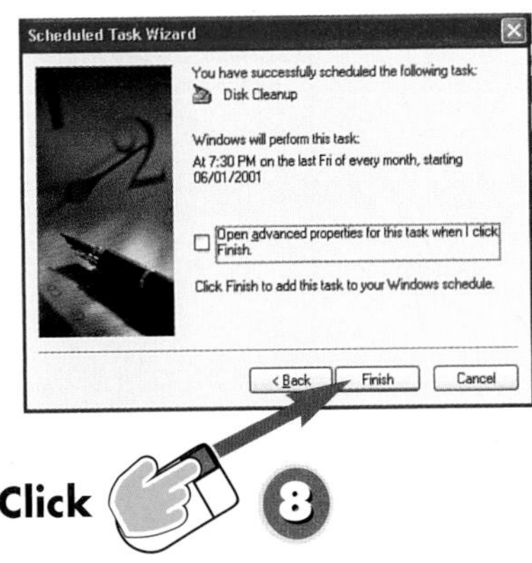

5. If you are not satisfied with the default name, enter a new one; then select how often to perform this task. Click **Next**.
6. Select the time and date to start. (Depending on how often you select to perform this task, you will see different options for selecting the date and time.) Click **Next**.
7. Type your user name and password, and then click the **Next** button.
8. You see a summary of the scheduled task. Click the **Finish** button.

TIP

Set Advanced Properties
Click the **Open advanced properties for this task when I click Finish** check box to view more configuration options for the scheduled task.

TIP

Removing a Task
To remove a task from the list, display the **Scheduled Tasks** list. Right-click the item, and then choose **Delete**. Confirm the deletion by clicking the **Yes** button.

TIP

Changing Settings
To change the settings for the task, display the **Scheduled Tasks** list. Right-click the item you want to modify, and then choose **Properties**. Make any changes to the tabs in the Properties dialog box, and then click **OK**.

Task 7: Transferring Files and Settings from Another PC

Start

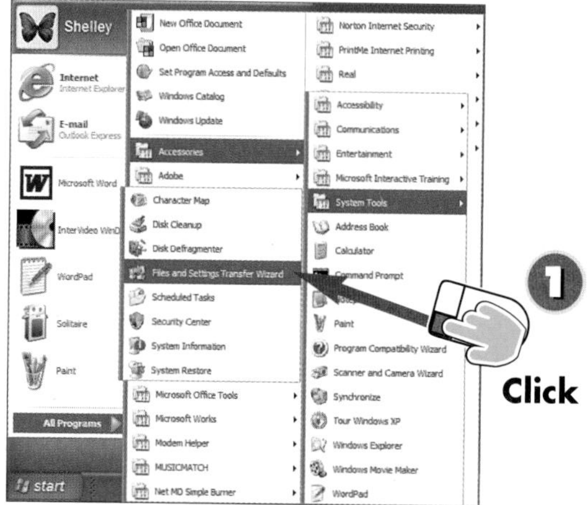

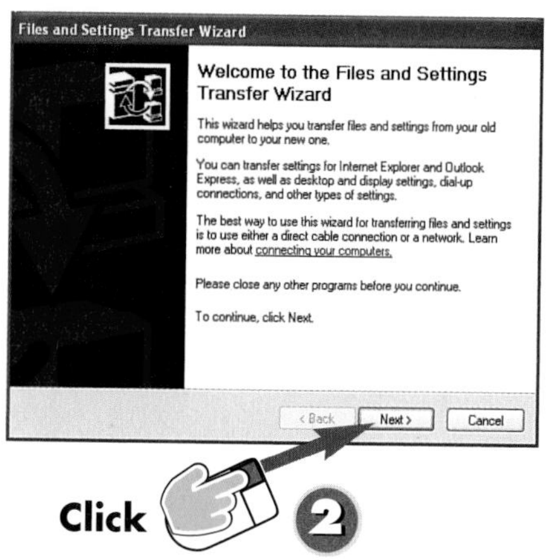

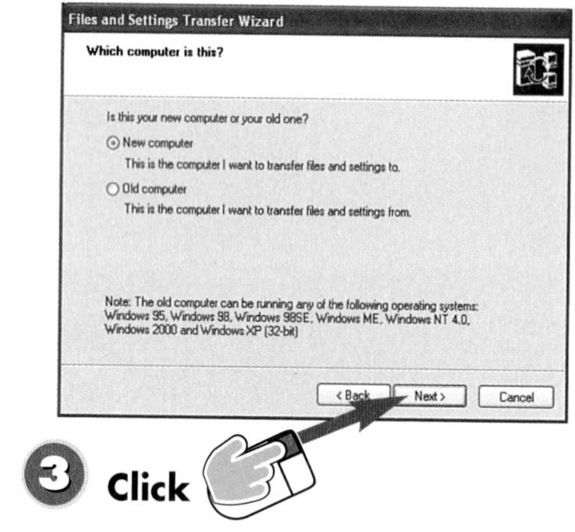

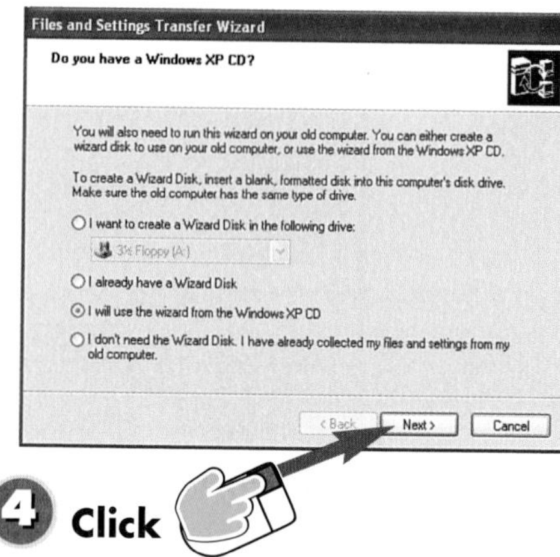

1. Click the **Start** button, choose **All Programs**, select **Accessories**, click **System Tools**, and choose **Files and Settings Transfer Wizard**.
2. The wizard starts. Click the **Next** button.
3. When asked whether you are currently using your new computer or your old one, select the **New computer** radio button, and click **Next**.
4. The wizard asks whether you have a Windows XP CD. Click the **I will use the wizard from the Windows XP CD** button, and click **Next**.

INTRODUCTION

If you're using Windows XP on a brand new computer, you can use XP's Files and Settings Transfer wizard to migrate files, documents, and settings from your old computer to your new machine via a floppy disk (or other removable media), LAN, or known network path.

TIP

No CD?

If you don't have a Windows XP CD handy, click the **I want to create a Wizard Disk in the following drive** button in step 4, select an option from the drop-down list, and follow the instructions to create a wizard disk of your own. It enables you to pull the files and settings you need from your old computer just as if you had an XP disk, and transfer your files and settings to your new machine.

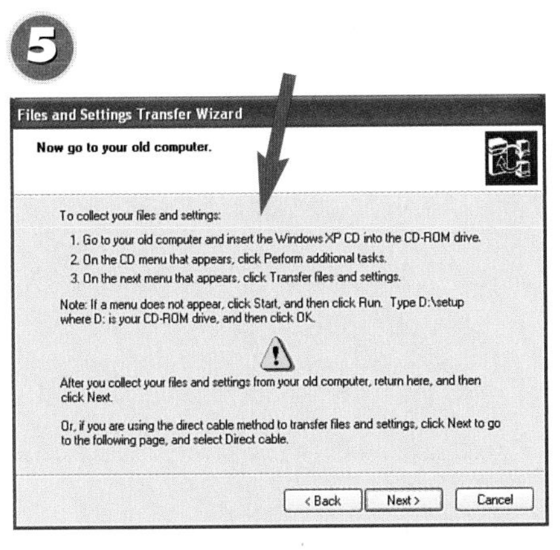

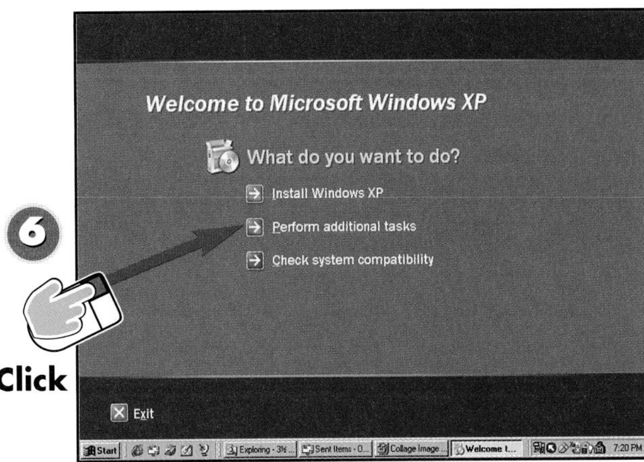

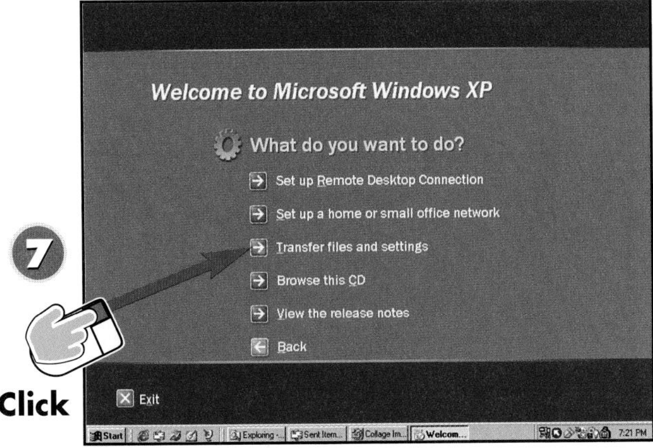

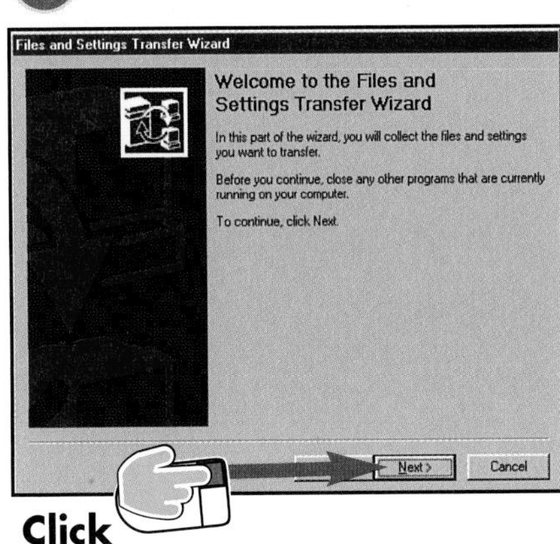

5. The wizard instructs you to insert your Windows XP CD in the CD drive of your old computer; do so now.
6. Using your old computer, wait for the Windows XP CD to start, and then click the **Perform additional tasks** link.
7. Windows asks what you want to do next. Click the **Transfer files and settings** link.
8. The Files and Settings Transfer Wizard starts. Click the **Next** button.

See next page

TIP

Office Settings

In addition to transferring your system settings, the File and Settings Transfer wizard can transfer a limited number of application settings for Microsoft Office. You should note, however, that the wizard does not migrate the applications themselves. These you must install on your new computer using your own two hands (if they are not already installed).

Transferring Files and Settings from Another PC (Continued)

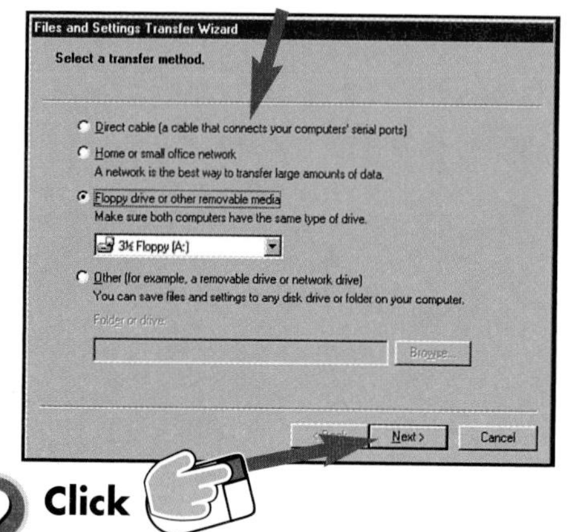

9 Click

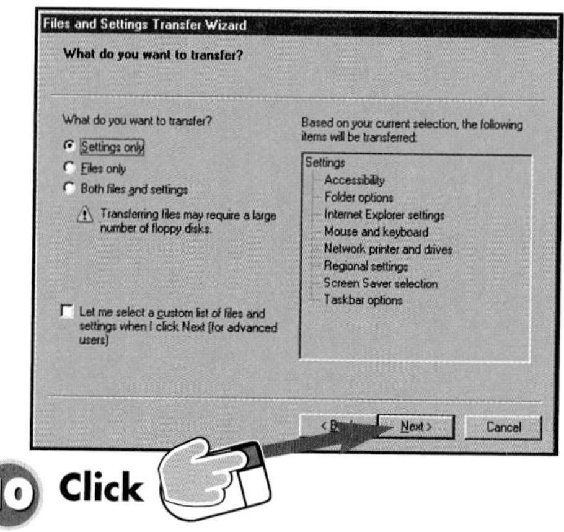

10 Click

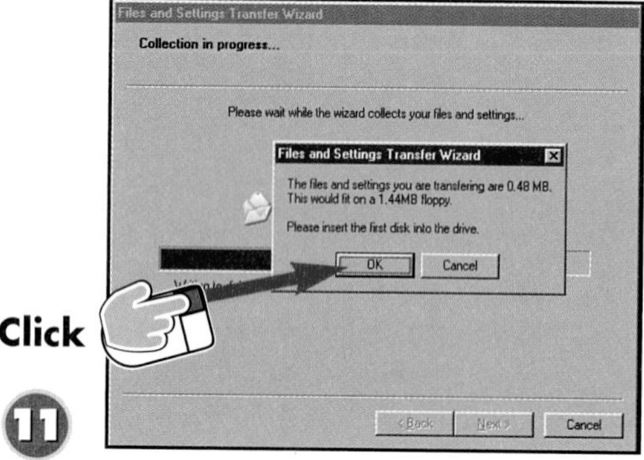

Click

11

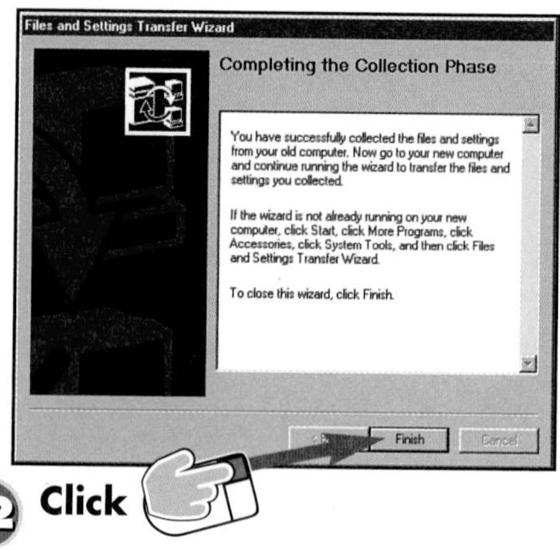

12 Click

9 After a moment, the wizard asks you to select a transfer method. Do so (I've chosen **Floppy drive or other removable media**), and click the **Next** button.

10 Decide what you want to transfer—settings, files, or both. Select the appropriate radio button (in this case, **Settings only**), and click the **Next** button to continue.

11 Wait while the wizard collects your files and settings. When prompted, insert an empty floppy into your old computer's disk drive drive, and click the **OK** button.

12 Windows notifies you when the wizard finishes transferring your files and settings onto the floppy disk(s), and instructs you to return to your new computer. Click the **Finish** button.

TIP

Transfer Media

If you want to transfer files ***and*** settings, you'll probably need several (read: dozens or hundreds) of floppy disks to finish the job. If you have the option of using some other media, for example, a Zip disk, a CD, or a network connection, take advantage of it.

TIP

Using Alternative Transfer Media

This task illustrates the use of floppy disks to transfer settings; the steps vary slightly if you choose another option in step 9. Follow the onscreen prompts.

TIP

Performing a Custom Transfer

If you want to transfer only some of your files and settings, click the check box at the bottom of the screen shown in step 10. You'll be given the opportunity to remove from the list any folders, file types, and settings you do not wish to transfer.

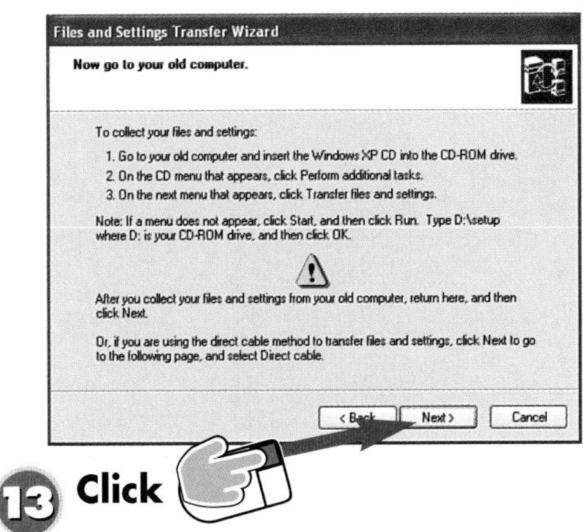

13 Click

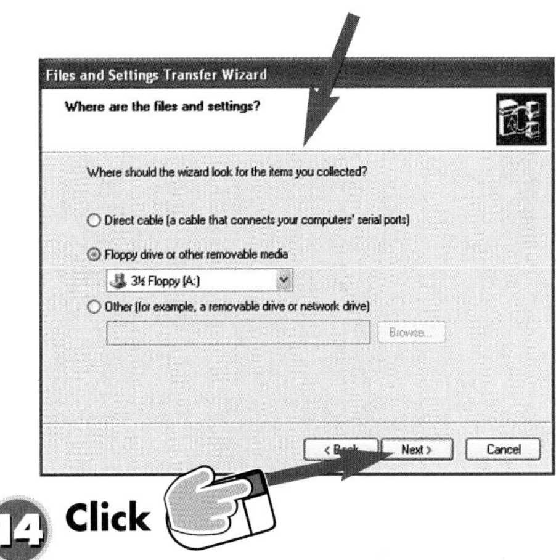

14 Click

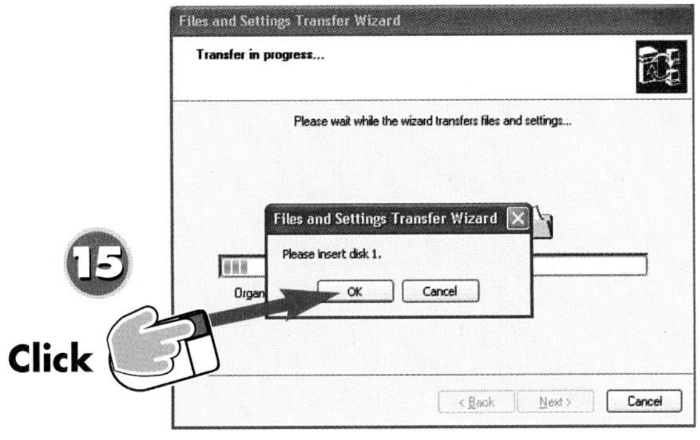

15 Click

16 Click

13 Return to your new computer, and click the **Next** button.

14 Specify where the wizard should look for the items you collected—a floppy drive, a network, or some type of removable device—and then click the **Next** button.

15 If the files and settings you collected are on a floppy, Zip disk, or CD, you'll be prompted to insert the appropriate disk. Do so, and click the **OK** button.

16 XP transfers the files and settings from your old computer to your new one (this could take some time). When the transfer is complete, click **Finish**.

TIP

Logging Off

When the transfer process is complete, you'll be prompted to log off so that the changes can take effect.

Task 8: Installing New Hardware

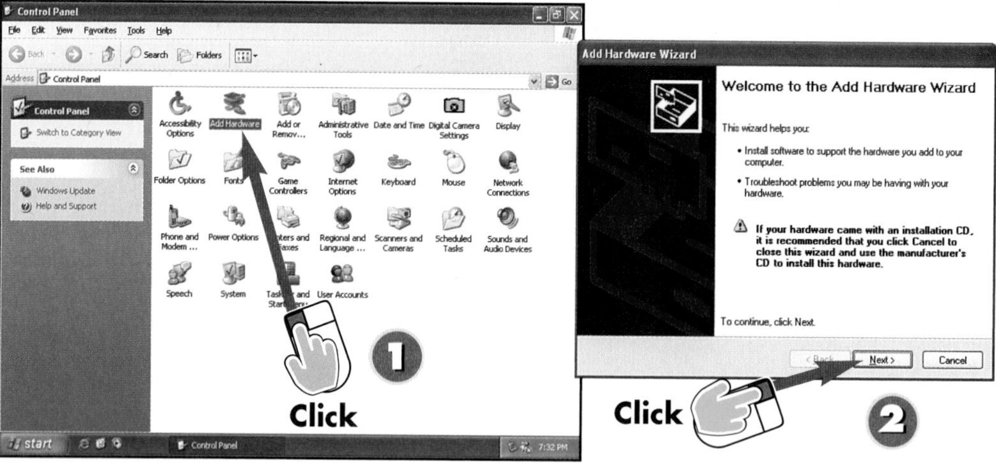

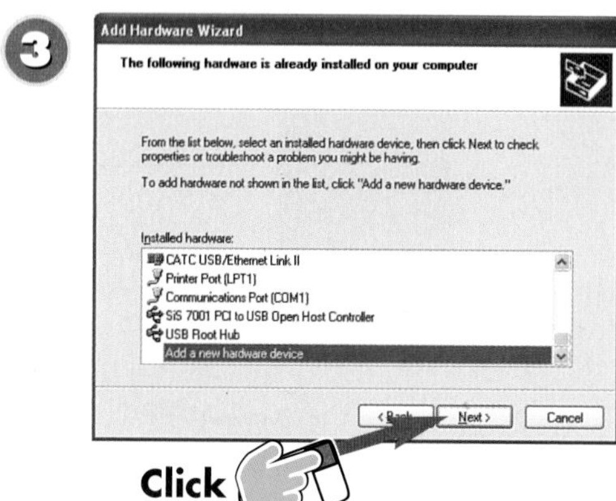

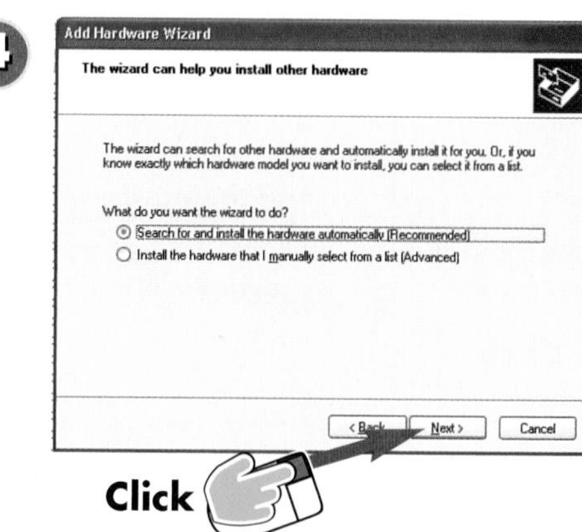

1. After you've connected the device to your computer, open the **Control Panel**, and double-click the **Add Hardware** icon.
2. The Add Hardware Wizard starts. If you don't have an installation CD, click the **Next** button to continue. Otherwise, insert the CD, and skip the remaining steps.
3. Windows determines whether the new device is Plug and Play. If not, click the **Add a new hardware device** option in the Installed hardware list, and click **Next**.
4. Click the **Search for and install the hardware automatically** radio button, and then click the **Next** button.

INTRODUCTION

You can install a new hardware device by using Windows XP's Add New Hardware wizard, which asks you questions about the hardware. If you do not know the answers, Windows can detect the type of hardware and install it with little input from you. Windows calls this handy feature Plug and Play.

TIP

Automatic Setup

If Windows detected your hardware, it is set up automatically. You might be prompted to insert the appropriate software disks to set up the hardware. Follow the onscreen directions.

TIP

Opening Control Panel

To open the Control Panel, click the **Start** button and choose **Control Panel**.

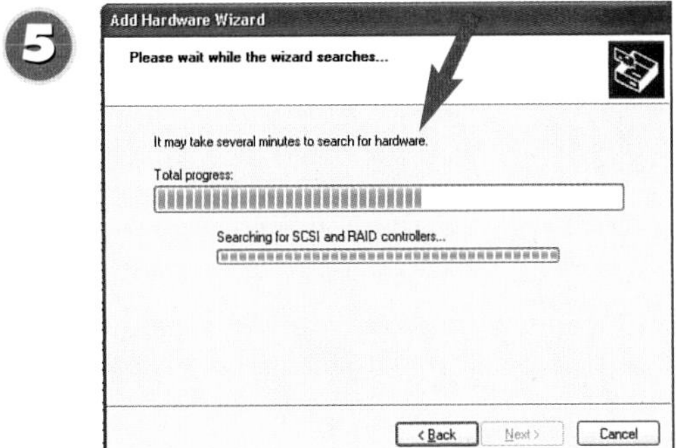

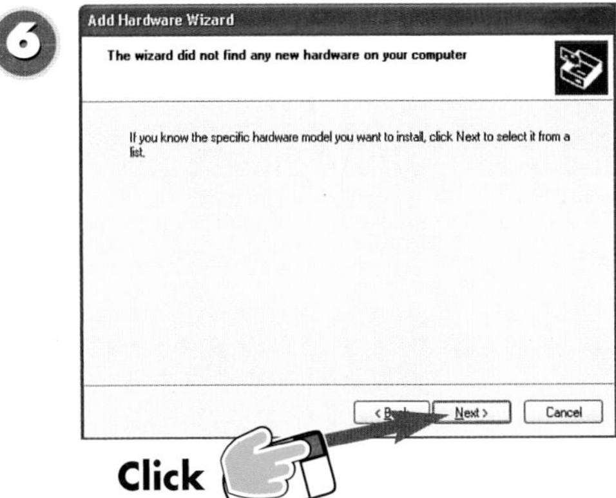

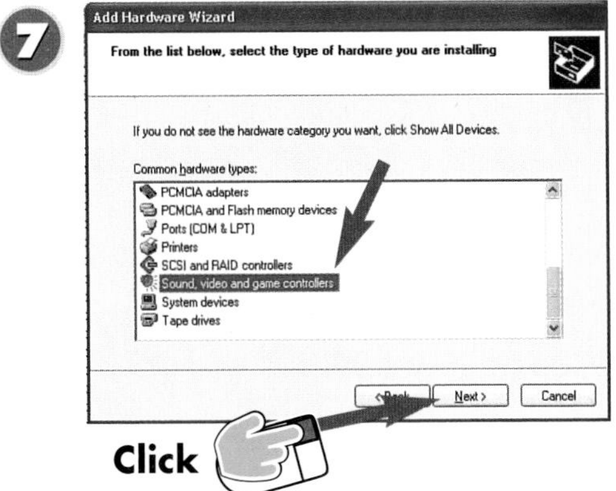

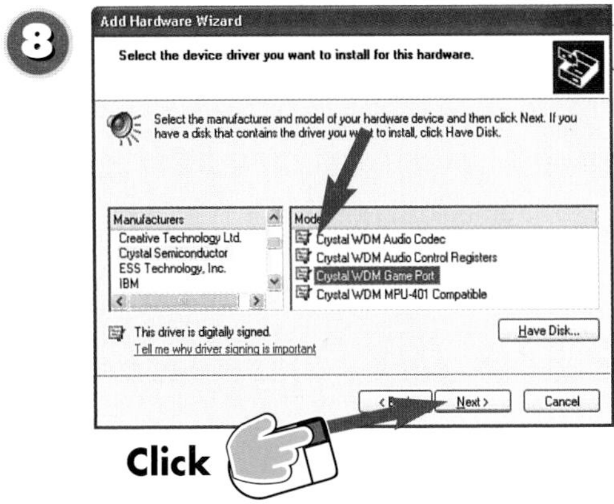

5 Windows searches your machine for non–Plug and Play devices.

6 If a device is detected, Windows installs it automatically; click the **Finish** button to close the wizard. If no devices are found (as shown here), click the **Next** button to continue.

7 A list of common hardware types appears. Click the category that best describes the type of device you want to install, and then click the **Next** button.

8 Click the device manufacturer, select the model, and click **Next**. What happens next depends on the hardware you're installing; follow the wizard's instructions to complete the process.

TIP

Plug and Play
Most newer devices are Plug and Play, so chances are you won't need to go beyond step 4.

TIP

Steps Vary
Depending on the type of device, the steps you follow will vary. Simply follow the wizard's instructions, clicking **Next** to go to the next step.

Task 9: Restoring Your System

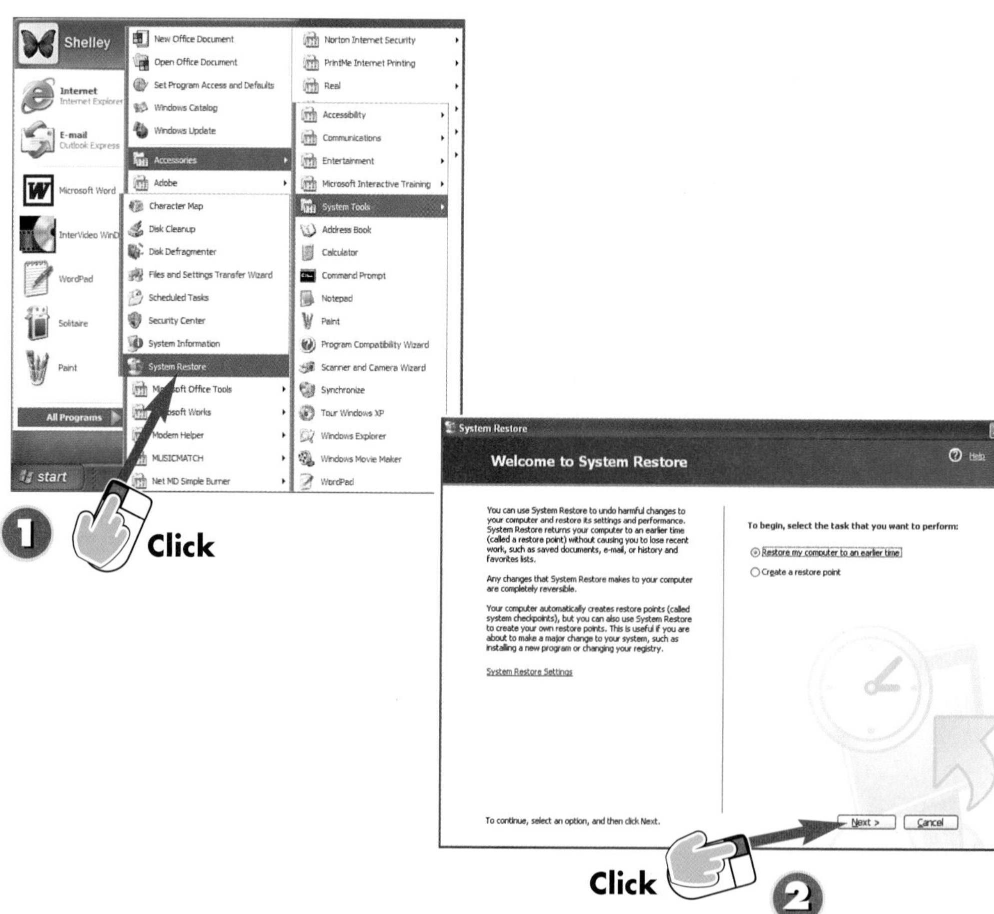

1. Click the **Start** button, select **All Programs**, choose **Accessories**, click **System Tools**, and select **System Restore**.
2. The System Restore window opens. Click the **Restore my computer to an earlier time** radio button, and then click **Next**.

INTRODUCTION

If you add new programs or hardware, you might find that your system does not work properly. To help, Windows XP includes System Restore, which you can use to go back to a previous setup that did work.

TIP

Restore Points
Instead of relying on you to create backups, System Restore monitors changes to your system and creates ***restore points*** each day by default. There are several types of restore points, many of which are created automatically.

TIP

Canceling Restore
You can cancel the restore by clicking **Cancel** in any of the windows. Also, you can go back a step and make a change by clicking **Back**.

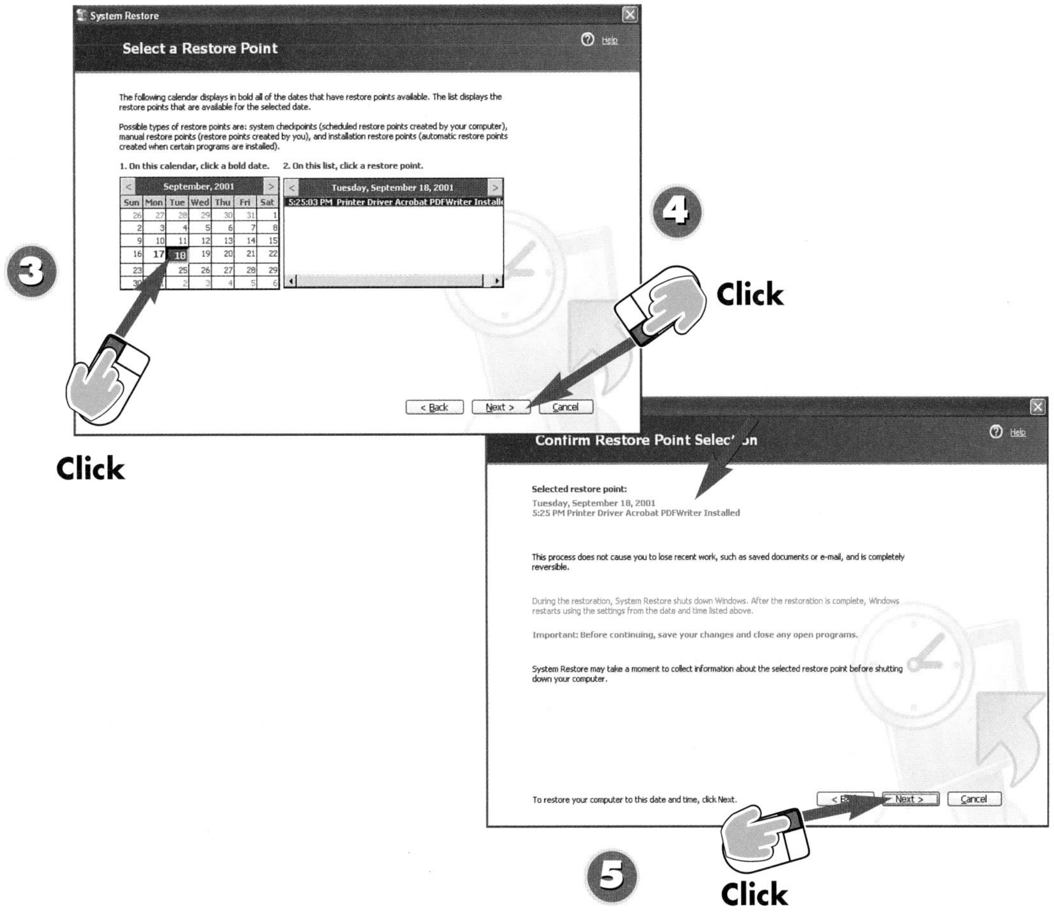

3. Some dates in the calendar appear in bold; these are days on which System Restore generated a restore point. Click the most recent bold date on which your computer worked properly.

4. Click a restore point in the list on the right side of the screen, and then click the **Next** button.

5. You see a confirmation of the restore point as well as a list of changes that will be undone. Click **Next**. Windows restores and restarts your system.

TIP

Displaying a Different Month
Click the arrows on either side of calendar to display a different month.

TIP

Saving Your Work
Save your work and close any open programs before restoring your system.

TIP

Creating a Restore Point
You might create a restore point before installing a major application or fiddling with your Registry. To do so, click **Create a restore point** in the System Restore window, and then click **Next**. Type a descriptive name for the restore point, and then click the **Create** button.

Task 10: Checking Virus Protection

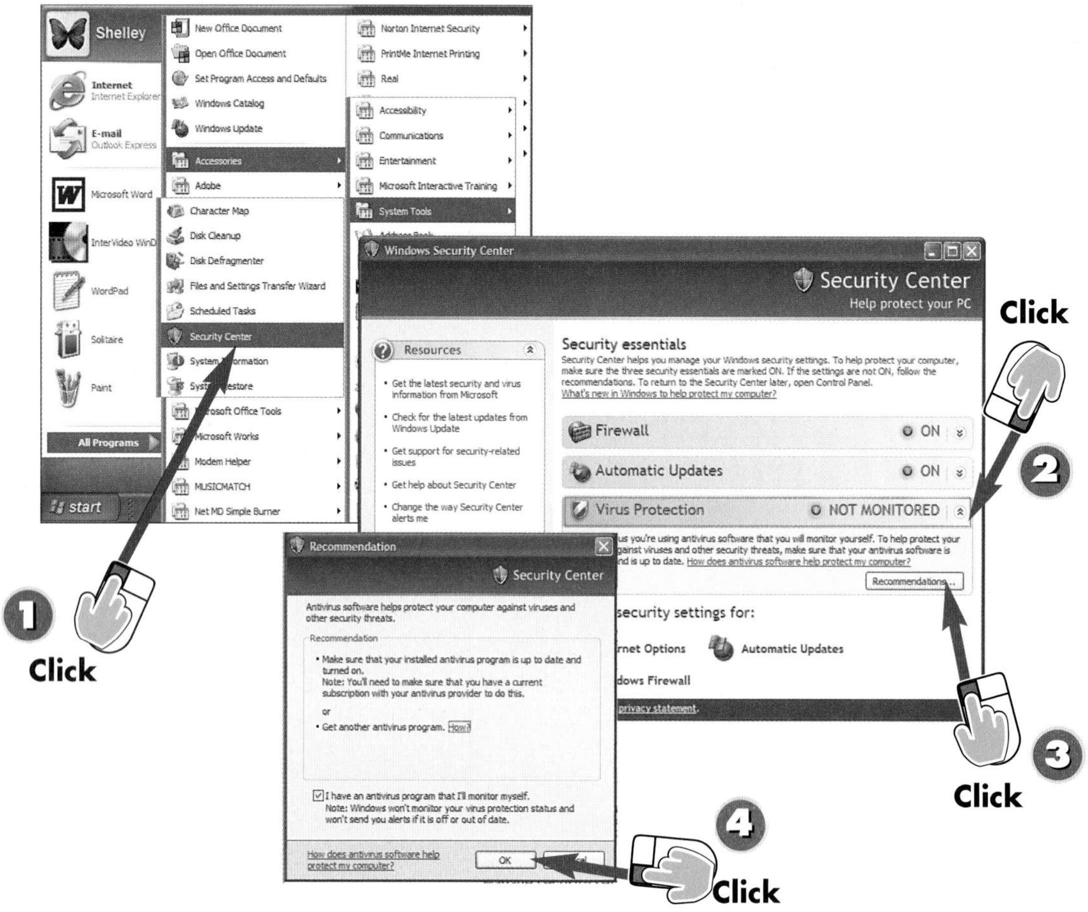

1. Click **Start**, **All Programs**, **Accessories**, **System Tools**, and then **Security Center**.
2. You see the Windows Security Center window with current system status. If necessary, click the down arrow in the Virus Protection area.
3. To view Windows Virus Protection recommendations, click the **Recommendations** button.
4. You see any suggestions, based on your current setup. Click **OK** to close this window.

INTRODUCTION

Most often viruses are spread via email (usually file attachments) or from downloading files form the Internet. You can also get viruses from files you share with others via a disk. You should use an antivirus program to periodically check your whole system for viruses as well as scan any attachments or files you open from someone else. Many new computers come with antivirus programs. You can check the status of virus protection on your system by using the Windows Security Center.

TIP

Caught a virus?

In addition to checking for viruses, these programs often can repair the problem. Because new viruses are created all the time, you should keep your antivirus program up to date. Usually you do this by subscribing to the update service.

Task 11: Checking a File for Viruses

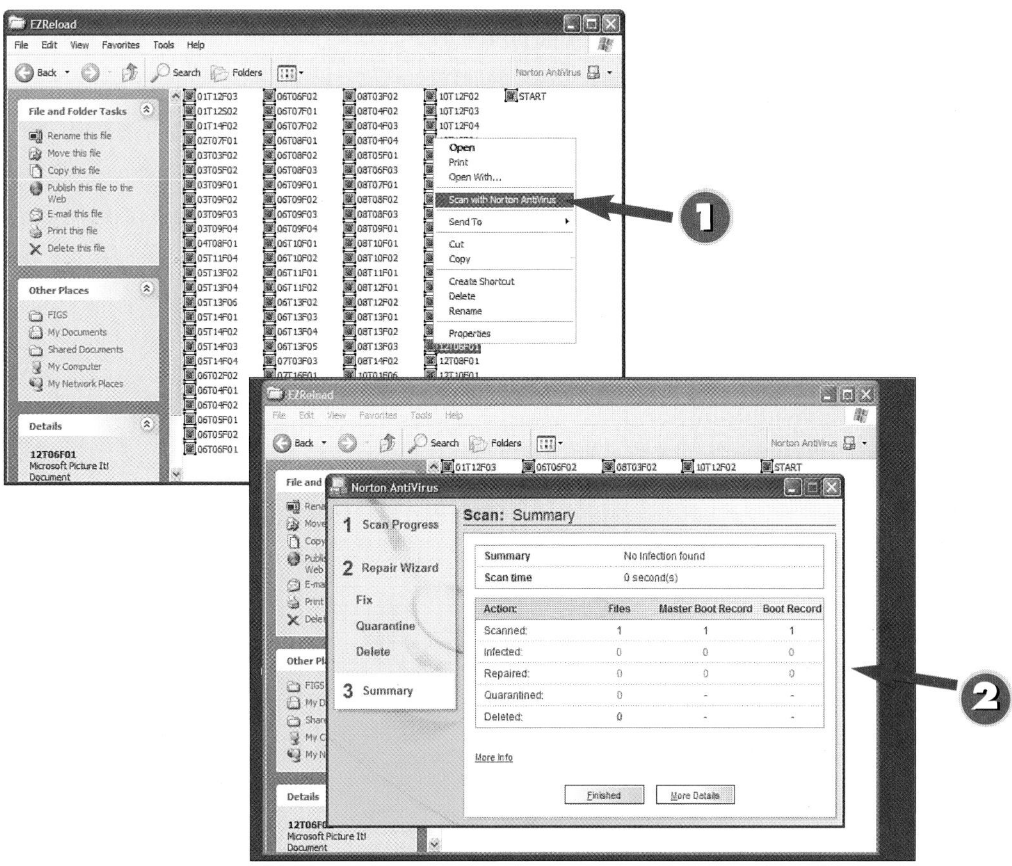

1. Right-click the file you want to scan and select the scan command. For instance, if you use Norton Antivirus, click **Scan with Norton Antivirus**.

2. View the results of the scan and take any appropriate action. For instance, if the file is okay, you can close the window. If the file is infected, you can delete, quarantine, or fix it.

INTRODUCTION

You should set up your antivirus program to automatically scan file attachments, files you open from a disk, and files you open from the Internet. You can also manually scan a file.

TIP

Options Vary

What you see after a scan and what options you have depend on the antivirus program you use.

TIP

Scan Disk

You can also scan your disk by starting your antivirus program and initiating a scan. Or, you can right-click the disk icon and select the scan command.

Home Networking Basics

If your household contains multiple computers (one equipped with Windows XP and Internet access, and one equipped with XP, Windows ME, Windows 98, or Windows 95), you can create a home network. Doing so enables you to share an Internet connection, hardware (such as a printer, scanner, and so on), and files and folders and play multi-computer games.

There are three basic steps: planning your network, installing and configuring the appropriate network hardware on each computer on the network, and running the Windows XP Network Setup wizard. Although an in-depth discussion of the first and second steps is beyond the scope of this book, you will find ample information about it in Windows XP's Help area (click the Networking and the Web link in the main Help and Support page). When planning your network, you must determine what type of network you want to build (Ethernet, HPNA, or wireless) and which machine will serve as your host computer (it should run Windows XP and be connected to the Internet). You must equip each computer on your network with a network interface card (NIC), or network adapter. If you want to network more than two PCs, you will need a hub (separate box into which cables from each network card connect).

The third step enables you to quickly and easily configure each PC for networking. The Network Setup wizard is covered in this part, as are the tasks associated with using a home network, including accessing network files, mapping networking drives, securing your network, and more.

Tasks

Task 1: Using the Network Setup Wizard

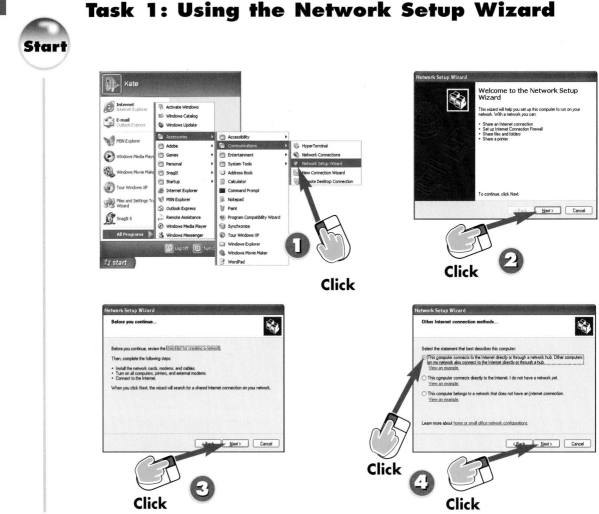

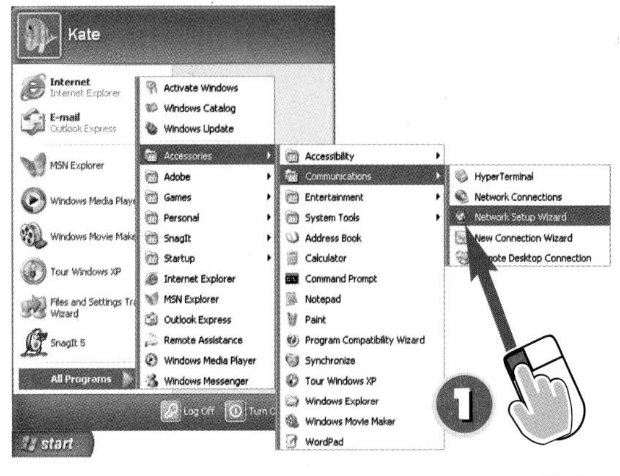

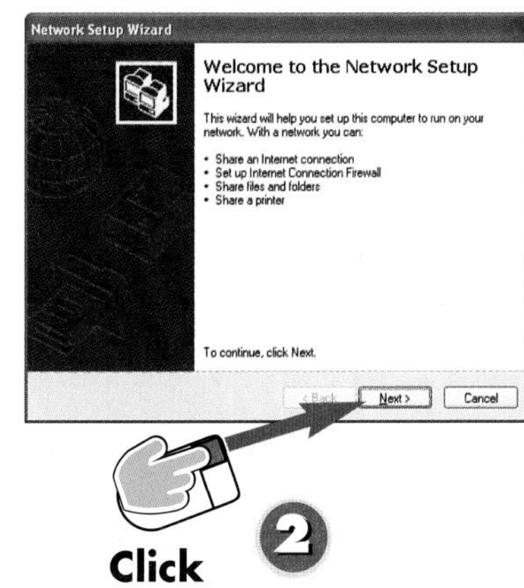

Click

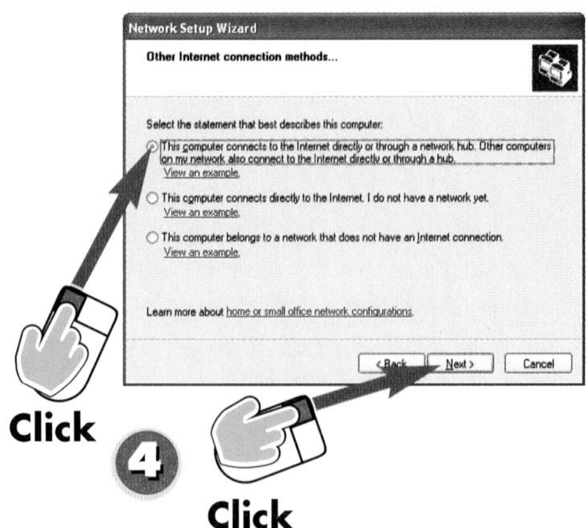

1. Choose **Start**, **All Programs**, **Accessories**, **Communications**, **Network Setup Wizard**.
2. When the Network Setup Wizard window appears, click **Next** to begin setting up your home network.
3. Be sure you've installed all network cards, modems, and cables; turned on all computers, printers, and external modems; and connected to the Internet. Then click **Next**.
4. Select the statement best describing the computer you are configuring (I've selected **Other**, and then **This computer connects to the Internet directly or through a network hub**). Click **Next**.

INTRODUCTION

After you have installed the necessary networking hardware, you can configure each computer to use the network by working through the Network Setup Wizard.

TIP

Checklist for Creating a Network

Before continuing beyond step 3, click the **checklist for creating a network** link. Doing so opens a help file that covers the basics of setting up your network.

TIP

Other Network Configurations

The steps I must take to configure my network may differ from yours if your network employs a different configuration. If so, consult XP's Help information for guidance.

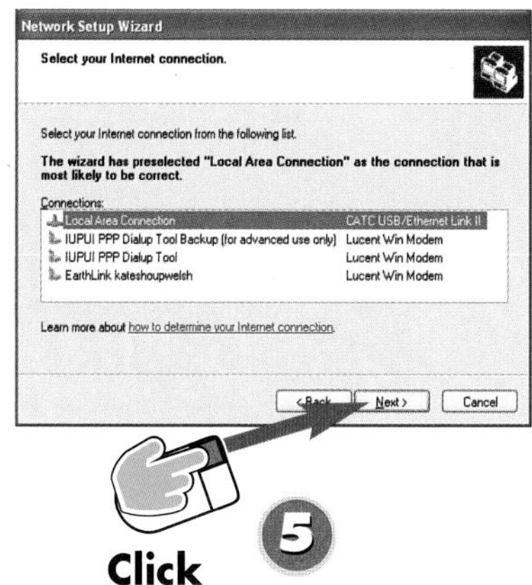

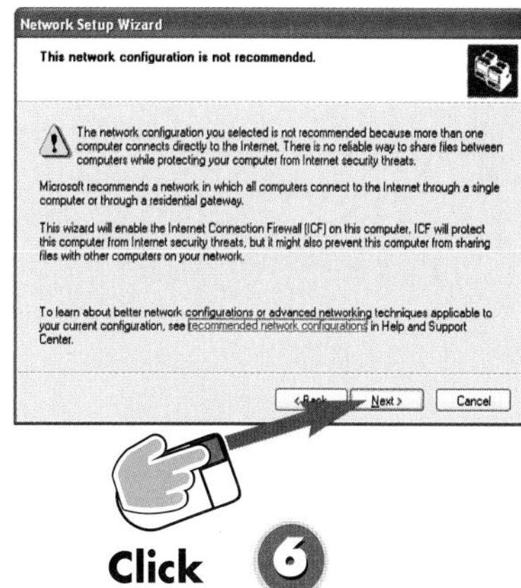

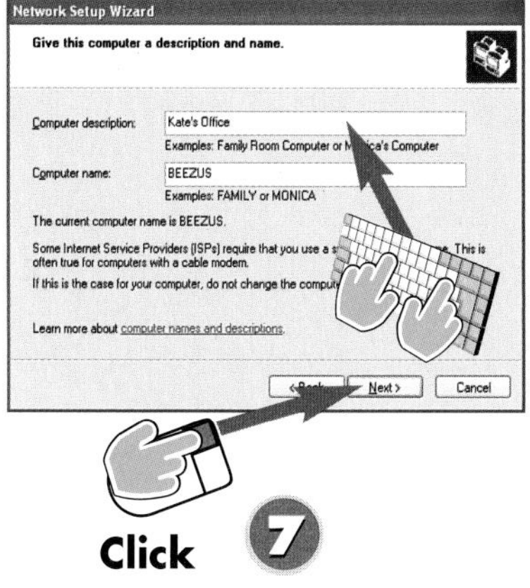

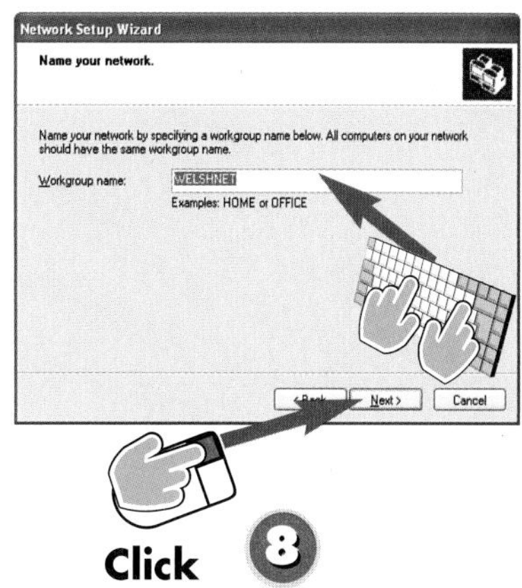

5. Select your Internet connection from the list, and click **Next**.

6. A warning about the network configuration I have chosen appears, indicating that this configuration is less secure than others. Click **Next**.

7. Enter a name and description of the computer (unless your ISP requires that you use a certain name, these can be anything you like), and click **Next**.

8. Name the network you are creating. This can be anything you like. Click **Next**.

TIP

Recommended Network Configurations

For information about recommended network configurations, click the **Recommended network configurations** link on the screen shown in step 5.

TIP

Mixing Network Types

Thanks to Windows XP's network bridging capabilities, you can use a combination of network adapter types within the same network. Windows XP's bridging components are implemented by default if the Network Setup wizard detects multiple adapter types.

TIP

Workgroup Name

All the computers on your home network must use the same workgroup name.

Using the Network Setup Wizard (Continued)

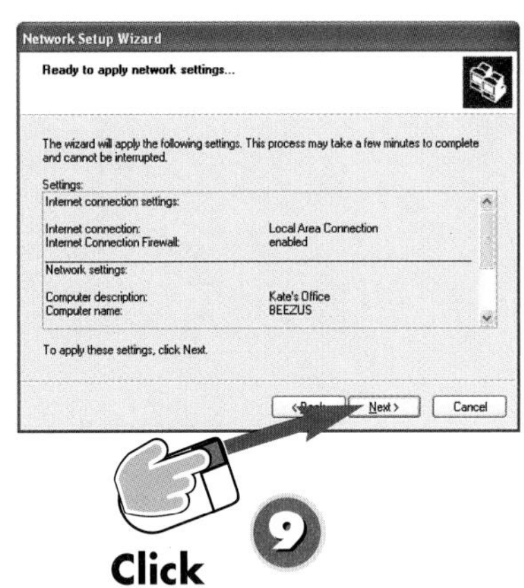

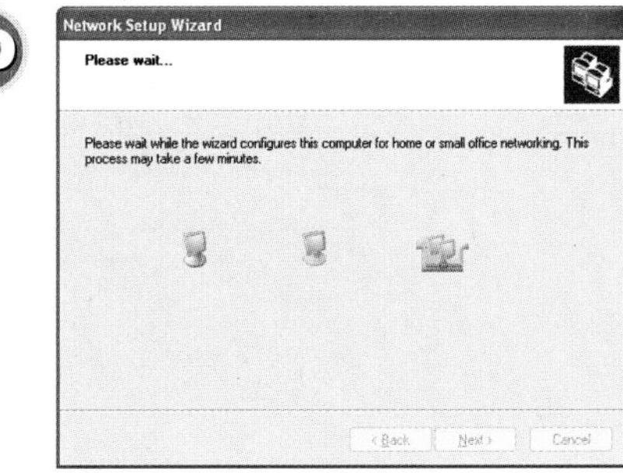

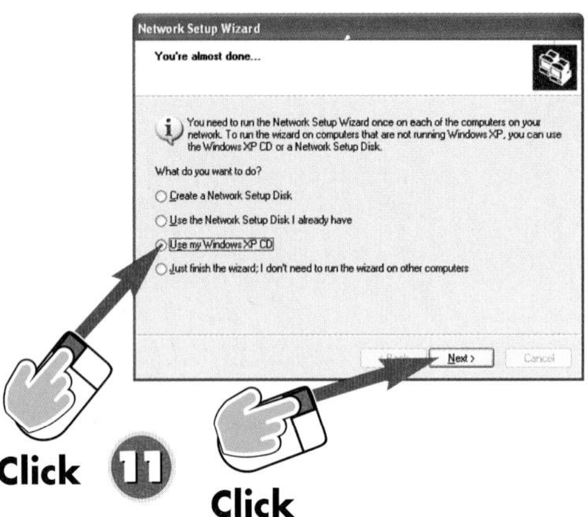

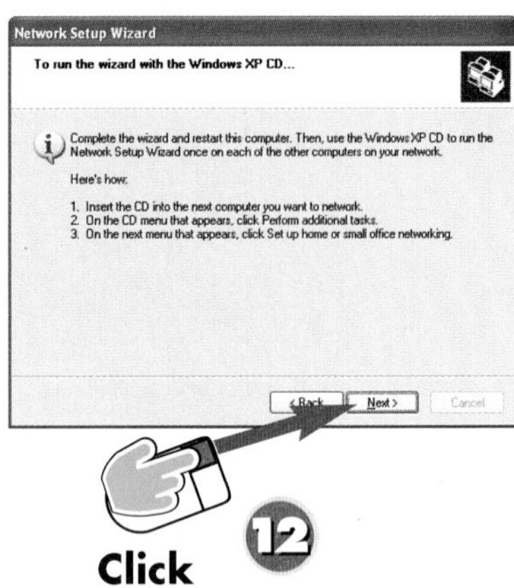

9. The wizard displays the settings to be applied to your network. Click **Next**.

10. Wait while the settings are applied. (This may take a few moments.)

11. After the wizard applies the settings, it prompts you to configure all other machines on your network. Choose U**se my Windows XP CD**, and click **Next**.

12. Read the instructions for running the wizard on the other computers on your network, and click **Next**.

TIP

Network Setup Disk

If you don't have your Windows XP CD handy, select Create a Network Setup Disk in the window shown in step 10, and follow the wizard's prompts.

TIP

Problems Sharing the Internet Connection

Some versions of AOL do not allow you to share a single Internet connection among multiple machines. Likewise, other ISPs may charge you extra to use a single Internet connection for multiple computers.

TIP

Printing to a Network Printer

A network printer works the same as a local printer in all your applications. Simply select **Network the printer** from the Print dialog box in whatever program you are printing from.

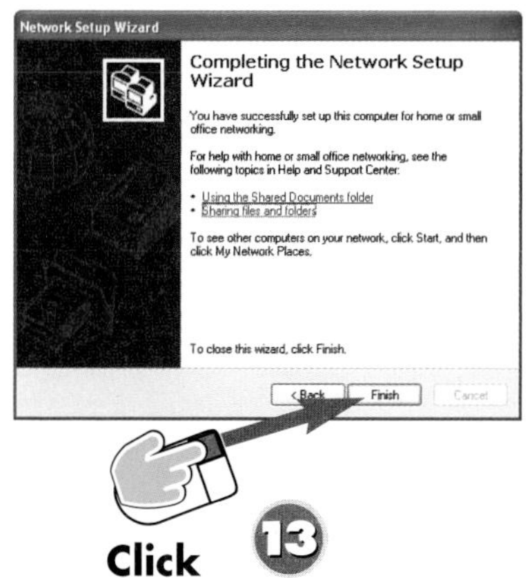

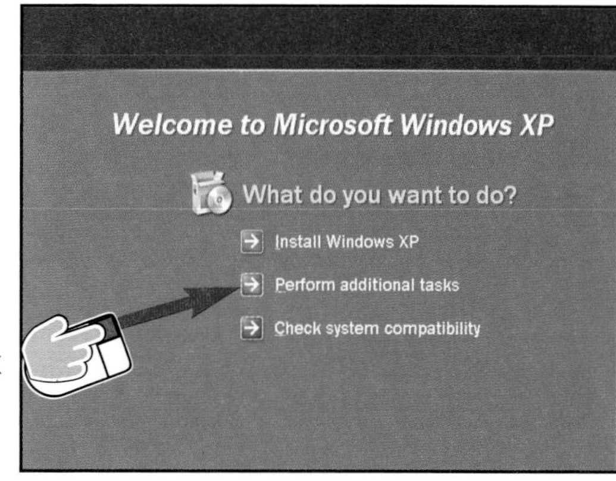

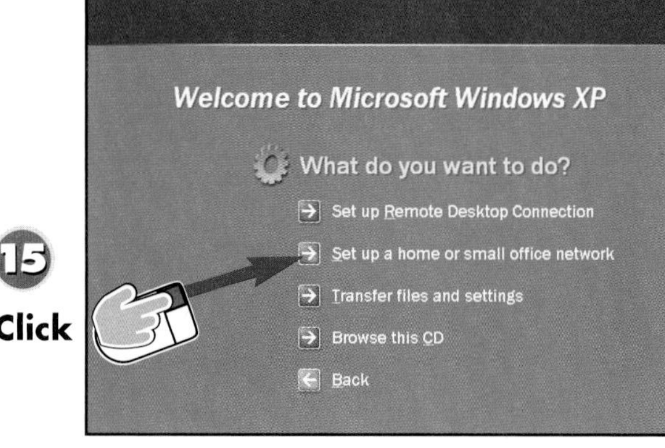

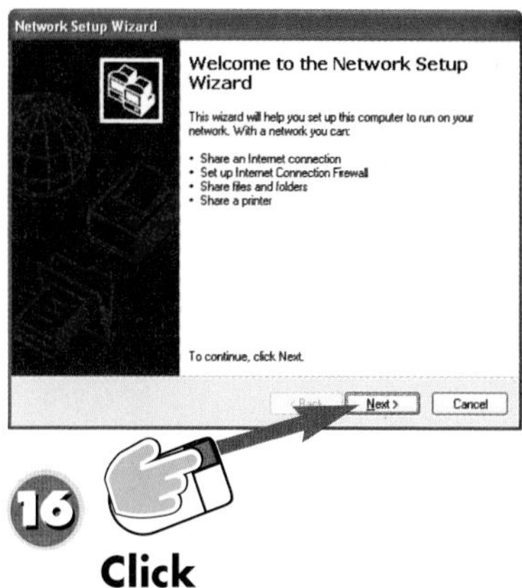

13. Windows XP informs you that you have successfully completed the wizard on this machine. Click the **Finish** button. You'll be prompted to restart your computer; do so now.

14. After moving to the next computer you want to configure and inserting your Windows XP CD-ROM, click **Perform additional tasks**.

15. Click **Set up a home or small office network**.

16. If the computer you are configuring is running Windows XP, the Network Setup wizard starts automatically. Click the **Next** button, and repeat steps 3-13 as needed.

TIP

Not Running XP?

You don't have to run Windows XP on every computer on the network. As long as at least one machine runs XP, the others can run Windows 95, Windows 98, or Windows 2000 Professional. (In truth, your network can include Macintosh or UNIX/Linux computers as well, but discussion of such a network is beyond the scope of this book.) If the computer you're configuring is running a supported version of Windows other than XP, you'll be prompted to allow Windows to install some network support files and possibly restart your computer. Click the Yes button, and follow the system prompts; the Network Setup wizard will start automatically.

TIP

Other PCs

You must run the Network Setup wizard on each computer you want on your network.

Task 2: Enabling File Sharing

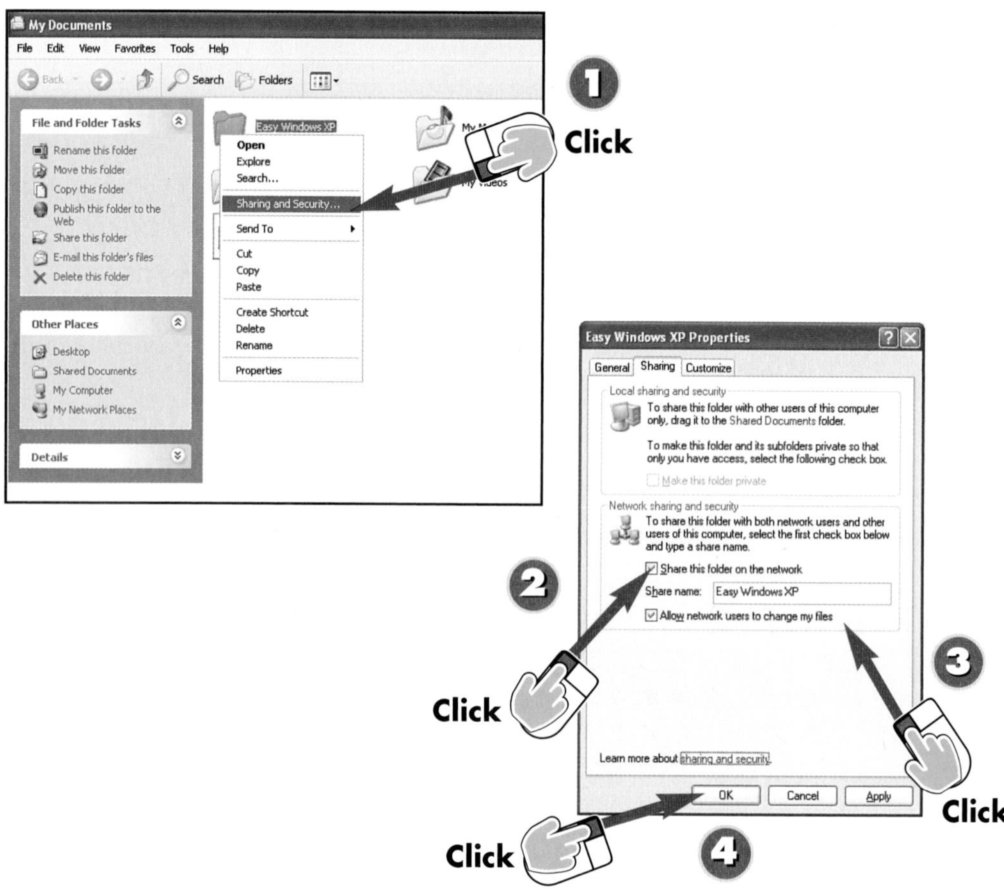

1. In My Documents, right-click the folder you want to share on your network, and select **Sharing and Security** from the menu that appears.
2. The folder's Properties dialog box opens, with the Sharing tab displayed. Click to select the **Share this folder on the network** check box.
3. If you want users on other machines to be able to change the contents of this folder, click to select the **Allow network users to change my files** check box.
4. Click the **OK** button.

INTRODUCTION

By default, certain folders are made available to all computers on your network. To make other folders on a computer available to other machines on your network, you must enable file sharing for those folders.

TIP

Sharing Drives and Devices

In addition to sharing folders and files, you can share drives and devices, such as printers, scanners, and so on. Follow the steps in this task, but instead of right-clicking a folder in step 1, right-click a drive instead.

TIP

Learn More

To learn more about sharing and security, click the sharing and security link in the folder's **Properties** dialog box.

Task 3: Browsing Shared Files

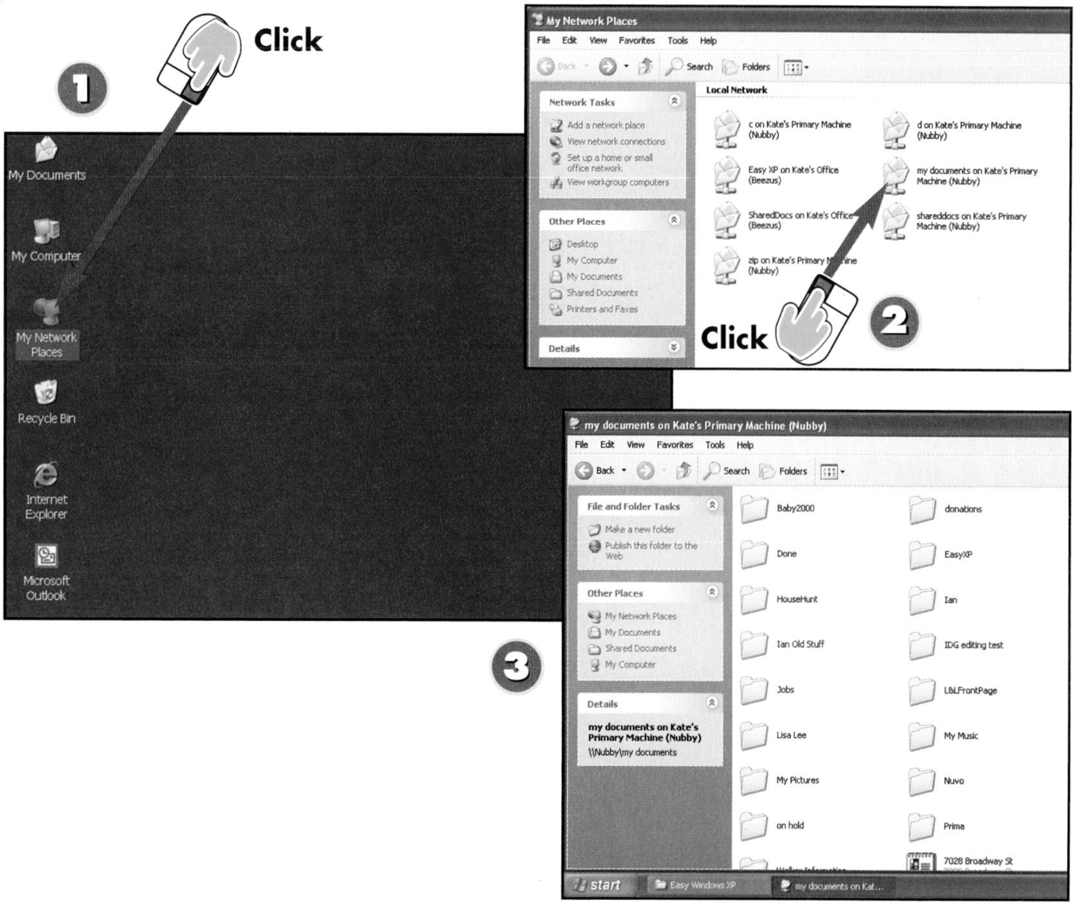

1. Double-click the **My Network Places** icon on the desktop.
2. The My Network Places window opens, displaying all shared folders on the network. Double-click a folder icon to open that folder.
3. The contents of the folder are displayed in My Network Places. Work with the files and folders normally, as you would files on your local hard disk.

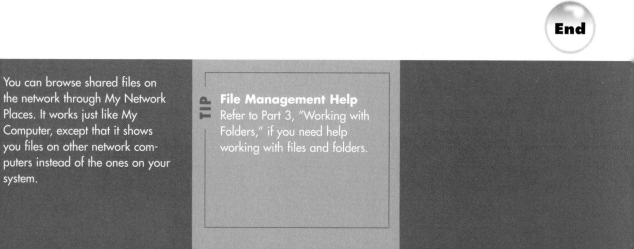

INTRODUCTION

You can browse shared files on the network through My Network Places. It works just like My Computer, except that it shows you files on other network computers instead of the ones on your system.

TIP

File Management Help
Refer to Part 3, "Working with Folders," if you need help working with files and folders.

Task 4: Mapping a Network Drive

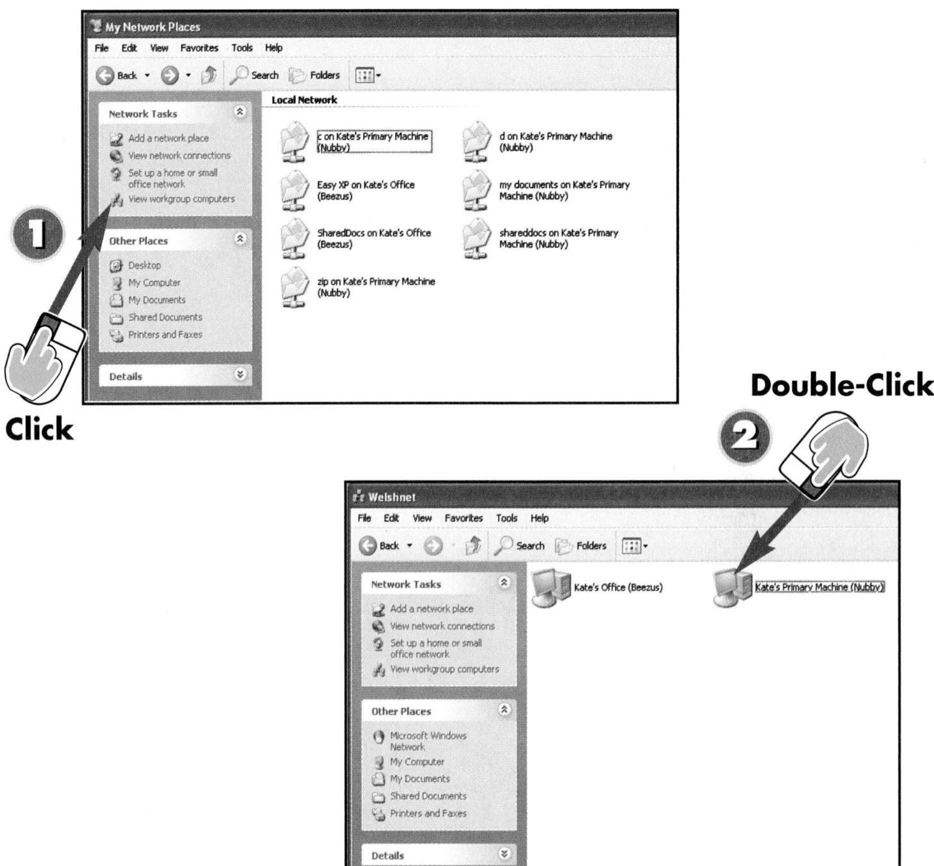

1. In the My Network Places window, click the **View workgroup computers link**.
2. Double-click the machine containing the drive you want to map.

INTRODUCTION

Not all programs enable you to browse network locations when opening or saving files. Some programs can only recognize drives on your computer. Fortunately, you can trick Windows into thinking that a particular drive or folder on the network is actually located on your system. This is called mapping a network drive. To do this, you create a connection that leads all programs from an imaginary new drive letter on your system to the network location you want. After you map a drive, the new letter appears in all drive listings.

TIP

Opening My Network Places

Refer to the preceding task if you need help opening the My Network Places window.

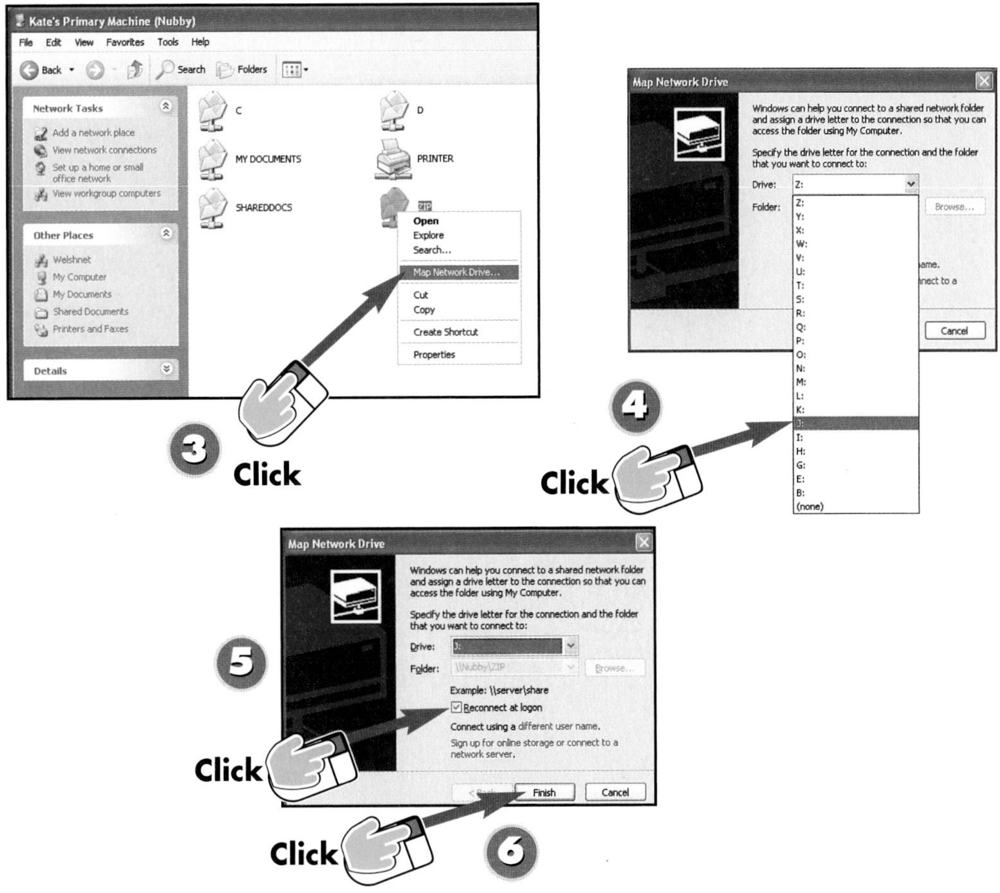

3. Right-click the drive you want to map, and choose **Map Network Drive** from the menu that appears.
4. Open the **Drive** drop-down list and click the drive letter you want to use for the drive.
5. Mark the **Reconnect at logon** check box if you want this mapping to be active every time you log on.
6. Click **Finish**.

TIP

Drive Letter

You can leave the default drive letter assigned, which is the first available letter, or you can assign a different available letter. Some people like to assign network drives later letters, such as X, Y, or Z, to avoid confusing them with local drive letters.

TIP

Reconnecting at Logon

Reconnecting a drive mapping each time you log on can slow things down. If you don't use the drive mapping every day, or if the mapped computer is not always turned on, it's better not to reconnect it automatically at logon.

Task 5: Creating Network Shortcuts in My Network Places

Start

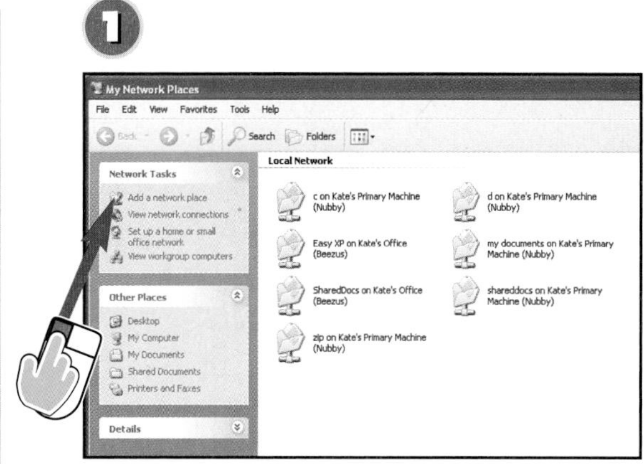

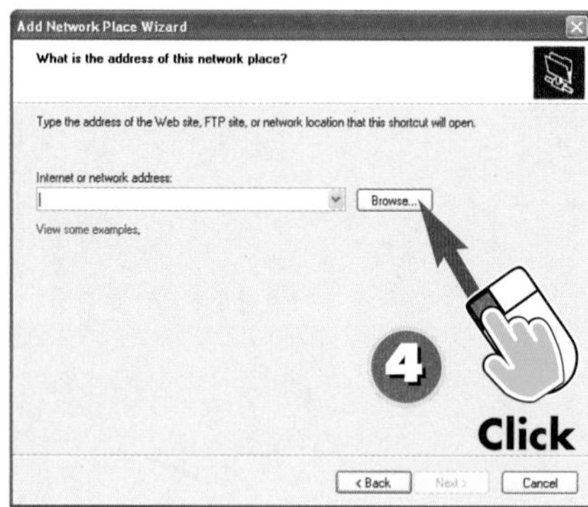

1. In the My Network Places window, click the **Add a network place** link.
2. The Add Network Place Wizard opens. Click the **Next** button.
3. Select **Choose another network location**, and click **Next**.
4. Click the **Browse** button to locate the computer, drive, or folder for which you want to create a shortcut.

INTRODUCTION

If you find yourself constantly rooting around in the My Network Places window to locate a particular computer, drive, or folder, you might want to create a shortcut to it. This shortcut can point to any computer, drive, or folder on the network.

TIP

Opening My Network Places
Refer to Task 3, "Browsing Shared Files," if you need help opening the My Network Places window.

TIP

Creating Shortcut to Web Pages or FTP Sites
You can create shortcuts to Web pages or FTP sites. Simply enter the URL of the page or site in the Internet or network address box on the window shown in step 4.

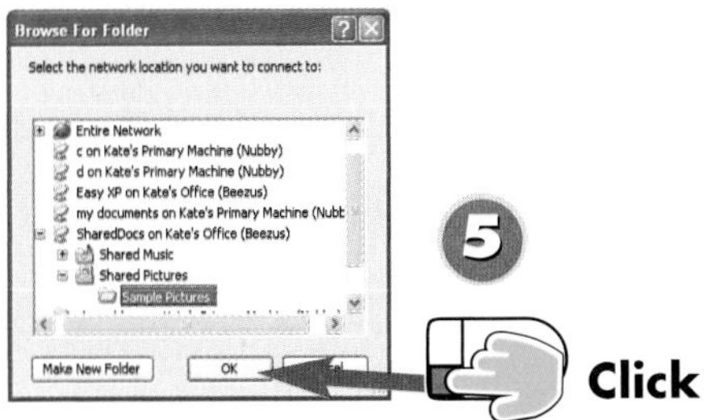

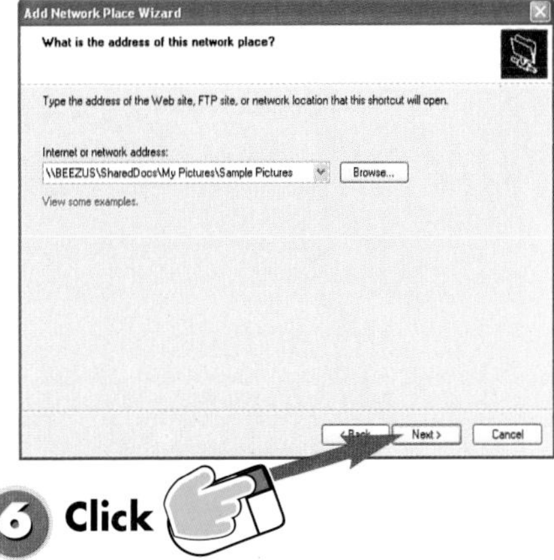

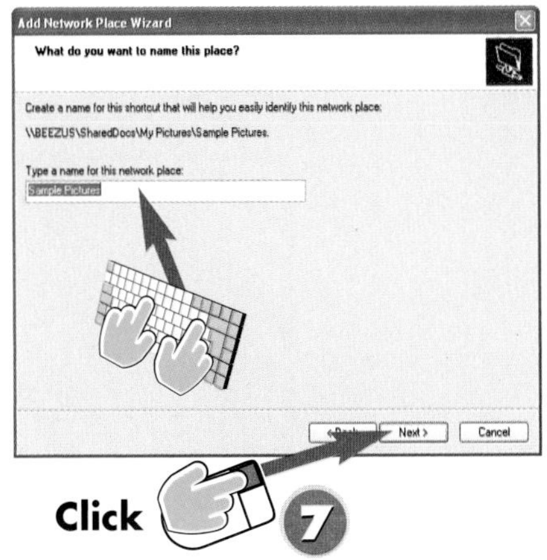

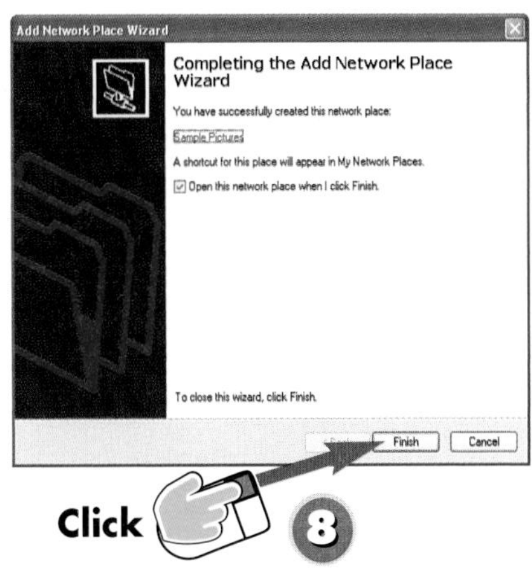

5. Navigate to the computer, drive, or folder to which you want to create a shortcut. Select it and click **OK**.
6. Click **Next** to continue.
7. If asked, type a name for the shortcut (or leave the default), and click **Next**.
8. Click **Finish**.

TIP

Shortcut Name
The shortcut name can be a "friendly" or descriptive name; it need not match the actual drive or folder name.

TIP

Adding Shortcut to the Desktop
In addition to creating a network shortcut that appears in the My Network Places window, you can create one that appears on your desktop. To do so, simply right-click and drag the icon representing the computer, drive, or folder for which you want to create a shortcut from the My Network Places window to the desktop. Choose **Create Shortcut(s) Here** from the menu that appears when you release your mouse button. Windows will place the shortcut on your desktop.

Task 6: Enabling the Security Log

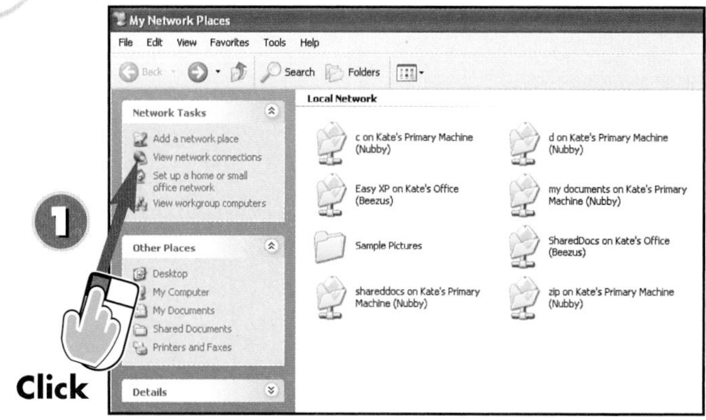

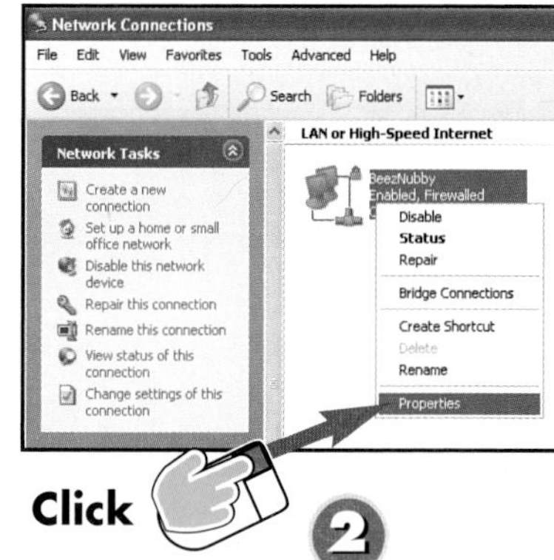

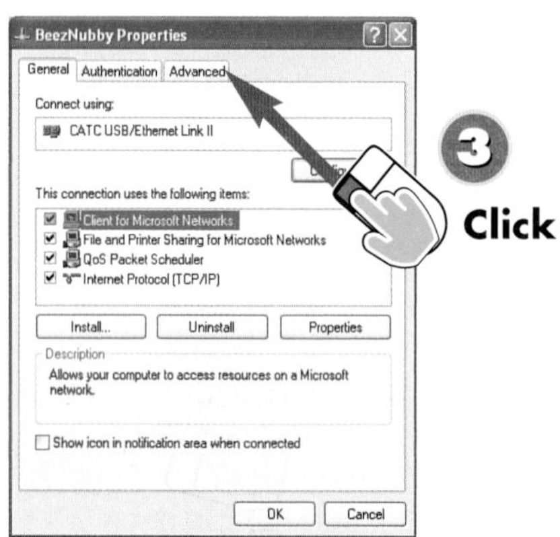

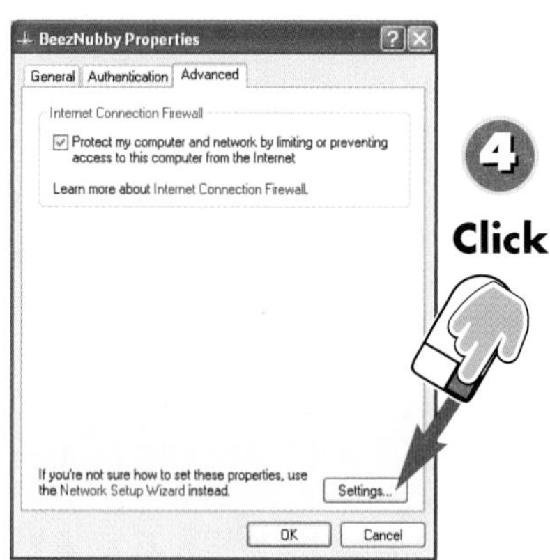

1. In the My Network Places window, click the **View network connections** link.

2. The Network Connections window opens. Right-click the icon representing your network, and choose **Properties** from the menu that appears.

3. The network's Properties dialog box opens; click the **Advanced** tab.

4. On the Advanced tab, click the **Settings** button. (If this button is grayed out, click the **Protect my computer...** check box to enable it.)

INTRODUCTION

If your home network is connected to the Internet, you suffer an increased risk of hackers obtaining access to the computers on that network. One way to obstruct unauthorized users is to erect a *firewall*. Windows XP ships complete with a firewall that is installed automatically when you run the Network Setup Wizard on a machine with a direct connection to the Internet. A key component of the firewall is a security log that tracks unsuccessful inbound connection attempts as well as successful outbound connections. To use the log, you must first enable it.

TIP

Opening My Network Places

Refer to Task 3, "Browsing Shared Files," if you need help opening the My Network Places window.

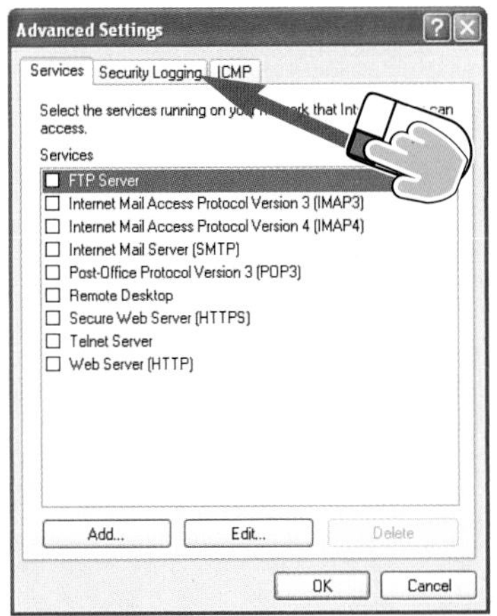

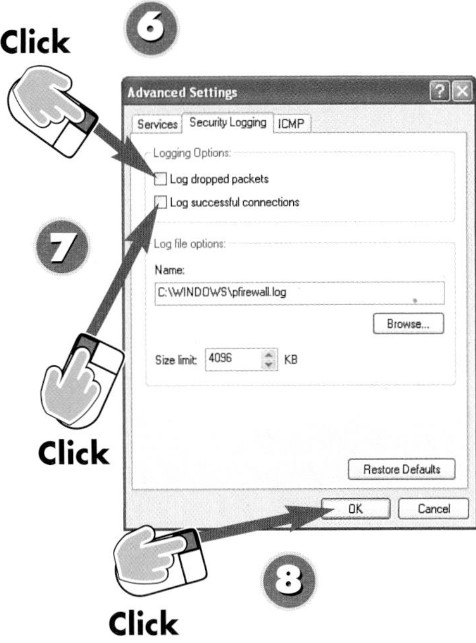

5 The Advanced Settings dialog box opens. Click the **Security Logging** tab.

6 In the Security Logging tab, click to select the **Log dropped packets** checkbox.

7 Click the **Log successful connections** checkbox to select it.

8 Click the **OK** button.

TIP

Changing the Size of the Log File

If the default setting for the size of the log file is too large or too small, change the setting in the Size limit spin box on the Security Logging tab of the Advanced Settings dialog box.

TIP

Viewing the Log File

To view the security log file, note its location in the Name box on the Security Logging tab. Then, right-click the **Start** button, click **Explore**, and locate the file. Double-click it to open it.

TIP

Changing the Path

If you have trouble locating the security log on your system, you can change its path and filename. Click the **Browse** button on the Security Logging tab, navigate to the location where you want to store the log file, and click **Open**.

Glossary

A

accessory One of the miniapplications that comes free with Windows XP. Examples include WordPad, Paint, and Calculator.

active window The window you're currently using. You can tell a window is active by looking at its title bar: If the bar shows white letters on a dark background, the window is active. Inactive windows show light gray letters on a dark gray background.

application Software that accomplishes a specific practical task. Same thing as a program.

application window A window that contains a running application, such as Paint or WordPad.

ASCII text file A file that uses only the American Standard Code for Information Interchange (ASCII) character set (techno-lingo for the characters you see on your keyboard).

B

boot To start your computer. The term *booting* comes from the phrase "pulling oneself up by one's own bootstraps," which refers to the fact that your computer can load everything it needs to operate properly without any help from you.

bps Bits per second. The rate at which a modem or other communications device sends data through a phone line or cable.

browser A program that you use to view sites on the World Wide Web. The browser that comes with Windows XP is called Internet Explorer.

byte A single character of information.

C

cascade menu A menu that appears when you select certain pull-down menu commands.

CD-ROM drive A special computer disk drive that's designed to handle CD-ROM discs, which resemble audio CDs. CD-ROMs have enormous capacity (about 500 times that of a typical floppy disk), so they're most often used to hold large applications, graphics libraries, and huge collections of shareware programs.

character formatting Changing the look of text characters by altering their font, size, style, and more.

character spacing The amount of space a font reserves for each character. In a monospaced font, every character gets the same amount of space regardless of its true width. In a proportional font, the space allotted to each letter varies according to the width of the letter.

check box A square-shaped switch that toggles a dialog box option on or off. The option is toggled on when a check mark appears in the box.

click To quickly press and release the left mouse button.

Clipboard An area of memory that holds data temporarily during cut-and-paste operations.

command button A rectangular "button" (usually found in dialog boxes) that, when clicked, runs whatever command is spelled out on it.

commands The options you see in a pull-down menu. You use these commands to tell the application what you want it to do next.

D

data files The files used by you or your programs. See also ***program files***.

desktop A metaphor for the screen that you see when Windows XP starts. Starting a Windows XP application is similar to putting a folder full of papers (the application window) on your desk. To do some work, you pull some papers out of the folder (the document windows) and place them on the desktop.

device driver A small program that controls the way a device (such as a mouse or printer) works with your system.

dialog boxes Windows that pop up on the screen to ask you for information or to seek confirmation of an action you requested.

digital camera A special camera that saves pictures using digital storage (such as a memory card) instead of film.

directory See ***folder***.

diskette See ***floppy disk***.

document window A window opened in an application. Document windows hold whatever you're working on in the application.

double-click To quickly press and release the left mouse button twice in succession.

double-click speed The maximum amount of time Windows XP allows between the mouse clicks of a double-click.

drag To press and hold down the left mouse button and then move the mouse.

drag-and-drop A technique you use to run commands or move things around; you use your mouse to drag files or icons to strategic screen areas and drop them there.

drop-down list box A list box that normally shows only a single item but, when selected, displays a list of options.

DVD A type of storage medium similar to a CD-ROM but with better sound, graphics, and video quality. Some computers now come with a DVD drive rather than a CD-ROM drive. You can find movies and programs on DVDs. You can also use standard data and audio CDs in a DVD drive.

E–F

Explorer bar The left pane of a folder window. You can choose to display different lists in this area, including a Folders list, a History list, or a Favorites list.

Favorites A list of folders, files, or Web sites. You can add items to the Favorites list and then quickly access the item.

file An organized unit of information inside your computer.

floppy disk A portable storage medium that consists of a flexible magnetic disk protected by a plastic case. Floppy disks are available in a variety of sizes and capacities.

folder A storage location on your hard disk in which you keep related files together.

Folder list A list of the drives and folders on your system. In folder windows, you can display the Folder list by clicking the Folders button.

font A character set of a specific typeface, type style, and type size.

format bar A series of text boxes and buttons that enable you to format the characters in your document. The format bar typically appears under the toolbar.

formatting The process of setting up a disk so that a drive can read its information and write information to it. Not to be confused with character formatting.

fragmented When a single file is chopped up and stored in separate chunks scattered around a hard disk. You can fix this by running Windows XP's Disk Defragmenter program.

gigabyte 1,024 megabytes. Those in the know usually abbreviate this as GB when writing, and as gig when speaking. See also ***byte***, ***kilobyte***, and ***megabyte***.

hard disk A storage medium that consists of several metallic disks stacked on top of each other, usually protected by a metal outer case. Hard disks are available in a variety of sizes and capacities and are usually the main storage area inside your computer.

History A list of folders, files, or Web sites you have opened recently. You can display the History list and then select to view any of the items in the list.

hover To place the mouse pointer over an object for a few seconds. In most Windows applications, for example, if you hover the mouse over a toolbar button, a small banner pops up that tells you the name of the button.

I

icons The little pictures that Windows XP uses to represent programs and files.

infrared port A communications port, usually found on notebook computers and some printers. Infrared ports enable two devices to communicate by using infrared light waves instead of cables.

insertion point cursor The blinking vertical bar you see inside a text box or in a word-processing application, such as WordPad. It indicates where the next character you type will appear.

Internet A network of networks that extends around the world. You can access this network by setting up an account with an Internet service provider.

intranet The implementation of Internet technologies for use within a corporate organization rather than for connection to the Internet as a whole.

IR Short for infrared. See also ***infrared port***.

ISP Stands for Internet service provider. The company that provides access to the Internet. You dial and connect to this network. You have access to the entire Internet through the ISP's network.

J–K

Jaz drive A special disk drive that uses portable disks (about the size of floppy disks) that hold 1 gigabyte of data.

Kbps One thousand bits per second (bps). Today's modern modems transmit data at either 28.8Kbps or 56Kbps.

keyboard delay The amount of time it takes for a second character to appear when you press and hold down a key.

kilobyte 1,024 bytes. This is often abbreviated K or KB. See also ***megabyte*** and ***gigabyte***.

L

LAN See ***local area network***.

list box A small window that displays a list of items such as filenames or directories.

local area network A network in which all the computers occupy a relatively small geographical area, such as a department, an office, a home, or a building.

M

maximize To increase the size of a window to its largest extent. A maximized application window fills the entire screen except for the taskbar. A maximized document window fills the entire application window.

Mbps One million bits per second (bps).

megabyte 1,024 kilobytes, or 1,048,576 bytes. This is often abbreviated in writing to M or MB and pronounced meg. See also ***gigabyte***.

memory-resident program A program that stays in memory after it is loaded and works "behind the scenes." The program normally responds only to a specific event (such as the deletion of a file) or key combination. Also called a terminate-and-stay-resident (TSR) program.

menu bar The horizontal bar on the second line of an application window. The menu bar contains the application's pull-down menus.

minimize To remove a program from the desktop without closing it. A minimized program appears as a button on the taskbar.

modem An electronic device that enables two computers to exchange data over phone lines.

multitasking The capability to run several programs at the same time.

N–O

network A collection of computers connected using special cables or other network media (such as infrared ports) to share files, folders, disks, peripherals, and applications. See also ***local area network***.

newsgroup An Internet discussion group devoted to a single topic. These discussions progress by "posting" messages to the group.

option buttons See ***radio buttons***.

P–Q

point To place the mouse pointer so that it rests on a specific screen location.

port The connection into which you plug the cable from a device such as a mouse or printer.

program files The files that run your programs. See also ***data files***.

pull-down menus Hidden menus that you open from an application's menu bar to access the commands and features of the application.

R

radio buttons Dialog box options that appear as small circles in groups of two or more. Only one option from a group can be chosen. These are also called **option buttons**.

RAM Stands for random access memory. The memory in your computer that Windows XP uses to run your programs.

repeat rate After the initial delay, the rate at which characters appear when you press and hold down a key.

right-click To click the right mouse button instead of the usual left button. In Windows XP, right-clicking something usually pops up a shortcut menu.

scalable font A font in which each character exists as an outline that can be scaled to different sizes. Windows XP includes such scalable fonts as Arial, Courier New, and Times New Roman. To use scalable fonts, you must have a software program called a type manager to do the scaling. Windows XP comes with its own type manager, TrueType.

scrollbar A bar that appears at the bottom or on the right side of a window when the window is too small to display all its contents.

shortcut A special file that points to a program or a document. Double-clicking the shortcut starts the program or loads the document.

shortcut menu A menu that contains a few commands related to an item (such as the desktop or the taskbar). You display the shortcut menu by right-clicking the object.

surf To travel from site to site on the World Wide Web.

system resources Memory areas that Windows XP uses to keep track of things such as the position and size of open windows, dialog boxes, and your desktop configuration (wallpaper and so on).

T–V

taskbar The horizontal strip across the bottom of the Windows XP screen. Each running application is given its own taskbar button, and you switch to an application by clicking its button. Sometimes called the system tray.

text box A screen area in which you type text information, such as a description or a filename.

text editor A program that lets you edit files that contain only text. The Windows XP text editor is called Notepad.

title bar The area on the top line of a window that displays the window's title.

toolbar A series of application-specific buttons that typically appears beneath the menu bar.

tracking speed The speed at which the mouse pointer moves across the screen when you move the mouse on its pad.

TrueType A font-management program that comes with Windows XP.

type size A measurement of the height of a font. Type size is measured in points; there are 72 points in an inch.

type style Character attributes, such as regular, bold, and italic. Other type styles (often called type effects) are underline and strikethrough.

typeface A distinctive graphic design of letters, numbers, and other symbols.

W–Y

Web integration The integration of World Wide Web techniques into the Windows XP interface. See also ***Web view***.

Web view A folder view that enables you to single-click an icon to open it. You can also add Web content to your desktop.

window A rectangular screen area in which Windows XP displays applications and documents.

word wrap A word processor feature that automatically starts a new line when your typing reaches the end of the current line.

write protection Floppy disk safeguard that prevents you from changing any information on the disk. On a 3 1/2-inch disk, write protection is controlled by a small movable tab on the back of the disk. If the tab is toward the edge of the disk, the disk is write protected. To disable the write protection, slide the tab away from the edge of the disk.

Z

Zip drive A special disk drive that uses portable disks (a little smaller than a Jaz drive disk) that hold 100 megabytes of data.

Index

A

B-C

F

G-H

I

J-K-L

M

P

Q-R

T

U

V

W-X-Y-Z